I. M. Pei

Lead Sponsor

Generously supported by

Travel Partner   Hotel Partner

Cover: Portrait of I. M. Pei at his office in 1967.

This book has been typeset in Neue Haas Unica (body text) and URW Clarendon (display type), a version of the original Clarendon typeface created in 1845. Clarendon was used for company branding by I. M. Pei & Associates, I. M. Pei & Partners, and Pei Cobb Freed & Partners.

First published in the United Kingdom in 2024 by Thames & Hudson Ltd, 181A High Holborn, London WC1V 7QX, in collaboration with M+, West Kowloon Cultural District, 38 Museum Drive, West Kowloon, Hong Kong

First published in the United States of America in 2024 by Thames & Hudson Inc., 500 Fifth Avenue, New York, New York 10110

Published on the occasion of the exhibition *I. M. Pei: Life Is Architecture* at M+, Hong Kong, 29 June 2024 to 5 January 2025

I. M. Pei: Life Is Architecture © 2024 Thames & Hudson Ltd, London, and M+, Hong Kong
Text and illustrations © 2024 M+, Hong Kong, unless otherwise stated on pages 394–395
Design © 2024 Thames & Hudson Ltd, London

Editors: Shirley Surya, Aric Chen
Assistant editor: Naomi Altman
Project editor: Andrew Goodhouse
Senior researcher and advisor: Janet Adams Strong
English editing: William Smith, Jacqueline Leung, Juliet Cheung
Chinese editing: Lam Lap Wai, Zhong Yuling, Or Ka Uen
Translations: Charles Lai, Chun Wai, Joanna Wong
Publication management: Dustin Cosentino, Sasha Anderson
Rights and reproductions: Jacqueline Chan, Crystal Yu, Tom Morgan
Cover and interior layout designed by Johanne Lian Olsen
Chinese typesetting: HATO

All Rights Reserved. No part of this publication may be reproduced or transmitted in any form or by any means, electronic or mechanical, including photocopy, recording, or any other information storage and retrieval system, without prior permission in writing from the publisher.

British Library Cataloguing-in-Publication Data
A catalogue record for this book is available from the British Library

Library of Congress Control Number 2023952398

ISBN 978-0-500-48102-8

Printed in Malaysia by Papercraft

Be the first to know about our new releases, exclusive content and author events by visiting
thamesandhudson.com
thamesandhudsonusa.com
thamesandhudson.com.au

I. M. Pei

Life Is Architecture

Edited by
Shirley Surya & Aric Chen

With more than 400 illustrations

Contents

Foreword
Suhanya Raffel   6

Introduction: Architecture Is Life
Shirley Surya & Aric Chen   8

1

Transcultural Foundations

'I don't think I shall feel strange in a strange land'   14

The American Education of I. M. Pei
Joan Ockman   42

4

Material & Structural Innovation

'The totality of the form'   148

I. M. Pei and the Tools of Invention
Janet Adams Strong   224

5

Power, Politics & Patronage

'I had a client from beginning to end'   228

OCBC Centre: The Iconic Turn of the Singapore Model of Asian Global Capitalism
Jiat-Hwee Chang   288

2

Real Estate & Urban Redevelopment

'We are going to change all this'   48

I. M. Pei and Urbanism in North America, 1948–1960
Eric Mumford   100

3

Art & Civic Form

'The play between solids and voids'   104

I. M. Pei's Museum of Chinese Art, Shanghai: Modernism between East and West
Barry Bergdoll   144

6

Regenerating Cultural & Historical Archetypes

'Like embedded rocks and rooted trees'   292

I. M. Pei and Chinese Spatiality at Expo '70
Wu Kwang-tyng   363

I. M. Pei's Pictorial Vision of Space
Liu Linfan   366

Timeline of I. M. Pei's Life and Work   369

Notes   382
Selected Bibliography   386
Contributors   391
Acknowledgements   392
Image Credits   394
Index   396

Foreword

Few lives embody the vision of global cultural exchange at the heart of M+ as thoroughly and elegantly as that of Ieoh Ming Pei. From its position in Kowloon along Victoria Harbour, the M+ building looks across to the skyline of Hong Kong Island, where Pei's Bank of China Tower stands prominently. With this dramatic structure, Pei left his mark on Hong Kong. At the same time, the city where Pei spent his formative years influenced the nuanced vision of international connectivity that underlies both his life and his architectural practice.

As a global museum of contemporary visual culture, M+ is uniquely suited to produce this comprehensive publication on Pei's life and work. We are also honoured to host the first major retrospective devoted to this architect, whose designs shaped the built environment for the twentieth and twenty-first centuries. This project reintroduces Pei and his contributions to a contemporary audience worldwide while bringing to the surface important facets of his career that have long been overlooked.

Born in Guangzhou, Pei grew up among the elite in Hong Kong, Shanghai, and Suzhou. As a student, he seized the opportunity to learn from leading figures of the modern movement in architecture in the United States. Although he would not return to China for nearly four decades, Pei maintained a strong bond with his native country throughout his life as he rose to prominence in America and found a place in the corridors of power and influence in culture, commerce, and politics in North America, Europe, and Asia. Sought after by clients around the world, Pei consistently pursued opportunities in China after the 1970s. By stewarding his legacy at M+, we feel privileged to be part of this history.

Through an extensive exploration of the archive of Pei Cobb Freed & Partners and other holdings, we have gained unique insights into Pei's practice as an architect as well as his personal aspirations. This volume provides new perspectives on the pivotal role his education played in the trajectory of his practice, as well as his early success working with a commercial developer to reshape post-war American cities. The archive reveals how Pei, always a master of understated aesthetics, can be recognised equally as an innovator of construction techniques. The coalescing of his interests and his supreme technical abilities brought him commissions that touched

FOREWORD

on core expressions of national identity. Expanding on his role as an architect, Pei became an adept diplomat and cultural mediator.

Pei's deep engagement with works of art remained consistent throughout his career. His museum designs have inspired millions with their sensitive display spaces and sightlines. But readers of this volume will also see that artworks are intertwined with Pei's plans for housing and his civic buildings, an acknowledgement of the fundamentally humanistic nature of his work. This connection between art, architecture, and urban design expresses what we mean at M+ by 'visual culture', namely, that the diverse areas of cultural practice are ultimately inseparable.

For their work to realise this ambitious project, my thanks go to the project team, led by Shirley Surya, Curator, Design and Architecture, M+. With her co-editor Aric Chen, General and Artistic Director of Het Nieuwe Instituut and former Lead Curator, Design and Architecture, M+, and supported by Naomi Altman, Curatorial Assistant, M+, and Senior Researcher and Advisor Janet Adams Strong, Surya approached her work tirelessly, with the same care, attention to detail, and sensitivity that her subject brought to his field. This publication draws on original scholarship presented at 'Rethinking Pei', a two-part symposium organised in 2017 by M+ in collaboration with the Harvard Graduate School of Design and the Faculty of Architecture at the University of Hong Kong. I am grateful to both institutions for their partnership in the earliest stages of our investigations. This volume and the exhibition are also made possible by the support of Lead Sponsor Bank of China (Hong Kong), Bei Shan Tang Foundation, the Family of S. P. Tao, Travel Partner Cathay, and Hotel Partner The Ritz-Carlton Hong Kong, and I would like to thank them for their generosity. Finally, and most importantly, I thank the Pei family for entrusting us with a presentation of the life and architecture of this remarkable figure in contemporary global culture. Their belief in this project and their unflagging support have been instrumental at every stage of its development, culminating in this book. Read today, the life and architecture of I. M. Pei offer an expressive example of the ability of a resolutely transnational and cross-cultural approach to speak to us all, together.

— Suhanya Raffel, Museum Director, M+

Introduction

Architecture Is Life

I. M. Pei (1917–2019) is one of the most recognised figures in twentieth-century architecture. His high-profile projects, realised with an exceptionally wide geographic reach, have solidified his prominent position in architectural history and popular culture. In the familiar, conventional view of Pei, the same set of reductive associations cling to his image: monumental geometry, a traversing of 'East' and 'West', and corporate structures that, while sophisticated, remain technical exercises.[1] Architecture placed in the public eye and on the front page over and over again inevitably becomes distilled to an easy shorthand. Moreover, Pei himself was averse to considering his practice on theoretical terms, a reluctance that doubtless contributed to the simplistic perspective that has come to be the dominant view of his work. But there is much more to Pei. His life and architecture weave together a tapestry made up of twentieth-century power dynamics, geopolitical struggles, cultural traditions, and the life of cities around the world. This book and the exhibition it accompanies were motivated by the need to reappraise the work of this familiar figure, and to examine its significance globally and for the Asia Pacific region in particular. Uncovering the conditions that informed his projects reveals what Pei once described as 'the functional currents swirling around them'—a network encompassing clients, cultures, governments, and financial interests.[2] The book's focus is as much on the context of Pei's life as it is on the dynamics of architectural practice. By taking a close look at Pei's long life, it becomes possible to describe his distinct approach through several themes, each representing a direction or area of focus that remained remarkably consistent throughout his career.

This book is organised into six chapters that correspond to these themes: 'Transcultural Foundations', 'Real Estate and Urban Redevelopment', 'Art and Civic Form', 'Material and Structural Innovation', 'Power, Politics, and Patronage', and 'Regenerating Cultural and Historical Archetypes'. For more than seventy years, Pei carried out close readings of regional and local contexts around the world, defined a role for architecture as a facilitator for the production of art and the formation of urban and civic space, and continuously investigated new interpretations of the idea of tradition. Taken together, these themes place Pei's practice in close dialogue with social, cultural, and biographical trajectories. Architecture and life become inseparable.

To provide an expanded view as well as a closer look at Pei's practice, as opposed to a comprehensive survey, the book studies the intentions and effects in a broad range of projects, both built and unbuilt. Pei is positioned not as a singular author, a lone genius moving through time and contexts, but rather an architect at the head of a large corporate office who embraced collaborative work and who fostered a company culture that privileged shared responsibility. For Pei, embracing multiple perspectives and bringing in the right collaborators were crucial to his method. He introduced his own perspective to each project, but recognised that any reading of a specific context would benefit from a gathering-together of relevant voices to arrive at an architecture that is the sum of experiences taken from life.

Each chapter of this book consists of a visual narrative drawn from archival documentation. Personal correspondence, photographs, material samples, newspaper clippings, and other documents, alongside sketches, drawings, presentation models, and site studies, present a picture of how Pei's work was produced, consumed, and mediated. Starting from the archive allows the material record of the work and its setting to speak for themselves. The picture that emerges is one of a practice that was fundamentally intertwined with crucial developments in urban renewal, nation building, and institutional identities in a range of circumstances. The selection of material makes it clear that architectural practice is as much tied to events as it is to projects; the records of meetings, correspondences, and receipts are just as important as direct documentation of the design process.

The selection foregrounds projects that illuminate Pei's contribution to regional and national narratives, particularly in Asia. These projects were important to specific contexts, and they also contribute to a larger portrait of Pei's career, marked by technical mastery, ingenious problem-solving, and serendipity, but also frustration and struggles with the limits of control. The material presented here comes from the archives of Pei Cobb Freed & Partners, the Library of Congress, the Pei family, clients, as well as Pei's collaborators at various points in his career, both institutional and individual. For example, documents and insights from Chang Chao-kang and Chen Chi-kwan, project architects on Tunghai University and the Luce Memorial Chapel in Taichung; from Liu Thai Ker of Singapore's Housing and Development Board and Urban Redevelopment Authority; and from Aslıhan Demirtaş, lead architectural designer on the Museum of Islamic Art in Doha, address the context of each project and discuss aspects of its design, development, and legacy. Alongside the archival documents, reflections and recollections from collaborators shed light on the working relationships that gave form to each project, while comments from observers and contemporary practitioners emphasise the broad resonance of Pei's work.

Pei's fame is due in no small part to the prodigious reproduction of photographs of his buildings in both architectural debates and popular culture. On the whole, these images treat the projects as icons, monuments that stand apart and speak on their own terms rather than as part of a larger urban strategy. The pyramid of the Louvre becomes like the pyramids of Giza. However, much can be gained from considering Pei's projects in their contexts and through a contemporary lens. This publication features newly commissioned images of eleven projects by seven photographers, taken during the Covid-19 pandemic: Kips Bay Plaza in New York, the National Center for Atmospheric Research in Boulder, Dallas City Hall, and the National Gallery of Art East Building in Washington DC by Naho Kubota; Fragrant Hill Hotel in Beijing and the Suzhou Museum by Tian Fangfang; Tunghai University in Taichung by Lee Kuo-Min; the Bank of China Tower in Hong Kong by South Ho; the Grand Louvre in Paris by Giovanna Silva; the Miho Museum in Shiga prefecture, Japan, by Yoneda Tomoko; and the Museum of Islamic Art in Doha by Mohamed Somji. The images document the buildings as elements rooted in their specific places and, taken together, show the relevance of Pei's projects to current conversations on architecture's relationship with cities and the public over time.

A study of the personal and professional dimensions of Pei's life relies on privileged access to both spoken and written records of his activities. This project would have been impossible without the support and trust of the Pei family: Didi, Sandi, Liane, and Patricia. We are particularly grateful to Sandi Pei, who as early as 2014 facilitated our discussions with I. M. Pei himself. In 2017, we organised the 'Rethinking Pei' symposium, a collaboration between M+, the Harvard Graduate School of Design, and the University of

Hong Kong's Faculty of Architecture. The discussions that took place in Cambridge, Massachusetts, and Hong Kong as part of this transcontinental symposium formed the foundation of our research for the exhibition and this publication. We are grateful to the late Henry N. Cobb, one of the three founding partners of Pei Cobb Freed & Partners, and José Bruguera, current partner, for supporting this project by granting us access to the firm's archive. Our extensive study of the archive was facilitated by the work of Emma Cobb, senior editor at Pei Cobb Freed & Partners, and in particular by Janet Adams Strong, senior researcher and advisor for this project, and formerly director of communications at Pei Cobb Freed & Partners, whose vast insight into Pei's work became immediately indispensable to the project.

Pei once described the process of overcoming difficulties in distinct social contexts as a cornerstone of his practice.[3] Examining how he interacted with the people and places involved in each project reveals a portrait of an architect as a savvy operator, a sophisticated thinker, and above all a humane conversation partner. Pei's ability to navigate complex situations with apparent grace and to realise projects for a range of places was due as much to his readiness to connect with others as it was to his abilities as an architect. He consistently addressed civic culture, the responsible and innovative use of materials and resources, and the place of a building in its surroundings. Along with other corporate offices of his era, Pei's firm set the standard for a global, transnational architecture practice that has today become routine. But, seen in this light, Pei's life and architecture can tell us something else, something subtler and more important than a simple statement of geographical breadth and a rigorous approach to design. Throughout his life, Pei remained committed to a belief in speaking across cultures, contexts, and territories and in working together for an architecture that could be part of a global discussion as much as a local or national one. Today, this kind of cosmopolitan perspective seems antiquated. As cities and countries turn increasingly inward, responding to anxiety about the loss of local culture and emphasising contrast and opposition, the easy, worldly sophistication that Pei demonstrated in his practice and relationships with others appears increasingly out of place. Pei's life and architecture show us an alternative, one built on understanding, curiosity, and intelligence. Examining his work as a record of his interactions with people, places, and ideas, it becomes clear that it is possible to recover this alternative, and to feel at home in the wider world.

— Shirley Surya and Aric Chen

M.I.T. Dorms.
Cambridge, Mass.
May 15, 1939

Dearest Dad,
 You have to be lenient with me when I remind you that this should have reached you ten days ago. Lately, I have been very much occupied; but aside from that, I can offer no other excuses.
 I am a bit puzzled by the complications over the scholarship. All I do know is that I have been granted the scholarship of $200.00 a year this last winter. This sum shall continuously be granted to me from then on till my graduation. I drew only $200.00 for my tuition last term (instead of $300.00) and I hope this will check with the report of the Irving Trust Co.
 During spring recess, I went to New York with a group of architectural students on an inspection tour. Through previous arrangements, we had a chance to see most of the outstanding structures built and being built. We also obtained permission to visit the New York' fair ground. I was there four months ago, and I could

could hardly believe my eyes when I saw it again five months afterwards. As I recall, the site chosen was originally a dumping swamp. Dead cows, junked automobiles and even wrecked baby carriages were of common sight. Now, it's a gigantic spectacle dazzling with color and glistening with light. Though, we laughed at its "false" architecture, we nevertheless were impressed by this masterpiece of broadway showmanship.

Regarding my summer practise, everything was settled two weeks ago. Thanks to Mr. Hellman's effort, I have been promised work at the architectural firm of Walker and Eisen of Los Angeles. School will be over by June 2nd, and I have promised Mr. Walker that I will report for work on or before June 20th. At present I am still undecided as to whether to take a transcontinental bus or to drive across with Audrey Li (李昭忠之子). The former is much faster but the latter promises more fun. In any way, I have saved enough to cover the passage. I have already written to two of my friends now in Los Angeles and I don't think I shall feel strange in a strange land.

Last week, I was elected treasurer of both the Chinese Students' Club and the Architectural Society. I begin to ponder that I should be studying banking instead of architecture.

Yesterday, at the Students' Club meeting, I found myself truly an old-timer of the occasion. I am in the last lap of my fourth year in this country and time no longer flies as it used to. I hope that I will see you, mother, sisters and brothers soon.

Your loving son,
Ioh Ming

I was awarded Chandler Prizes No. 4 & No. 5 at the Boston Society of Architects. Enclosed is a clipping from a local news paper. Dean William Emerson will retire this summer. He offered me a scholarship of $500.00 if I come back for graduate year work (6 th year). This I have declined.

**I. M. Pei, letter to Tsuyee Pei, 13 May 1939.
Second Historical Archives of China. Original stored at Second Historical Archives of China**

Transcultural Foundations

1

'I don't think I shall feel strange in a strange land'

PAGE 14:
**I. M. Pei, A Bankers' Club in Hong Kong, 1938–1939.
MIT Museum**

For his fourth-year student project at the Massachusetts Institute of Technology, Pei selected a site near Victoria Peak in Hong Kong. The choice reflects how the urban environment of Hong Kong—where Pei spent the first decade of his life, from 1918 until 1927—continued to capture his imagination. The building's plain rectilinearity and flexible asymmetry show the formal influence of the International Style. But the structure's position within the steep topography of the Peak, oriented towards Victoria Harbour, and the response of its programme to financial work in the city make this project one of Pei's earliest exercises in geographical and cultural specificity.

TRANSCULTURAL FOUNDATIONS

This book begins with a letter written by I. M. Pei in Cambridge, Massachusetts, to his father, Tsuyee, who had recently moved to Chongqing to escape the Japanese invasion of Shanghai. Dated 13 May 1939, the letter shows the ease with which the younger Pei inhabited multiple cultures. He relays news from his last year at the Massachusetts Institute of Technology (MIT) in English as comfortably as he would have done in Chinese, describing his participation in a Chinese students' club, receiving the Boston Society of Architects' Chandler Prize, his fascination with New York and the 1939 World's Fair, and—in jest—the idea of studying banking instead of architecture. Like the other documents illustrated in this chapter, this letter offers a picture of how I. M. Pei came to thrive within the differences in cultures and environments he encountered throughout his life as a Chinese-born American architect practising around the world.

This chapter explores the ways in which Pei reconciled multiple identities as a young man, against a backdrop of social, cultural, and political upheaval in wartime China and the United States. This formative period—beginning with his birth in Guangzhou in 1917 and ending with him embarking on his first design projects as part of the real-estate firm Webb & Knapp in 1948—provided a foundation of cultural and architectural references that would inform his later built projects, especially those in Shanghai, Taichung, Beijing, Hong Kong, and Suzhou. The material presented here expands and complicates how we interpret the effects of Pei's upbringing—how the cosmopolitan modernity of Hong Kong and Shanghai, the historic gardens of Suzhou, and the giants of the modern movement who were teaching in Cambridge influenced his life and practice. Pei's engagement with ideas of tradition, modernity, regionality, and internationalism transcends simplistic cultural duality and instead portrays an architect grappling with Chinese nationalism and global citizenship, the lack of racial and ideological diversity in the academy and the architectural profession in post-war America, and architecture's role in society.

The influence of Tsuyee Pei (1893–1982) on his son extended far beyond the architect's early years. The elder Pei's transnational banking network and connections with the Chinese diaspora played a direct role in his son's commissions. In his own work as a banker,

Tsuyee Pei espoused a kind of cosmopolitan nationalism, a sense of duty to place one's knowledge and skills at the service of national interests, in the context of a globalised economy.[1] He developed this sensibility at least in part in response to the political turmoil that raged around him as a financier in Republican China. He persuaded his employer, the Bank of China, to establish a main branch in Hong Kong to take advantage of the foreign-exchange market in the British colony and enrolled his children in missionary schools in Hong Kong and Shanghai, steeping them in both Chinese and American pedagogy.[2] Tsuyee Pei's adroit manoeuvring and deliberate decision-making connected his son with members of high society, many of whom would go on to become power brokers between China and the rest of the world.

In 1930s Shanghai, I. M. Pei was fascinated by the recently constructed Park Hotel, at that time Asia's tallest building. It was established by the Joint Savings Society—a bank founded in the 1920s and managed by members of the Chinese elite—and symbolised a shift from the Euro-American–dominated, quasi-colonial legacy of the Bund to the bourgeois Chinese society of Midtown. In the milieu of explosive urban growth in Shanghai, Pei identified a current of national sentiment and a sense of social responsibility in the rise of a generation committed to the city's development beyond the dictates of foreign investors. He articulated this sense of nationalism in his undergraduate thesis at MIT, completed in 1940, which focuses on the design of modular mobile pavilions for staging exhibitions, films, and plays across rural China, as a way to disseminate information related to Republican campaigns promoting sanitation and national education. Titled 'Standardized Propaganda Units for War Time and Peace Time China' and conceived soon after the fall of Shanghai to Japanese forces, Pei's thesis reflected a desire upheld by many Chinese students of his generation to align their professional skills with the charge of *shi ye jiu guo* (rescuing the nation through one's enterprise). This sense of responsibility corresponded with the prevailing call among American architects to contribute to the war effort in Europe, as reflected in such magazines as *TASK*, published by students at the Harvard Graduate School of Design (GSD), MIT, and Smith College, which featured excerpts from Pei's thesis project.

Pei's brand of nationalism was neither essentialist nor oppositional. His views were not centred on the definition of a singular and invariant ethnic, national, or cultural entity set against the 'other', even as he demonstrated a sustained interest in questions of Chinese identity in architecture. A project for a museum of Chinese art at the politically significant civic centre of the Greater Shanghai Plan, the subject of his final-year thesis project at the GSD in 1946, signals the beginnings of Pei's nuanced nationalist consciousness. His incorporation of a Chinese walled garden in the museum's spatial organisation was more than a nod to tradition and an evocation of childhood memories of Shizi Lin, the fourteenth-century garden in Suzhou that his family owned. The integration of landscaped courtyards with gallery spaces emphasises a spatial and visual dialogue between the Chinese artefacts and works of art on display and the natural elements outside—a way of encountering traditional Chinese art that differed from the way art is typically experienced in a European context. Pei's design was also motivated by a search for a 'national' form of expression that would address what he saw as the 'limit to the internationalisation of architecture' in its response to differences in 'climate, history, culture and life'.[3] Reacting to the anti-historic curriculum and notion of modernism as an 'international style' that Walter Gropius was championing at Harvard, Pei asserted an alternative model that reflected local customs and conditions.[4]

Like his later projects sited in China, from the unbuilt Huatung University campus in Shanghai to the Suzhou Museum, Pei's Harvard thesis refers to historical precedents of vernacular and landscape architecture, in carefully scaled buildings set amid landscaped gardens featuring meandering paths, bodies of water, rock work, and miniature trees. For Pei, the Chinese garden was not an unchanging prototype but a historically and culturally embedded conceptual framework that mediates change in nature, and nature's interdependence with human intervention. Pei expressed ambivalence towards such historicist 'Chinese' architectural elements as the *da wuding* (big roof) with an upturned roofline, which was popular in early twentieth-century Shanghai and is notable in the buildings of the YMCA (Young Men's Christian Association) and St John's University missionary schools attended by Pei. The architect believed that forms arising from a particular locality, history, and cultural framework should not be mimicked, but rather reinterpreted through site and programme. This view aligned with modern architecture's commitment to formal abstraction, economy, industry, and civic consciousness, while remaining attuned to specific conditions.

In the context of wartime China and the lack of ideological diversity in his architectural education, Pei's embrace of the persistence and mutability of tradition was more than an exercise in modern architecture's universal relevance. It was an attempt to recover an endangered past, to represent a minority perspective, and to reconcile these intentions with modern architecture's engagement with particular cultural identities and geographic settings. The foundation of an approach composed of aligning multiple specific contexts without homogenising them would have enabled Pei to contribute to the construction of a new China. Instead, it led him to the visionary project of rebuilding cities in post-war America and, later, to work in places beyond.

— Shirley Surya

1.1 | **Pei family portrait, from left: I. M. Pei's sister Denise; his father, Tsuyee; his mother, Chuang Lien Kwun; sister Cecilia; I. M.; and brother Yu Kun, 1919. Bank of China (Hong Kong)**

Pei's father, Tsuyee Pei, chief accountant of the Bank of China's Canton branch, recommended that the institution focus its business away from Canton (now Guangzhou) and towards Hong Kong. This was in response to the political turmoil caused by warlords in Canton and a recognition of the business opportunities afforded by the foreign-exchange market in Hong Kong, a centre of intense trading activities among the Chinese diaspora across Southeast Asia. It led to the Pei family's relocation to Hong Kong in 1918 and to huge profits for the bank. In the British colony, Pei was exposed to a cosmopolitan and multicultural environment. Like his father had done in Suzhou, Pei attended an Anglican missionary school in Hong Kong, St Paul's College Primary School. He nevertheless considered his family life to be 'absolutely Chinese'.

1.2.1 | **China's delegation to the Bretton Woods Monetary Conference, held at the Mount Washington Hotel in New Hampshire (1–22 July 1944), including Tsuyee Pei (front row, second from left), former Chinese ambassador to the US Hu Shih (front row, fifth from left), and Minister of Finance Kung Hsiang-Hsi (front row, sixth from left), 1944. Patricia Pei**

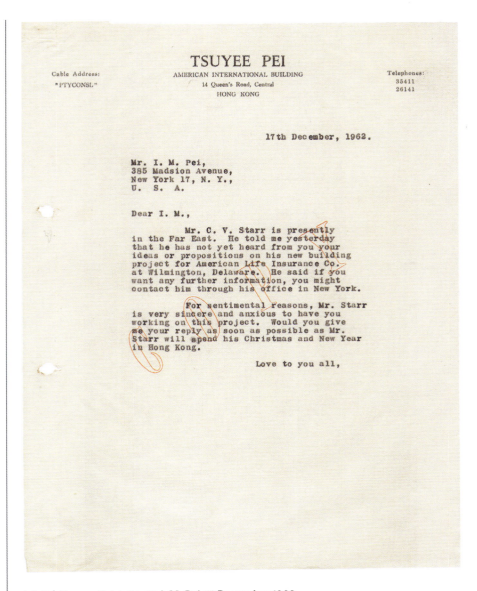

1.2.2 | **Tsuyee Pei, letter to I. M. Pei, 17 December 1962.**
Patricia Pei

1.2.1–1.2.2
Tsuyee Pei continued to have an instrumental role not only in the growth of the Bank of China but also in China's standing in global finance, especially in relation to the United States. In 1944, as the then director of the Bank of China, and having travelled to America in the 1930s to study the US banking system, Tsuyee Pei played a key role in drafting China's proposal for the Bretton Woods Monetary Conference, which established the World Bank. There, China successfully lobbied to ensure equitable loans for its post-war development. Tsuyee Pei's strategic outlook and transnational network had an influential role in his son's life and career. Notably, Tsuyee Pei had a connection with C. V. Starr, who, in Shanghai, had founded what came to be the world's leading global insurance and investment company, American International Group. I. M. later designed the Wilmington Tower (1963–1971) in Delaware as the headquarters of the American Life Insurance Company, a subsidiary of Starr's corporation.

I think it happens in many childhoods. You see things or hear stories that make the existence of another world seem concrete—another world informed by knowledge unknown to you, guided by an entirely different logic, and adorned with exciting details and expressions. It makes you want to explore. For me, this was the Jinling Hotel in Nanjing, where I grew up. Seeing its towering presence in the city, strolling through its grand, column-free lobby, and looking out of its monumental glass storefront, I was as excited as Pei must have been when he saw the Park Hotel being built in Shanghai as a boy. Some of us go on to become architects and aspire to make buildings and structures that inspire.

Pei, who became one of the most successful architects working with the institutional leaders, political elites, and corporate tycoons of his generation, understood very well the power of architecture to evoke child-like excitement in his clients.

– Jing Liu

Jing Liu is a Nanjing-born architect and co-founder of the New York–based practice SO – IL.

1.3 | **Map of Shanghai featuring major landmarks in the International Settlement, in** *Oriental Skyscraper: The New J. S. S. Building*, **1934. László Hudec Collection, University of Victoria Special Collections and University Archives**

Tsuyee Pei's transfer to the Bank of China's Shanghai branch as manager brought the Pei family from Hong Kong to an even more cosmopolitan metropolis. Shanghai owed much of its vitality and diversity to the quasi-colonial nature of the International Settlement and the French Concession. This illustrated map from a 1934 booklet commemorating the opening of the Park Hotel, in the J. S. S. Building developed by the Joint Savings Society in Shanghai's Midtown, features the main attractions in the settlement. This was the environment Pei grew up in—his secondary school at the YMCA, the cinemas he visited, and the traditional and modern landmarks he saw around him. For Pei, Midtown and its new buildings represented the future as opposed to the downtown Bund of the colonial past. The Park Hotel, Asia's first skyscraper, fascinated Pei and sparked an early interest in architecture.

1.4 | 'The Park Hotel, Shanghai—and Its Automatic Sprinkler Installation', *The Sprinkler Bulletin* 151 (30 June 1935): 1354. University of Victoria Special Collections and University Archives

The automatic sprinkler system installed at the Park Hotel was one of its many technologically advanced features. The twenty-two-storey structure's frame of lightweight, German-made chrome steel, supported by four hundred timber piles atop a concrete base, prevented it from sinking into Shanghai's loose soil. Designed by László Hudec, a Hungarian architect who lived and worked in China, the building is a three-tiered stepped volume in the Art Deco style. Rather than typical ornamentation, the brick facade is distinguished by vertical bands formed by regularly aligned windows. The two lowest floors housed the Joint Savings Society bank, founded and directed by members of the Chinese elite. The building was a symbol of the new cosmopolitan Shanghai bourgeoisie, a segment of society that included the Peis.

1.5 | Burr Photo Co., Chinese YMCA, Shanghai, ca.1920. Kautz Family YMCA Archives, University of Minnesota Libraries

The Shanghai YMCA was built in 1907 on Sichuan Road. Designed by expatriate British architects Algar & Beesley, the building housed a gymnasium—the first in Shanghai to feature an indoor swimming pool—in addition to the classrooms, dormitories, and lecture hall of the YMCA Middle School, where Pei was a student from 1927 to 1931. With its symmetrical layout, brick facade, and neoclassical arches and keystones, it resembled YMCA buildings in the United States and across East Asia, representing the organisation's international missionary reach.

1.6 | The Memorial Arch at Schereschewsky Hall, St John's University, Shanghai, ca.1925. Archives of the United Board for Christian Higher Education in Asia, Yale Divinity Library

Founded in 1879 by the Episcopal Church, St John's University was a prestigious private school accredited by the US university system. Between 1931 and 1935, Pei attended high school there and then studied engineering. Designed in 1894 by Brenan Atkinson, a Shanghai-based British architect, the main building featured a *da wuding* (big roof) with an upturned roofline, atop a symmetrical reinforced-concrete structure. Generations of architects, both Chinese and foreign, reproduced the *da wuding* as a means of connecting with China's building traditions. At various points throughout his career, Pei would ask how regional characteristics can be expressed in architecture without resorting to the imitation of historical forms.

1.7 | I. M. Pei (middle row, eighth from right) and classmates at St John's Middle School on the occasion of the retirement of Chinese literature teacher Wang Xiang Yin, 1931. Estate of I. M. Pei

The frame of this photograph is inscribed with a poem expressing gratitude to Wang Xiang Yin and the desire for a future reunion. This parting memento given to Pei by his classmate Wang Tung speaks to the close-knit community of St John's and its unique curriculum, taught by Western and Chinese professors to students who were steeped in both cultures. Pei became part of a network of bilingual St John's alumni who formed important links between China and the rest of the world.

1.8 | Pei family portrait, back row, from left: Tsuyee Pei and Chuang Lien Kwun with I. M. Pei's youngest brother, Yu Tsung; front row, from left: I. M., Denise Pei, Cecilia Pei, I. M.'s grandfather Bei Li-tai and step-grandmother, and Yu Kun, ca.1927. Papers of I. M. Pei, Library of Congress, Washington DC

This photograph was taken when Pei first visited Suzhou. As one of the eldest of his siblings, he spent his summers with his paternal grandfather, studying the history of the family and learning rituals of ancestral worship. Suzhou provided him with an important counterpoint to Shanghai. Its environment and the figure of his grandfather embodied China's past and a society where human relationships and traditional Confucian values were paramount. This experience shaped much of Pei's sense of responsibility and connection with his roots, and eventually came to influence his practice.

1.9 | **Illustration of Shizi Lin, in *Nanxun shengdian* (The Great Canon of the Southern Tours) by Gao Jin (fasc. 99), 1770. National Diet Library**

Located in the Jiangnan region to the south of the Yangtze River, Suzhou was for centuries an economic and cultural centre of southern China. The city is home to an unrivalled collection of classical walled gardens. The gardens are admired for their complex interplay between openness and interiority, with labyrinthine but flexible layouts of meandering streams, elaborate rock work, caves, rich plantings, and such architectural elements as bridges, pavilions, and corridors. In the eighteenth century, the Qianlong Emperor commissioned detailed documentation of the gardens during his six tours of southern China. At his imperial residence in Beijing, the emperor recreated Shizi Lin (the Lion Grove Garden) built by monk and scholar Tian-ru in Suzhou during the Yuan dynasty. The garden is best known for its lion-shaped rock work made from intricately water-worn limestone from nearby Lake Tai. Shizi Lin was acquired by Pei's paternal grand-uncle, Bei Runsheng, in 1917.

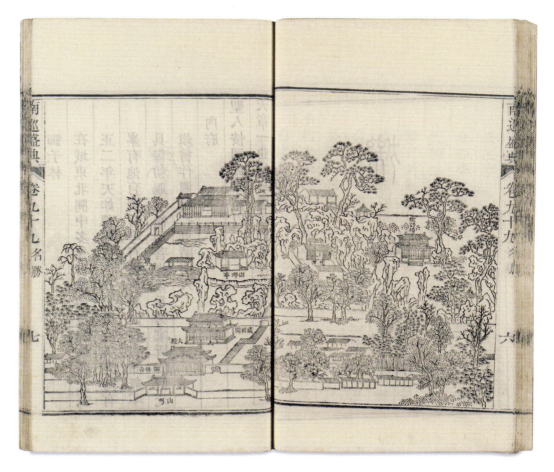

1.10.1 | **I. M. Pei on a bridge in Shizi Lin in front of the Huxin Ting (Mid-lake Pavilion), 1930s. Family of I. M. Pei**

On our first family visit to Shizi Lin in Suzhou around 1978, my father told childhood stories about running around and hiding among the rocks. Today, the garden is teeming with tourists, but when he visited, which was not that often, he was alone. That's the real way to appreciate Chinese gardens.

– Chien Chung (Didi) Pei

Chien Chung (Didi) Pei is I. M. Pei's second son. He joined I. M. Pei & Partners in 1972 before establishing Pei Partnership Architects (now PEI Architects) in 1992.

1.10.2 | Plan of Shizi Lin, in *Suzhou gudian yuanlin* (Chinese Classical Gardens of Suzhou) by Liu Dunzhen, 1979. China Building Industry Press

1.10.1–1.10.2
Shizi Lin underwent several reconstructions in the Qing era as its successive owners redesigned the garden to pique the emperor's interest. Renovations by Bei Runsheng—reflected in a 1960 study by architectural historian Liu Dunzhen—included the addition of an ancestral hall and the Huxin Ting (Mid-lake Pavilion). Through its various transformations, the garden retained its Taoist-influenced conceptual framework as an interpretation of landscapes in canonical works of painting and literature and as a meditation on change in nature. Pei recalled how, as a child playing among its rocks and grottoes, the garden stimulated his imagination. As an adult, he recognised the importance of the interdependence of nature and human intervention in the garden, and of the multivalent search for scenery when one is in motion and at rest.

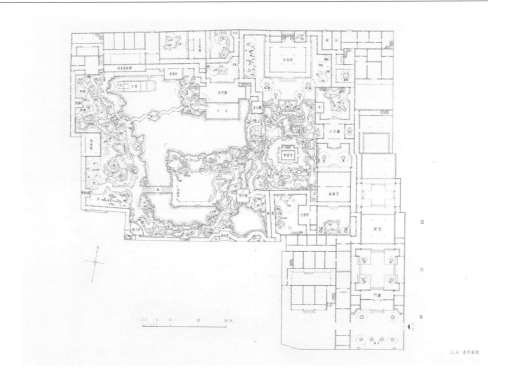

It was only years later that I recognised how experiential I. M.'s approach to the National Gallery of Art East Building was. While working in Hong Kong, I flew to Shanghai and took the soft-seat train to Suzhou. It was there that I fully understood the impact of I. M.'s early experience in his family garden. Each garden in Suzhou feels like a universe, even if it's only a quarter acre. You feel that you're no longer in a city. Everything is designed from the perspective of what one sees, how one walks there, and the experience of the space.

– Yann Weymouth

Yann Weymouth was the design architect for the National Gallery of Art East Building.

1.11 | Zigzag corridor at Shizi Lin, in *Suzhou gudian yuanlin* (Chinese Classical Gardens of Suzhou) by Liu Dunzhen, 1979. China Building Industry Press

In Chinese gardens, straight and winding paths coexist, creating transitions between houses, pavilions, gardens, and gates. This interplay slows the viewing experience and provides different vantage points from which to enjoy scenes of plants or rocks, or look through latticed windows onto another courtyard.

The foundations of I. M.'s perception and understanding were Chinese, but he was very worldly and open-minded. He knew there might be a different way of looking at something, and he could learn how to shape things according to the situation. He was able to swim in many ponds, combining sensibilities from China, the United States, and Europe.

– Liane Pei

Liane Pei is I. M. Pei's daughter.

1.12 | **I. M. Pei (front row, sixth from left) and other students aboard the SS *President Coolidge* in Shanghai, sailing for San Francisco, 1935. Papers of I. M. Pei, Library of Congress, Washington DC**

Pei left China with the intention of making the most of his forthcoming education in the United States and of returning to contribute to his native country's projects of reform and modernisation, just as earlier generations of US-trained youth had done. However, he would not return to China until 1974. The community of expatriate Chinese students became an important way for him to maintain a link with his distant home.

1.13 | I. M. Pei, letter to his parents, 12 October 1935. Shanghai Municipal Archives. Original stored at Shanghai Municipal Archives

Pei wrote this letter shortly after transferring to MIT from the University of Pennsylvania. The latter had trained a generation of influential Chinese architects, but Pei was uninterested in its Beaux-Arts curriculum, which emphasised aesthetic success based on monumental planning, symmetry, and hierarchy, and he left the school after two weeks. In the letter, Pei describes the first courses he took at MIT: Graphics, Shades and Shadows, Perspective, Mechanics, and Architecture Design I. While MIT's architecture school also broadly followed the Beaux-Arts model, its dean at the time, William Emerson, introduced contemporary issues into the curriculum. Pei expresses the difficulties he had with studying English and French, but also his eagerness to enrol in an additional course in order to graduate a year early—a sign of his ambition.

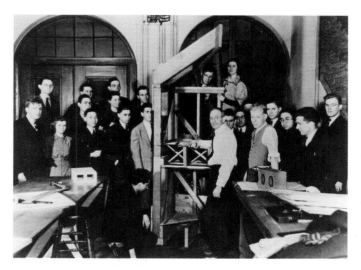

1.14 | I. M. Pei (front row, third from left) and classmates at MIT during Pei's sophomore year, ca.1936. Papers of I. M. Pei, Library of Congress, Washington DC

By this point, Emerson had persuaded Pei to focus on architecture as opposed to architectural engineering. Although he was dissatisfied with the school's Beaux-Arts emphasis on historicism, Pei became exposed to the writings of Le Corbusier at MIT—as well as to the man himself, at a November 1935 lecture. Le Corbusier's ideas of economy, industry, and abstraction would play an influential role in the formation of Pei's language as an architect.

1.15 | Frederick K. Morris, letter to William Emerson, 2 October 1936. Papers of I. M. Pei, Library of Congress, Washington DC

MIT geology professor Frederick K. Morris wrote this letter to Emerson in reference to Pei's request to forego a general science course, which he had made on the grounds of credentials earned from his studies at St John's University in Shanghai. Morris's doubts about the ability and prospects of an 'Oriental student' reveal the deep-seated discrimination Pei faced in a profession marked by little racial or cultural diversity.

1.16.1 | **I. M. Pei, nude figure drawing, ca.1938. MIT Museum**

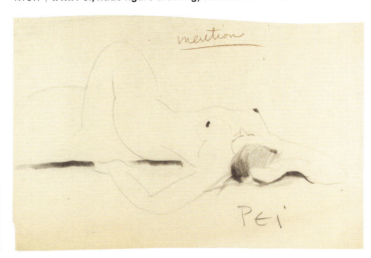

1.16.2 | **I. M. Pei, nude figure drawing, ca.1938. MIT Museum**

1.16.1–1.16.2
In his freehand drawing course, part of MIT's third-year curriculum, Pei learned foundational drawing techniques that would be indispensable to the architectural design process. Pei's life drawings demonstrate a focus on gradients of light and shade and an emphatic use of regulating lines to create decisive contours.

1.17.1 | **I. M. Pei, 'Standardized Propaganda Units for War Time and Peace Time China', 1940, cover, 6, 14. MIT Libraries**

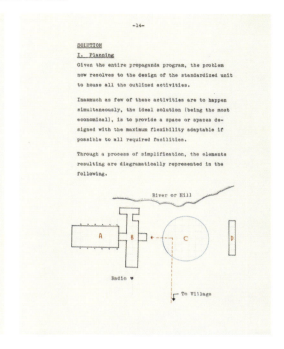

1.17.2 | **I. M. Pei, model of a propaganda unit, 1940. MIT Museum**

1.17.1–1.17.2

The Japanese occupation of China in the late 1930s instilled in Pei a patriotic sense of responsibility to contribute to the country's nationalist project. For his undergraduate thesis at MIT, Pei proposed a prototype propaganda pavilion composed of a movable, prefabricated bamboo shelter housing a 1,200-square-metre theatre (A), an exhibition space (B), an outdoor forum for radio broadcasts and public speeches (C), and a shed for livestock and agricultural equipment (D). Pei defined 'propaganda' as information on public health and economic development disseminated to a largely illiterate populace through plays, films, and exhibits. He proposed that units be used to spread messages at the local level in often remote areas, where populations were swelling owing to migration from Japanese-occupied cities. With its position at the centre of village life and its use of readily available bamboo as a building material, the pavilion design refers to traditional village theatres in rural China.

1.18.1 | **I. M. Pei, relationship diagram showing a propaganda unit at the centre of a village, 1940. MIT Museum**

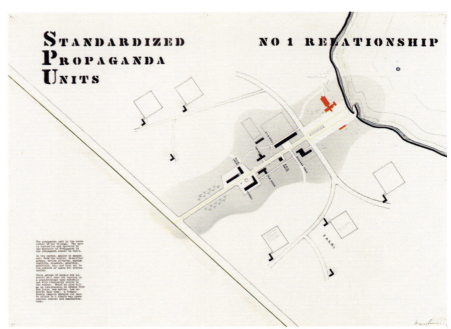

1.18.2 | **I. M. Pei, floor plan of a propaganda unit, 1940. MIT Museum**

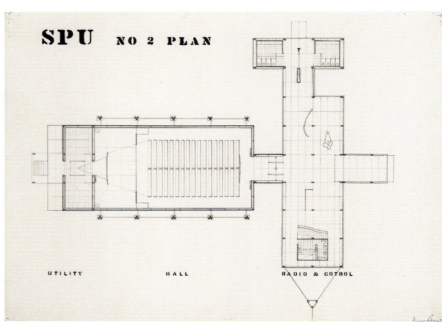

1.18.3 | **I. M. Pei, elevations of a propaganda unit, 1940. MIT Museum**

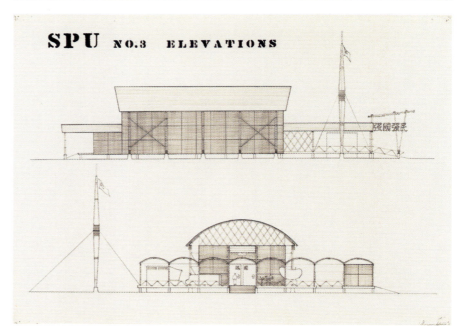

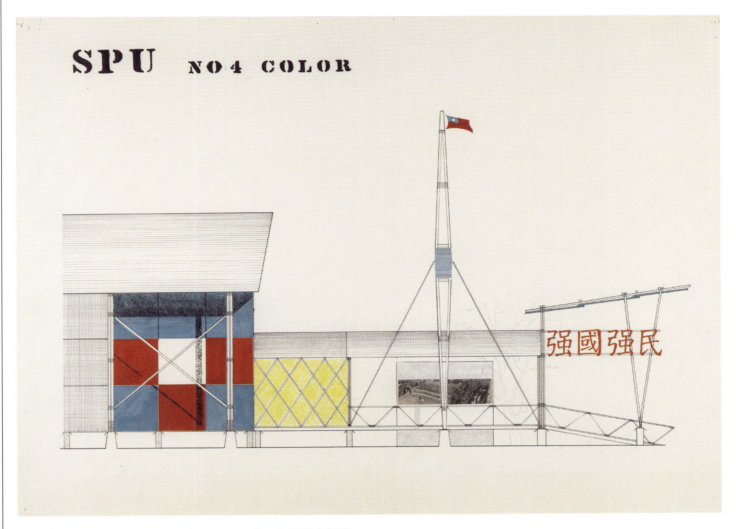

1.18.4 | **I. M. Pei, elevation study of a propaganda unit, 1940. MIT Museum**

1.18.1–1.18.4
The flexible, low-cost design of Pei's standardised propaganda unit would allow it to be adapted to a range of uses. The walls of the theatre hall can be reconfigured to control lighting and divide spaces for smaller-scale activities. The exhibition hall features an open floor plan, with woven-bamboo wall panels painted with colour-coded messages in yellow, red, and blue, including the slogan *qiang guo qiang min* (strong nation, strong people).

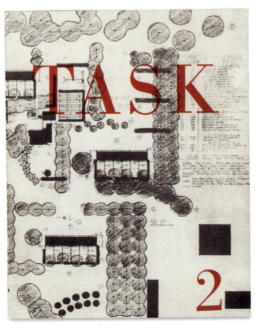

1.19 | **Cover, *TASK* 2 (Summer 1941). Frances Loeb Library, Harvard University Graduate School of Design**

Pei's MIT thesis was included in the second issue of *TASK*, a magazine published by the GSD, MIT, and Smith College between 1941 and 1945. The publication addressed architecture's relevance to the war effort, a focus that aligned with the Chinese nationalist charge of *shi ye jiu guo* (rescuing the nation through one's enterprise) taken up by Pei. Presented alongside articles on defence housing in the United States and post-war reconstruction in Europe, Pei's proposal for a new building type responding to China's political transformations widened the geographical reach of *TASK*'s contents.

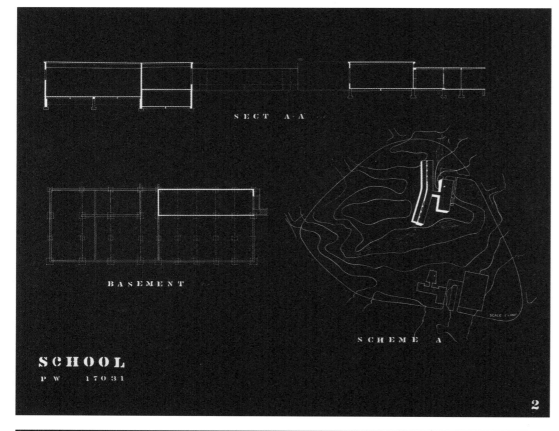

1.20.1 | **Eileen Pei, site, plan, and elevation drawings of Post-war Housing (with Community Center, School, and Shop), made as part of Marcel Breuer's studio course, 1943. Frances Loeb Library, Harvard University Graduate School of Design**

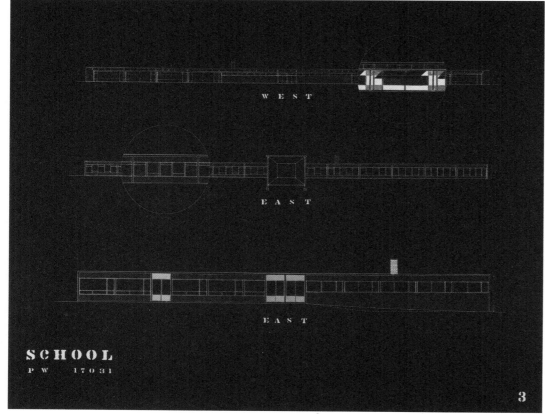

1.20.2 | **Eileen Pei, elevations of Post-war Housing (with Community Center, School, and Shop), 1943. Frances Loeb Library, Harvard University Graduate School of Design**

1.20.3 | **I. M. Pei, elevations of Post-war Shelter for the Average Family, made as part of Walter Gropius's studio course, 1943. Frances Loeb Library, Harvard University Graduate School of Design**

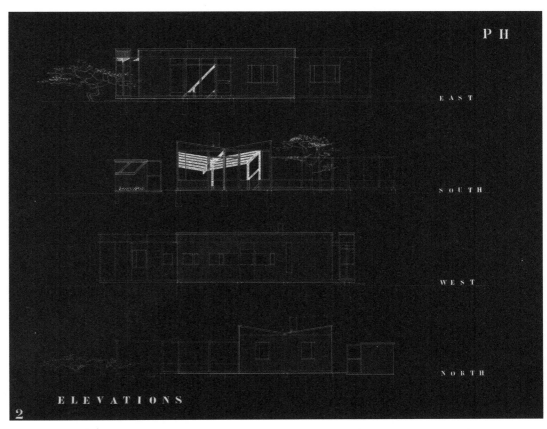

1.20.4 | **I. M. Pei, design variations for Post-war Shelter for the Average Family, 1943. Frances Loeb Library, Harvard University Graduate School of Design**

1.20.1–1.20.4
I. M. and Eileen Pei (née Loo) produced these drawings in design studios at the GSD in the spring of 1943—I. M. for Walter Gropius and Eileen for Marcel Breuer. The couple had married in 1942, and, after completing her studies at Wellesley College, Eileen had enrolled in the landscape architecture programme at the GSD. I. M.'s interaction with Eileen's professors had significant influence on his decision to enrol at the GSD himself, which he did in December 1942. He was drawn to the school's forward-looking curriculum, which integrated architecture with design, landscape architecture, and planning. He received his Master of Architecture degree in 1946. Eileen, however, withdrew from her studies after the birth of the couple's first child, T'ing Chung, in 1945.

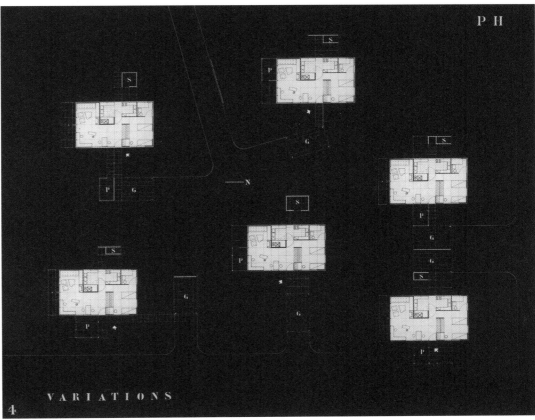

1.21 | **Jerry Cooke, Walter Gropius at the GSD, ca.1945. Jerry Cooke Archives**

Pei was attracted to Gropius's Bauhaus methodology of developing formal solutions for an efficient and humane built environment through consideration of technical, economic, and social conditions. While he was influenced more by Marcel Breuer at the GSD, Pei saw Gropius—who had become chair of the GSD in 1938—as 'a great teacher' whose commitment to logic and rigour nevertheless allowed for vigorous debate. The Bauhaus master's definition of the 'international style' was a point of contention for Pei, who found a basic 'limit to the internationalisation of architecture' (as he would put it in a later interview) in the discipline's relationship with culture, climate, and history.

TRANSCULTURAL FOUNDATIONS

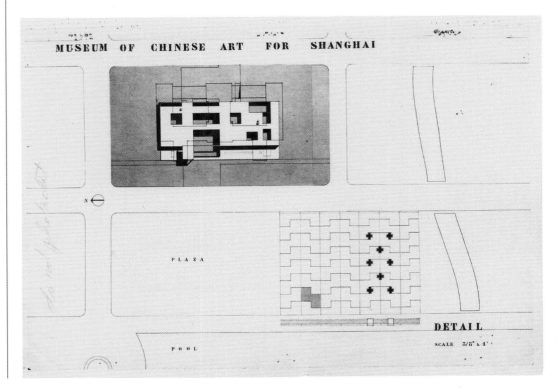

1.22.1 | **I. M. Pei, site plan of the Museum of Chinese Art for Shanghai, 1946. Frances Loeb Library, Harvard University Graduate School of Design**

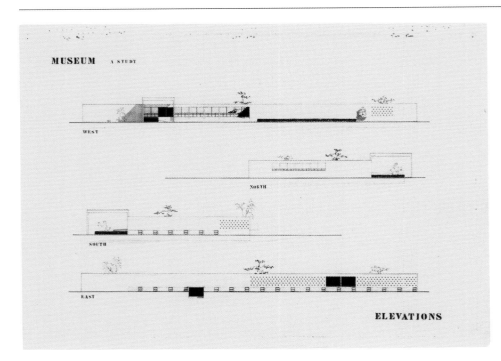

1.22.2 | **I. M. Pei, elevations of the Museum of Chinese Art for Shanghai, 1946. Frances Loeb Library, Harvard University Graduate School of Design**

1.22.1–1.22.2
To demonstrate the potential of a regional or national expression in architecture, Pei proposed a museum of Chinese art for Shanghai as the subject of his master's thesis. The museum was designed to house artefacts and works of art from all periods of China's history. In contrast to the upturned *da wuding* and symmetrical elevation of the buildings in the Greater Shanghai Plan, Pei's museum is a low, two-storey, flat-roofed orthogonal structure of reinforced concrete with marble veneer. A left-aligned entrance canopy on a ramp leads to the museum's lower and upper floors. The building is sunk half a level below ground, and semi-permeable walls allow views into the landscaped courtyards from outside. By incorporating specific elements of Chinese culture—bare, whitewashed walls and walled gardens of the kind found in traditional homes, in addition to the works of art on display—and integrating them into a modernist language of form, material, and structure, Pei presented an alternative to modernism's universality while questioning the Beaux-Arts model adopted by China's Republican government. The project was featured in the February 1948 issue of *Progressive Architecture*—the only student work to be included—with Walter Gropius describing it as 'highly prized by the Harvard Design faculty'.

1.23.1 | **I. M. Pei, lower-floor plan of the Museum of Chinese Art for Shanghai, 1946. Frances Loeb Library, Harvard University Graduate School of Design**

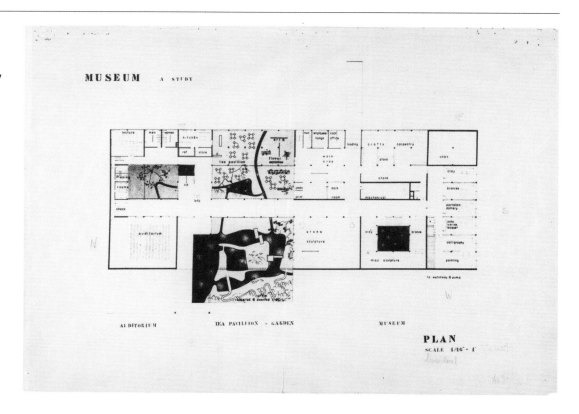

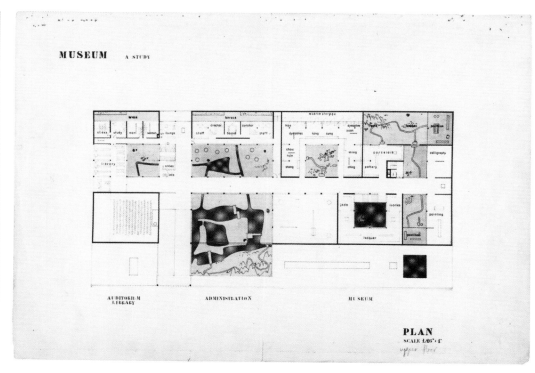

1.23.2 | **I. M. Pei, upper-floor plan of the Museum of Chinese Art for Shanghai, 1946. Frances Loeb Library, Harvard University Graduate School of Design**

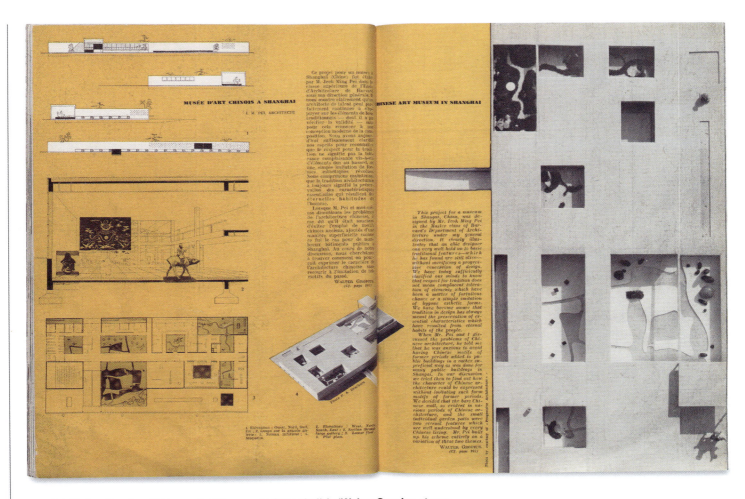

1.23.3 | **Walter Gropius, 'Chinese Art Museum in Shanghai', in 'Walter Gropius et son école/The Spread of an Idea', special issue,** *L'architecture d'aujourd'hui* **28 (February 1950): 76–77. Bibliothèque d'architecture contemporaine—Cité de l'architecture**

1.23.1–1.23.3

The galleries in Pei's museum of Chinese art are organised around landscaped courtyards. In the February 1950 issue of *L'architecture d'aujourd'hui*, which focused on Walter Gropius's influence, Gropius identified the 'small individual garden patio' and the 'bare Chinese wall' in Pei's design as the two traditional features that enabled Pei to express the 'character of Chinese architecture' without 'sacrificing a progressive conception of design'. The introduction of these walled landscaped gardens, which feature circuitous paths, bridges crossing streams, rock compositions, miniature trees, and a bamboo tea pavilion, resulted from Pei's observation of the inextricable link between Chinese scholars' intimate delight in works of art and the natural beauty of the scholar's garden. While in section it resembles Mies van der Rohe's Museum for a Small City (1941–1943), the project never loses sight of its cultural specificity, with Pei's collage of three ancient artefacts (see page 144) and his introduction of indoor–outdoor connectivity through the long gallery corridors and central tea garden.

Huatung University (1946–1948; unbuilt)
Shanghai

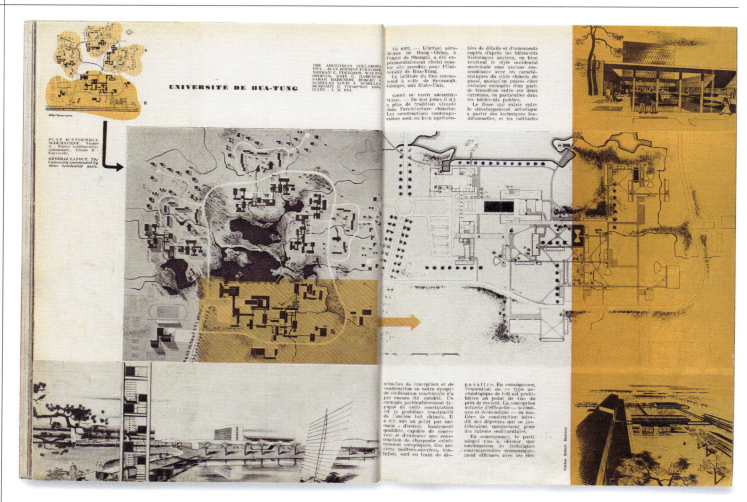

1.24 | **Walter Gropius, 'Université de Hua-tung', in 'Walter Gropius et son école/The Spread of an Idea', special issue,** *L'architecture d'aujourd'hui* **28 (February 1950): 26–27. Bibliothèque d'architecture contemporaine—Cité de l'architecture et du patrimoine**

The February 1950 issue of *L'architecture d'aujourd'hui* features Huatung University in Shanghai, designed by The Architects Collaborative (TAC)—a firm co-founded by Walter Gropius in 1945—with Pei as an associate. The project was commissioned in 1946 by the United Board for Christian Colleges in China (UBCCC), the organisation behind St John's Middle School, Pei's alma mater in Shanghai. Gropius invited Pei, who was then an assistant professor at the GSD, to collaborate on the project. Like Pei's project for his master's thesis, a museum of Chinese art for Shanghai, the design of Huatung campus demonstrates a keen sensitivity to the human scale and an intimate dialogue with the landscape. Apart from the library and clock tower, academic buildings and residential areas are two- or three-storey tile-roofed structures with terraces placed among landscaped courtyards, artificial lakes, and ponds. The buildings are lofted on stilts and connected by covered walkways, a response to the swampy conditions of the sixty-hectare site.

1.25 | **I. M. Pei, letter to Walter Gropius, 25 October 1948. Bauhaus-archiv**

As part of his work with Gropius and TAC for the Huatung University project, Pei met with the executive secretary of the UBCCC, Dr Robert J. McMullen. In his letter to Gropius telling him of this meeting, he notes how the project's model was still on display, and attributes its 'atmospheric' character to observations gleaned from the drawing process. Pei remained involved with the project until the UBCCC suspended all work in mainland China following the founding of the People's Republic in 1949. Pei also writes confidently to Gropius about his work to remake American cities with New York real-estate developer William Zeckendorf, beginning with an ambitious proposal for an apartment block known as the Helix.

The American Education of I. M. Pei

Joan Ockman

Eighteen-year-old I. M. Pei set foot in the United States for the first time in late August 1935, newly arrived from Shanghai and eager to begin his studies in architecture. Disembarking in San Francisco, he and a comrade spent a few days sightseeing and then boarded a train for Philadelphia. It was a tumultuous time. America was in the throes of the Great Depression. In Europe, fascism was on the march. Two years later, the Second Sino-Japanese War would erupt in a bloody battle in Pei's home city of Shanghai. Meanwhile, in China's northwestern provinces, Mao Zedong was consolidating his communist insurgency, precipitating the struggle with Chiang Kai-shek's Nationalist government.

Against this fraught backdrop—the Chinese portion of which would have major repercussions for Pei's family and alter Pei's plans to return home after he finished school—architectural education too was undergoing a momentous change. The Beaux-Arts system that had been dominant since the end of the nineteenth century was being challenged by a new culture and pedagogy, one that reflected the realities of the modern world and ushered in a pragmatic, technically orientated outlook. The epicentre of the change in American academia was Cambridge, Massachusetts, where in 1936 Joseph Hudnut was appointed dean of Harvard's School of Architecture, with an implicit mandate from the university president to reshape the programme in a forward-looking, scientific direction. Hudnut had previously been dean of architecture at Columbia University in New York City, where he succeeded in overturning the Beaux-Arts 'conspiracy of bewilderment', as he put it, whose authority rested on the ability of professors to 'distinguish a Corinthian capital from a cauliflower'.[1] At Harvard, Hudnut presided over the school's name change to the Graduate School of Design (GSD) and set about hiring a chair of the architecture department. In Germany, the Nazi takeover had set in motion an exodus of the country's intellectuals and cultural figures, among them Walter Gropius, the eminent founder of the Bauhaus, who had temporarily taken refuge in England. In 1937, Hudnut brought Gropius to the GSD, soon to be followed by a stream of other important émigré practitioners and pedagogues—not just at Harvard—bearing the message of modern architecture.

This was the historical and educational milieu in which the young Pei soon found himself. To say that the school at which an architect trains often has a decisive impact on their subsequent career is hardly a surprising observation, especially when the school in question is a prestigious institution with world-renowned teachers and a pronounced ideology. But the influence is all the more pronounced at a time of upheaval and change. Pei's experiences as an American architecture student, first at MIT from 1935 to 1940, and then at Harvard from 1942 to 1946 (with a two-year interruption between 1943 and 1945), would be both formative and transformative in shaping his future trajectory. As Pei's long-time friend and associate Henry N. Cobb later said of Pei's master's thesis, completed in 1946, 'I doubt if there has ever been a piece of student work that was more predictive of a professional life to come.'[2] More exceptional in Pei's case, however, were the maturity and assurance with which he navigated his encounter with American society and architectural education during this period, skilfully absorbing the culture and knowledge that were being transmitted to him while at the same time retaining a remarkably clear sense of his own identity and direction. His original and precociously accomplished master's thesis would even have a reciprocal effect on those around him, not least Gropius himself.

Pei had initially enrolled at the University of Pennsylvania. This was a logical choice, as a series of Chinese students had passed through the architecture school in Philadelphia in the 1920s and returned home afterwards to illustrious careers. Among the best known were Liang Sicheng and his wife, Lin Huiyin, both of whom matriculated at Penn, as it is known, in 1924. Under the direction of French *maître* Paul Philippe Cret, Penn's Beaux-Arts programme was internationally famous, its students winning more competitions in the mid-1920s than all other American schools combined. Notably, half the winners were Chinese.[3] Yet by the time of Pei's arrival, Cret was nearing retirement and the school was past its prime. Pei's first impression was decidedly negative; he was especially put off by an enormous watercolour drawing of a Tibetan monastery hanging in a school stairwell, expertly rendered in the gauzy Beaux-Arts manner by a student with an American-sounding name.[4] Pei had originally been drawn to a career in architecture after witnessing the construction of the Park Hotel in downtown Shanghai—an audaciously modern skyscraper built by the expatriate Hungarian architect László Hudec between 1931 and 1934, inspired by Raymond Hood's Radiator Building in New York. At twenty-two storeys, the hotel was the tallest building in Asia. Now, excited by the possibilities of modern construction, Pei had little interest in immersing himself in esoteric and exotic projects. With his characteristic aptitude for sizing up situations quickly, he realised that Penn was not for him. A visit from two friends who happened to be studying at MIT convinced him that it offered a preferable alternative, and, with his father's banking connections easing his way, he transferred to the school in Boston.[5]

Pei arrived at MIT two weeks later, in October 1935. Like Philadelphia, Boston was a historic city with a conservative architectural culture, and the architecture school at MIT—the oldest in the country, founded in 1865 just after the American Civil War—was located in an imposing classical building in an elite area of the city centre. It too was under the sway of the Beaux-Arts at this date. Dean William Emerson, who warmly welcomed the new student and took him under his wing, was among the staunchest supporters of the Beaux-Arts in America. Unlike at Penn, however, which would remain mired in the antiquated system until the beginning of the 1950s, new winds were starting to blow.

Based on what he had seen at Penn, Pei considered focusing on architectural engineering or civil engineering at MIT. Emerson, however, sensing Pei's promise as a designer, persuaded him to focus on the artistic side of the profession. Pei's initial semester at MIT thus had a strong Beaux-Arts flavour. Despite his lack of enthusiasm for drawing, he spent long hours mastering the ritual techniques of drafting. His principal classes during the first semester, in addition to a course in mechanical engineering, consisted of Graphics, Shades and Shadows, Perspective, Mechanics, and Architecture Design I. He also took English literature, a mandatory French class, and—ambitious to finish his degree early—another non-vocational course. It was a heavy load, especially for a student still struggling with English pronunciation, but Pei tackled his schoolwork with discipline and determination, and in letters written home to his family he expressed satisfaction with both the school and his own progress (see 1.13, page 28).

The most consequential event of Pei's first semester did not occur in the classroom or studio, however. In early November 1935, Le Corbusier was invited to speak at MIT and Harvard. Emerson viewed the Parisian architect as 'a much over-rated individual' and was against paying 'good money' for the lecture.[6] Yet there was clearly plenty of interest at both schools in hearing what he had to say, and Le Corbusier did not disappoint. Wearing his signature heavy-rimmed glasses and a black bowtie with red dots, he expounded on the subject of 'modern architecture'. Never one to mince words, he criticised Americans for developing advanced methods of industrial production but no 'philosophy of living', and denounced the skyscrapers he had seen in New York and other cities for failing to function as rational 'tools of city planning'.[7] In a book about his experiences in the United States, *When the Cathedrals Were White: A Journey to the Country of Timid People*, written after his return to France, Le Corbusier commented on the schools he had visited. American architecture students were 'serious, balanced, calm', he observed, but they seemed to harbour 'a sort of fear of seeing the doors open on the unknown of tomorrow'. Of his visit to Boston, he noted:

> In the halls of MIT I saw huge machines hung on the walls, wash drawings, representing palaces or mausoleums. Boring, shameful. Surrounded by students and some of their teachers, I said: 'How is it that you have not done away with these horrors?'[8]

Pei, who was in the audience at both talks, found himself 'mesmerised'. The talk at MIT and the one the following day at Harvard were 'the two most important days in my professional life', he recalled half a century later.[9] '[Le Corbusier] was insolent. He was abusive. But he did everything right [...] we had to be shocked out of our complacency.'[10] After the lectures, Pei headed for the architecture school's library to pore over the two volumes of Le Corbusier's *Œuvre complète* that had been published to date. The school's well-endowed library would continue to be a haven throughout Pei's years at MIT, with new books and journals providing evidence of the radically new approach to architecture that was emerging in many places around the world.

In Pei's third year at MIT, the architecture school moved from its venerable pile in Boston to the main university campus in Cambridge; the following year, acknowledging the changed climate at the school, Emerson resigned as dean. A new swimming pool complex—one of the first modernist buildings to be constructed on an American campus, designed between 1938 and 1939 by Lawrence Anderson and Herbert Beckwith, two faculty members—was one sign of MIT's new direction. Another was the launching in 1938 of the Albert Farwell Bemis Foundation, a research institute bequeathed by a former trustee, dedicated to the study of rationalised housing and prefabricated construction methods. The Bemis Foundation established early contacts with Alvar Aalto, whose appointment as a research professor at MIT had to be aborted because of the Soviet invasion of Finland in 1939, but who would return to the university to design the Baker House dormitory on campus right after the war. Pei would find employment at the Bemis Foundation shortly after graduating, hired to do preliminary research on problems of shelter in China.[11] But it was the arrival of Gropius just down the road at Harvard that likely had the most galvanising effect on MIT's transition to modernism. The architecture schools at the two institutions had long enjoyed a close relationship, formalised during the Beaux-Arts period by the 'conjunctive' sketch problems in which fourth- and fifth-year students from each programme took part. These were eliminated in 1935/1936, but Pei participated in a subsequent interschool exercise that brought him into closer contact with the work of his GSD peers.

In 1939/1940, his final year in the undergraduate programme at MIT, Pei came up with an unusual topic for a thesis. Titled 'Standardized Propaganda Units for War Time and Peace Time China', the proposal clearly must have raised some eyebrows among both the faculty and Pei's fellow students for its focus on 'propaganda'. This is suggested by the written document that Pei submitted together with his final drawings, in which he begins by explaining that 'the propagation of falsities' commonly associated with the term was in no way the intended meaning. Instead, his project was meant to address the 'deplorable' level of illiteracy in China by finding a way to 'instil into the masses the consciousness of the importance of education'.[12] This, he wrote, would amount to 'a program of progressive propaganda'. Moreover, the recent outbreak of war with Japan had caused massive migrations inland, overwhelming cities and leading to the creation of a multitude of informal villages that lacked basic services, sanitation, and schools. The situation, Pei stated, demanded a realistic and coordinated response from 'scientists, economists, socialists, educationalists, and architects'. But as his own 'humble' contribution to a solution, he proposed to create a system of standardised 'propaganda units' that could be deployed to remote locations around the country and accommodate presentations by touring theatre groups as well as 'motion pictures, museum exhibits, speakers, graphical materials, etc.' Administered by a 'Ministry of Propaganda'—a central authority located in the capital that would communicate by radio with its far-flung network—the units would be designed for flexibility of function and have a modern but festive and familiar atmosphere. Pei envisaged them constructed largely of bamboo in combination with other easily available local materials, 'in strict accordance with the traditional native usages and methods'.[13]

Most notable about Pei's novel thesis was his thoughtful and imaginative adaptation of modernist thinking—standardised construction, flexible functionality, and advanced technology, as well as a reformist social project—to the context of his native China. A year later, the thesis would be published in the second issue of *TASK*. A short-lived magazine subtitled *A Journal for the Younger Generation in Architecture*, the magazine was edited by progressively orientated students at the GSD, MIT, and Smith College. The purpose of *TASK*, as the editors explained it in their editorial in the issue in which Pei's thesis appeared, was to involve architecture students and professionals more deeply in real-world social and economic problems and, specifically in the context of wartime emergency, 'to prove that the architectural profession has a place in the war effort' and to 'find out what civil and military problems our training has fitted us to solve'.[14] Pei's thesis exemplified all of these objectives. Giving it even more currency was the Japanese bombing of Pearl Harbor in December 1941, which finally forced President Roosevelt's hand and caused the United States formally to declare war on the Axis powers.

Upon his graduation from MIT in 1940, Pei received a gold medal from the Boston chapter of the American Institute of Architects and a travelling fellowship. It was impossible for him to take advantage of the latter, however, because of wartime hostilities. He also wanted to return home to China but was dissuaded by his family for the same reason. After completing his work at the Bemis Foundation, he secured a job at the Boston engineering firm of Stone & Webster, which was heavily involved in military contracts at the time. He gained some experience with concrete construction there before deciding to enrol in the master's programme in architecture at the GSD, where his wife, Eileen Loo, whom he had married in the spring of 1942, was already a landscape student. Following an interview with Hudnut, Pei obtained admission to the programme in December 1942.

It was an unusual time to be a student at Harvard. Enrolment was in steep decline because of the war. Prospective students were off fighting on the front, and the academic ranks were now being filled out with different types of students, including women for the first time, ethnic and racial minorities, and foreigners, giving Pei's cohort an unusually diverse complexion.[15] Members of the faculty had little professional work, which gave them ample time to devote to their students. Gropius, for his part, was busy working on a collaborative project, the Packaged House System, with Konrad Wachsmann, another German émigré architect who had made his way to Cambridge, Massachusetts, with Gropius's aid after managing to escape from occupied France. The Packaged House System, commissioned by the General Panel Corporation, was a scheme for the rationalised production of prefabricated wooden houses. Wood was the only material readily available on the domestic US market during the war, and the houses were designed to be assembled by unskilled workers on-site as cheaply and efficiently as possible. Gropius involved his GSD students in projects related to the scheme, as can be seen in an article that appeared in *New Pencil Points* magazine in December 1943 featuring designs for single-family houses by four Harvard students, including Pei, utilising General Panel Corporation components. The article was intended to demonstrate that a standardised production process did not necessarily restrict an architect's creativity or an owner's expression of individuality.[16] The message was clearly a departure from the ideology of the European modern movement of the 1920s, which had promoted collective housing based on minimum functional requirements. As Gropius now appreciated and proselytised, modern architecture in the United States would have to accommodate the social and economic expectations of American consumers and corporations, who were already eagerly looking ahead to an era of post-war plenitude. The single-family suburban house designed for growth and transformability thus became one of the preferred design programmes at the GSD. As reflected in a series of winning competition projects carried out in the first half of the 1940s, Pei was an early and adept master of the new formula.

Pei had hardly begun his studies at GSD, however, when, in December 1942, he realised he could not in good conscience remain in academia with the war going on. Ineligible to serve in the armed services because of nationality requirements and weak eyesight, he volunteered to work for the National Defense Research Committee (NDRC), an organisation set up to conduct top-secret scientific research into warfare devices and mechanisms. The NDRC was the beginning of the military-industrial-academic complex in America, and predictably the Cambridge establishment was well connected with it. The presidents of Harvard and MIT were both on the original executive committee, and John Burchard, the first director of the Bemis Foundation, had been seconded from MIT to work there. Burchard became one of the organisation's prime movers, as did Marc Peter Jr, a Harvard MArch graduate to whom Pei would report directly after a year. A number of other expatriate modernist architects, loosely known as 'the Gropius group', were also involved.[17] Pei was assigned to Division 2, based in Princeton, New Jersey, a branch of the NDRC responsible for 'structural defense and offense' and 'effects of impact and explosion'. He arrived for

I. M. Pei's design of a prefabricated unit, in 'Variety of Houses from Identical Prefabricated Units of General Panel Corporation designed by Harvard Students', *New Pencil Points* (December 1943): 81. M+, Hong Kong

I. M. Pei and Frederick G. Roth, 'Pencil Points – Pittsburgh Competition Winners', *Pencil Points/Progressive Architecture* 26 (May 1945): 58. USModernist

service in January 1943 and would spend the next two years studying bombs and incendiaries intended for targets in Europe and Japan, using his architectural and constructional expertise to analyse how best to deploy these devices in different urban and material contexts. Not surprisingly, he found the work anathema: 'I would be brought photographs of Japanese towns,' he recalled, 'and I was supposed to figure out the best way to burn them down. It was awful.'[18] Whether to distract himself or simply to keep his hand in, he took part in a number of architectural competitions during this time, as noted earlier, either together with a partner or alone, winning several prizes and mentions and seeing his work published in national architecture magazines. Most of the projects were for single-family houses with prefabricated components, of the type at which Gropius's GSD students had come to excel.

In 1943, designs by Pei and a fellow GSD student, E. H. (Emilio) Duhart, a Chilean who also collaborated with Gropius and Wachsmann on the Packaged House System, came second in two competitions co-sponsored by *California Arts & Architecture*, appearing in the magazine's August 1943 and January 1944 issues respectively. In the first competition, responding to an open-ended call for 'Designs for Postwar Living', Pei and Duhart produced a two-storey rectangular volume made of standardised panels adjoined on one of its long sides, through a covered neck, by a prefabricated service unit made of corrugated aluminium and containing bathrooms on the upper floor and a kitchen below. In a statement typical of the moment, the designers envisaged a client 'who has no prejudice against mass-produced houses' and emphasised the house's flexibility and 'livability'.[19] Their second competition entry, a 'House for the Post War Worker', likewise featured an industrially produced service unit with kitchen and bathrooms; in this instance, however, the house was a single storey and the service unit was located in the central bay of a nine-square plan. Designed to be shipped to the dwelling site in standardised sections, the service unit included such high-tech conveniences as a 'precipitron' to eliminate dust and a built-in garbage disposal system. The kitchen, with its own sliding-glass windows and venetian blinds, was conceived as a panoptic centre 'from which the wife controls the whole house', as Pei and Duhart elaborated in their accompanying text. Their main aim, as they stated, was to 'vitalize the family as the most important cell of democracy' and community life, noting that they were opposed to a 'completely collectivistic form of living'.[20]

In 1944, Pei submitted an entry on his own to a competition entitled 'Design of a Small House'—co-sponsored by the same publication, now simply called *Arts & Architecture*, and the United States Plywood Corporation—and received an honourable mention. Like his and Duhart's first competition entry, it utilised a prefabricated service unit that plugged into the basic house plan from the exterior. But in an original move, and anticipating a concept that architects would explore (at larger scale) in the 1960s, the plug-in appendages were designed to be mobile and replaceable, as well as having a variety of functions. Options included not just plug-in kitchens and bathrooms but also plug-in laundry, storage, and sleeping utilities. Termed 'Community Share Units' by Pei, they were to be rented out to the residents of the local community on a cooperative basis.[21]

Finally, in a fourth competition project, also for a 'post-war house', Pei collaborated with Frederick G. Roth, an MIT classmate who was also working at the NDRC, and won second prize in a field of more than nine hundred entries. Published in *Progressive Architecture* in May 1945, the scheme received an additional prize for a sliding glass screen and storage partition designed to separate the kitchen from the dining room, and this detail appeared on the magazine's cover. The jury commended the project overall for its 'easy directness' and 'purposeful planning'.[22]

In 1945, with the war finally over, Pei returned to the GSD and began to focus on his master's thesis under the supervision of Gropius and Marcel Breuer. Breuer had been brought to Harvard by Gropius shortly after his own arrival in 1937. 'Lajko', as the students called the Hungarian-born Bauhaus émigré, was the teacher with whom Pei would develop the closest affinity. He was warm and down to earth, and a more fluent and gifted designer than Gropius. 'From Breuer I learned that to understand architecture, one must understand life,' Pei stated.[23] Gropius, on the other hand, remained more detached from day-to-day interactions with students. He was nevertheless an elegant and charismatic presence in the school and an oracular authority on the ethical obligations of the modern architect. Pei respected him for his role as a public architectural intellectual. Ironically, however, even as Gropius preached his gospel of 'teamwork' against the 'cult of the ego', he and Breuer had a bitter falling out in 1941 and dissolved their design partnership. Gropius's relationship with Hudnut was even worse, deteriorating to the point where, by the end of the 1940s, the two were barely speaking; Hudnut accused Gropius of a reductively formalist and ahistorical approach to teaching architecture, while Gropius saw Hudnut's stance as 'applied archaeology'.[24] The collaboration with Wachsmann fizzled out as well. With Wachsmann endlessly tinkering with the details, the Packaged House System failed to be put into production. More significantly, the wartime dream of the prefabricated house rapidly faded as a new period of affluence unfolded in the United States. Gropius increasingly turned his attention to his new firm The Architects Collaborative, founded in 1945—himself the *éminence grise* among equal partners—and intensified his schedule of international travel and public appearances, embracing the role of modern architecture's elder statesman.

Pei too, for his part, was glad to leave the technocratic ethos of the war behind him. The subject he chose for his master's thesis, a museum of Chinese art for Shanghai, reflects a renewed desire to return to his roots, picking up on the cultural and national thrust of his undergraduate thesis, yet now with a focus on art and the natural beauty of the Chinese garden. It was also a direct, and strongly critical, response to the monumental complex built for the Greater Shanghai Plan in Pei's home city between 1931 and 1936 by the architect Dong Dayou, who had received a Beaux-Arts education in the United States in the 1920s at the University of Minnesota and Columbia University. The Municipal Museum, one of the last-completed components of the complex, was a closed block of heavy masonry construction symmetrically disposed around an interior courtyard, recalling the architecture of Étienne-Louis Boullée except for the pagoda-like 'hat' atop the entry. Pei's building, for the same general site, could hardly have been more different.

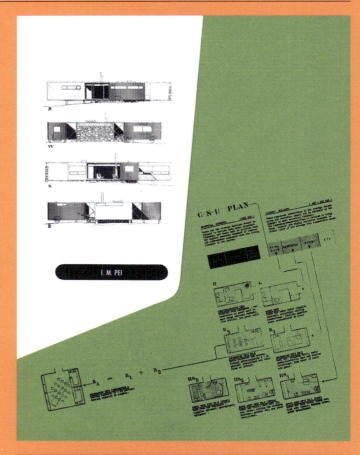

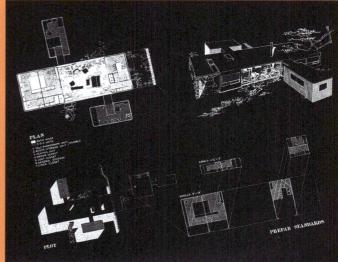

I. M. Pei, 'Community-Share-Use Plan', *Arts & Architecture* 62 (March 1945): 38–39. Joan Ockman

Weaving together the various strands of modern architecture that he had assimilated over the course of the previous decade, Pei produced an abstract, two-storey spatial composition of lightweight wall planes and luminous marble-veneer surfaces interspersed with freely landscaped garden courtyards open to the sky. Sunk half a level below ground to create exterior walls for the main garden and to permit views from outside in, the low structure lucidly combined simplicity of plan and circulation with a more lyrical sculptural quality, evoked by the free-form garden elements. While owing some inspiration to Mies van der Rohe's Museum for a Small City (1941–1943)—especially in its perspectival renderings with collaged-in works of art: a bronze Buddha head, a sculpture of a Chinese philosopher riding a buffalo, and a large embroidered tapestry with a dragon—and perhaps also to Le Corbusier's early pavilion designs for displaying art, the museum was a deeply original synthesis of Western and Eastern sensibilities.[25] Received with great admiration by everyone at Harvard, it was lauded by Gropius in a statement that accompanied its publication in *Progressive Architecture* in February 1948 (see 3.3, page 111):

> This project for a museum in Shanghai, China, was designed by Mr. Ieoh Ming Pei in the Master class of Harvard's Department of Architecture under my general direction. It clearly illustrates that an able designer can very well hold on to basic traditional features—which he has found are still alive—without sacrificing a progressive conception of design.

Gropius then went further, acknowledging that the project represented an important new direction for modern architecture, moving beyond the decontextualised and dehistoricised universalism to which he and other protagonists of the modern movement had previously subscribed:

> We have today sufficiently clarified our minds to know that respect for tradition does not mean complacent toleration of elements which have been a matter of fortuitous chance or a simple imitation of bygone esthetic forms. We have become aware that tradition in design has always meant the preservation of essential characteristics which have resulted from eternal habits of the people.[26]

The affirmation of tradition and of 'eternal habits' was indeed a profound revision of modernist ideology—part of a new humanism and an intellectual evolution that other members of Gropius's generation, among them Sigfried Giedion, would undergo in the wake of the war.[27] It also anticipated the more militant critiques of modern architecture soon to be levelled within the institutional framework of CIAM (Congrès internationaux d'architecture moderne) by Team 10, representatives of the post-war generation.

Two years later, in 1950, Pei's project would be republished, together with Gropius's statement, in a special issue of *L'architecture d'aujourd'hui*, 'Walter Gropius et son école/The Spread of an Idea', edited by Paul Rudolph, a classmate of Pei's at the GSD (see 1.23.3, page 39).[28] The publication of a student thesis project in a national magazine was already an unusual event; its reappearance in a leading foreign journal was exceedingly rare. After receiving his master's degree in 1946, Pei, having already received a teaching appointment in 1945 while still a student, would remain at the GSD for two more years as a much-valued faculty member. Henry N. Cobb, who entered the school in 1947, described him as 'the youngest and best of our design critics'.[29]

Later in 1948, Pei began a new chapter. Recruited by real-estate magnate William Zeckendorf to be in-house architect at his firm Webb & Knapp in New York, Pei entered the world of large corporate practice. Seven years later, he would open his own architectural office, initially called I. M. Pei & Associates. He would also, in 1954, become an American citizen. Over the next six decades, he would go on to design some of the most important cultural, educational, and corporate buildings in the world. Without doubt, however, the years he spent as a student in Cambridge were instrumental in shaping his future work and world view, even if his early American experiences also served to reinforce his abiding connection with his homeland. With his characteristic tact and goodwill, he maintained warm relations over the years with both of the schools he had attended, returning later to design four buildings on MIT's campus and continuing to be a generous benefactor to both institutions. Yet as an inordinately talented and sure-footed student, he was already honing an identity distinct from his mentors, reconciling his knowledge of two different cultures, and responding to the vicissitudes of mid-twentieth-century history.

It is interesting to conclude this essay with a reference to the photograph of Gropius in a studio at the GSD standing over a student (whom some authors have identified as Pei) as he works at his drafting board, possibly on his master's thesis (see 1.21, page 36). The photo has been widely reproduced; often, however, the figure of this student and that of another at left, also turned away from the camera, are cropped out, thereby keeping the focus on the famous pedagogue in an iconic act of teaching.[30] In the uncropped version, the student in the foreground looks as if he is waiting expectantly for a word or two from the 'great man'. Yet scrutinised more closely, it appears to be a two-way colloquy, with the teacher absorbing as much from his encounter with an exceptional student as the other way around.

Walter Gropius (second from left), A. P. Kanvinde (centre), and I. M. Pei (far right) at a GSD studio review, ca.1946. Kanvinde Rai & Chowdhury Archives

Real Estate & Urban Redevelopment

2

'We are going to change all this'

PAGE 48:
I. M. Pei explains his proposal for Oklahoma City's new downtown to one of the 'city fathers', ca.1964. The Oklahoman Archive

Typical of the work of Webb & Knapp, the presentation model in this image covers a much larger area than the site of intervention, conveying the firm's conception of urban design in which 'each part functionally and visually relates to the others and to the whole'. The scale and degree of detail expressed the firm's ambition to transform cities and did much to aid its ability to win competitions for municipal development projects.

I. M. Pei's public reputation rests on his designs for such prestigious commissions as the National Gallery of Art East Building and the modernisation of the Grand Louvre. Less known are his contributions to real estate and urban development in the United States in the 1950s and 1960s. The under-representation of this period—a critical, defining one—is due to Pei's own ambivalence towards it in later years, as well as the architecture fraternity's long-held bias against commercial real-estate and government-led urban development projects. This chapter focuses on Pei's work for Webb & Knapp, the largest real-estate development company in post-war America, as well as the urban design and planning projects undertaken by Pei's own firm in the United States and beyond after 1960. It addresses how Pei and his team marshalled urban economics, land use, city leadership, government regulations, material resources, urban histories, and civic planning as part of a strategy to respond to opportunities and tackle urban and architectural challenges.

After the Second World War, a housing crisis for returning servicemen, discriminatory mortgage lending, and suburbanisation left American city centres in a state of decay and led the US government to declare urban renewal a national priority. The Title I provision of the Housing Act of 1949 offered significant federal subsidies to cities and private developers for the purchase and clearing of land to rebuild ailing urban hubs. William Zeckendorf, head of Webb & Knapp, saw rejuvenating inner-city areas through new forms of urban living as an ethical obligation. Unlike the developers behind the rapidly expanding suburbs, Zeckendorf devoted his attention to the city, while also being aware of the most important issues in architectural discourse. This aligned him with the 'heart of the city' position on the development of the urban core proposed at the eighth meeting of CIAM (Congrès internationaux d'architecture moderne) in 1951. He extended these ideas through direct action by merging the expertise of real-estate economists, designers, engineers, and city planners in his firm in order to develop residential, industrial, and commercial architecture of 'beauty, functionalism, and economic soundness'.[1] His nationwide urban redevelopment campaign, begun in 1956, resulted in a suite of speculative projects that catalysed architectural and urban experimentation. Attracted by Zeckendorf's vision and ambition, and having an interest in architecture's relationship with real estate, Pei arrived at Webb & Knapp in New York City in 1948. His move made headlines. But Pei's direct involvement with a commercial enterprise was decried as a crass 'violation of professional ethics' by the American Institute of Architects.[2]

Webb & Knapp was committed as much to 'architecture as craft' as to 'architecture of an urban scale'.[3] The firm's experimental projects began with the Helix, an apartment block with a system of floors designed to allow tenants to customise their living space, and continued with the structural innovation of the 108-storey Hyperboloid for Grand Central Terminal. In the firm's cylindrical New York penthouse office, perched atop a commercial building, and Kips Bay Plaza, for which Pei pioneered the use of poured-in-place reinforced concrete, its visions took built form.

For Zeckendorf, Pei, and their colleagues, the success of urban redevelopment was inseparable from broad programmatic thinking intended to alleviate social and economic ills.[4] Webb & Knapp placed consistent emphasis on public space and the circulation of pedestrian and vehicular traffic in its projects. This approach is evident in strategies for mixed-use buildings first applied in the design of the Mile High Center and Courthouse Square, whose close ensemble of offices, hotel, convention halls, retail space, and plazas created a focal point in downtown Denver. For Roosevelt Field Shopping Center on Long Island—the largest suburban mall in America at the time of its completion—Zeckendorf assigned part of the site to the construction of highway ramps that would direct traffic to the parking lot. The project sought to introduce urban conditions into a suburban context by being designed as a compact cluster of blocks around an open-air plaza with mixed-use indoor and outdoor space, including a skating rink and an art gallery.

In his urban renewal work, Pei attempted to bridge the gap between new and historical structures, as well as racial and income divides. The rehabilitation of Society Hill in Philadelphia was an early model of incremental redevelopment that included newly built low-rise town houses designed in dialogue with preserved historical row houses. For the massive redevelopment of Southwest Washington, a district of the US capital, Pei and Zeckendorf waded through bureaucratic morass to realise a scheme that unified the historically segregated residential area with the city's core.[5] Pei's concern for the social fabric is also evident in his pro bono intervention to regenerate the majority-Black neighbourhood of Bedford-Stuyvesant in Brooklyn. To foster the community's sense of ownership in the redesign of urban space, he collaborated with Franklin Thomas, founding leader of America's first community development corporation (CDC), Bedford Stuyvesant Restoration Corporation, and the first Black man to head the Ford Foundation.

In the context of nation-building in post-colonial Southeast Asia in the 1960s and the oil crisis that brought wealth to the Middle East in the 1970s, Pei was presented with opportunities to realise grand urban development projects outside America. While they were crucial for Pei's large office—formally established as I. M. Pei & Associates in 1960—in the 1970s, these projects were also significant demonstrations of his sensitivity to government aspirations and urban histories in various cultural contexts. In Singapore, the expansion of the central business district (CBD) led Pei to propose the thirteen-hectare mixed-use Raffles International Centre complex, eventually partially completed as Raffles City. The Kapsad development in Tehran involved arranging buildings of various heights to reference Iran's historic walled courtyards. Having been invited to design a high-rise hotel near the Forbidden City in Beijing, Pei made an alternative proposal to build a low-rise structure in the city's western hills, to protect sightlines from the palace complex. His choice led to a policy in urban planning around the Forbidden City known colloquially as the 'Pei Height Limitation'.

Pei had described the Southwest Washington project as aspiring to 'the highest goal of the art of civic design—that of a new urban organism, each part functionally and visually related to the others and to the whole'.[6] While he rarely took on large, difficult-to-control planning projects in his later career, he remained committed to designing buildings that responded to and reorganised a city's spatial and circulatory systems for greater productivity and liveability. Regardless of a project's scale, Pei always aspired to an inventive redesign of the city—as he once expressed to a Webb & Knapp colleague while looking up Madison Avenue: 'We are going to change all this.'[7]

— Shirley Surya

2.1.1 | 'Going On in Real Estate—Pei Joins Webb & Knapp', *New York Herald Tribune*, 12 September 1948. Papers of I. M. Pei, Library of Congress, Washington DC

2.1.2 | I. M. Pei (standing at right) and William Zeckendorf (seated at front right) with executives of Webb & Knapp, 1954. Pei Cobb Freed & Partners

2.1.1–2.1.2
Pei's decision to practise architecture for a developer, as director of the architectural research division of Webb & Knapp, was considered a violation of professional ethics by many of his fellow architects. Drawn to William Zeckendorf's vision of remaking cities in post-war America, Pei took the leap and made a name for himself with projects that addressed large-scale urban and suburban challenges. Pei demonstrated not only skill in design and planning, but also a keen sensitivity to the dynamics of power. Zeckendorf recognised this and involved Pei in important meetings with clients.

Webb & Knapp Headquarters (1949–1952)
New York

2.2 | 'Big Operator's Base—Realty tycoon Bill Zeckendorf dreams up far-flung deals in a dream of an office', *New York Sunday News*, 22 May 1955. Pei Cobb Freed & Partners

A decade before the heyday of corporate high style, Pei designed a swish two-storey penthouse office for Webb & Knapp. The office was equal parts control room, lounge, and art gallery, and featured a dining pavilion on the upper level set amid landscaped terraces, and a sculpture by Gaston Lachaise. Pei's design underscored Zeckendorf's vision of defining a new kind of real-estate development company that pursued architectural excellence as much as financial success.

2.3 | **Wurts Brothers, Webb and Knapp's headquarters at 383–385 Madison Avenue, New York, 1952. Museum of the City of New York**

In addition to giving Webb & Knapp's office lobby and interiors a facelift, Pei built a freestanding cylindrical structure on the rooftop of 383–385 Madison Avenue. This address was to be the home for Pei's team—beginning with Henry N. Cobb and Ulrich Franzen—which he began to assemble for this penthouse office project.

REAL ESTATE & URBAN REDEVELOPMENT 57

2.4 | **Ezra Stoller, William Zeckendorf's circular office, 1952. Esto**

Zeckendorf's office was surrounded by a single circular teak wall, measuring seven and a half metres in diameter, and a glass clerestory window. His desk, designed by Ulrich Franzen, was equipped with two built-in telephones and a control panel that could change mood lighting. Notable decorative elements included a blue-and-white Chinese vase selected by Pei, and a bronze sculpture by Henri Matisse.

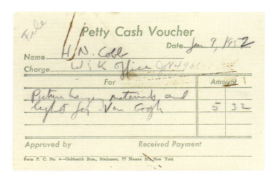

2.5 | **Henry N. Cobb, Webb & Knapp office petty-cash voucher for the purchase of materials to hang a Van Gogh painting, 1952. Pei Cobb Freed & Partners**

Thanks to Zeckendorf's relationship with Nelson Rockefeller and Richard Abbott of the Museum of Modern Art, New York, works from the museum's collection were sometimes loaned for display in the offices of Webb & Knapp. This petty-cash voucher documents Cobb's expenditure on materials used to hang a painting, *Landscape from Saint-Rémy* (1889), by Vincent van Gogh.

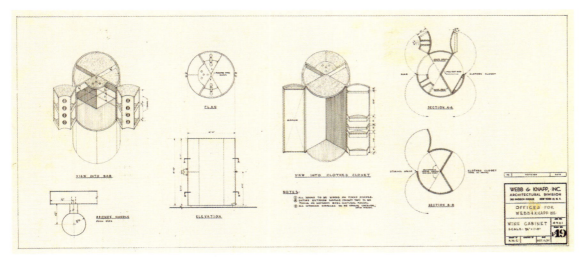

2.6 | **Henry N. Cobb, drawing of wine cabinet for Webb & Knapp offices, 1951. Pei Cobb Freed & Partners**

Cobb designed this cylindrical wine cabinet in thuya-burl wood. It became the focal point of the upper-level semi-circular dining room where Zeckendorf entertained guests.

Hyperboloid (1954–1955; unbuilt)
New York

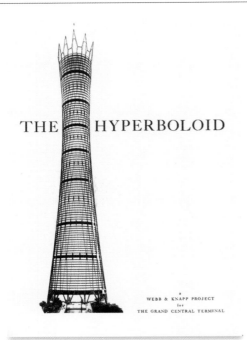

2.7.1 | **I. M. Pei & Associates, cover, *The Hyperboloid—A Webb & Knapp Project for the Grand Central Terminal*, 1956. Pei Cobb Freed & Partners**

2.7.2 | **Model of the Hyperboloid, 1956. Pei Cobb Freed & Partners**

2.7.1–2.7.2
The Hyperboloid was Pei's first skyscraper design. A 108-storey tower meant to be part of a new transportation centre and green space on Park Avenue, it would have been the world's largest office building. Its construction would have necessitated the reconfiguration of traffic flow along curved viaducts, as well as the demolition of Grand Central Terminal. Robert R. Young, chairman of the close-to-bankrupt New York Central Railroad, saw this radical redevelopment as essential to the survival of the railroad industry in the context of the post-war boom in commercial aviation and the growth of suburbs designed for automobiles. The Hyperboloid project was abandoned following Young's death in 1958.

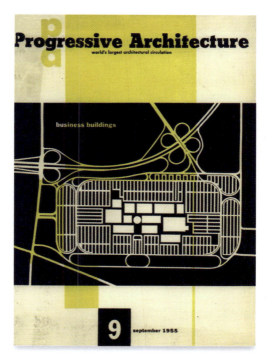

2.8.1 | **Cover, *Progressive Architecture* 36 (September 1955). USModernist**

Roosevelt Field Shopping Center (1951–1956)
Garden City, New York

2.8.2 | **I. M. Pei & Associates, model, in 'Roosevelt Field Shopping Center—a Webb & Knapp Project', *Progressive Architecture* 36 (September 1955): 94. USModernist**

2.8.1–2.8.2
With rapid suburbanisation in the 1950s, consumer activities shifted from the streets to the mall. In 1951, Zeckendorf acquired a disused airfield in Garden City, Long Island, to develop a regional shopping centre. Three years later, he donated a portion of the site to New York State's highway extension, leading to the construction of cloverleaf-shaped on- and off-ramps that funnelled traffic into the shopping centre's 11,000-car parking lot. Unlike the sprawling complexes that would become typical of suburban shopping mall developments, the fifty-hectare Roosevelt Field Shopping Center was designed to include urban elements, such as a heightened core and mixed-use indoor and outdoor recreational space. Pei concentrated more than one hundred shops into a compact cluster of blocks around an open-air plaza (which, in an unbuilt scheme, features a futuristic glass-and-steel canopy) in an asymmetric grid that created 'streets' of various widths and minimised walking distances. Roosevelt Field, the largest mall in the United States at the time of its completion, also contained an outdoor skating rink, meeting rooms, an art gallery, and a broadcasting studio.

2.9.1 | **Lionel Friedman, Water Mall, ca.1956. Pei Cobb Freed & Partners**

2.9.2 | **Aerial view of Franklin National Bank as part of Roosevelt Field Commercial Center, ca.1958. Pei Cobb Freed & Partners**

2.9.1–2.9.2
Individualised storefronts of glass and whitewashed brick along the mall's 'streets' are characterised by a modular rhythm of exposed structural steel frame and a continuous cantilevered roof framing system. The shaded walks of the Water Mall contain seating, trees, flowers, and fountains, while facades feature distinct architectural treatments to aid shoppers' orientation across the complex. The mall was not immediately successful following its opening in 1956, but the gradual increase in its popularity led to the construction of eighteen hectares of office buildings nearby, including the circular brick kiosks of Webb & Knapp's Franklin National Bank, with its drive-through facilities.

2.10 | **Site plan of Mile High Center (1952–1956) and Courthouse Square (1954–1960) in downtown Denver, ca.1954. Pei Cobb Freed & Partners**

Located a block apart from each other, Mile High Center and Courthouse Square were Webb & Knapp's earliest mixed-use urban redevelopment projects, comprising office, retail, hotel, exhibition, and recreational use. For his part, Zeckendorf secured financing from remote investors to break into the local real-estate market, while Pei envisioned each site's assemblage of forms and interconnected spaces and signed off on various design elements that were assigned to individual architects. The plaza was a key component of the overall design, a means of place-making and raising land value. Webb & Knapp's integration of architectural design, urban sensitivity, and real-estate acuity gave a new focal point to Denver that attracted businesses and drew suburbanites back to the city centre.

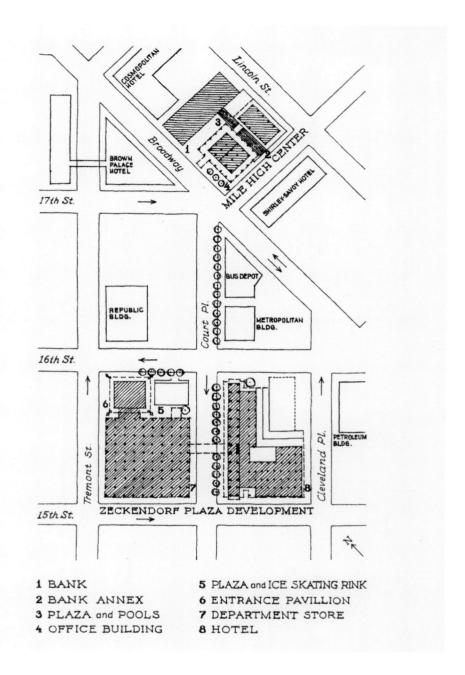

1 BANK
2 BANK ANNEX
3 PLAZA and POOLS
4 OFFICE BUILDING
5 PLAZA and ICE SKATING RINK
6 ENTRANCE PAVILLION
7 DEPARTMENT STORE
8 HOTEL

Mile High Center (1952–1956)
Denver, Colorado

2.11.1 | **Ezra Stoller, lower plaza with a view of Mile High Center's exhibition pavilion, 1955.** Esto

2.11.3 | **Ezra Stoller, interior of Mile High Center's exhibition pavilion, 1955.** Esto

2.11.1–2.11.3
For Mile High Center, Pei convinced Zeckendorf to devote more than three quarters of the site to public use. This move was intended to attract tenants, mollify locals who opposed the redevelopment, and raise rental values. Pei's plan entailed a complex composed of a twenty-three-storey glass-and-steel office tower, a two-storey thin-shell concrete-roofed exhibition pavilion with retail and dining spaces on its lower level, and reflective pools and landscaped plazas enlivened with custom lighting. The 'gift' of open plazas convinced city officials to allow the tower to be the first to surpass the height limit of twelve storeys, which had been established to preserve views of the Rocky Mountains. Denver's first skyscraper was also Pei's first built high-rise. On the intricate structural facade, dark-grey cast aluminium and beige enamel panels interweave with the heating and cooling units under each window and the vertical air ducts, lending an interpenetrating visual texture to an otherwise flat surface.

2.11.2 | **Ezra Stoller, office tower of Mile High Center, 1955.** Esto

Courthouse Square (1954–1960)
Denver, Colorado

2.12.1 | **Convention hall seen against the May-D&F department store (right) and the Denver Hilton (left), Courthouse Square, ca.1958. Pei Cobb Freed & Partners**

2.12.2 | **George Cserna, Columbine Bar and Lounge at the Denver Hilton, ca.1958. Avery Architectural and Fine Arts Library, Columbia University**

2.12.1–2.12.2
Courthouse Square was completed fifteen years after Zeckendorf purchased the site of a former courthouse, a delay caused by difficult legal negotiations and the Korean War, which led to a shortage of steel. The development consists of an 884-room hotel linked to a shopping centre via a skybridge, a convention centre, underground parking, and a public plaza. The slender hotel slab, the department store's rectangular block, and the sculptural convention centre are arranged around the sunken plaza, which becomes an ice-skating rink in the winter. The ensemble forms a cohesive urban field with an inviting relationship to its surroundings. Artistic detailing pervaded the buildings' exteriors and interiors. The facade of the Denver Hilton by Araldo Cossutta had an ornamental screen of cast stone that transitioned to waffle-pattern windows as it rose. Interiors were designed by Alexander Girard, while one of Harry Bertoia's metal dandelion sculptures graced the bar. The May-D&F department store by Henry N. Cobb was clad in golden anodised aluminium and was accessed through the convention pavilion, which is characterised by its soaring hyperbolic paraboloid concrete-shell roof.

Southwest Washington Urban Redevelopment (1953–1959)
Washington DC

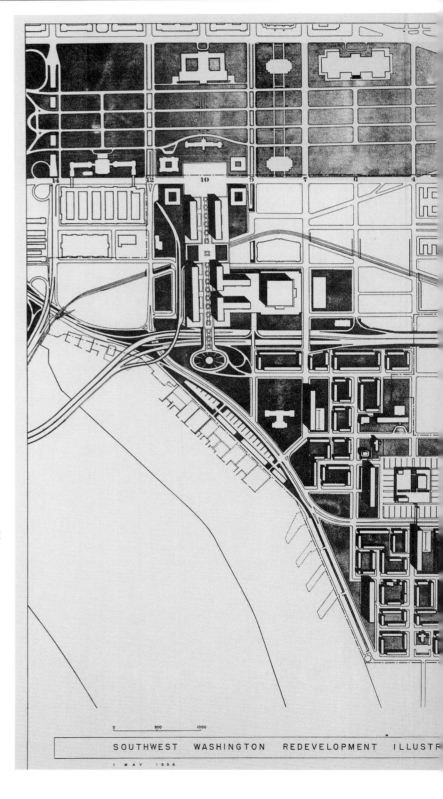

2.13 | **Illustrative site plan, in *Urban Renewal Plan—Southwest Urban Renewal Project Area C* by the National Capital Planning Commission, 1956. Avery Architectural and Fine Arts Library, Columbia University**

Webb & Knapp's first foray into Title I redevelopment saw the firm tackle 173 hectares of an impoverished neighbourhood in the heart of Washington DC, an area to the south-west of the Capitol that national media outlets had identified as an ideal testing ground since the passing of the legislation in 1949. Despite the community's perceptions of Pei and Zeckendorf as outsiders, the latter built credibility with an extensive public relations campaign. He secured support from the Redevelopment Land Agency, local politicians, and the public leading up to his successful bid to design the master plan of Southwest Washington in 1954. Webb & Knapp's scheme, which Pei conceived with Harry Weese and William L. Slayton, called for wholesale clearance of existing structures, and was anchored by the transformation of Tenth Street into a ninety-one-metre-wide cultural mall. Bridging a railroad track and dip in a proposed highway, this key intervention would unify the historically segregated residential neighbourhood with the city's core while introducing a new cultural hub called L'Enfant Plaza. Sensitive to the shift in urban scale, Pei's team proposed a pedestrianised town-within-a-town to the south, designed as a self-contained community with mixed low- and high-rise residential buildings, shopping, and amenities to articulate an urban vision that combined suburban ideals with the cosmopolitan fabric.

REAL ESTATE & URBAN REDEVELOPMENT

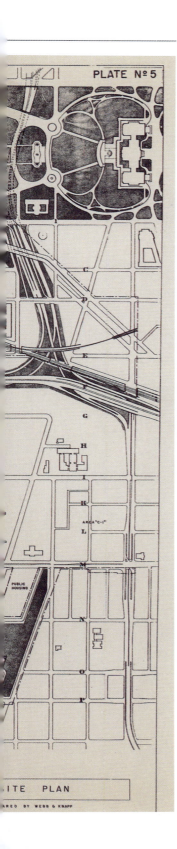

2.14 | **Ezra Stoller, L'Enfant Plaza with a view of its underground pedestrian and vehicular network, 1968. Esto**

The complex bureaucracy and competing interests of government agencies resulted in delays and compromises to Webb & Knapp's proposed plans for Southwest Washington. By the first phase of development in the 1960s, increasing strain on Zeckendorf's finances and Pei's expanding responsibilities meant that the realisation of L'Enfant Plaza—one of the plan's few elements that remained under the firm's domain—was put in the hands of Araldo Cossutta. As depicted in Webb & Knapp's master plan, grand boulevards between large commercial buildings mirrored those found in namesake Pierre Charles L'Enfant's historic plan of the city. Underground parking established direct automobile access from the newly built expressway to the square, which adjoins an interconnecting network of over- and underground walkways leading to office and retail areas. However, failed negotiations around a proposed multipurpose cultural centre in L'Enfant Plaza represented one of many fragmentations to Pei's larger vision of Southwest Washington as a 'new urban organism'.

2.15.1 | Naho Kubota, park at Kips Bay Plaza, 2022. Photo commissioned by M+

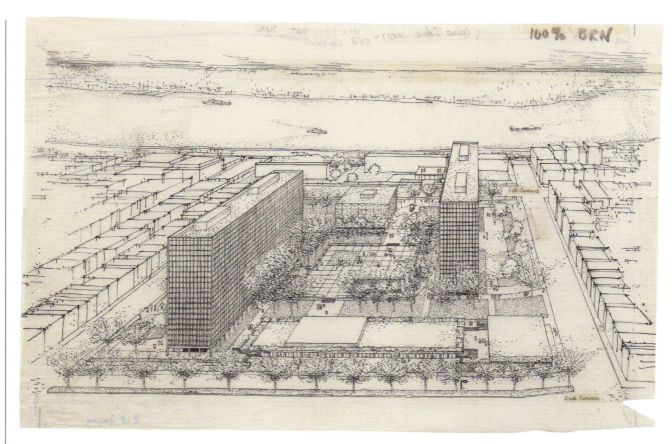

2.15.2 | **Aerial perspective of Kips Bay Plaza, ca.1957. Pei Cobb Freed & Partners**

Kips Bay Plaza (1957–1962)
New York

2.15.3 | **Newly constructed south tower of Kips Bay Plaza, ca.1960. Pei Cobb Freed & Partners**

2.15.1–2.15.3
At the invitation of the chairman of New York's Committee on Slum Clearance, Robert Moses, Zeckendorf took on the task of reviving Kips Bay Plaza. The project was part of Moses's grand scheme to redevelop low-income neighbourhoods in New York. Reluctant to introduce more of the symmetrical blocks of brick-clad buildings typical of low- and middle-income housing, Pei instead proposed two 125-metre slabs constructed entirely of exposed concrete that aligned with the city grid at opposite ends of the site. Small streets lead into an enclosed park between the two towers, occupying more than half of the four-hectare site and appearing as a contained unit amid the brownstones of a historical Italian neighbourhood. The choice of material resulted from budget constraints, which precluded the use of a steel structure with concrete skin. By relying entirely on cast-in-place concrete, Pei pioneered a solution within the financial constraints. As someone elected to the advisory board of the Federal Housing Administration's Multifamily Housing Committee, Pei entered into negotiations to ensure that the project would qualify for government-subsidised mortgage insurance. He succeeded in having Kips Bay Plaza's deep window recesses allotted as balconies.

2.16.1 | **George Cserna, north-east view of midtown Manhattan from a Kips Bay Plaza apartment, ca.1962. Avery Architectural and Fine Arts Library, Columbia University**

```
                                              Eileen Hunter
                                              330 East 33rd Street, #16-H
                                              New York, New York 10016

26 July 1993

Mr. I. M. Pei
Architect
600 Madison Avenue - 8th Floor
New York, New York 10022

Dear Mr. Pei:

For "logical" reasons I've been resisting writing you. Your genius has been recognized by acclaim
and awards throughout your career and I've told myself that you didn't need to hear my little middle
class observations. But this letter wouldn't let go of me and so I'm writing.

I moved into Kips Bay May 7th. Having lived in the neighborhood twenty-four years, I've always
wanted to live there. I consider it the premiere place to live in Manhattan, the north building,
particularly, as it's raised above the street permitting a person to step back from this frenetic city;
leaving isn't necessary, just removing to a safe place for a while to replenish one's spirit.

I love the generosity of dimension and space at Kips, the land, the wide halls, and especially the part
of the building I don't know what to call (is it a portico, a colonnade, an overhang, a porch?) that
when entered from east or west allows the eye a long, restful and renewing length of visual space. It
reminds me of a monastery, a cathedral and yet not reaching up to some deity but human scale, one
built for her and him and me -- that warm, that personal. The garden is a gift wherein I have felt safe
outdoors to sit and dream with relaxed posture, the first time ever in all the years I've lived in
Manhattan.

Coming home is a happy experience. Since I've moved here I've thought of you often as the man
who had the vision, the humanity, even the romance to design a place so truly for people, an ever
more valued oasis in a world increasingly uncivil. Stepping onto Kips Bay property with its kind
personnel (I believe made more so by their surroundings) and congenial neighbors is a little like
stepping into Camelot. These words, flowery though they may be, still inadequately describe what I
experience living in this environment you envisioned and made real.

Without even considering the magnitude of all your other works, I am sure of one thing:

    Your life and work have mattered and been a blessing to so many people.
    Having the privilege of living in Kips Bay, I count myself one of those lucky ones.

    Thank you.

    Sincerely,

    Eileen Hunter
    Eileen Hunter
```

2.16.2 | **Eileen Hunter, letter to I. M. Pei, 26 July 1993. Papers of I. M. Pei, Library of Congress, Washington DC**

2.16.3 | Naho Kubota, living room of an apartment at Kips Bay Plaza, 2022. Photo commissioned by M+

2.16.1–2.16.3
With Kips Bay Plaza, Pei demonstrated that a development's economic viability did not have to come at the expense of architectural detail or tenants' quality of life. The building's deep concrete window frames doubled as the building's structure, offering floor-to-ceiling windows that provided natural light, privacy, and shade, in addition to introducing a visual texture to the facade. Outside, the park provided residents with a refuge in the city. When budget limitations prevented him from installing a Picasso sculpture on the grounds, Pei instead populated the green space with fifty saplings. Converted to condominium apartments in the 1980s, Kips Bay Plaza has today become a prized New York address.

Society Hill (1957–1964)
Philadelphia

2.17.1 | **Early site plan of Society Hill, ca.1957. Pei Cobb Freed & Partners**

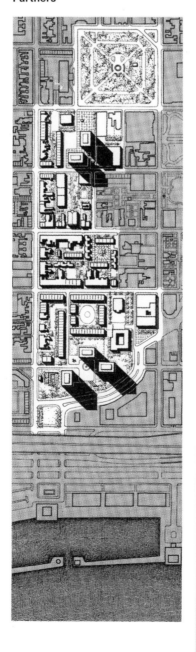

2.17.2 | **Perspective plan of Society Hill, 1958. Pei Cobb Freed & Partners**

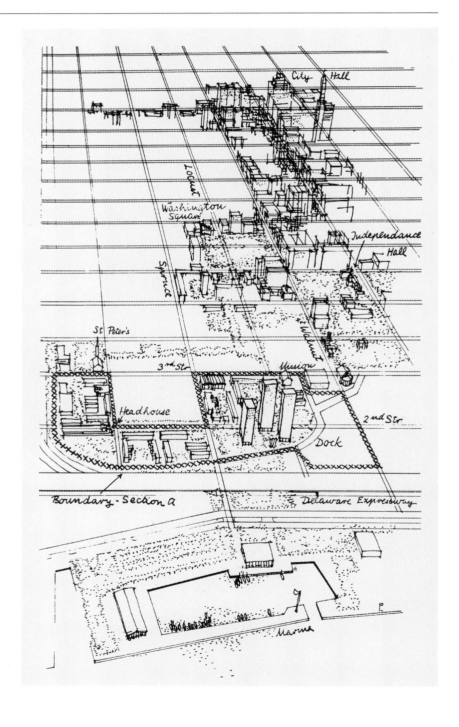

2.17.3 | **Ara Derderian, rendering of town houses at Society Hill with the towers behind, ca.1957. Pei Cobb Freed & Partners**

2.17.1–2.17.3
Pei established I. M. Pei & Associates as an independent practice in 1955. At the invitation of Edmund Bacon, director of Philadelphia's City Planning Commission, his new firm partnered with Zeckendorf to submit a plan for the rehabilitation of Society Hill in Philadelphia as part of a comprehensive urban renewal of the Washington Square East area of the city. In response to Bacon's wishes to protect existing architecturally significant buildings, Pei and Zeckendorf proposed a redevelopment that would be incremental rather than wholesale. Historic red-brick row houses were preserved, while new, low-rise town houses matched the scale and materiality of the colonial structures, providing a transition from the old to the new urban fabric. The scheme also extended Bacon's pedestrian greenway system, connecting Society Hill with Washington Square and introducing three apartment buildings. Instead of the twelve-storey slabs Bacon initially suggested, Pei chose to build slender, thirty-one-storey towers that not only fulfilled the density requirement of providing 720 apartments, but also preserved views, precisely framing historical landmarks. Funding for the towers came from the Federal Housing Administration, adding a further constraint to the project's already tight budget.

2.18.1 | **Wurts Brothers, Society Hill town houses with a view of the United States Custom House, ca.1964.** Architectural Archives, University of Pennsylvania; National Building Museum

2.18.2 | **Robert Damora, view of Society Hill towers with the New Market Headhouse in the foreground, ca.1964. Estate of Robert Damora**

2.18.1–2.18.2
Grouped in residential squares and with extensive use of brick, the three-storey town houses were designed to integrate with their historical neighbours. The horizontal strip of windows stretching across the roofline echoes the proportion of the colonial windows and resonates with the rectilinearity of the residential towers' concrete frame. The towers' facades combine framing, exterior walls, and window openings in a single structural system, a solution that gives each apartment large windows to maximise views. The towers are set back from the historic buildings on a park along the Delaware River, with each tower orientated towards a specific urban node. The view pictured here shows an axis aligned with the New Market Headhouse just to the south of the complex.

2.19 | **George D. McDowell, rubble on future site of the Delaware Expressway with view of Society Hill towers, 1970. Temple University Libraries, Special Collection Research Center**

The pristine towers of Society Hill photographed from South Front Street contrast with the debris left from recent demolitions to make way for the Delaware Expressway. The image represents the extent to which Philadelphia's city centre was still catching up with the reinvention of Society Hill six years after its completion. Within a decade, the transformation of Society Hill attracted new waves of ownership, displacing lower-income residents and transforming the area into a neighbourhood that remained affluent throughout the following decades.

2.20 | **I. M. Pei (centre) and members of I. M. Pei & Associates, ca.1960. Pei Cobb Freed & Partners**

Needing an identity separate from Webb & Knapp in order to take on institutional commissions, Pei registered the firm of I. M. Pei & Associates in 1955 with design partner Henry N. Cobb and managing partner Eason Leonard. They remained under Zeckendorf's employment until formal separation in 1960, when they brought with them a seventy-person architectural team. The success and stability of the firm over the following decades owed much to Pei's mix of idealism and practical ingenuity. Pei was as involved in securing commissions and maintaining client relationships as he was in the conceptual phases of the design process. In the firm's early years, his collaborations with each project team created a shared language of design and culture of work.

REAL ESTATE & URBAN REDEVELOPMENT

2.21.1 | **Norman McGrath, reception area at the new office of I. M. Pei & Partners at 600 Madison Avenue with a blown-up graphic of the Everson Museum of Art, in 'I. M. Pei & Partners',** *Architecture Plus* **1 (February 1973): 55**

This photograph [opposite] presages the later firm of I. M. Pei & Associates, established in the mid-1950s. From left to right: Leonard Jacobson, project manager and future partner; Eason Leonard, Pei's long-term business partner; Martin Daum (standing), older, with practical bricks-and-mortar knowledge about building; my brother Pershing Wong, I. M.'s trusted detail-oriented designer; and Don Page, head of the graphics department. It's all there: design, technical knowledge, exacting detail, refined presentation, management. Drawings were everywhere, whether in design sessions, production meetings, or just out on tables in the drafting room for all to see. In the early days, everyone knew about every project. It remained a collaborative atmosphere in which everyone understood the goal of striving for perfection. The mentality was: no one would know, or care, that you laboured under a punishing deadline, that you didn't eat lunch, or that you hadn't slept. The work had to be done correctly. No shortcuts! That's the kind of pressure the office, and an uncompromising person like I. M., demanded. During overnight charrettes—intense work sessions to meet project deadlines—some people napped under their desks. Constant charrettes were a way of life.

– Kellogg Wong

Kellogg Wong was a member of I. M. Pei's team for more than fifty years, serving as associate partner, chief administrative architect, and lead designer for a wide range of major projects.

2.21.2 | **Dennis Brack, I. M. Pei and staff reviewing a drawing, 1978. Papers of I. M. Pei, Library of Congress, Washington DC**

2.21.1–2.21.2
By 1966, the volume of new projects being undertaken by the firm necessitated a move to an office befitting a large New York corporate practice. In its new space at 600 Madison Avenue, Pei changed the firm's name from I. M. Pei & Associates to I. M. Pei & Partners to reflect the contributions of his partners, in particular Henry N. Cobb and James Freed.

Bedford-Stuyvesant Superblock (1966–1969)
New York

2.22.1 | Lael Scott, 'In the News: Architect I. M. Pei—Man with a Plan to Beautify the Ghetto', *New York Post*, 20 May 1967. Wright's Media

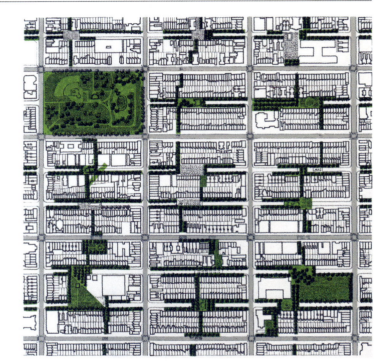

2.22.2 | Early planning scheme, ca.1966. Pei Cobb Freed & Partners

2.22.1–2.22.2

As part of his commitment to the Civil Rights Movement in the United States, New York Senator Robert F. Kennedy proposed an urban regeneration of Bedford-Stuyvesant, Brooklyn, one of the largest majority-Black neighbourhoods in the country. Pei's pro bono involvement in the project followed his selection to design the John F. Kennedy Presidential Library and Museum in Boston in 1964. After studying the six-hundred-block neighbourhood, Pei's office identified under-utilised gridded streets that had no community focus and proposed linking groups of two to three parallel blocks to form seventeen 'superblocks', organised by interlocking landscaped paths, parks, and playgrounds. Making use of a grant from the Vincent Astor Foundation, Pei collaborated with landscape architect M. Paul Friedberg and the Bedford Stuyvesant Restoration Corporation—America's first community development corporation, led by Franklin Thomas—to begin the project with a small-scale intervention that would not involve the relocation of residents.

2.23 | **Gil Amiaga, redesigned St Mark's Avenue, ca.1969. Amiaga Photographers, Inc.**

Following the advice of Thomas, Pei strove to engage the community's sense of ownership in selecting the blocks for redevelopment. Residents chose a middle-class block at Prospect Place and an adjacent one largely occupied by welfare tenants. For Pei, the contrast between the two areas demonstrated the importance of repairing the social fabric in addition to revitalising the urban space. Block committees were organised to define desired improvements, a Black construction contractor was hired, and residents' children were paid to help with planting trees and paving sidewalks. Prospect Place gained expanded, well-lighted sidewalks with street furniture and speed bumps to slow traffic. St Mark's Avenue was pedestrianised, and a playground, paddling pool, seating, and access for a mobile library were introduced, with parking concentrated at the ends of the block. Following Robert F. Kennedy's assassination in 1968, the Bedford-Stuyvesant project stalled. The completion of its pilot phase nevertheless raised enthusiasm for the later regeneration of nearby blocks.

Raffles International Centre Redevelopment (1969–1972) / Raffles City (1973–1986)
Singapore

2.24.1 | **Site plan for Raffles International Centre, 1970. Pei Cobb Freed & Partners**

We arrived in the small city-state of Singapore in 1969 to masterplan a half-mile-long, thirty-two-acre mega site, the most ambitious commercial enterprise in all of Southeast Asia. Our mandate was to demonstrate the stability and economic prosperity of Singapore's recent independence and signal the nation's auspicious future. There was no programme as there was no clear vision of what was needed and building codes and guidelines had not yet been developed. Our firm had a solid knowledge of how cities work and a deep commitment to learn everything about the forces impacting a site: its history, culture, urban axes, open spaces, traffic and growth patterns, revenue sources, influences from neighbouring countries, behind-the-scenes players, etc. Singapore was to become a destination. Understanding the integrated commercial, residential, office, shopping, tourism, convention, and entertainment functions of cities, we anticipated the need for hotels not just for lodging but also for the activity they generate, the pizzazz. We appreciated the importance of punctuating the skyline with a tall structure, as if planting a flagpole, to create an identity from afar and clearly signal the nucleus of the site. Other than a small cluster of mid-rise buildings in the financial district, Singapore was a dense accretion of low shophouses and uncoordinated private development. Our prime objective was to define the city centre with a grand design, built in phases, that would create order and unity over time. We completed master planning in 1973, making multiple revisions to accommodate the changing market. Ultimately, only Raffles City was realised, on a single superblock at the head of the site.

– Kellogg Wong

Kellogg Wong was project architect for Raffles City and was involved in the project when it was first known as Raffles International Centre.

2.24.2 | **Early scheme for Raffles International Centre, ca.1970. Pei Cobb Freed & Partners**

2.24.3 | **Robert Schwartz, interior view of early scheme for Raffles International Centre, ca.1970. Pei Cobb Freed & Partners**

2.24.1–2.24.3
As underwriter of real-estate developments in the newly independent city-state's Urban Renewal Programme, the Development Bank of Singapore invited I. M. Pei & Partners to identify possible uses for a thirteen-hectare area in the CBD. Part of the Singaporean government's plan to maximise land value, the project led Pei to propose Raffles International Centre, a 'city within a city' consisting of a hotel, office buildings, a convention centre, shopping facilities, apartment blocks, and a park. The global economic recession in the 1970s and a change in investors meant that only one superblock was realised, in 1986. Named Raffles City, the multipurpose complex privileged retail space to encourage all-day traffic. The large atrium is animated with intersecting escalators, bridges, balconies, and screen walls that create a visual and programmatic complexity, which Pei considered to be important for sustaining interest in the large space.

Tête de la Défense (1970–1971; unbuilt)
Paris

A decade before the Grand Louvre, a little-known design for two linked slabs at La Défense was I. M. Pei's introduction to Paris. During the late 1960s, the state-sponsored business district experienced its first quantum leap in high-rise construction, leading to the involvement of US firms. The office tower was designed to be worthy of the grand east–west axis of the Voie triomphale, which stretches to the Louvre. The slight incline at La Défense was meant to terminate in a monumental gesture. Here, Tête de la Défense was to house managerial functions in a 'head', marrying the business world with the ceremonial urban landscape of the French capital. Tackled by numerous designers before and after Pei, the formal challenge would not be solved until 1989 by the Grande Arche de la Défense. Johan Otto von Spreckelsen's gateway occupies the same footprint as the designs proposed before the oil crisis of 1973, which stalled La Défense's development for almost decade. In the aftermath of the student protests of 1968 and the controversial demolition of Les Halles market in the heart of Paris, the budding skyline was met with increasing hostility. Pei and his associate Araldo Cossutta took public opinion into account. They included sightlines from the Place de la Concorde and perspectives through the Arc de Triomphe in their design iterations between 1970 and 1971. Pei would later revisit the axial sequence of voids and stereometric volumes with the Louvre pyramid. Like Tête de la Défense, the Grand Louvre is a superblock project; both interventions are premised on a pedestrian superblock loaded with hidden layers of infrastructure and circulation systems. Although excluded from Pei's monographs, Tête de la Défense is a turning point in his career. The pinwheel compositions of late-modernist urban renewal are superseded by an increasingly abstract formalism, in this case a tribute to the French tradition of urban composition while bringing New York corporate professionalism to Paris.

– André Bideau

André Bideau is an architectural historian who contributed to the discussion on urban design for the 'Rethinking Pei' symposium organised by M+ and the GSD in 2017.

2.25.1 | **Model of I. M. Pei's initial scheme for La Défense, ca.1970. Pei Cobb Freed & Partners**

REAL ESTATE & URBAN REDEVELOPMENT   83

2.25.2 | Robert Schwartz, rendering of Araldo Cossutta's scheme for La Défense, 1971. Pei Cobb Freed & Partners

2.25.1–2.25.2
The large office tower at La Défense would serve as an end point of the city's grand historical axis extending from the Louvre through the Place de la Concorde and the Place de l'Étoile. In addition to wanting to preserve Paris's historic sightlines, Pei approached the project as a finely grained problem of urban design, examining questions of access, vehicular circulation, and infrastructure in the new business district. He proposed two towers that curve towards each other at the base, calculated to reach 189 metres in height, so as not to obstruct views through the Arc de Triomphe. Araldo Cossutta's later iterations of the scheme connected Pei's two towers to form a parabolic structure while accentuating the civic square that extends from underneath the complex. Ultimately, neither proposal was selected by the project's commissioners.

2.26.1 | **Kouo Shang-Wei, street view of OCBC Centre, ca.1976. Pei Cobb Freed & Partners**

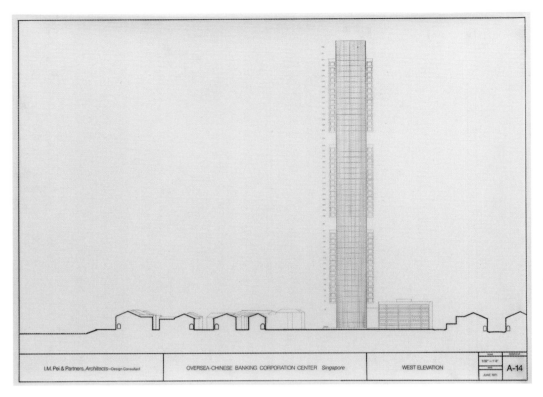

2.26.2 | **West elevation of OCBC Centre, June 1971. Pei Cobb Freed & Partners**

2.26.1–2.26.2

Pei's first built project in Singapore arose from the second Sale of Sites in the city's financial district. The sale was carried out by the Urban Renewal Department (now the Urban Redevelopment Authority) to offer state land around the historic commercial area of Raffles Place for private development. Pei's redesign of the OCBC's headquarters reflected the bank's ambition with an imposing hall and a structure that was then the tallest building in the city-state. The design, created by spanning two freestanding cores with steel trusses, not only allowed a column-free banking hall but also met the Singaporean government's requirement of constructing the building quickly. Set back with an open plaza facing the narrow streets of shophouses, the tower, with its slender rounded ends, relates to the public realm in a way that most buildings in the financial district did not—as they were largely of a podium–tower configuration with almost 100 per cent site coverage.

Oversea-Chinese Banking Corporation (OCBC) Centre (1970–1976)
Singapore

Kapsad Development
(1975–1978; unbuilt)
Tehran

2.27.1 |
Plan of Kapsad Development, ca.1975. Sazeh Consultants

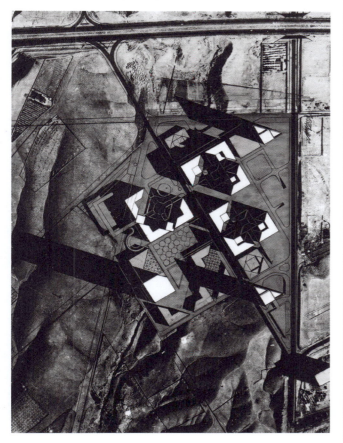

2.27.2 | **Model of Kapsad Development, ca.1978. Pei Cobb Freed & Partners**

2.27.1–2.27.2
The 1973 oil crisis that had caused a recession in the United States also led to an increase in wealth and a building boom in the countries of the Middle East. Among them was Iran, which attracted many American architectural offices, including Pei's. The firm's initial design for the headquarters of the Industrial Credit Bank in Tehran's new city centre was expanded to a project for a fourteen-hectare urban block. In line with the Iranian state's desire for large-scale infrastructural developments, public buildings, and modern housing, Pei proposed a tightly knit mixed-use scheme combining low-, medium-, and high-rise structures, including residential apartments, office towers, a hotel, and a shopping centre. The plot was divided into square parcels, with buildings arranged to reference Iran's historic walled courtyards. Plans for the project's development were abandoned at the beginning of the Islamic Revolution in 1978.

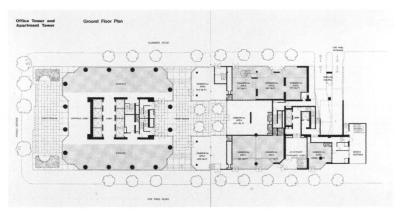

2.28.1 | **I. M. Pei & Partners and W. Szeto & Partners, ground-floor plan of Sunning Plaza, 1981. Hysan Development Company Ltd**

Sunning Plaza (1977–1982)
Hong Kong

The idea of the set-back was Pei's. This was his first project in Hong Kong, and he wanted to create something unique, rather than just another elevated podium and tower design. Hong Kong building regulations allowed commercial developers to build with 100 per cent land coverage for the first fifteen metres in height, but Pei proposed setting the office tower back on the long, linear site to create a more generous frontage between the main entrance and the edge of the street. Similar to how the Seagram Building in New York was set back to create an open plaza, Sunning Plaza stands out as it does not completely fill its site—unlike many buildings in Hong Kong. Pei understood that Hong Kong is a commercially orientated city. To increase the project's commercial value, he introduced two podiums devoted to shops and restaurants, one submerged below the office tower, and the other under the residential building designed to take advantage of the street exposure created by the wider pavements along the perimeter. This led to a courtyard-like space framed with palm trees that became a unique outdoor dining area in the busy heart of Causeway Bay.

– Sherman Kung

Sherman Kung was a project architect at W. Szeto & Partners, which designed Sunning Plaza with I. M. Pei & Partners. Kung subsequently collaborated with Pei's office on the Bank of China Tower in Hong Kong as executive architect.

2.28.2 | **I. M. Pei & Partners and W. Szeto & Partners, cover of lease brochure for Sunning Plaza, 1981. Hysan Development Company Ltd**

2.28.1–2.28.2
Composed of a thirty-floor office tower and an eighteen-floor residential block on a single-storey podium housing retail space, Sunning Plaza was developed by Lee Hysan Estate Company, which owns most of the prime real estate in Hong Kong's Causeway Bay neighbourhood. The 2,900-square-metre high-rise development replaced a 1950s apartment and hotel building, marking Causeway Bay's transformation into a high-end commercial area. Contrary to the city's lot-line development and conventional maximising of the use of habitable land, Pei convinced Hysan to set the office tower's entrance back from the tree-lined street edge. This enhanced the building's vertical sculptural articulation, which was already emphasised by the Kawneer silver reflective curtain-wall system—the first such system to be installed in Hong Kong. A twenty-metre-wide walkway along a landscaped dining courtyard below the apartment tower provided an emergency exit for residents and linked the two roads bordering the site.

REAL ESTATE & URBAN REDEVELOPMENT   87

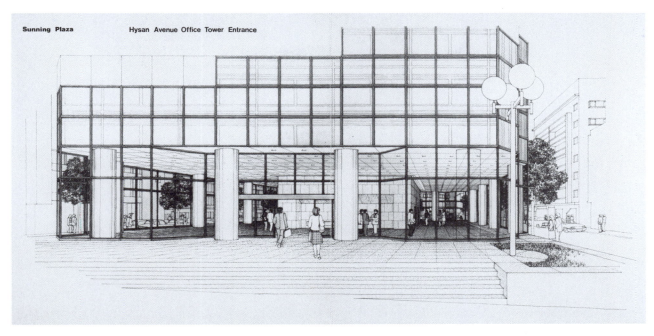

2.29.1 | **I. M. Pei & Partners and W. Szeto & Partners, perspective of Sunning Plaza along Hysan Avenue, 1981. Hysan Development Company Ltd**

2.29.2 | **A scene from *A Better Tomorrow* (1986) by John Woo, filmed at the entrance of Sunning Plaza, 37:48. Fortune Star Media**

2.29.1–2.29.2

The demolition of Sunning Plaza was announced in 2013. Amid the resulting outcry from the Hong Kong media and public, many recalled a memorable scene from John Woo's 1986 triad melodrama *A Better Tomorrow* set at the office tower. A crew of flashily dressed gangsters led by the villainous Shing (played by Waise Lee) strides out of the building—with a reflection of the Lee Gardens Hotel visible in the glass curtain-wall facade behind them—across the stepped granite pavement and towards a waiting Mercedes-Benz, whose windshield has just been cleaned by Mark, the film's down-on-his-luck protagonist (Chow Yun-fat). The building's set-back created an urban stage for dramatic entrances and exits. This grand gesture and the tower's diagonal position on its site, formed by four corners chamfered at a forty-five-degree angle, made Sunning Plaza a prototype for office buildings in Hong Kong in the 1980s.

Marina South Development Plan (1982–1983; unbuilt)
Singapore

The site of the Marina South Development was on land reclaimed in the late 1970s, adjacent to Singapore's colonial and post-independence-era CBD. As CEO of the Housing and Development Board, which oversaw the city's land reclamation, I suggested that this piece of prime land should be planned for Singapore's future CBD, instead of a housing development. The government agreed and asked me to suggest a planner. Having worked with I. M. Pei in New York in the late 1960s—on several urban planning and design projects, including the renewal of Bedford-Stuyvesant—I recommended him for the task. Pei made a model that covered an area much larger than the proposed site in order to relate his proposal well with the surrounding urban context. He straightened the curved shape of Marina Bay on one side of the reclamation shoreline, turning the bay into a squarish aquatic plaza.

The street plan was a grid integrated into the adjoining CBD's own grid pattern, allowing an incremental development of land parcels that made the area look complete at any stage. Bearing in mind that a CBD is not just a commercial area but a city's most important civic space, Pei created an urban panorama and a civic identity. He introduced a central green axial line, terminating at a promontory with a pair of towers as the focal point. However, after I left the civil service, Pei's proposal was no longer in use.

– Liu Thai Ker

Liu Thai Ker was an architect and planner at I. M. Pei & Partners (1965–1969) before returning to Singapore to join the Housing and Development Board as chief architect and chief executive (1969–1989) and then the Urban Redevelopment Authority as chief planner and chief executive (1989–1992).

2.30 | **Model of Marina South Development Plan, ca.1982. Pei Cobb Freed & Partners**

Pei's office was selective in taking on planning projects owing to their indefinite outcomes. It accepted the Marina South Development Study project on the condition that it was solely commissioned to the firm. The Singapore Cabinet, however, required an alternative proposal, which led to a similar commission being given to Kenzo Tange. Tange's radial plan, which matched the curve of a highway, differed from Pei's rectilinear grid. Pei's plan was preferred as its rectilinearity could seamlessly integrate the old CBD's grid pattern with the new city centre. Despite many changes, Pei's project laid the groundwork for the eventual master plan, which proved influential in shaping an economically viable and visually arresting Marina Bay.

REAL ESTATE & URBAN REDEVELOPMENT 89

2.31 | **Perspective rendering of Gateway, in** *Gateway—Office Development Proposal for Land Parcel 8*, **1981. Tao Shing Pee; Singapore Land Ltd**

The Gateway was proposed for the Urban Redevelopment Authority's ninth Sale of Sites in an area termed the Golden Mile, envisioned as a mixed-use commercial strip lining Singapore's seafront. The design was determined by its location, a prominent parcel of land bounded by Beach Road, Nicoll Highway, and newly built flyovers. The simplicity of the two parallelogram forms sought to bring cohesion to the area's skyline, which was characterised by a loose collection of building masses. The towers' geometry, placement, sharp angles, and notched planes elicit dynamic views of the building when seen from moving vehicles. Precise detailing of the surface cladding enhances the interplay of light and shadow as metal panels wrap around each floor in continuous bands.

Gateway (1981–1990)
Singapore

2.32.1 | **Kellogg Wong, sketch recommending a height limit on buildings built around the Forbidden City, ca.1979**

Fragrant Hill Hotel (1979–1982)
Beijing

We were shown a site for a hotel on Coal Hill, behind the Forbidden City, in the heart of Beijing. I'm sure it was the most valuable location as tourists would want to stay near the emperor's palace. No matter the convenience of close proximity, a tall building here would forever diminish the Forbidden City's image of invincibility and destroy its defining relationship with the open sky. I made a sketch [above], explaining that no building should ever be so high that it could be seen from the central axis of the palace and gave the drawing to my guide. In my debriefing, I. M. agreed in rejecting the Coal Hill site. Meanwhile, my sketch made its way to Beijing's city planners; in due course, strict height regulations were imposed. I bumped into this twenty or thirty years later when a local planner asked me to review a proposed building on an outer Ring Road. When I asked about plot ratio and height limits, he replied incredulously, 'You're not aware of the Pei Height Limitation? Buildings may not be seen from the Forbidden City.'

– Kellogg Wong

Kellogg Wong was a member of I. M. Pei's team for more than fifty years and worked on the planning and site-selection phase of Fragrant Hill Hotel.

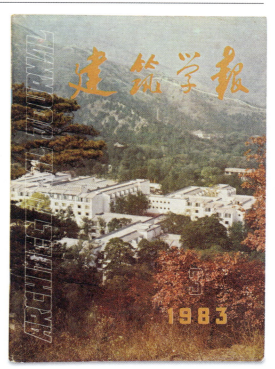

2.32.2 | **Cover, featuring Fragrant Hill Hotel,** *Jianzhu xuebao* (*Architectural Journal*) 175 (20 March 1983). M+, Hong Kong

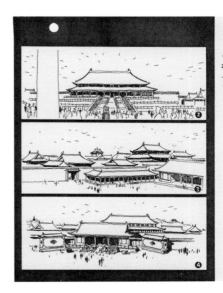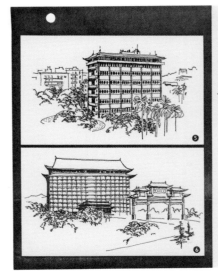
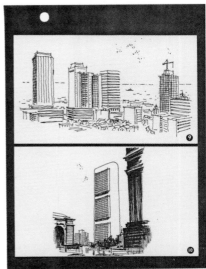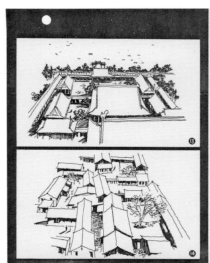

2.32.3 | **I. M. Pei and Wang Tianxi, illustrations of urban contexts in Beijing and Singapore from Pei's lecture 'Urban Planning in Beijing and the Problem of the Nationalisation of Architectural Creation in China', delivered to delegates from Beijing's Tsinghua University at the Tsinghua Alumni Association of Greater New York, 30 May 1980. Papers of I. M. Pei, Library of Congress, Washington DC**

2.32.1–2.32.3
Pei's lecture 'Urban Planning in Beijing and the Problem of the Nationalisation of Architectural Creation in China' reflected his call for a more nuanced and careful approach to identifying, interpreting, and applying national, cultural, or regional identity in architectural design and city planning in mainland China. The lecture stressed the importance of protecting the relationship between the Forbidden City's roofscape and the open sky by not building towering structures around it. Pei also critiqued the tendency of constructing *da wuding* (big roofs) atop high-rise buildings. Using the examples of the Summer Palace and Beijing's *siheyuan* (courtyard dwellings), he noted how the distinct features of traditional imperial and vernacular structures in China are found not only in the form of roofs with upturned eaves, but also in the modular spatial configuration of the courtyard and garden typology—which he would apply in the design of the Fragrant Hill Hotel.

Bank of China Tower (1982–1989)
Hong Kong

2.33.1 | **Cover, featuring Bank of China Tower,** *Shidai jianzhu* (*Time + Architecture*) 1 (November 1984). M+, Hong Kong

2.33.2 | **Yang Yuan-loong (second from left) and Jiang Wen-gui (third from left), vice chairman of the Bank of China, reviewing a model of the Bank of China Tower, ca.1983. Esquel Group**

2.33.1–2.33.2
The commission for the Bank of China Tower in Hong Kong's CBD came on the heels of the Fragrant Hill Hotel in Beijing. Yang Yuan-loong, one of the founding partners of YTT Tourism, which had financed the hotel's development, recommended Pei to design the bank's new headquarters. In light of the impending handover of Hong Kong from the United Kingdom to China, the project was significant as a symbol of the city's development through China's policy of modernisation. Pei's father's former position in the bank's senior leadership gave the project a personal resonance. However, Pei was reluctant to work with a mainland Chinese entity owing to the mismatch in expectations for contractual conditions between client and architect that he had experienced with Fragrant Hill. He accepted the commission once he had ensured that the project would follow Hong Kong law and construction regulations, and only after verifying his team's ability to construct a typhoon-proof tower, one that would dwarf the recently completed headquarters of rival HSBC, at one-third of the construction budget.

REAL ESTATE & URBAN REDEVELOPMENT

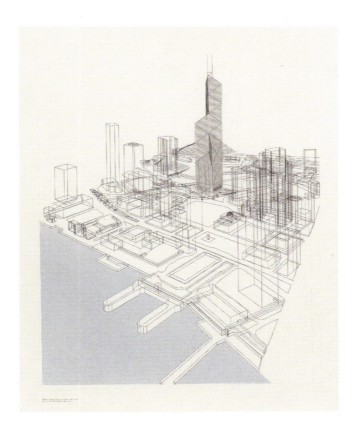

2.34.1 | **AutoCAD site study of the Bank of China Tower, 1986. Pei Cobb Freed & Partners**

2.34.2 | **John Nye, Bank of China Tower seen from Ocean Terminal in Tsim Sha Tsui, ca.1989**

2.34.1–2.34.2
With an inland site pressed between existing tall buildings, a mountain, and Victoria Harbour, a tower of great height was necessary for the symbolically significant project to be visible on the Hong Kong skyline. Determined to diverge from the standard rectangular skyscraper typology, Pei envisioned a tower composed of four triangular segments that could address the streets, achieve visual prominence—particularly when seen from the Kowloon Peninsula—and be strong enough to withstand typhoon-force winds and earthquakes. Atop a four-storey base, the northern, harbour-facing quadrant tapers at the seventeenth floor, the western quadrant at the thirty-eighth, and the eastern quadrant at the fifty-first, with the southern quadrant, facing Victoria Peak, climbing to two additional thirteen-storey tiers topped by double masts. At 368 metres, it was the fifth-tallest building in the world upon completion. The glass-and-concrete structure supports an anodised-aluminium and reflective glass curtain wall, which creates vertical and sloped surfaces that mirror the neighbouring buildings and landscape under an ever-changing sky.

REAL ESTATE & URBAN REDEVELOPMENT 95

2.35.1 | **Site plan of the Bank of China Tower, ca.1988.
Pei Cobb Freed & Partners**

OPPOSITE:
2.35.2 | **South Ho, view of the old Bank of China building and Chater Garden from the top of the Bank of China Tower, 2021.
Photo commissioned by M+**

2.35.1–2.35.2
For its new headquarters in Hong Kong, the Bank of China acquired a nine-thousand-square-metre sloped parcel of land at the eastern edge of the Central district, on a corner site surrounded by major thoroughfares, flyovers, and a municipal car park. Pei expressed dissatisfaction with the plot of land and, even before he had finalised his design for the tower, began protracted, difficult negotiations with Hong Kong's Lands Department to exchange a public open space on one corner of the site for a space that would provide a parallelogram-shaped footprint for the tower, framed by triangular gardens on each side. The change of location would make the tower parallel to Central's grid, facing Chater Garden along the axis of the old Bank of China building and aligned with a road leading directly to Victoria Harbour. Pei also lobbied the Lands Department for a new transverse road along the site's upper boundary, to give the tower a formal entrance and make it accessible to cars and pedestrians.

Grand Louvre Phase I (1983–1989) & Phase II (1989–1993)
Paris

2.36 | **Early traffic study of roads and intersections surrounding the Louvre in Paris, ca.1984. Pei Cobb Freed & Partners**

Pei saw President François Mitterrand's decision to transform the Louvre into a single museum complex as an opportunity to knit together the left and right banks of the Seine. The yellow lines drawn on this map document an analysis of traffic circulation on major thoroughfares surrounding the Louvre. Pei's observations include serious congestion along rue de Rivoli, the road parallel to the Louvre, caused by tourist buses parked on the street, and gridlock at the intersection with avenue de l'Opéra, diagonal to the museum. Realised in collaboration with the city, the traffic department, and the mayor's office, this study led Pei to the solution of an underground road, a large car park, a new metro station, and a passage linking the Louvre to the Jardin des Tuileries—all of which facilitated greater ease of access.

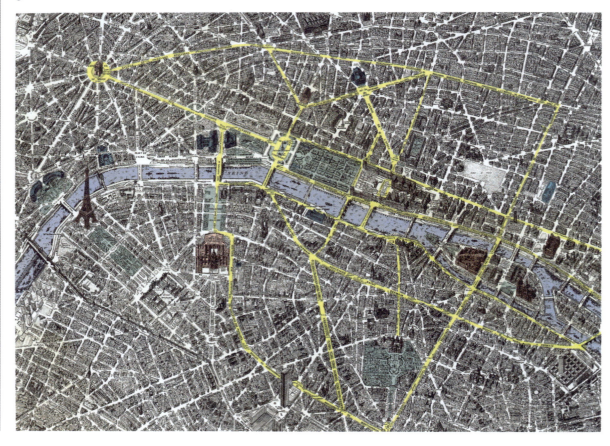

2.37 | Tracy Turner, I. M. Pei-opoly game board, 2017

I. M. Pei-opoly was created in 2017 for Pei's one-hundredth birthday by his daughter Liane Pei and graphic designer Tracy Turner, who had developed the visual identity of the Fragrant Hill Hotel in Beijing three decades earlier. Using the popular Parker Brothers board game Monopoly as a template, I. M. Pei-opoly offers a tongue-in-cheek representation of Pei's life and legacy of built projects, as well as his enduring entanglement with political and financial power brokers and real-estate machinations. Decorated with the cracked-ice pattern that features prominently at Fragrant Hill, the game's twenty-two properties are named after buildings designed by Pei, arranged loosely chronologically from the 1960s onwards and with the most emblematic projects—such as the National Gallery of Art East Building and Grand Louvre— having the highest value. Other squares on the board refer to essentialised elements of Chinese culture and the rewards and challenges of Pei's jet-setting lifestyle.

Suzhou Museum (2000–2006)
Suzhou

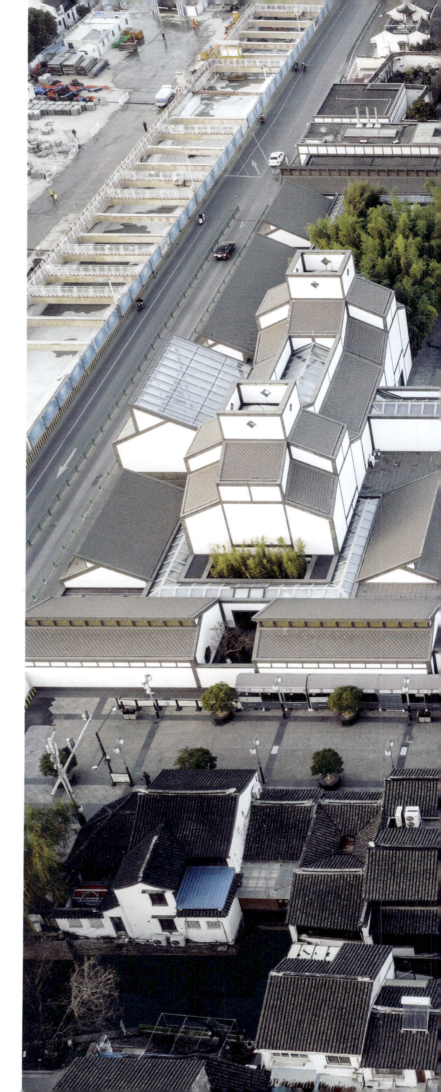

2.38 | **Tian Fangfang, aerial view of the Suzhou Museum, 2021. Photo commissioned by M+**

Suzhou Museum was sited in Suzhou's most historic quarter. To keep the historical integrity of the area, Pei recommended that Qimen Road—the street running parallel to a canal fronting the museum entrance—be converted into a pedestrian-only thoroughfare. Paved with local *jinshan* stone and lined with shops, Qimen Road would be a public open space for circulation and commercial activities. Pei's recommendation was informed by the historic preservation and urban revitalisation guidelines proposed by a team led by his son T'ing Chung Pei in 1996, and supported by the mayor of Suzhou, Zhang Xinsheng, who saw the museum project as an opportunity for economic growth and the development of heritage tourism. The guidelines also informed the parameters for the design of the museum itself, including the definition of height limits and the need for the form and materials of roofs to correspond with historical precedents.

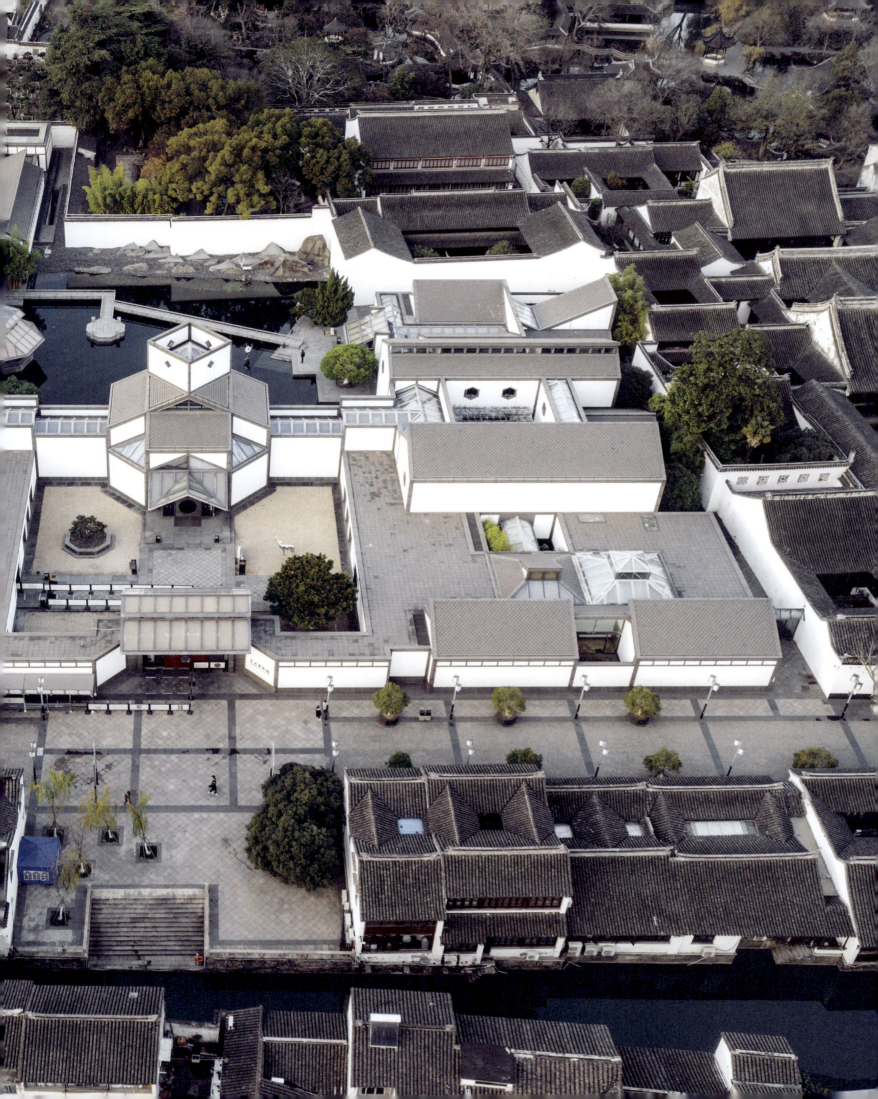

I. M. Pei and Urbanism in North America, 1948–1960

Eric Mumford

I. M. Pei's projects for New York developer William Zeckendorf's firm Webb & Knapp between 1948 and 1960 were widely publicised and remain relatively well known, but the intellectual context that informed them and their importance to the history of urbanism are not as clearly understood. These projects include two in downtown Denver, the Place Ville Marie in Montreal, and large mixed-use urban renewal projects in Washington DC, Chicago, New York, and Philadelphia. Pei's work for Zeckendorf was closely related, in part, to the modernist approach that began to be advocated in the early 1950s by Josep Lluís Sert, Louis Kahn, and Philadelphia city planner Edmund Bacon—an approach they called 'urban design'.[1] In a 2008 interview with Maki Fumihiko, a former Sert student at the Harvard Graduate School of Design (GSD), Pei acknowledged the influence of CIAM (Congrès internationaux d'architecture moderne) concepts of urban design, but also said that, by necessity, his work in American cities in the 1950s was more pragmatic than ideological.[2] Pei's urban-design work for Zeckendorf merits a close reading in relation to the intellectual development of urban design as a field, particularly after Sert became dean of the GSD in 1953 and organised, with Jaqueline Tyrwhitt, a series of urban-design conferences.

Beginning in the late 1940s, Zeckendorf outlined his vision for large-scale, pedestrian urban development in American cities in magazine articles and public speeches.[3] At about the same time, Bacon had begun to use the term 'urban design' in his Philadelphia planning efforts, which until 1954 also involved Louis Kahn. Sert knew Kahn well from their involvement in the American Society of Planners and Architects (ASPA), a short-lived group of modernist American architects with CIAM ties that also included Pei's former GSD professor Marcel Breuer. Kahn had served as vice president of ASPA in the mid-1940s, and his architectural partner at the time, Oscar Stonorov, was a CIAM and ASPA member. Zeckendorf's approach ran counter to the urban renewal based on slum clearance pioneered by New York City Construction Coordinator Robert Moses, who publicly denigrated the 'long-haired planners' of CIAM. Zeckendorf created pedestrian spaces and routes to connect new developments with their existing urban surroundings.[4] These efforts were in line with the concepts in modern architecture advocated by Sert at CIAM, where he was president from 1947 to 1956. Pei's work for Zeckendorf also sometimes involved retaining existing historic neighbourhoods and landmarks while modernising parts of cities, notably in his plans for

REAL ESTATE & URBAN REDEVELOPMENT

Southwest Washington; the Hyde Park area of Chicago (with Harry Weese); and the Society Hill neighbourhood of Philadelphia.

Pedestrian connectivity is at the heart of Pei's initial plan for the Washington DC redevelopment, which included an urban armature with a ninety-one-metre-wide pedestrian promenade called L'Enfant Plaza. The plaza was named for Pierre Charles L'Enfant, who created the original urban plan of the city in 1791. Pei's plan was intended to provide a link from the nineteenth-century Smithsonian Institution, prominently sited on the National Mall, to the areas then being rebuilt to the south of it, including a new waterfront marina. The new linkages spanned an existing railway line and a proposed eight-lane interstate highway (now I-395) to create pedestrian access to a previously isolated part of the city. Like many such plans in the immediate post-war years, this proposal was premised on the clearance of an existing area, which was majority Black. Pei and Zeckendorf negotiated with twenty-seven government agencies and extensively modified the plan, resulting in two widely separated built fragments: the two Town Center Plaza apartment buildings and L'Enfant Plaza.

The core concepts behind Pei and Zeckendorf's proposal are also evident in Sert's unbuilt urban-design projects for cities in Brazil, Peru, and Colombia from the same period.[5] At a 1953 American Institute of Architects (AIA) lecture, Sert criticised many North American planners for 'turning their backs on what we can call the city proper', because of what they saw as its 'inhuman scale, the traffic congestion, the air pollution, the overcrowding, etc.' The result has been 'much more suburbanism than urbanism'.[6] In contrast to nearly all his planning predecessors since the 1920s, Sert understood the potential of city centres. The challenge for architects would be the 'carrying out of large civic complexes: the integration of city-planning, architecture, and landscape architecture; the building of a complete environment' in existing urban centres, much as Pei was then doing for Zeckendorf.[7] This position combined Sert's post-war CIAM focus on the pedestrian heart of the city with the GSD efforts begun in 1936 by the then dean of the school, Joseph Hudnut, to synthesise the three professions of architecture, landscape architecture, and city planning under the rubric of design. For Sert, however, this return to a focus on the core of the city was only one component of CIAM urbanism, which remained based on the idea that cities had to be reorganised to better serve the needs of the working classes for improved housing conditions, more efficient infrastructure, and better opportunities for mass recreation near the city. Pei's work in Washington DC demonstrates closely related ideas, in a more pragmatic commercial and official context.

Both Sert and Pei, like Kahn and other members of ASPA, had seen Le Corbusier's New York presentation of the model of his plan for Saint-Dié (1945), which combined his earlier CIAM urbanism based on widely separated housing slabs with a new sensitivity to places for pedestrian gathering. In his 1946 essay 'Ineffable Space', Le Corbusier calls attention to the emotional importance of architectural spaces that could not be easily described in words. In his 1953 AIA talk, Sert noted that historic central urban areas, such as the Piazza San Marco in Venice and the Place de la Concorde in Paris, were 'a miracle repeated through the ages'.[8] He saw these places as spatial and functional models for sites of face-to-face pedestrian interaction, and he argued they were the only

Robert Schwartz, drawing of early scheme for the Southwest Washington Urban Redevelopment, ca.1957. Pei Cobb Freed & Partners

places where a post-war civic culture could continue. In the unpublished version of the talk he gave at the eighth meeting of CIAM, he suggested that face-to-face interactions that took place in such places were the only way to resist the centralising and undemocratic forces of mass media–based politics.[9] In general, however, Sert offered this vision of urban design in the same apolitical spirit as other kinds of post-war modernism, which distanced themselves from CIAM's highly politicised socialist roots in Europe and the Soviet Union before 1932.

This ideal of urban design appeared as planners and the urban real-estate industry were attempting to 'save' American cities by clearing and redeveloping them at higher densities. In the mid-1940s, for example, Robert Moses oversaw the development of Stuyvesant Town, a massive housing project on the east side of Manhattan intended for middle-income white people built on a site cleared of multi-ethnic slums. Moses applied bureaucratic standards that had been set by the New York City Housing Authority in the 1930s on a large scale.[10] Criticised by modern architects like Breuer, this direction also had little appeal to the target population itself; the white middle class was then beginning to move en masse to new segregated suburban subdivisions. Those developments, now often symbolised by Levittown, New York (1944–1951), were the antithesis of modernist urban planning, based as they were not on creating a collective public realm but on privately owned, often widely spaced, and traditionally styled single-family dwellings sited on gently curving streets. Yet they also resembled modernist developments in their standardised designs and large scale, with routine plans and site layouts determined by existing property lines and the subdivision guidelines of the Federal Housing Administration.

Suburban developments intentionally omitted the kind of pedestrian public realm at the heart of Sert's design philosophy. Such public spaces could instead still be found, more or less, in city centres served by mass transit systems. By the 1950s, these urban cores were deteriorating, extremely congested, and had changed in terms of racial composition. Rather than remaining centres of culture, cities were starting to become residential areas of last resort for those excluded from the suburbs for racial or economic reasons. To address this emerging problem, the US Congress, supported by President Truman, passed the 1949 Housing Act. The Title I provision of this legislation made federal funds available for cities to use eminent domain—the requisitioning of private property for public use—to clear and redevelop their central areas with high-density housing and, later, mixed-use developments.

These directions continued under the administration of President Eisenhower and informed the National Housing Act of 1954, which launched a federal urban renewal programme. As many histories of urban development attest, this legislation, like its Truman-era predecessors, led to the displacement of hundreds of thousands of people of colour and the removal of existing urban areas for new infrastructure. One of the best-known examples of urban renewal prompted by the National Housing Act was Mill Creek Valley in St Louis, cleared in 1959, where the Pei–Zeckendorf team's proposal for row houses for the rebuilt site was rejected in favour of Chloethiel Woodard Smith's LaClede Town (1962–1965, demolished) and adjacent projects.

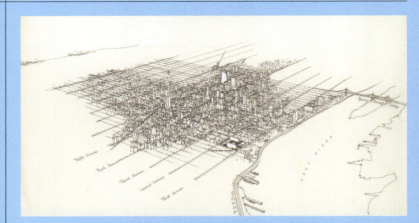

Perspective study of the areas around Kips Bay Plaza, ca.1957. Pei Cobb Freed & Partners

Robert Schwartz, rendering of Kips Bay Plaza, ca.1957. Pei Cobb Freed & Partners

It was in this context of debate over the future of American cities that Sert launched the field of urban design as a professional discipline at the First Urban Design Conference at the GSD in 1956. The speakers at this event included Victor Gruen, Charles Abrams, Richard Neutra, and Jane Jacobs, all of whom challenged in different ways what had become conventional decentralised planning wisdom. Many would return at the Second Urban Design Conference, to which Zeckendorf was also invited, and collectively their ideas would have a profound influence on thinking about cities in the years that followed. Sert put forward the social and political value of pedestrian encounters as a central element of the agenda of CIAM. In addition, alternative justifications for pedestrianised cities emerged, primarily from Edmund Bacon and Gruen. Instead of spaces for political assembly, each in different ways offered an aesthetic basis for pedestrian spaces. Bacon emphasised the historical and symbolic qualities of the city, while Gruen underscored the importance of spatial and perceptual experiences. Bacon stressed that his approach was based on the articulation of urban space 'for its experiencing by people' as 'a series of sensations in sequence'.[11] His presentation was particularly relevant to Pei's work, as the Zeckendorf team would win a design and development competition for the historic Society Hill area the following year, 1957.

One of Pei's most significant built projects for Zeckendorf, Kips Bay Plaza in New York, can be considered in relation to this emerging field of urban design. Even so, by his own account, Pei's design was inspired more by Mies van der Rohe's landscape-focused urbanism than Sert's urban theories. Pei was faced with tight per-unit cost constraints on this Title I project, designed in a New York planning context that was still dominated by Moses and his general disdain for architects. Pei's design placed 1,120 units into two 125-metre-long, 21-storey exposed-concrete slab buildings, with underground parking and a shopping arcade with a supermarket. It was an immense success, in part owing to Zeckendorf's hiring of a contractor who normally built bridges and highways, and to his insistence on planting fifty trees in the open areas of the site, instead of installing the large Picasso sculpture Pei favoured.[12]

Pei's work for the Society Hill area of Philadelphia continued some of the architectural aspects of Kips Bay Plaza and was also intended to combine modern architecture with pedestrian amenities and mixed-use development. Formally known as the Washington Square East Renewal project, it involved the redevelopment of 50 hectares around the former Dock Street city market and included 700 designated historic landmarks. Title I funding was approved for the project in 1957, after Zeckendorf was selected as the developer in a limited competition. Headed by Bacon, the Philadelphia City Planning Department staff included architects Preston Andrade and Willo von Moltke (the latter would go on to be the director of the Urban Design programme at the GSD following the Society Hill project). They prepared a master plan that called for three towers near the waterfront, a concept based on Kahn's Mill Creek towers, and housing slabs and three additional towers near Washington Square. In Pei's project, the second set of towers was replaced by town houses, reviving a then-extinct American urban housing type that Pei had also introduced with Harry Weese in their work at Hyde Park, Chicago, around the same time.

At the Third Urban Design Conference in 1959, Pei's Society Hill project was discussed, along with his unbuilt proposal for town houses at Mill Creek Valley (presented by Washington University in St Louis Dean of Architecture Joseph Passonneau), with the goal of examining differing approaches to town houses in Sert's definition of urban design.[13] Pei's Society Hill project was analysed by an invited panel composed of Sert, Bacon, Pei, and Stonorov, along with Martin Meyerson, then a chaired professor of city and regional planning at the GSD; Boston developer Jerome Rappaport; federal urban renewal administrator William L. Slayton; and landscape architect Garrett Eckbo. The panel report stressed the importance of urban-design guidelines visually expressed for projects of this kind, as well as the need for better training, the goal of the newly founded GSD Urban Design programme. In his panel comments, Pei said he saw immense financial value in the approach taken at Society Hill, in light of the fact that Bacon's city planning department had built up a knowledge base about the project over the past decade.

The goal of the conference, according to Sert, was 'to arrive at certain principles which can guide the design of large-scale residential developments of an urban character', which he called 'residential sectors'.[14] Robert Geddes, a GSD alumnus who had been teaching in the architecture department at the University of Pennsylvania since 1951 and in 1953 had founded the Philadelphia firm of Geddes & Brecher, took a positive attitude towards Pei's unbuilt Mill Creek Valley project, but was most enthusiastic about his Society Hill plan, saying, 'The greatest value of the Philadelphia project is in its linkage with the past and its spatial linkages which create focal points ... This is a project which does not imply a completion date in itself at all, because it started in the 18th century, has 19th and 20th century buildings and can grow on to have buildings of the future.'[15] The panel concluded that Pei had successfully developed the project's basic concept, that the relationship between high and low buildings expressed in the project was a positive one, and that at the same time 'an attitude of conservation toward all existing useful elements, buildings, trees, water, land is desirable'.[16] They also noted that 'people's needs and preferences and their ability and willingness to pay for what they want as expressed in "marketability" must be taken into account'.[17]

In almost total contrast to the general American trends of the time, which included the construction of the federal interstate system and massive demolition of many urban neighbourhoods, the focus of the GSD programme was on the thoughtful interweaving of new and old, high and low buildings in existing urban neighbourhoods, along with the careful design of pedestrian and vehicular circulation systems. At the Third Urban Design Conference, Bacon and Pei's work at Society Hill was held up as the best new example of this approach, while the more conventional modernist projects by Mies and Skidmore, Owings & Merrill, as well as Lúcio Costa's Brasília, were criticised in terms that anticipated much of the later criticisms of modernist urbanism. Monotony, lack of pedestrian scale, large undefined open spaces, and blank scaleless facades were all identified as aspects of these projects, which were part of an internal debate within modernism, and would soon also become part of the post-modernist critique.

Art & Civic Form

3

'The play between solids and voids'

PAGE 104:

Marc Riboud, atrium of the National Gallery of Art East Building, ca.1978. Association Les amis de Marc Riboud

The 1,500-square-metre atrium of the East Building of the National Gallery of Art in Washington DC embodies Pei's belief in the modern museum as a site for social encounters as much as for the display of art. With a space-frame roof made up of glass pyramids and an Alexander Calder mobile overhead, the atrium is enlivened by patterns of shadows on the walls and changing perspectives on the space. Its theatricality is heightened by the movement of people on bridges, stairs, and an escalator recessed into a wall, connecting all five levels and providing an underground link to the gallery's West Building.

In 1971, four years before its planned completion, I. M. Pei's National Gallery of Art East Building in Washington DC was already being declared 'a great building for all time'.[1] Proclaimed so by *New York Times* architecture critic Ada Louise Huxtable, the exaltation, she admitted, was based only on the architect's yet-to-be-realised plans. But it presaged the near unanimous praise that would be heaped on the building when it finally opened in 1978, three years behind schedule, when Huxtable could announce without qualification that 'Pei has delivered a structure in which the art of architecture unites with the painting and sculpture of its own time for a symbiotic relationship of singular grandeur.'[2]

Pei, like many architects of international stature, was best known for his museums, and his museums became most identified with their geometries: the cantilevered pinwheel boxes of the Everson Museum of Art in Syracuse, the interlocking triangles of the National Gallery of Art East Building, the pyramid at the Grand Louvre. However, beyond the sense of timelessness, permanence, and dignity that these forms were meant to instil, a more profound story emerges. This chapter addresses Pei's belief in the civic, social, and urban role of museums, his personal relationship with art and artists, and his sensitivity not only to the painting and sculpture of his time, as Huxtable noted, but also to place—a fact that becomes more salient as one looks more broadly at his museums across the temporal and geographic span of his career.

When it came to museums, Pei was precocious. Having already investigated them as a student at Massachusetts Institute of Technology (MIT), his 1946 thesis project at Harvard Graduate School of Design (GSD)—a proposal for a museum of Chinese art in Shanghai—deftly negotiated the modernism of his training with traditional Chinese garden and spatial typologies. 'All forms of Chinese art are directly or indirectly results of a sensitive observation of nature,' Pei reasoned in the 1948 issue of *Progressive Architecture* in which the project was published.[3] Contradicting his own anti-historical impulses, the then dean of the GSD, Walter Gropius, conceded in the same feature that Pei had shown how 'an able designer can very well hold on to basic traditional features—which he has found are still alive—without sacrificing a progressive conception of design'.[4] This was an ability that endured in Pei, as he would most explicitly prove sixty years later when he completed his first museum building in China, the Suzhou Museum.

In the meantime, from his base in New York, Pei once proclaimed that modern art, and specifically Cubism, was the genesis of modern architecture, and so museum buildings naturally represented the synergetic heights of the two disciplines.[5] Whether in the United States, China, or elsewhere, Pei saw architecture as 'the play between solids and voids', an art form unto itself that was shaped by, and could shape the experience of, art.[6]

His earliest built museums, the Everson Museum of Art and his addition to Eliel and Eero Saarinen's Des Moines Art Center in Iowa, already showed his own sculptural inclinations with their soaring, light-filtering atriums (voids) articulated by his geometries in concrete (solids). In these spaces, large-scale works by such post-war abstract artists as Al Held and Morris Louis—in many cases specially commissioned, often by Pei—expressed the inseparability between art, architecture, and the public that he argued for. It was a spatial–social strategy that would continue in later projects like the National Gallery of Art, with its iconic, skylit atrium animated by a kinetic mobile by Alexander Calder—a space that Pei intended to exude 'a life-giving force' for the 'art-loving public'.[7]

Just as Pei had designed atriums as socially activating spaces in both museums and other projects, his commissioning of public sculptures to anchor outdoor spaces was also not limited to museums. He installed sculptures by Henry Moore at the entrance to the Everson Museum of Art, but also at the headquarters of the OCBC Bank in Singapore. There was the monumental Picasso at the University Plaza housing complex in New York, and the Calder in front of MIT's Cecil and Ida Green Center for Earth Sciences. With an astute eye and deep art-world connections (he and his wife, Eileen, were also—minor, they would insist—art collectors), Pei returned again and again to these and other abstract artists because, as Seng Kuan writes later in this chapter, their work was 'effective across scales and especially suited to the context of the city'.

For Pei, the combination of art, building, and city formed a potent triumvirate in civic projects. (The connection was no doubt ingrained early on when he was working for William Zeckendorf, the New York developer who aimed to tackle the woes of America's cities from an office decorated with, among other works, a Vincent van Gogh painting borrowed from the Museum of Modern Art.) The cultural firmament of Pei's day largely saw art as an embodiment of higher values to be bestowed upon the public—a sense of *noblesse oblige*, however well-intentioned, that might nowadays be criticised for its elitist and patriarchal undertones. For Pei, however, the civic potential of museums was also closely linked to broader social and urban agendas.

Indeed, while Pei's museums are often remembered for their singular gestures, one should not ignore the specificity with which those schemes addressed their contexts. At the height of America's urban renewal era, the Everson design sought to provide both a sculptural highlight and a connective public space that would facilitate plans to reinvigorate a troubled urban centre over time. The geometry of Pei's National Gallery of Art project in Washington DC, arose from its need to fill an odd, trapezoidal site on the National Mall. The pyramid at the Louvre brilliantly reconciled the museum's spatial and functional needs with the historical sensitivity of its site to produce a clear result that has seemed, to many, to have always been there.

In other words, Pei was consistent, but he was no one-trick pony. In his later years, he continued to broaden his museum work and art commissioning in such countries as China, Japan, and Qatar. As he did so, cultural and historical context would become an ever more noticeable influence on his work. Nevertheless, perhaps reflecting his own transcultural background, Pei sought from art— whether his own art of architecture or that of artists—a language that could resonate universally.

Having commissioned the Paris-based Chinese artist Zao Wou-Ki to create works for his Fragrant Hill Hotel in Beijing, Pei asked the artist Cai Guo-Qiang to produce a work for the opening of the Suzhou Museum in 2006. Cai responded with *Exploding Tower*, a structure set alight with gunpowder. It was a project about ephemerality, the passage of time, and tradition's relationship with the present, but it was also a spectacle anyone could understand. 'Pei always said that artistic concepts and techniques have to be worldwide and universal,' Cai recalls in this chapter, 'in order to evoke sentiments of connection and resonance with different cultures.'

— Aric Chen

3.1 | **I. M. Pei, A Member's Lounge for the Museum of Modern Art, fifth-year project in architectural design at the Massachusetts Institute of Technology, 1940. MIT Museum**

Responding to an inter-school competition brief from the Boston Society of Architects to imagine the interior of a members' lounge for the Institute of Modern Art, Boston (formerly associated with the Museum of Modern Art in New York), Pei proposed a resourceful intervention of surface colour and texture while incorporating the functional needs of a lounge and board meeting room. His design relies on the reuse of existing materials, dyeing textiles, and reupholstering furniture already in place. The proposal called for the installation of an abstract mural created by students, a reflection of his belief in the potential of cultural institutions to be inclusive spaces for the wider community.

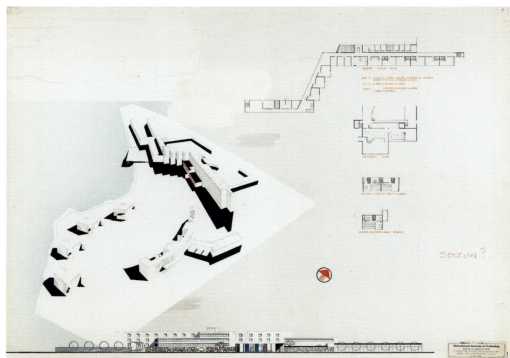

3.2 | **I. M. Pei, A Centre of Research for Creative Art, fifth-year project in architectural design at the Massachusetts Institute of Technology, 1939. MIT Museum**

Revolving around a wing of clustered workshops for a wide range of disciplines, the centre of research for creative art also contains a library and exhibition spaces and is accompanied by freestanding housing units for members of its community. The programme of interdisciplinary collaboration and production echoes the activities of progressive movements in the arts, perhaps most notably the Bauhaus campus in Dessau. Pei's project introduces an urbanistic logic to the complex, defining it as a series of interconnected nodes in a network.

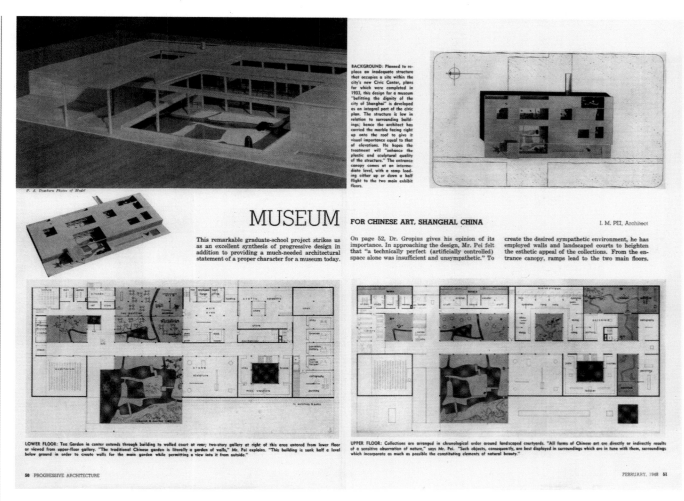

3.3 | **'Museum for Chinese Art, Shanghai, China'**, *Progressive Architecture* 29 (February 1948): 50–51. USModernist

Drawings and models of Pei's proposal for a museum of Chinese art in Shanghai were published in *Progressive Architecture* alongside commentary from Walter Gropius describing the project's environment designed to display calligraphy, paintings, porcelain, jade, and stone sculptures. In Pei's view, the fact that these works were conceived through close observation of nature meant that they should be experienced in relation to the natural environment. He therefore designed a central tea garden and smaller landscaped courtyards that can be seen from the galleries. The tea pavilion and bamboo garden are accessible via a ramp connecting the upper and lower floors, demonstrating Pei's vision of a museum that is as much a space for social encounters as it is for the display of art.

3.4.1 | Frank Lerner, Alexander Calder's *La grande voile* (1965), installed to anchor McDermott Court, the open plaza in front of the Cecil and Ida Green Center for Earth Sciences at MIT, 1966. Pei Cobb Freed & Partners

3.4.2 | Alexander Calder and I. M. Pei at the dedication ceremony of *La Grande Voile* (1965), 1966. Papers of I. M. Pei, Library of Congress, Washington DC

3.4.1–3.4.2
As part of MIT's campus expansion—his first commission outside of Webb & Knapp—Pei designed a tower as the first of three science buildings clustered together to frame a large open space and pedestrian connections in between the buildings. Intending to align it with the twenty-one-storey Cecil and Ida Green Center for Earth Sciences along a new axis, Pei commissioned a twelve-metre-high stabile from Alexander Calder, titled *La Grande Voile*, to act as a focal point. For Pei, the abstract nature of Calder's works made them ideally suited to high-rise structures. The sculptor's use of overlapping painted steel plates allowed for the adoption of industrial production methods to realise the work at an architectural scale.

Cecil and Ida Green Center for Earth Sciences (1959–1964)
Massachusetts Institute of Technology
Cambridge, Massachusetts

University Plaza (1960–1966)
New York University
New York

3.5 | **Margaret Heit, photo showing the installation of Pablo Picasso's** *Bust of Sylvette* **(1968) at University Plaza, in 'Picasso's Prestressed Sculpture',** *Engineering News-Record* **(8 August 1968): 20. Pei Cobb Freed & Partners**

University Plaza's three thirty-storey residential towers are arranged in a pinwheel formation. The complex's central court presented an opportunity for Pei to experiment with scaling sculpture in proportion to high-rise buildings. His securing of USD75,000 in additional funding allowed him to commission the enlargement of Pablo Picasso's *Sylvette* (1954), which had originally been proposed for Kips Bay Plaza. An eleven-metre-high blown-up reproduction of the sculpture was executed by Picasso's long-time collaborator Carl Nesjar in buff-coloured concrete to complement the exposed-concrete structures on the site. The result was as much a work of construction as it was a work of art. The sculpture was informed by and integrated into the development, even requiring steel support columns running through the underground garage.

For many of his large, institutional projects, I. M. Pei commissioned outdoor sculptures as crucial components of the architectural scheme. In particular, he believed the figural but abstract sculptural work of artists such as Pablo Picasso, Henry Moore, Joan Miró, and Jean Dubuffet was effective across scales and especially suited to the context of the city. Pei saw these sculptures as tools for positioning the human body in urban space.

In 1968, Pei commissioned Picasso and the Norwegian artist Carl Nesjar to create a work for University Village, his recently completed housing project in New York. Nesjar had been collaborating with Picasso since the late 1950s, rendering Picasso's forms in concrete using the technique of *Naturbetong*. In this method, developed by the architect Erling Viksjø and patented in 1950, dark basalt aggregate is combined with a soft, light-tone mortar and then sand-blasted to achieve the desired surface texture. For University Village, Picasso and Nesjar realised *Bust of Sylvette* (1968), a massive, sixty-ton figural sculpture three storeys in height. The artists determined the dimensions of the work by floating balloons in the middle of the courtyard, using the urban scale of the surrounding residential towers to shape their intervention.

In his design for the Cleo Rogers Memorial County Library in Columbus, Indiana, completed in 1971, Pei created a plaza for civic gatherings and approached Henry Moore for a work that would anchor this space. The artist proposed *Large Arch* (1971), a sculpture in bronze that reproduced his smaller *Large Torso: Arch* of 1963 at a monumental scale. The form is unmistakably figurative, and at this larger scale it can also be seen as an allusion to the triumphal arches of ancient Roman architecture. Moore created a 1:1 maquette of the work in Styrofoam, selecting a size that would be large enough for a pedestrian to pass under, but too small for a car. Following the Columbus commission, which was installed in 1971, Moore became one of Pei's most frequent collaborators as well as a close friend.

– Seng Kuan

Seng Kuan is an architectural historian. He contributed to the 'Rethinking Pei' symposium organised by M+ and the GSD in 2017.

3.6 | **Balthazar Korab, Henry Moore's *Large Arch* (1971) seen against Cleo Rogers Memorial County Library, ca.1971. Balthazar Korab Collection, Library of Congress, Washington DC**

With an open plaza accompanying the boxy brick design for the Cleo Rogers Memorial County Library, Pei's plan called for a centrepiece that would unite the library with its significant neighbours, Eliel Saarinen's First Christian Church (1942) and the Victorian mansion of Irwin Gardens (1864). Support and funding from industrialist J. Irwin Miller—who established the Cummins Foundation to subsidise buildings by prominent modern architects in Columbus—made it possible for Pei to commission a six-metre sculpture from Henry Moore. Recalling his young daughter's playful engagement with Moore's earlier works, Pei negotiated with the artist to enlarge *Large Torso: Arch* (1963) to an architectural scale that the public could interact with.

Cleo Rogers Memorial County Library (1963–1971)
Columbus, Indiana

3.7.1 | **Helmut Jacoby, drawing of the Everson Museum of Art in Community Plaza, ca.1961. Pei Cobb Freed & Partners**

Everson Museum of Art (1961–1968)
Syracuse, New York

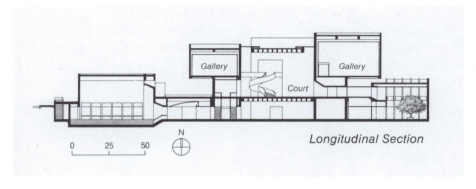

3.7.2 | **Longitudinal section of the Everson Museum of Art, ca.1961. Everson Museum of Art Archive**

3.7.1–3.7.2
The Everson Museum of Art was the first building to be completed as part of the Community Plaza, a cultural complex intended to rejuvenate downtown Syracuse, New York. The plan to develop the museum was prompted by *Architectural Forum*'s call in the 1940s to redesign post-war American cities. Viewing the museum as part of a larger project of urban renewal, Max W. Sullivan, its director at the time, entrusted Pei with the project as a result of the architect's experience with urban planning and his vision of museums as cultural centres for communities. Pei spent a year developing a design that would be sculptural enough to stand on its own on a site consisting of empty lots, an industrial building, and a sports hall. The main galleries are expressed as four cantilevered cubes hovering over a paved plaza with a reflecting pool, which formed the open area around the museum that Pei lobbied for, and which was also meant for future developments. By resting the building on a submerged podium and thereby concealing most of the museum's facilities, Pei was free to sculpt the distinct massing of the museum's above-ground galleries. This also created ground-level access to the two-storey lobby and sculpture court. The four gallery blocks, linked by bridges on the second floor, surround this central space in a series of solids and voids. Likewise, two volumes flanking the main structure on the plaza, housing the museum's auditorium and administration, contribute to this dynamic exterior.

3.8.1 | **William Henderson, early drawing of the Everson Museum of Art's sculpture court, 1962. Pei Cobb Freed & Partners**

3.8.2 | **Robert Damora, Rosamond Gifford Sculpture Court, ca.1968. Estate of Robert Damora**

3.8.1–3.8.2
Pei designed the museum to provide nine differently sized spaces for its growing permanent collection, as well as for travelling exhibitions. The majority of the galleries are distributed throughout the four elevated cubic volumes, with the central sculpture court acting as both a gallery for monumental works and a unifying social space. Featuring a concrete helix stairway, upper-level balconies and catwalk bridges, and a waffle-grid ceiling flanked by skylights of clear glass, the building's composition creates changing views of light, space, artworks, and the movement of people.

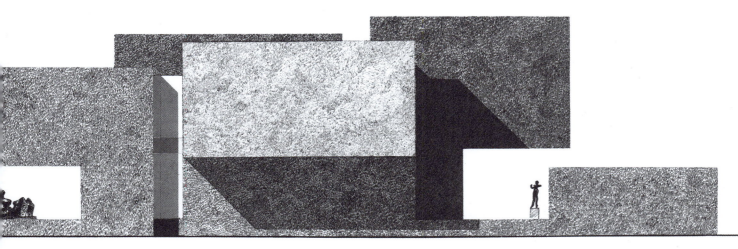

3.9.1 | **Dale Byrd, elevation drawing of the Everson Museum of Art, 1962. Pei Cobb Freed & Partners**

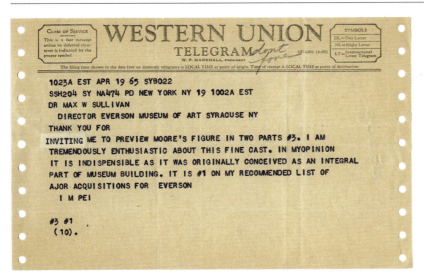

3.9.2 | **I. M. Pei, telegram to Max W. Sullivan, director of the Everson Museum of Art, 19 April 1965. Everson Museum of Art Archive**

3.9.1–3.9.2
Pei's belief in an inextricable link between art and architecture is evident in the design of the Everson Museum of Art. He attributed the building's sculptural form to his early interest in Cubism. The museum was described in *Progressive Architecture* as 'a work of art for other works of art'. Such a view, which was also held by Paul Mellon, a philanthropist and the then president of the National Gallery of Art in Washington DC, contributed to the decision to commission Pei to design the National Gallery's East Building. Pei's close relationships with artists also enabled him to be directly involved in the Everson's acquisitions, which included newly commissioned works by Al Held and Morris Louis. The Everson Museum of Art project also saw the first of Pei's many collaborations with Henry Moore, whose *Two Piece Reclining Figure No. 3* (1961) formed an integral part of the design of the museum's entrance plaza from the earliest drawings. Helen Frankenthaler's *The Human Edge* (1967) was also acquired expressly for the sculpture court, in direct response to the architectural context.

Des Moines Art Center Addition (1965–1968)
Des Moines, Iowa

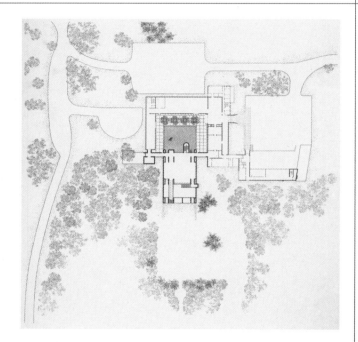

3.10.1 | **Site plan of Des Moines Art Center, ca.1965. Pei Cobb Freed & Partners**

3.10.2 | **Ezra Stoller, north facade and courtyard of the Des Moines Art Center Addition, 1968. Esto**

3.10.1–3.10.2
Completed at the same time as the Everson Museum of Art, the Des Moines Art Center Addition was humble in scale but significant in establishing Pei as an architect of choice for cultural institutions. As an extension to the 1948 building designed by Eliel and Eero Saarinen, the new wing would house the centre's growing collection of large sculptural works while deferring to the entrance, height, and parkland setting of the existing structure. Pei's strategy was to enclose the U-shaped courtyard facing the park with a rectangular volume on the site's sloping topography. This created a continuous circulation loop as well as providing a loftier space for the centre's sculpture galleries, with a roofline to match the existing S-shaped complex. A deep pool was turned into a shallow surface of water, with Pei's dense, reinforced-concrete structure—bush-hammered to expose the limestone aggregate that reflects the colour of the Lannon stone used by the Saarinens—sitting precisely on the edge, allowing the courtyard's ground plane to flow through the building.

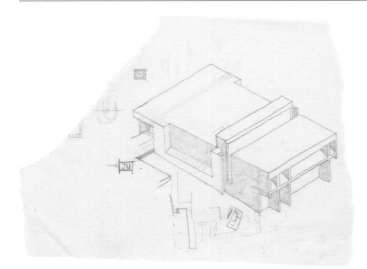

3.11.1 | **Early axonometric drawing of the Des Moines Art Center Addition, 1965. Pei Cobb Freed & Partners**

3.11.2 | **Ezra Stoller, upper gallery of the Des Moines Art Center Addition's sculpture court, 1968. Esto**

3.11.1–3.11.2
Upon entering the upper sculpture court from the Saarinen building, visitors experience a vessel of solids and voids designed to house naturally illuminated sculptural works and orchestrate views along an axial connection between the interiors and the landscape beyond. The seemingly heavy envelope is filled with daylight of varying intensity through the use of horizontal or vertical concrete fins, end walls—some with four-metre-deep embrasures with plate glass—and a large, butterfly-shaped vault on the roof supported by a single beam, bringing light in at an angle. Solid walls are arranged in parallel to the north–south axis, directing views and movement towards either the courtyard framed by the dolomite walls of the original Saarinen building to the north, or the landscape of Greenwood Park to the south.

Herbert F. Johnson Museum of Art (1968–1973)
Cornell University
Ithaca, New York

3.12 | **J. Henderson Barr, view of the Herbert F. Johnson Museum of Art from the Arts Quadrangle, ca.1968. Pei Cobb Freed & Partners**

The Herbert F. Johnson Museum at Cornell University sits by the Arts Quadrangle, the boundary of the central campus. Constructed in yellow pigmented site-cast concrete, the cantilevered volume towers over its nineteenth-century neighbours. Approaching the museum from the Arts Quadrangle, the visitor follows a concrete path approximately twelve feet wide that rings the quad and extends to the west. A set of concrete steps descends to a landing with a concrete bench that seems to fold the width of the path back upon itself, like a concrete ribbon. A void that cuts through the mass of the building, also twelve feet wide, creates a line of sight towards the landscape beyond. The museum at first glance appears monolithic and distant from its context, but its careful alignment constructs a relationship to the context of the campus.

– Eric Höweler

Eric Höweler is principal of Höweler + Yoon and an associate professor at the Harvard Graduate School of Design. He moderated a panel on technology at the 'Rethinking Pei' symposium organised by M+ and the GSD in 2017.

Cornell University alumnus and benefactor Herbert F. Johnson requested that the school's trustees commission Pei to design a new museum for the campus. The museum would be built on a hilltop site at the far end of the historic Arts Quadrangle, set against a gorge to the north and creating views on three sides. Pei's initial visit in 1968 revealed the constraints of the site; a strong architectural statement would be a capstone on the campus's three-hundred-metre-long slope, but transparency was required to preserve views of the natural vistas. Pei decided on a compact rectangular structure opened on the east, south, and west sides. The resulting form introduced new vantage points from an elevated outdoor sculpture court—matched in height to neighbouring buildings—and a cantilevered student lounge.

ART & CIVIC FORM   121

3.13.1 | **Section of the Herbert F. Johnson Museum of Art, ca.1968. Pei Cobb Freed & Partners**

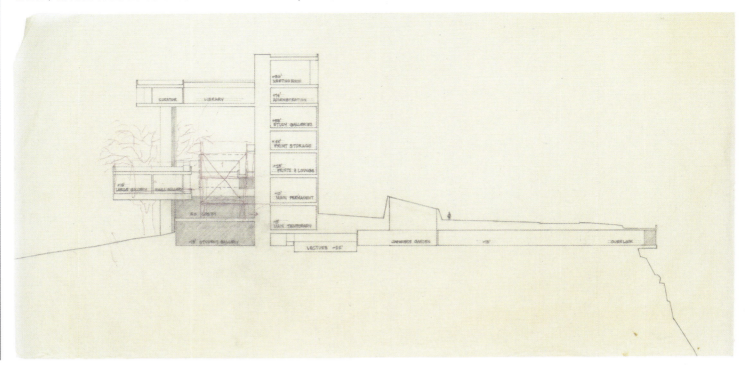

3.13.2 | **Thorney Lieberman, second-floor outdoor sculpture court of the Herbert F. Johnson Museum of Art, 1973. Pei Cobb Freed & Partners**

3.13.1–3.13.2
Cornell required a multipurpose building to house a permanent collection of paintings, prints, and works of decorative art. Pei maximised programmatic space on the small building site by stacking floors in a slim tower. Spatial sequencing was informed by an extensive analysis of functional requirements, potential users, and accessibility. From the lobby, visitors need only ascend or descend a maximum of two floors to reach all public areas, moving through intersecting walkways and galleries that end in either the underground lecture room or the sculpture court. In response to university administrators' fear of vandalism during an era of anti-war and anti-establishment protests on campuses across the United States, and recognising that a high water table made excavation impossible, Pei elevated the sculpture court above ground level to protect the artworks. Storage spaces were placed below ground, while Pei designated the upper floors as being for administrative offices and spaces for students.

3.14.1 | **Site plan of Roosevelt Field Shopping Center, in 'Roosevelt Field Shopping Center: A Webb & Knapp Project',** *Progressive Architecture* **36 (September 1955): 93. USModernist**

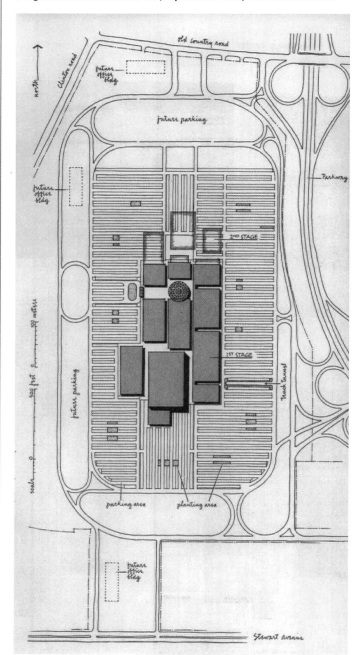

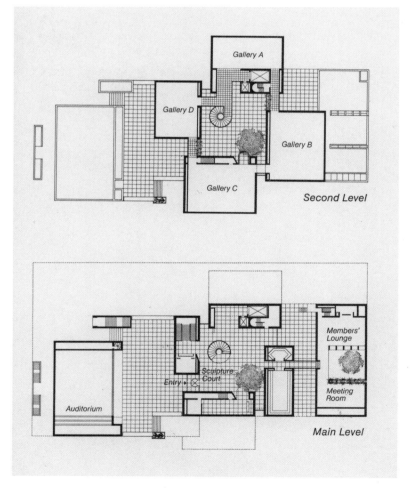

3.14.2 | **Site plan of the Everson Museum of Art, ca.1961. Everson Museum of Art Archive**

ART & CIVIC FORM   123

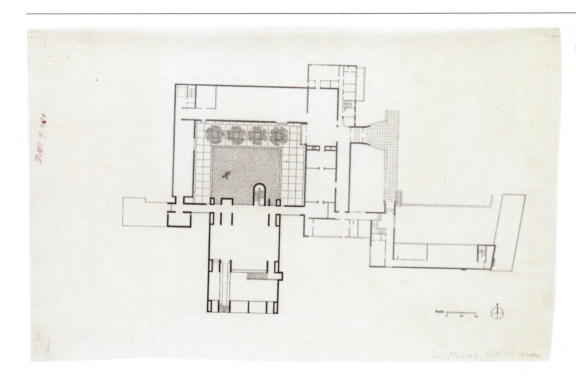

3.14.3 | **Site plan of the Des Moines Art Center, ca.1965. Pei Cobb Freed & Partners**

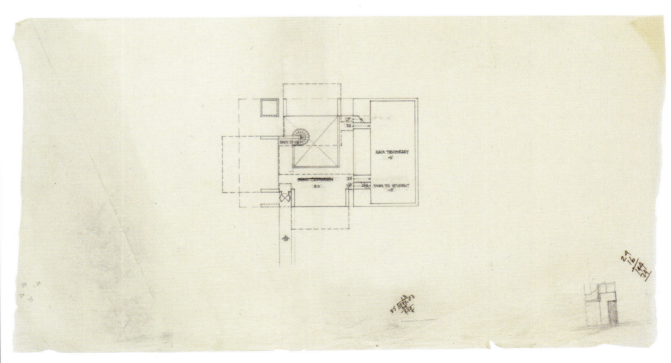

3.14.4 | **Site plan of the Herbert F. Johnson Museum of Art, ca.1968. Pei Cobb Freed & Partners**

3.14.1–3.14.4
Pei's approach to designing museums was informed by a keen understanding of how to experience different forms of art, whether the intimate viewing of traditional Chinese paintings or the open display of large-scale modern sculptures. With his background in designing mixed-use retail and residential spaces and offices, Pei believed in the importance of creating a central open space that could function as a focal point for spatial orientation as well as providing a shared experience of the building.

National Gallery of Art East Building (1968–1978)
Washington DC

I. M. had the concept of interlocking triangles almost immediately. He took the trapezoidal site, which is an awkward shape for a building, and sliced it into two pure triangles with a gap between them. It was quite some time before we understood how best to make the triangle work as a museum. That finally happened after Carter Brown [the then deputy director of the National Gallery] attended a museum conference in Mexico City, where he heard about 'museum feet', the fatigue experienced by a person—young or old, art connoisseur or simply someone who appreciates art—who spends roughly fifty minutes in a gallery. This is not because your feet are tired; you really haven't walked that much. It's because your mind is so focused. Great art engages you, pulls you in, fires many neurons and burns calories. You need a break. How much space do you cover in those fifty minutes? Usually under ten thousand square feet, but the National Gallery needed thirty thousand square feet of new galleries plus a temporary exhibition gallery. Carter felt that the thirty thousand square feet could be broken into three ten-thousand-square-foot parcels. Bill Pedersen [design architect on the project] and I went directly back to our desks to see how to do this and came back the following day to I. M. with a cardboard model showing three prismatic volumes in the three corners of the triangle connected by a glass atrium. That was the beginning of the design.

– Yann Weymouth

Yann Weymouth was design architect for the National Gallery of Art East Building and the Grand Louvre.

3.15.1 | **West facade and plaza of the National Gallery of Art East Building, 1980. National Gallery of Art, Washington DC, Gallery Archives**

3.15.2 | **Yann Weymouth, site plan of the East Building in relation to the West Building and surroundings, 1969. National Gallery of Art, Washington DC, Gallery Archives**

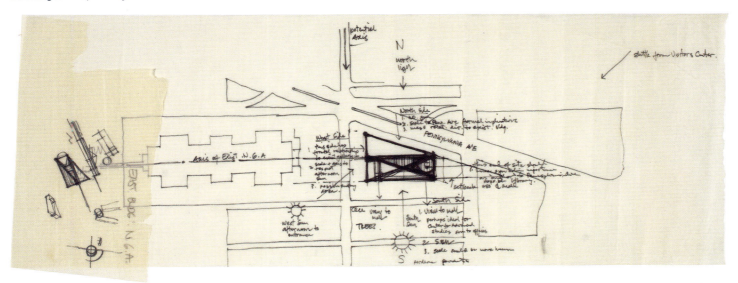

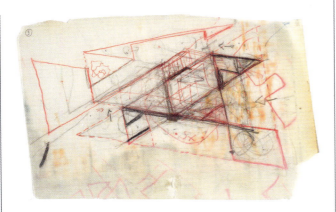

3.15.3 | **Yann Weymouth, early sketch of the East Building, 1969. National Gallery of Art, Washington DC, Gallery Archives**

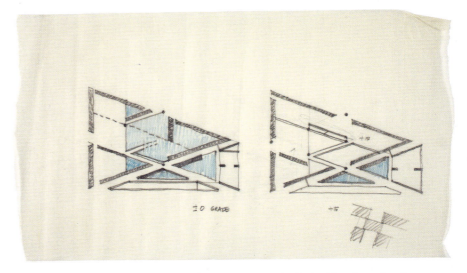

3.15.4 | **Yann Weymouth, early sketch of the East Building's double-triangular plans, 1969. National Gallery of Art, Washington DC, Gallery Archives**

3.15.1–3.15.4

The site for the expansion of the National Gallery of Art was trapezoidal, the point at which Pennsylvania Avenue converges with the National Mall at a 19.5-degree angle. Pei sought to maximise the site by drawing a line connecting the original museum and the new building on the former's east–west axis. He defined a diagonal crossing the trapezoid, with two triangles serving as a basis for the design. With the eastern side of the northern-most triangle acting as a broad post-and-lintel entrance facing John Russell Pope's West Building across a one-and-a-half-hectare plaza, the new building reflects the neoclassical symmetry of its counterpart. To provide space for a research centre as well as galleries for temporary exhibitions and a growing collection of twentieth-century art, one triangle is organised into three diamond-shaped towers for display, while the other contains the library, archives, and offices.

3.16.1 | **Yann Weymouth, early study of multi-level viewing and movement within the gallery, 1969. National Gallery of Art, Washington DC, Gallery Archives**

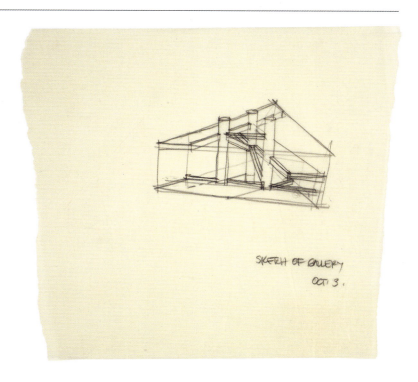

3.16.2 | **Marc Riboud, interior of a hexagonal gallery, ca.1978. Association Les amis de Marc Riboud**

3.16.1–3.16.2
The design of the East Building's galleries was informed by a month-long visit to museums across Europe made by Pei and Carter Brown, the then deputy director of the National Gallery of Art. The decision to divide the galleries between three independent towers—described as 'house museums' by the project team—with one at each corner of the triangular plan and an atrium at the centre, was inspired by Pei and Brown's experience of the Museo Poldi Pezzoli in Milan, where galleries connected by stairs offer a museum experience at a refreshingly human scale. Each of the three towers in the East Building was designed to house five levels of galleries, which would be small enough to reduce fatigue on the part of visitors, and whose ceiling heights would differ to accommodate both intimate and monumental displays. The galleries' natural lighting could be manipulated through a UV filtering film newly developed by the Mellon Institute.

ART & CIVIC FORM 127

3.17.1 | Yann Weymouth, early sketch of a bridge over the atrium connecting two 'house museums', 1969. National Gallery of Art, Washington DC, Gallery Archives

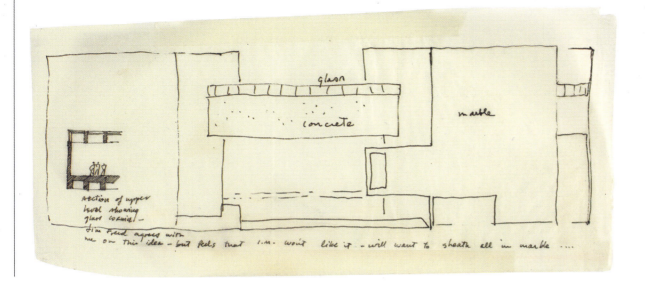

3.17.2 | Ezra Stoller, bridges and balconies in the glass-roofed atrium, 2008. Esto

3.17.1–3.17.2
The East Building's triangular layout introduces multiple vanishing points that exceed the experiential possibilities of an orthogonal grid. The balconies, mezzanines, and bridges connecting the galleries allow visitors to navigate a sequence of spaces and views overlooking the expansive atrium.

3.18.1 **Naho Kubota, view of the West Building from the East Building, 2021. Photo commissioned by M+**

ART & CIVIC FORM 131

3.18.2 | **Naho Kubota, underground café and concourse cascade at the National Gallery of Art East Building, 2021. Photo commissioned by M+**

3.18.1–3.18.2
Developing a visual and spatial connection between the West and East buildings was of primary importance to Pei and the client. Upon entering the East Building's atrium, visitors are greeted with a view of the West Building's eastern facade—in the same Tennessee pink marble as its new counterpart. A road between the two buildings led Pei to design a double-height underground concourse housing a cafeteria, shops, and a moving walkway conveying visitors between buildings. Opposite the cafeteria, Pei introduced a waterfall inspired by the *chadar*, a Mughal design created by directing a channel of water over a slope of carved stones.

3.19.1 | **I. M. Pei and Henry Moore reviewing a full-scale polystyrene model of** *Large Reclining Figure* **(1984), 1983. Papers of I. M. Pei, Library of Congress, Washington DC**

3.19.2 | **I. M. Pei with Henry Moore's** *Large Reclining Figure* **(1984) installed at the entrance to the OCBC Centre, 1986. Papers of I. M. Pei, Library of Congress, Washington DC**

3.19.1–3.19.2
Pei designed the entrance to the new headquarters of the OCBC Bank as a public plaza, set back from the street in the heart of Singapore's growing financial district. He approached Henry Moore for a new commission, and together they decided on a monumental cast of Moore's *Reclining Figure* (1938), enlarged to a length of nine and a half metres from the original thirty-three-centimetre sculpture. At Pei's suggestion, the abstract nude figure was first modelled at full scale in polystyrene before it was cast in bronze—the largest bronze sculpture Moore ever realised.

Oversea-Chinese Banking Corporation (OCBC) Centre (1970–1976)
Singapore

Fragrant Hill Hotel (1979–1982)
Beijing

3.20 | **Ogawa Taisuke, ink painting by Zao Wou-Ki installed in a room next to the Four Seasons Courtyard lobby of Fragrant Hill Hotel, 1982. Pei Cobb Freed & Partners**

Pei first encountered the paintings of Paris-based Chinese artist Zao Wou-Ki in 1951. In an essay for a catalogue of Zao's work at Pierre Matisse Gallery in 1980, Pei writes that they recalled for him 'at once the mystical imagery of Klee on the one hand, and the dry brush landscapes of Ni-Tsan on the other'. Invited by Pei to participate in the Fragrant Hill project, Zao produced two large black-and-white compositions for a room next to the hotel's atrium lobby. Zao's paintings, inspired by the white walls and grey tiles of Chinese vernacular dwellings, employ a dialogue between form and void to harmonise with the simplicity of the hotel's design. This commission became a prototype for the artist's later series of monumental ink works.

Wiesner Building/Center for Arts & Media Technology (1978–1984) Massachusetts Institute of Technology
Cambridge, Massachusetts

3.21.1 | **I. M. Pei and sculptor Scott Burton with a model of Burton's stone benches and curved balustrades, 1986. Papers of I. M. Pei, Library of Congress, Washington DC**

Collaborating with artists on the Wiesner Building was an exciting idea, especially for me as it was my first big project. I remember my father saying, 'Art and architecture are kindred, so we should bring them together. Let's try.' Three artists were selected to participate in the project. All had to surrender the freedom of private studio work for architecture's team approach, larger scale, longer schedule, and practical constraints. In turn, we architects had to relinquish control over aspects of the building that we would typically regulate very carefully. Everyone learned from the experience.

Scott Burton's work included stone benches and railings in the atrium. He ran into problems because the railings didn't comply with the building code and had to be redesigned to satisfy safety concerns. The railing's final horizontal plate and tube solution was truly an artist–architect collaboration.

Richard Fleischner designed the courtyard pavements and stone benches. It wasn't easy. He disagreed with a lot of what we wanted to do and held his ground. Ultimately my father acquiesced: 'Let's do it your way.' It wasn't the detail but the give-and-take that was important.

The third artist, Kenneth Noland, focused primarily on the atrium wall but was really flummoxed by such a giant canvas. We made a quarter-size mock-up for him, and I came up with the idea of putting three-dimensional strips in the interstices between the aluminium wall panels. Adding these different lengths and colours really animated the surface; all of a sudden, Noland came into his own.

– Li Chung (Sandi) Pei

Li Chung (Sandi) Pei is I. M. Pei's third son. He was design architect for the Wiesner Building/Center for Arts & Media Technology.

ART & CIVIC FORM   135

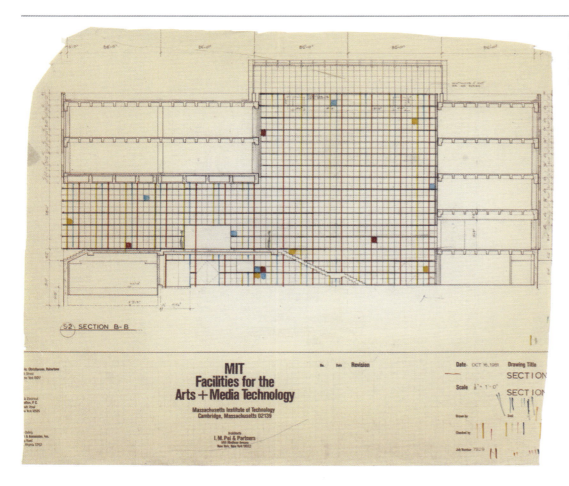

3.21.2 | **Section drawing detailing painter Kenneth Noland's polychromatic additions between the square aluminium panels on the atrium wall, 1981. Pei Cobb Freed & Partners**

3.21.3 | **Steve Rosenthal, portion of Kenneth Noland's** *Here—There* **(1985) commission along with balustrades by Scott Burton in the atrium of the Wiesner Building, ca.1985. Historic New England**

3.21.1–3.21.3
To represent the interdisciplinary programme of its new arts and media technology facility, MIT's Committee on the Visual Arts used the building project as a site for experimental collaborations between art and architecture. Pei was eager to explore the potential of integrating art beyond a decorative component and quickly embraced the initiative. At the juncture of MIT's old and new campuses, the square form and gridded surfaces of Pei's design became the canvas for artists Richard Fleischner, Scott Burton, and Kenneth Noland. Pei worked closely with the artists, adapting plans in response to their proposals.

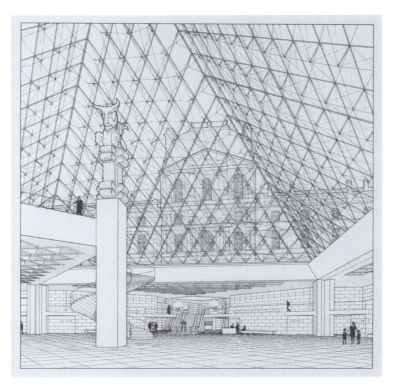

3.22 | **Early CAD drawing of the Hall Napoléon, 1986. Archives nationales de France**

Pei's intervention for the Grand Louvre in the Cour Napoléon defined a single, central point of entry into the Louvre, fundamentally reorganising the museum's space. The glass pyramid commands a distinct presence in the historical complex, yet its transparency blends the contemporary addition with the stone facades of the palace while also introducing light into the underground hall. The hall orientates visitors in relation to the vast museum's diverse collections, presented in three wings. This study drawing shows a twenty-metre-tall ancient Persian bull-shaped capital installed in the hall.

Grand Louvre
Phase I (1983–1989) &
Phase II (1989–1993)
Paris

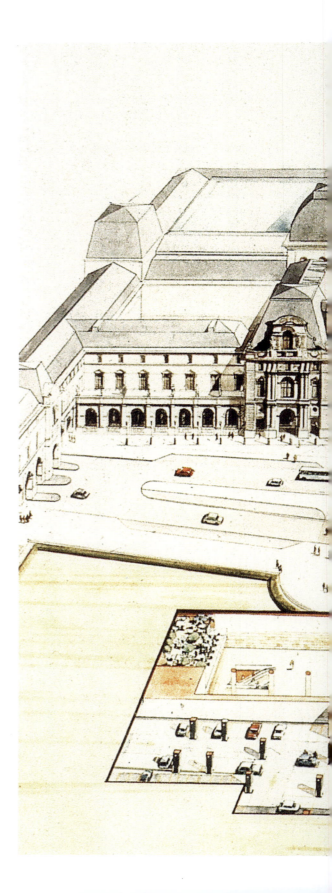

3.23 | **Perspectival view of the Louvre's underground network of spaces, ca.1993. Pei Cobb Freed & Partners**

Pei aimed to revitalise the Louvre by establishing a modern museum infrastructure and embedding the museum within the urban circulation network of Paris. This drawing shows part of the underground complex of spaces in relation to structures above ground. Extending from the entrance hall in the Cour Napoléon, the complex houses temporary exhibition galleries, auditoriums, underground parking for cars and tourist buses (which used to clog rue de Rivoli), and the Carrousel du Louvre shopping space. It also connects with the metro and the nearby Jardin des Tuileries.

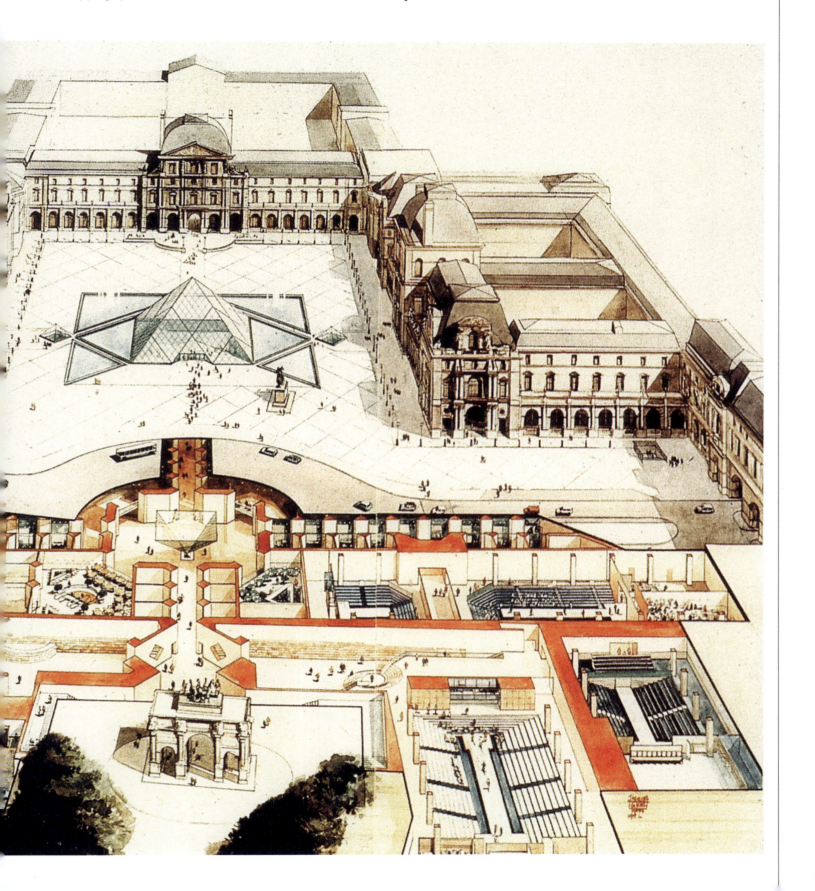

3.24.1 | Longitudinal section of the Richelieu wing, ca.1989. Pei Cobb Freed & Partners

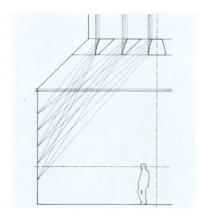

3.24.2 | Diagram illustrating light reflection from overhead sun-shading louvres, ca.1989. Pei Cobb Freed & Partners

3.24.3 | Stéphane Couturier, overhead skylight in a gallery in the Richelieu wing, ca.1993. Pei Cobb Freed & Partners

3.24.1–3.24.3
In 1981, President François Mitterrand announced that the Ministry of Finance would be moving out of the Richelieu wing of the Louvre palace. This transformed the Grand Louvre into a U-shaped complex and made it accessible from rue de Rivoli. In the process of converting the offices into galleries, which began in 1989, Pei preserved the palace's enfilade as well as the historic facade. Sun-shading louvres were installed to protect the paintings, while escalators were introduced to bring visitors seamlessly to the upper floors and provide views of the interior court.

3.25.1 | **Michel Macary, early perspective drawing of the Cour Marly, 1990. Archives nationales de France**

PAGES 140–141:
3.25.2 | **Giovanna Silva, Cour Puget of the Richelieu wing, 2021. Photo commissioned by M+**

3.25.1–3.25.2
Pei installed a soaring glass canopy over two courtyards that were formerly used for parking and deliveries, creating two sculpture courts: the Cour Puget and the Cour Marly. The new spaces provide a naturally lit indoor environment for sculptures from the seventeenth to the nineteenth centuries, protecting them from damage caused by the elements. The terraced design allows the works to be displayed on different levels according to historical period and curatorial theme. Without the support of Jean-René Gaborit, head of the Louvre's sculpture department, and that of his colleagues, Pei might not have been able to complete his redesign of the museum, which faced much opposition.

I. M. Pei often associated me with Zao Wou-Ki, who was from his generation. Zao and I are both Chinese and acquired international recognition for our work. In Pei's view, one should not simply represent one's own traditional culture, but ingest the contemporary and transform it into a culture of the world. He felt this was what Zao and I had achieved. For the opening of the Suzhou Museum, he invited me to create a large installation as a symbol of contemporaneity. Pei always said that artistic concepts and techniques have to be worldwide and universal in order to evoke sentiments of connection and resonance with different cultures.

– Cai Guo-Qiang

Cai Guo-Qiang is a New York–based artist. Pei first collaborated with Cai in 2006, when the artist's work was displayed at the opening of MUDAM Luxembourg, which Pei designed.

3.26.1 | Cai Guo-Qiang, *Chun Qiu: Project for the New Galleries of Suzhou Museum, Invited by I. M. Pei*, 2006, gunpowder on paper, mounted on wood as nine-panel screen, 230 × 697 cm. Hiro Ihara, Cai Studio

3.26.2 | Tatsumi Masatoshi, installation view of Cai Guo-Qiang's works for the exhibition *Searching for Dreams in the Canals* at Suzhou Museum, 2006. Cai Studio

3.26.1–3.26.2
After being commissioned to design a new home for the Suzhou Museum—known for its collection of historical and cultural artefacts—Pei recommended that galleries for the display of modern art be constructed. At his recommendation, the museum presented work by the international Chinese artists Zao Wou-Ki, Xu Bing, and Cai Guo-Qiang at its opening exhibition. Cai's installation included a new gunpowder painting titled *Chun Qiu*, based on the ancient history of Suzhou. Its composition of indistinct figures of humans, horses, and objects alludes to the warring and sword-making activities of the kings of the Wu state, which controlled lands south of the Yangtze River during the Spring and Autumn period (770–476 BCE).

Suzhou Museum (2000–2006)
Suzhou

ART & CIVIC FORM

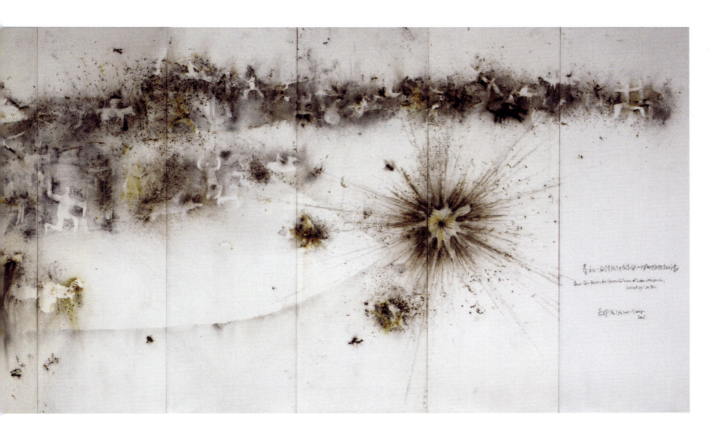

3.27 | Stills from a video of Cai Guo-Qiang's *Exploding Tower* **(2006), 40 sec. Cai Studio**

Cai Guo-Qiang staged one of his signature explosion events in the museum's central garden to celebrate the opening of Suzhou Museum and Pei's upcoming ninetieth birthday. The artist laid a gunpowder fuse along one side of the garden's perimeter and around a structure built to resemble Suzhou's famous seven-storey Tiger Hill Pagoda. As the lit fuse worked its way towards the tower, it set off a sequence of fireworks along the garden's white walls, Pei's rock composition, and the bridge. The tower then exploded into flames, leaving behind a bare metal frame. The event highlighted the garden's spatial and formal features, but Cai also intended to evoke the twin realities of *zao* (constructing) and *zha* (exploding) the pagoda, an archetype of traditional Chinese architecture.

I. M. Pei's Museum of Chinese Art, Shanghai
Modernism between East and West

Barry Bergdoll

In the immediate aftermath of the Second World War, I. M. Pei concluded his stellar progress through the Harvard Graduate School of Design (GSD) with a thesis project that marked an original position in debates of the period over the renewal of civic space and on the form of a modern museum. Pei's choice of subject, a museum of Chinese art for Shanghai, made clear enough his ambition to take his new design training home to his native China and to contribute to debates on the appropriate form for a modern Chinese architecture. With this choice, he raised the fascinating question of cultural relativity: does Chinese art require a distinctive type of architectural frame for viewing? This question extended the then current debate among architects and museum curators over whether or not modern art was better shown in new types of spaces. In his complex, two-storey frame of widely spaced reinforced-concrete piers, featureless so as to make reference neither to Western colonnades nor to Chinese timber traditions, Pei proposed a museum space that was as much community centre as museum, and equally as much landscape, with its garden flowing through the building and interior tea pavilions. Pei's remarkable design catapulted him onto the international stage—before he had ever built a building—when his thesis project was published in two of the leading architectural journals of the day: *Progressive Architecture* in New York (see 3.3, page 111) and *L'architecture d'aujourd'hui* in Paris (see 1.23.3, page 39).[1]

Pei had left China at a moment when Shanghai was in the throes of discussing the creation of a new civic centre, of which a museum would be a key component. Throughout his studies in the United States, Pei had kept an eye on the situation at home, even during the height of the war. His undergraduate thesis project at the Massachusetts Institute of Technology (MIT), submitted in 1940 and titled 'Standardized Propaganda Units for War Time and Peace Time China', was in essence a design for an itinerant cultural centre to be deployed by the 'Ministry of Propaganda' in rural areas. The design paid homage in its tensile structures as well as in its conception of cultural propaganda, referring to both Soviet revolutionary architecture and Le Corbusier's Pavillon des temps nouveaux at the Paris Exposition universelle of 1937.[2]

Early on, Pei viewed architecture as an impetus for cultural transformation and community-building, with a sense of the urgent need to contribute to a spirit of nationalism in a country resisting

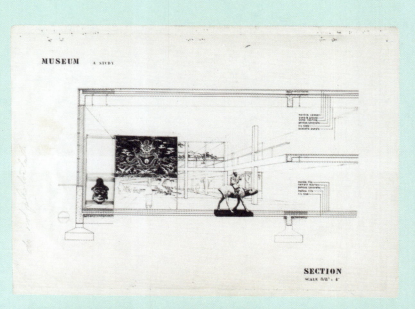

I. M. Pei, section drawing of the Museum of Chinese Art for Shanghai, 1946. Frances Loeb Library, Harvard University Graduate School of Design

Japanese invasion. In the text accompanying his MIT thesis, he underscored the political and social basis of his design with technical descriptions of the system of lightweight bamboo construction uniting Chinese tradition and a burgeoning interest in prefabrication. Two aspects of this project are relevant for his decision six years later to design a museum for Shanghai: the fact that the space would be modifiable, with equal weight given to exhibitions and to theatrical events, and that bamboo could be used in a mixed assembly to become a modern structural material, locally available and relying on existing labour know-how. Pei proposed a largely open-plan space with flexible partitions, notably so that the space could be changed from a darkened theatre to a light-filled display.[3]

When Pei enrolled at the GSD in December 1942—only to interrupt his studies almost immediately to work for the National Defense Research Committee in Princeton—his young wife, Eileen, was already studying landscape design there. Art periodicals were filled with articles on the need for museums to respond to the challenges of modernist art and of a changing society. In New York, Alfred Barr Jr, founding director of the Museum of Modern Art (MoMA), conceived of an entirely different concept of a museum and of its architectural space, influenced by his first-hand experiences at the Bauhaus and with the experimental installations undertaken by Alexander Dorner in Hanover in the late 1920s. After Dorner's emigration from Hitler's Germany, Barr was instrumental in finding him a position as director of the Museum of the Rhode Island School of Design. With his concept of the 'living museum', Dorner promoted museums as active parts of a community. Walter Gropius, likewise newly installed in the United States, would frequently assign museums and cultural facilities as studio assignments at Harvard.

In 1939, MoMA opened in its permanent home—a building designed by Philip Goodwin and Edward Durell Stone that represented a radical departure from the neoclassical temple type most recently promoted for a new national gallery of art in Washington DC. At MoMA, Goodwin and Stone discarded the conventions of classical columns in favour of a translucent curtain-wall facade, transparent on the ground floor to allow views from the street. Visitors entered at ground-floor level rather than ascending a flight of ceremonial stairs; they also had immediate access to an outdoor sculpture garden behind the museum that could be seen from the street through the glazed vestibule. Transparency and flexibility were to be hallmarks of a new generation of museums, qualities that were soon seen as echoing the stakes of national cultural politics. In his radio broadcast on the opening of MoMA's building, President Franklin D. Roosevelt declared: 'As the Museum of Modern Art is a living museum, not a collection of curious and interesting objects, it can, therefore, become an integral part of our democratic institutions—it can be woven into the very warp and woof of our democracy.'[4]

In 1943, two radically new, if diametrically opposed, visions of a future art museum were proffered by Frank Lloyd Wright and Mies van der Rohe. Wright had drawn up a variety of schemes for the future Solomon R. Guggenheim Museum's famous spiralling ramp suspended above an open ground floor penetrable from the street by both pedestrians and vehicles. In September 1945, as Pei was returning to complete his graduate work at the GSD, Wright's model was unveiled at the Plaza Hotel and heralded in the New York Times: 'Museum Building to Rise as Spiral, New Guggenheim Structure Designed by F. L. Wright Is Called First of Kind'.[5] Few knew that Le Corbusier had been working on a similar concept since 1929, although it is likely that, given Pei's enthusiasm for Le Corbusier, he was familiar with the project, titled Musée à croissance illimitée, which had been published in 1937 in the first volume of the architect's Œuvre complète.

In 1943, Architectural Forum published a special issue of designs by leading American architects that posited the form and institutions of a post-war city under the rubric '194X', since no one knew when the Second World War would come to an end. Together with its parent publication, Fortune, the magazine modelled all aspects of a medium-sized post-war city, choosing Syracuse, New York, imagined as if it had been bombed. Fortune proposed the economic and social dimensions of the city and Forum its architecture and urban layout, including a civic centre where city hall and museum would be brought into a taut composition at the core, something with echoes of the Greater Shanghai Plan debated during Pei's high-school days in China.[6] The future museum was entrusted to Mies van der Rohe, whom Architectural Forum called the nation's chief 'exponent of the "open" plan'.[7] Ironically, Syracuse would be remodelled in the 1950s and 1960s by bulldozers in the name of urban renewal, rather than by German or Japanese bombs. Syracuse's new Everson Museum of Art would be designed not by the elder statesman Mies—then at work on a new museum for West Berlin—but by the virtually untried Pei.[8]

To represent new display conditions for modern art, which had discarded all the perspectival traditions of painting, Mies used collage, a method that had become his standard teaching technique for the courtyard house projects with students at Illinois Institute of Technology, and which Pei would emulate in his GSD thesis. Mies collaged photographs of works of art that might be displayed—poignantly Picasso's Guernica, which depicts the horror of the Spanish Civil War—and enlarged colour details of nature, cut to represent the uninterrupted view of the landscape from his glazed box. All is held in place in the collage by thin ruled pencil lines, which represent the delicate steel frame of the future structure. Most importantly, Mies's building would be a new frame for looking at art from different vantage points. He writes: 'A work such as Picasso's Guernica has been difficult to place in the usual museum gallery. Here it can be shown to greatest advantage and become an element in space against a changing background.'[9]

Mies captured the larger ethos of the future city: 'The first problem is to establish the museum as a center for the enjoyment, not the interment of art. In this project the barrier between the artwork and the living community is erased by a garden approach for the display of sculpture.' (This element of the project corresponds interestingly with the sculpture garden in Goodwin and Stone's 1939 design for MoMA.) Mies concludes: 'The entire building space would be available for larger groups, encouraging a more representative use of the museum than is customary today, and creating a noble background for the civic and cultural life of the whole community.'[10]

Both Mies's design approach and his rhetoric would find echoes—emulation and critique—in Pei's design for Shanghai. Pei's project was published in *Progressive Architecture* in February 1948 together with a number of short texts, the editors noting that 'This remarkable graduate-school project strikes us as an excellent synthesis of progressive design in addition to providing a much-needed architectural statement of a proper character for a museum today.' As background, they add: 'Planned to replace an inadequate structure that occupies a site within the city's new Civic Center, plans for which were completed in 1933, this design for a museum "befitting the dignity of the city of Shanghai" is developed as an integral part of the civic plan.'[11]

Published under Gropius's guidance, the project is accompanied in both *Progressive Architecture* and *L'architecture d'aujourd'hui* by a statement from the former Bauhaus director that reflects some of his concerns in the 1940s, even if they perhaps overlook the extent to which Pei has taken on the museum debate that I am sketching in here. As Gropius explains:

> [The project] clearly illustrates that an able designer can very well hold on to basic traditional features—which he has found are still alive—without sacrificing a progressive conception of design. We have today sufficiently clarified our minds to know that respect for tradition does not mean complacent toleration of elements which have been a matter of fortuitous chance or a simple imitation of bygone esthetic forms. We have become aware that tradition in design has always meant the preservation of essential characteristics which have resulted from eternal habits of the people.[12]

This text could apply as easily to Gropius's relationship to New England clapboard houses as to Pei's evolving vision of a relationship between Chinese tradition and modernity. 'When Mr. Pei and I discussed the problems of Chinese architecture,' Gropius continues,

> he told me that he was anxious to avoid having Chinese motifs of former periods added to public buildings in a rather superficial way as was done for many public buildings in Shanghai ... We tried then to find out how the character of Chinese architecture could be expressed without imitating ... former periods. We decided that the bare Chinese wall, so evident in various periods of Chinese architecture, and the small individual garden patio were two eternal features which are well understood by every Chinese living. Mr Pei built up his scheme entirely on a variation of these two themes.[13]

Pei designed a two-storey concrete frame, entered by means of a dramatic ramp, cutting into it as needed to create sectional richness. The frame is clad in marble, an honorific befitting Shanghai's civic centre. The expansive roof is pierced with many more openings than those programmed by Mies in his steel frame and would be visible from taller buildings nearby, since the building is embedded in the ground by half a level. Influenced by both his wife's study of landscape architecture and his own memories of the gardens of

Ludwig Mies van der Rohe, interior perspective drawing for Museum for a Small City project, ca.1941, graphite and cut-and-pasted reproductions on illustration board, 76.1 × 101.5 cm. The Museum of Modern Art, New York/Scala, Florence

Suzhou, Pei weaves a garden through the open courts of the lower level. Gardens could be enjoyed both at eye level and from above, where the section of the building is opened to the sky. In place of Mies's pictorialised landscape in the distance, Pei interweaves a commemoration of the garden as one of the high forms of Chinese art-making and considers it for use, labelling it a tea pavilion on the plan. He notes of the landscaped courtyards: 'All forms of Chinese art are directly or indirectly results of a sensitive observation of nature. Such objects, consequently, are best displayed in surroundings which are in tune with them, surroundings which incorporate as much as possible the constituting elements of natural beauty.'[14]
As is clear from photographs of the model, now lost, Pei set out to capture the essence of Chinese domestic architecture using the courtyards, gardens, and semi-enclosed rooms that are present at every scale, from the hutong to the palace. 'This section looks toward the entrance garden court, at right of which is a modern translation of the traditional Chinese Tea Garden,' the editors note. 'Usually located in the market place, or near the temple grounds, to serve men of all classes as a social center and place for intellectual exchange, its inclusion here in a museum is with the hope that it will help make the institution a living organism in the life of the people, rather than a cold depository of masterpieces.'[15] The incorporation of a Chinese-style garden, which fragments experience towards greater enjoyment, enlightenment, and discovery of multiple facets of reality, makes it clear that Pei was conscious of the ways in which Chinese pictorial traditions with nature or ink and brush often incorporate multiple perspectives, rather than the unified construct of linear perspective.

As Pei was designing a museum to take home, the civil war between Nationalists and Communists made an immediate return impossible. In the next few years, he would teach at Harvard instead, notably a foundation course, Architecture 2b: Architectural and Landscape Design, which clearly underscored the interdependence of building and site, construction and nature, and which also, according to the 1946 course bulletin, assured that 'the social and economic factors underlying the design are constantly considered'. In 1947, Dorner was invited as a guest to work with students at the GSD on the design of a living museum. He took it as the occasion to pen a veritable manifesto on the role of the museum in relation to the specific spiritual state of mankind in modernity. The classroom brief was even reprinted in its entirety in Dorner's influential *The Living Museum: Experiences of an Art Historian and Museum Director*, published in 1958, a year after his death. The brief also served as the point of departure for his 1947 book *The Way Beyond Art*. 'The new type of museum', he wrote,

> would begin to partake of that energy [of the modern movement in art and architecture]. It would not only be more alive and stimulating but also much more easy to establish, for it would depend much less than the current type on quantitative accumulation, i.e. wealth. It would not require any gorgeous palaces of absolutistic ideal art but would be constructed functionally and flexibly of light modern materials ... Like all new movements this new type of museum would then be an important factor in the urgently needed integration of life and in the unification of mankind on a dynamic basis.[16]

In his Museum of Chinese Art for Shanghai, Pei synthesised a series of concerns: his ongoing desire to intervene in the civic centre in Shanghai, his commitment to imagining a cultural politics for his home country, and his attentiveness to the debate in the United States on the spaces and functions of an art museum. With its emphasis on landscape, the design possibly shows the influence of his wife, Eileen, who was at the time fully immersed in landscape architecture at the GSD. The first product of what would prove to be a lifetime engagement with museum design stood at the intersection of Pei's memories of the cultural needs of pre-war China and the debates about the appearance of a post-war United States. When he was suddenly catapulted to national attention with an innovative built design for the Everson Museum of Art in Syracuse, his interest in changing perspectives on space was largely internalised. He created a building that could take its place not in dialogue with the larger liberated landscape but in the hard realities of an American city being reconceived for urban renewal. It was the first sketch in many ways of the East Building of the National Gallery of Art in Washington DC, where the Chinese émigré architect would be one of the first to bring a modernist vision of exhibition space to the landscapes of the American National Mall.

Robert Damora, interior view of the Everson Museum of Art, ca.1968. Estate of Robert Damora

Material &
Structural
Innovation

4

'The totality of the form'

PAGE 148:
Marc Riboud, I. M. Pei, and French president François Mitterrand inspecting a glass sample for the Louvre pyramid, 1987. Association Les amis de Marc Riboud

Pei's vision for the Grand Louvre specified a structure that would respect yet break with architectural tradition through the use of steel and extra-clear glass. To achieve a truly transparent pyramid required a glass free of greenish tints, something that was not readily available on the open market. Sensitive to the national significance of the project, Pei first approached French glass manufacturer Saint-Gobain, which expressed reluctance to revive an abandoned technique for producing the low-iron glass required. With the alternative of turning to a German firm, it was with the direct intervention of President Mitterrand—a powerful client and a strong supporter of Pei's project—that Saint-Gobain produced the material.

MATERIAL & STRUCTURAL INNOVATION 151

In 1957, the then forty-year-old Pei was tasked by his employer, the larger-than-life New York developer William Zeckendorf, to design a new apartment complex as part of an urban renewal scheme on the east side of Manhattan. Although the prominent architect Gordon Bunshaft had warned Pei that nothing good could come of it—'housing is lawyers' work', Bunshaft said—Pei took on the assignment with enthusiasm and ingenuity.[1] The resulting pair of twenty-one-storey apartment blocks bracketing a large open space, together named Kips Bay Plaza, became a landmark in post-war American urban housing for its use of poured-in-place structural concrete. This achievement was one of the many groundbreaking techniques and methods that Pei and his colleagues pioneered throughout his career, and which are the subject of this chapter.

The formal aspects of Pei's work have long overshadowed the role that he and the teams of architects, engineers, and other specialists he assembled had in introducing structural and material innovations to the practice of architecture. For Pei, however, the formal and technical (as with the spatial and social) were inseparable, articulating confluences of concrete, glass, stone, and steel with structure, tactility, plasticity, and even locality across an oeuvre of often surprising diversity.

Pei had already demonstrated interest in new construction methods and materials in his 1940 thesis project, 'Standardized Propaganda Units for War Time and Peace Time China' at the Massachusetts Institute of Technology (MIT), with its modular, prefabricated components in locally sourced bamboo that could be easily mounted throughout rural parts of the country. After graduating from Harvard, Pei travelled across America visiting manufacturers of Masonite, Celotex, cement, and other prefabricated building materials with the intention to introduce them to China upon his return home.[2]

With war and political turmoil making China increasingly distant, however, Pei instead wound up at Zeckendorf's firm of Webb & Knapp. There, his striking 108-storey proposal for the Hyperboloid —a soaring hourglass-shaped tower that would have replaced Grand Central Terminal—never made it off the drawing board, but more modest proposals were just as noteworthy, including Pei's first built project: a small office building completed in 1952 in Atlanta. Leased to Gulf Oil, the simple glass box of prefabricated components—reminiscent of Mies van der Rohe's work—was built on a small budget but nevertheless featured a luxurious facade of Georgia marble spandrels (procured at a steep discount after Pei, already a master of persuasion, convinced the supplier of the project's PR value). *Architectural Forum* reported that rather than applying the stone cosmetically, Pei 'freed traditionally monumental marble from its use as a thin veneer on costly masonry walls and turned that veneer into the wall itself'.[3] Pei had devised a marble curtain wall, and the building was completed in only four months at a fraction of the cost of comparable projects.

Pei's inventiveness arose not only from an economy of means when needed—to meet a tight deadline, his 1976 OCBC Centre in Singapore was designed and engineered so that construction on its three vertical stages could proceed simultaneously—but also from his demanding creativity, rigour, and sensitive approach to materials. Completed in 1967 on a mesa beneath the Rocky Mountains outside Boulder, Colorado, his offices and laboratories for the National Center for Atmospheric Research offered a pioneering way of using bush-hammered concrete on a building facade. Made by workers using the forked chisel of a pneumatic hammer, the corduroy-like grooves of the centre's facades hid the concrete's seams while lending a stone-like tactility and revealing the locally quarried aggregate, specially chosen to match the surrounding landscape.

Pei would again employ bush-hammering at the Everson Museum of Art, but this time striated diagonally as a counterpoint to the building's boxy cantilevered galleries, which themselves required the development of a floating foundation to ensure the structure's stability. For the pyramid at the Louvre, a particular kind of glass had to be formulated to achieve the clarity that Pei desired, the pyramid's diamond-cut panels held in place by a specially designed system of wires held in tension. Clad in Tennessee pink marble, the impossibly sharp 19.5-degree knife-edge prow forming the south-west corner of Pei's East Building for the National Gallery of Art in Washington DC was as much an exercise in precision craftsmanship as it was a consequence of the site's odd angles. As Henry N. Cobb, a partner at Pei's firm, later recalled: 'We were fiercely committed to being on what we saw as the cutting edge of things, in two ways in particular: architecture at an urban scale—big things—and architecture as a craft.'[4]

Like many of his peers, Pei was inspired early on by the sculptural concrete of Le Corbusier and the clarity and detailing of Mies, whose influence could be seen in the house Pei designed for himself and his family in Katonah, New York. But Pei's design ambitions and exacting standards prompted him to push even further through relentless experimentation. For concrete alone, his firm assembled a library of cements, sands, and aggregates from across America. The team also experimented with the setting times and pouring and vibrating techniques, as well as various surface treatments, paying careful attention to the effects of cracking, weathering, and pollution.[5]

Throughout his career, Pei was skilful at finding expert collaborators: engineers like Leslie E. Robertson, Michael D. Flynn, and Peter Rice, to say nothing of the architects Henry N. Cobb, James Freed, and Araldo Cossutta, all three of whom would become partners in his firm. In Taiwan, the parabolic concrete-shell roof of Pei's Luce Memorial Chapel at Tunghai University was devised with his protégé Chen Chi-kwan. It was with Robertson, along with Pei's son Sandi, that Pei came up with the design of Hong Kong's Bank of China Tower, its exposed structural cross-bracing ingeniously resolving its stepped arrangement of four triangular tubes that, as Pei described it, evoke bamboo shoots.

Pei officially retired from his practice in 1990, aged seventy-three. Or so he claimed. Perhaps it was to be expected that the incorrigible architect would decide to take on one more project, which in fact turned out to be several projects in various countries. In 1988, for the Japanese religious movement Shinji Shumeikai, Pei had designed—reluctantly at first—a bell tower next to its Minoru Yamasaki–designed assembly hall outside Kyoto. This small project, whose flanged form was inspired by an ivory *bachi* (a pick used for Japanese stringed instruments), was soon followed by the Miho Museum and the organisation's Miho Institute of Aesthetics Chapel, his final building, completed in 2012.

For the Miho Museum, Pei convinced Shinji Shumeikai and local government authorities to expand the site to include an adjacent hill, allowing for the construction of a hidden tunnel leading to a suspension bridge that, in Robertson's hands, would gracefully traverse the valley below without any supporting pylons. To clad the chapel's conical form with custom-warped stainless-steel panels, Kikukawa, a firm known for its work for Apple stores, developed a special pressing technique and adjusted its milling machinery to manufacture the largest panels it had ever produced. Pei was ambitious until the end, lobbying clients and brokering relationships with builders to achieve the most precise implementation of his design and, in so doing, 'the totality of the form' that he sought in every project.[6]

— Aric Chen

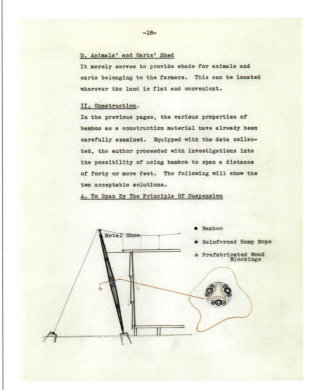
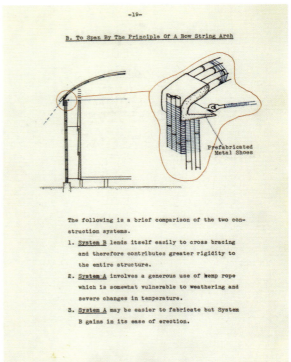

4.1.1 | **I. M. Pei, 'Standardized Propaganda Units for War Time and Peace Time China', 1940, 18–20. MIT Libraries**

'Standardized Propaganda Units for War Time and Peace Time China' (1940)

MATERIAL & STRUCTURAL INNOVATION   155

4.1.2 | **I. M. Pei, model of a standardised propaganda unit, 1940.**
Papers of I. M. Pei, Library of Congress, Washington DC

4.1.1–4.1.2
In Pei's MIT thesis, construction of the standardised propaganda units relies on materials and methods of assembly that would be available and economical in rural parts of China. Rather than timber, steel, or concrete—expensive and scarce in these areas—Pei selected bamboo for its availability locally and researched its use to demonstrate its suitability for his proposal. Drawing on the principles of a bowstring arch to span each unit's twelve-metre-wide main hall, he specified the use of bamboo for the columns and arched roof, leveraging the material's flexibility while strengthening the structure with metal connections and stabilising it with cross-bracing.

Helix (1948–1949; unbuilt)

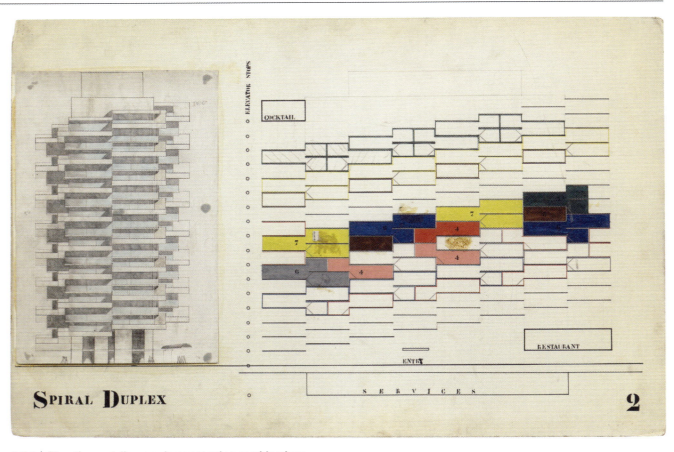

4.2.1 | **Elevation and diagram demonstrating combinations of adjoined apartments, ca.1948. Pei Cobb Freed & Partners**

MATERIAL & STRUCTURAL INNOVATION

4.2.2 | **Elevation showing entrance and lower floors, ca.1948. Pei Cobb Freed & Partners**

4.2.1–4.2.2
Pei's unbuilt Helix tower is made up of wedge-shaped apartments, stacked in a split-level spiral arrangement to produce a cylindrical volume reaching twenty-one storeys. While load-bearing walls between apartments are vertically aligned across floors, adjacent units are staggered by half a floor such that they can be adjoined diagonally to form duplexes or limitless larger configurations. This system would allow tenants to expand or contract their apartments as desired, introducing a fundamental flexibility in living space.

4.3 | **Plan and diagrams of the Helix's interior configuration, ca.1948. Pei Cobb Freed & Partners**

In the Helix's plan, Pei concentrated the building's utilities in the middle to create flexible living spaces. A slim circulation core houses the elevator and stairs and opens outwards onto looped corridors, with each floor containing four apartments. The area devoted to kitchens and bathrooms forms a mechanical ring in the building, centralising all utilities. The main living space extends seven and a half metres to the outermost perimeter of private balconies, amounting to more than seventy-four square metres for each apartment.

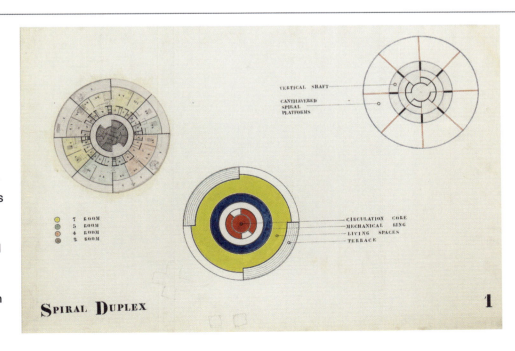

4.4.1 | **Henry N. Cobb, interior model of lower floors, ca.1949. Pei Cobb Freed & Partners**

4.4.2 | **Photomontage of model showing the Helix overlooking New York's East River, ca.1949. Pei Cobb Freed & Partners**

4.4.1–4.4.2
The Helix's modular design meant that it could be erected with prefabricated units, which Pei combined with poured-in-place concrete—construction methods made possible only by the latest advances in building technologies. Supported by eight radiating, load-bearing slabs, inverted U-shaped units of precast concrete would be stacked according to the structure's spiral arrangement, while the building's central core acted as a hoisting tower. The novel assembly methods Pei conceived, along with the project's flexible living concept, led William Zeckendorf to file a patent for the design. Zeckendorf's enthusiasm for the Helix's potential drove efforts to finance the project in such cities as New York and Havana, but he was ultimately unable to realise the unconventional proposal.

MATERIAL & STRUCTURAL INNOVATION

4.5.1 | 'Small Office Buildings—1. Marble Curtain Walls Hung from the Inside of Pre-fab Framing Cut Costs but Preserve Quality', *Architectural Forum* 96 (February 1952): 108. Pei Cobb Freed & Partners

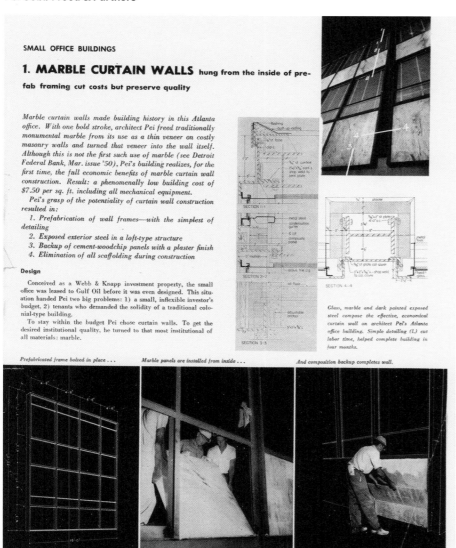

4.5.2 | Alternating marble and glass curtain wall of the Gulf Oil office building, ca.1952. Pei Cobb Freed & Partners

4.5.1–4.5.2
Confronted with an exceptionally limited budget for his first ground-up built project, Pei designed a simple Miesian box for a small office building leased to Gulf Oil. Pei negotiated a discount for locally sourced marble from Georgia in exchange for displaying the material prominently in the building's curtain wall. Alternating panels of thin marble and glass form the walls, which were installed directly onto the prefabricated steel frame from inside to eliminate the need for scaffolding and to reduce costly on-site labour. Completed in four months, the construction of the fully air-conditioned building and installation of mechanical systems cost a mere USD7.50 per square foot.

Gulf Oil Building (1950–1952)
Atlanta

Pei Residence (1952)
Katonah, New York

4.6.1 | **I. M. Pei, early elevation emphasising cross-layered cantilevers, 1952. Estate of I. M. Pei**

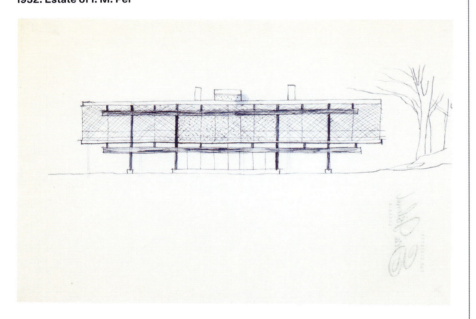

4.6.2 | **I. M. Pei, early plan and elevation of the Pei residence, 1952. Estate of I. M. Pei**

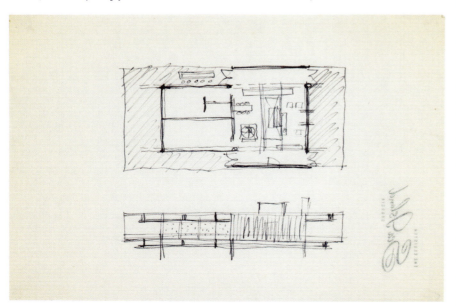

MATERIAL & STRUCTURAL INNOVATION

4.6.4 | **Robert Damora, Pei residence, 1952. Estate of Robert Damora**

4.6.1–4.6.4
While working on large urban-planning projects for Webb & Knapp, Pei designed and built a compact rural retreat for his growing family on a hillside in Katonah, New York. Deep verandas enclosed by a wrap-around screen surround a core structure of bedrooms, a freestanding kitchen, and a fireplace to express a house-within-a-house plan adaptable to seasonal changes. Pei used inexpensive prefabricated components that could be transported easily to the remote site and assembled rapidly. Inspired by timber construction systems he had observed in Chinese temples, Pei built the house on a base of cross-layered laminated pine beams that evenly distributes weight while preventing shrinkage. As wooden beams up to twenty-four metres in length cantilever out from supporting joists, the structure appears to float in the landscape, a striking aspect of the house highlighted in one of *Vogue*'s 'Fashions in Living' features.

4.6.3 | **'Small-House Perfection',** *Vogue* **138 (January 1961): 87. Condé Nast**

4.7.1 | **Model of the Hyperboloid, 1956. Pei Cobb Freed & Partners**

Hyperboloid (1954–1955; unbuilt)
New York

4.7.2 | **I. M. Pei & Associates, plan of the main lobby level, in *The Hyperboloid—A Webb & Knapp Project for the Grand Central Terminal*, 1956. Pei Cobb Freed & Partners**

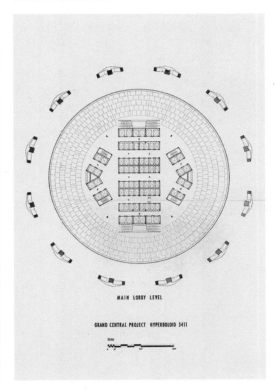

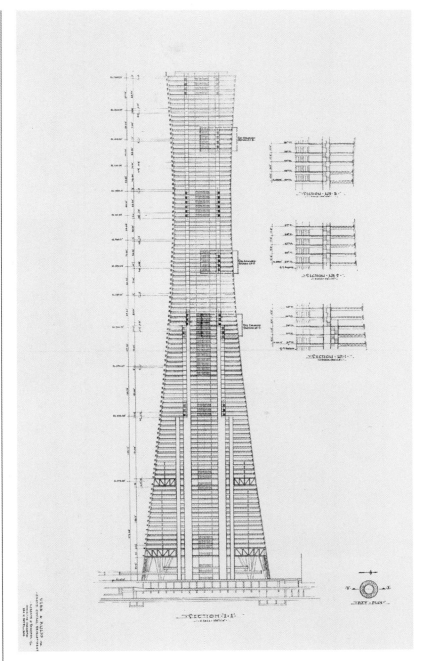

4.7.3 | **Roberts & Schaefer Company, section of Hyperboloid, in *Engineering Report for Proposed New York Central Building to be Erected at the Site of the Grand Central Terminal, New York City*, 1956. Pei Cobb Freed & Partners**

4.7.1–4.7.3

When he was invited to envision a new building that would make use of the air rights above New York's Grand Central Terminal and breathe life into an ailing rail industry, Pei proposed the Hyperboloid. The development was announced on the front page of the *New York Times* on 8 September 1954. As its name suggests, the 108-storey, 456-metre-high project was a three-dimensional closed hyperbolic paraboloid with a central core of vertical columns surrounding elevator shafts, corridors, and circulation, and exterior inclined columns intersecting to form a diagonally latticed shell. The efficiency of its braced perimeter tube structure meant that the Hyperboloid could have been built with the same amount of steel as was used in the Empire State Building—a tower 80 per cent smaller—and would have had stronger resistance to lateral wind loads. Pei's scheme represented a revolutionary use of the hyperboloid, a structural form that until then had only been applied to open-framed latticed infrastructural towers and long-span, thin-shell concrete structures.

Luce Memorial Chapel (1954–1963), Tunghai University
Taichung

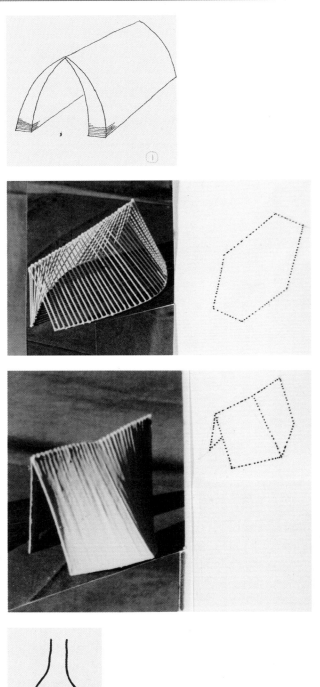

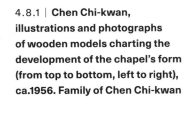

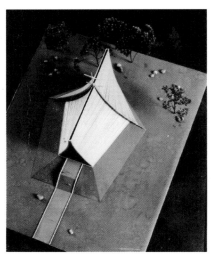

4.8.1 | Chen Chi-kwan, illustrations and photographs of wooden models charting the development of the chapel's form (from top to bottom, left to right), ca.1956. Family of Chen Chi-kwan

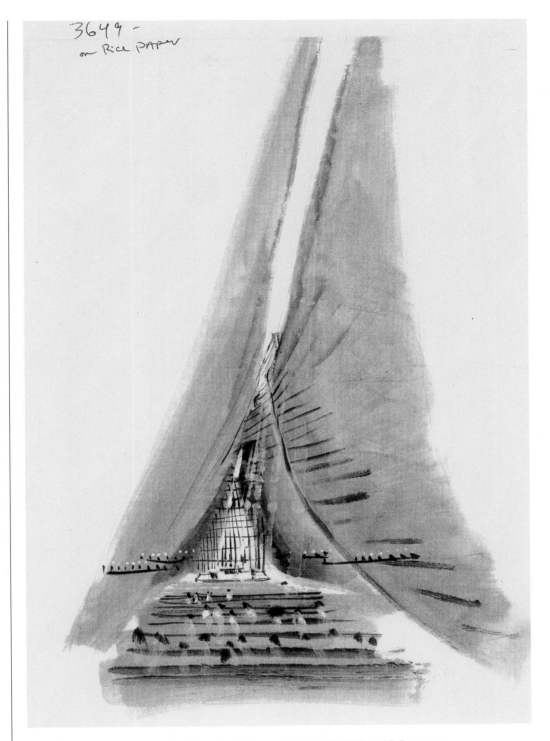

4.8.2 | **Ink drawing of the chapel's early design, ca.1956. Pei Cobb Freed & Partners**

PAGES 166–167:
4.8.3 | **Lee Kuo-Min, view of exposed lattice structure in chapel's interior, 2021. Photo commissioned by M+**

4.8.1–4.8.3
Situated on a slight elevation to the north of Tunghai University's main east–west axis, Luce Memorial Chapel was designed in collaboration with architect Chen Chi-kwan to express a distinct presence that represented the university's Christian mission. Inspired initially by the pointed arches typical of Gothic architecture, the concept for the building's form changed through Chen's modelled iterations to resemble the hull of a wooden ship. By integrating the curvature of traditional Chinese saddle roofs, the chapel's final hexagonal plan features four warped shells that converge at a narrow skylight, which stands out from the beam-and-column archetype of its neighbours. The curved walls soar skyward, enclosing a space for up to 450 people. The building's exposed lattice structure, lit by streams of natural light, is intended to create an atmosphere of the sublime.

4.9.1.1 | Chen Chi-kwan, drawing of lamella frame of the chapel's initial timber design, ca.1956. Pei Cobb Freed & Partners

4.9.1.2 | Chen Chi-kwan, drawing of interior and exterior diagonal sheathing of the chapel's initial timber design, ca.1956. Pei Cobb Freed & Partners

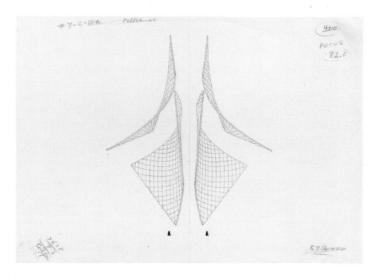

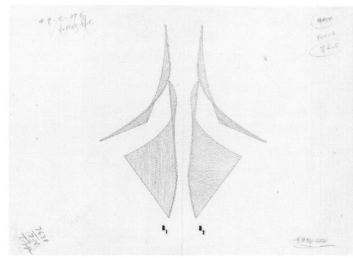

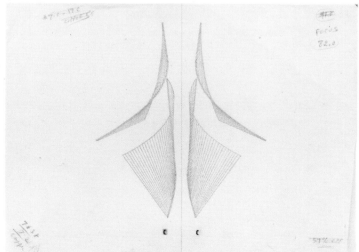

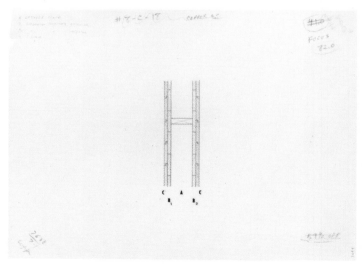

4.9.1.3 | Chen Chi-kwan, drawing of hinoki wood sheathing of the chapel's initial timber design, ca.1956. Pei Cobb Freed & Partners

4.9.1.4 | Chen Chi-kwan, section of shell structure showing the sandwiched lamella frame of the chapel's initial timber design, ca.1956. Pei Cobb Freed & Partners

MATERIAL & STRUCTURAL INNOVATION 169

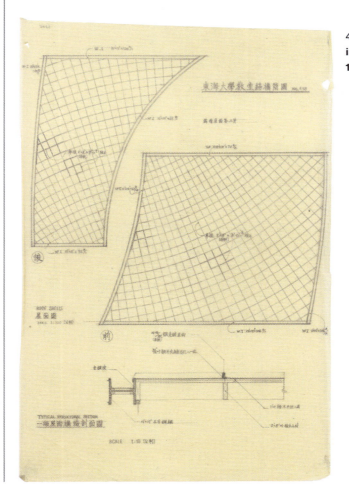

4.9.2 | **Section and components of the chapel's initial I-beam-reinforced timber structural shell, 1958. Pei Cobb Freed & Partners**

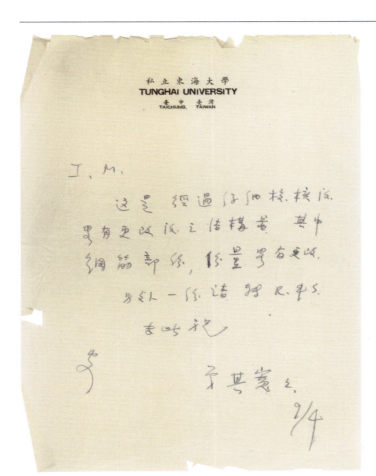

4.9.3 | **Chen Chi-kwan, memo to I. M. Pei accompanying drawings to convey refinements in the chapel's reinforced-concrete structure, copied and sent to engineers Roberts & Schaefer Company, ca.1960. Pei Cobb Freed & Partners**

4.9.1–4.9.3
The hyperbolic paraboloids of the chapel's warped shells were relatively novel architectural forms that proved challenging to engineer without the availability of digital technology. Pei's team originally designed these forms to be built with a lamella structure sandwiched between layers of wood and reinforced with a steel I-beam enclosing the edges. But Chen's studies revealed that a wooden structure of this design would not attain the needed stability, while also being susceptible to termite infestations and earthquakes. These concerns prompted him to explore a reinforced-concrete solution. Chen consulted structural engineer H. S. Fong to evaluate the feasibility of this approach, and the pair travelled to New York to convince Pei—whose engineering advisor disagreed with Fong's analysis—to agree to the design of a reinforced-concrete structure. Pei then entrusted Chen and Fong with overseeing the entire construction process.

4.10.1 | **T. T. Chiang, elevations and sections of Luce Memorial Chapel, ca.1962. Family of Chen Chi-kwan**

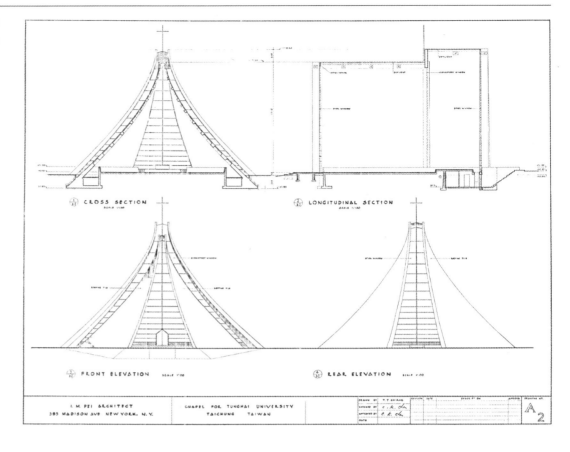

4.10.2 | **View of latticed cross ribs and longitudinal skylights, ca.1963. Pei Cobb Freed & Partners**

OPPOSITE:
4.10.3 | **Lee Kuo-Min, view of the glazed facade towards the altar, 2021. Photo commissioned by M+**

4.10.1–4.10.3
The chapel is made up of four conoidal shells of reinforced concrete, arranged as symmetrical pairs with glazed openings at the chapel's two ends. In a clear expression of its structural mechanisms, latticed cross ribs dominate the bare interior surfaces, which increase in thickness towards the shell's base, where greater strength is required to support heavier loads and bending moments. Each shell is structurally independent, and they are hinged together only with delicate, bowtie-shaped links to provide rigidity and stability during seismic events. Glass is inserted into the slender gaps between shells and a longitudinal skylight at the building's peak, allowing natural light into the space and emphasising the interior's texture through a play of light and shadow. The linearity of these components, paired with the optical effect of the lattice structure, highlights the soaring, twenty-metre height of the chapel.

On one of my short stays in Taiwan, I visited the Luce Chapel on the campus of Tunghai University. In 1963, when the chapel was completed, Taiwan was still recognised by the United Nations and the United States as the seat of the sole legitimate government of China. Robust activity was transforming the island's economy, and Tunghai was its first private university. Observers must have been in awe of the reinforced-concrete structure, rising from what had until recently been farmland and built by local craftsmen who had never before applied their skills to such soaring geometry.

I remember contemplating a certain appreciation for the human in the texture of the hardened surfaces, the scale of the intricate waffle formwork, and the gentle curvature of the leaf forms. It occurred to me that despite his progressive education and his eloquent arguments for modernism, Pei never strayed far from his interest in the relationship between ideas and the people who bring them into being.

– Jing Liu

Jing Liu is a Nanjing-born architect and co-founder of the New York–based practice SO – IL.

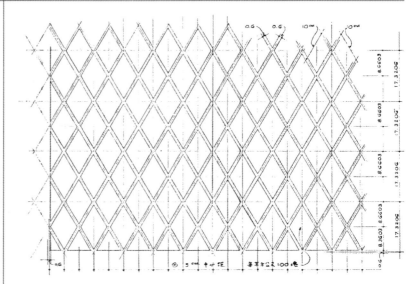

4.11.1 | **T. T. Chiang, diagram of ceramic tile pattern for the facade, ca.1962. Family of Chen Chi-kwan**

OPPOSITE:
4.11.2 | **Lee Kuo-Min, view of the chapel with a shadow cast on the glazed ceramic shell, 2021. Photo commissioned by M+**

4.11.1–4.11.2
The shift from the chapel's original timber design to a concrete structure called for a waterproof finish to protect the shell's porous surface. Chen opted for yellow glazed ceramic tiles, explicitly referencing the yellow tiled roofs characteristic of traditional Chinese palatial structures. Chen shaped the tiles to mirror the proportions of the interior lattice beams. Given the disparity in width between each shell's top and bottom edges, the number of tiles in each row increases towards the base, while the width of mortar between tiles is controlled to visually balance the pattern. Protrusions from the centre of every other tile create horizontal cues on the facade that appear to emphasise the curvature of the conoidal wall.

4.12.1 | **Builders pouring concrete from bamboo scaffolding on top of Luce Memorial Chapel, ca.1962.**
Papers of I. M. Pei, Library of Congress, Washington DC

4.12.2 | **Chen Chi-kwan, partially constructed wooden formwork for the chapel's reinforced-concrete shell, ca.1962. Family of Chen Chi-kwan**

4.12.3 | **Higashide Photo Studio, installation of steel cladding on the reinforced-concrete shell of the Miho Institute of Aesthetics Chapel, ca.2011. io Architects**

4.12.1–4.12.3
Realising the chapel's complex form required contemporary concrete construction techniques unfamiliar to local builders. Learning from construction practices in Japan, Guang-yuan Construction Company experimented with small-batch concrete mixtures to understand how the chapel would be built. Carpenters crafted wooden supports and framework from full-sized drawings, and bamboo scaffolding was erected, from which concrete was poured in a continuous rotation from shell to shell. Pei's design for the Miho Institute of Aesthetics Chapel some fifty years later—the only other religious building he completed—marks a similar use of the latest developments in technology to pursue a desired geometry.

4.13.1 | **Drawing of the interior of a typical Kips Bay Plaza apartment, ca.1957. Pei Cobb Freed & Partners**

OPPOSITE:
4.13.2 | **Naho Kubota, detail of a window frame's rounded corner, 2022. Photo commissioned by M+**

4.13.1–4.13.2
For Kips Bay Plaza, Pei developed an innovative lightweight concrete mixture that allowed the structure's load-bearing system and facade to be combined. The window modules were developed at a human scale and placed in a grid, creating uniformly spaced columns and introducing a visual rhythm to the facade. Within each opening, rounded corners add rigidity to increase the frame's overall wind resistance, while also allowing unframed glass panes to be directly fitted behind deep recesses. The depth of the window set-back is reduced at the fifth and tenth floors in response to the incrementally lessened loads of the building's upper floors. Highly priced bids from construction contractors resistant to new techniques nearly derailed the project. In order to complete it, William Zeckendorf purchased the concrete company Industrial Engineering.

Kips Bay Plaza (1957–1962)
New York

4.14.1 | **A member of I. M. Pei & Associates on a bend test built prior to the construction of Kips Bay Plaza, ca.1958. Pei Cobb Freed & Partners**

OPPOSITE:
4.14.2 | **Naho Kubota, detail of Kips Bay Plaza's gridded concrete facade, 2022. Photo commissioned by M+**

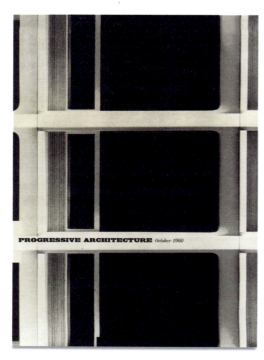

4.14.3 | **Cover, featuring details of Kips Bay Plaza model, *Progressive Architecture* 41 (October 1960). USModernist**

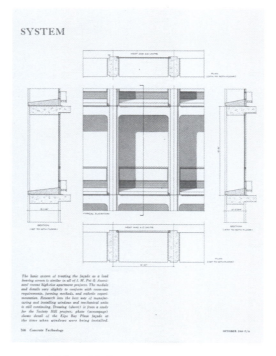

4.14.4 | **Edward L. Friedman, study of system of treating facade as load-bearing screen for Society Hill towers, in 'Concrete Technology in USA – Cast-in-Place Technique Restudied', *Progressive Architecture* 41 (October 1960): 166. USModernist**

4.14.1–4.14.4
When Pei conceived the fair-faced concrete design of Kips Bay Plaza, the techniques and technology required to achieve the smooth, exposed finish were lacking, as evidenced by defects in existing concrete structures, such as colour inconsistencies, surface spalling, shrinkage, and thermal cracks. With Zeckendorf's support, he began an extensive research programme in order to better understand the material and find a new solution. Pei's team developed a scale model of a proposed forming system to demonstrate to construction contractors the viability of the proposal. They then proceeded to test the performance of formwork, joints, and concrete mixture variations on full-sized facade sections. The formwork for Kips Bay Plaza was built to precise cabinet-making standards and faced with a fibreglass-reinforced plastic that would produce the finished facade straight out of the form. Key elements had to be considered from the project's design phase, rather than determined during construction. Kips Bay Plaza became a prototype for other low-cost housing projects and determined Pei's approach to later concrete structures, perhaps most notably Society Hill in Philadelphia.

4.15.1 | **George Cserna, view of complex from main entrance, ca.1967. Avery Architectural and Fine Arts Library, Columbia University**

National Center for Atmospheric Research (NCAR) (1961–1967)
Boulder, Colorado

MATERIAL & STRUCTURAL INNOVATION   181

4.15.2 | **Cliff dwellings at Mesa Verde National Park, Colorado, 2010. Alamy**

4.15.1–4.15.2
The headquarters of the National Center for Atmospheric Research—a government laboratory for research into atmospheric physics—was designed to be in harmony with the mesa overlooking Boulder, Colorado. Pei conceived two asymmetrical clusters of six-storey towers connected on a basement level and through a two-storey central building. The towers' hooded tops and irregularly placed keyhole windows were informed by cliff dwellings of the Ancestral Puebloan peoples of Mesa Verde. Cantilevers, overhangs, and vertical concrete slabs serve as buffers between windows and the outdoors, emphasising the totality of the form.

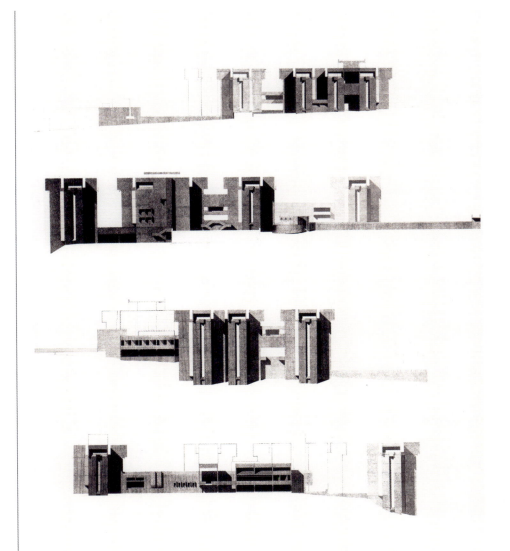

4.16 | **Elevation of intended final scheme, ca.1963. Pei Cobb Freed & Partners**

Visible in the elevations of NCAR's final scheme, vertical circulation takes the place of conventional horizontal hallways, which the scientists found undesirable. Staff descend from one cluster of towers and cross the central section of the building to reach the next set of towers. The third cluster seen here, designed to hug the southern edge of the mesa, was never built owing to budget cuts.

MATERIAL & STRUCTURAL INNOVATION 183

OPPOSITE:
4.17 | Naho Kubota, circular stairway, 2021. Photo commissioned by M+

The circular stairway at the front of the building alludes to the *kivas*—multipurpose ceremonial grounds—found in the cliff dwellings at Mesa Verde. It is an example of the occasional curves intended to offset the rectilinear forms that dominate the NCAR complex. It is also one of the many open spaces where staff can meet privately or semi-privately.

4.18.1 | I. M. Pei discussing a possible mottled texture for the concrete during a review of slabs erected on-site, 1965. University Corporation for Atmospheric Research

4.18.2 | A worker combing the dry concrete with a fork-like tool to create the bush-hammered effect, ca.1965. Pei Cobb Freed & Partners

4.18.1–4.18.2
Concerned with the texture of the poured-in-place concrete walls, Pei had a series of sample slabs erected on-site and experimented with various finishes. He eventually decided not to use any finish at all and instead to create texture through bush-hammering, which in this case involved using a pneumatic tool that drives a five-pointed chisel into concrete to break its surface. While the technique had been used for roughening concrete before a finish was applied, it had never before been used on its own. From a distance, the narrow vertical grooves of the bush-hammered facade are invisible; from a closer vantage point, however, they provide a clear alternative to the typical smoothness of concrete architecture. The process also fragmented the stone aggregate in the concrete, revealing shimmering mica when light hits the surface.

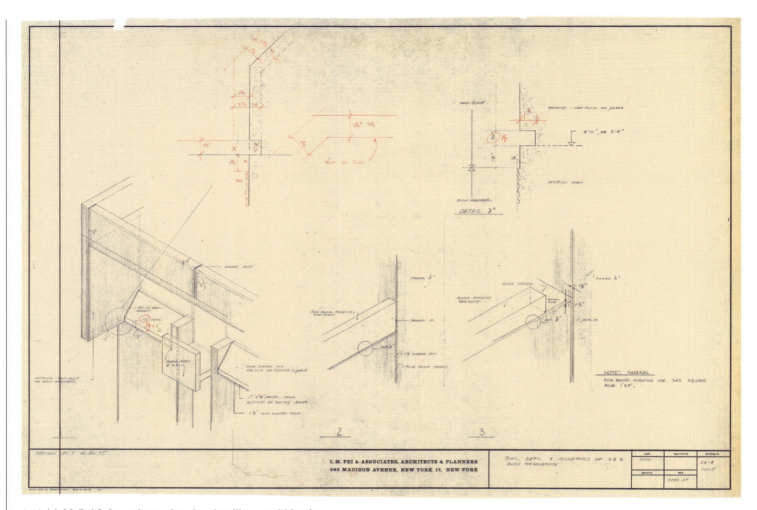

4.19 | **I. M. Pei & Associates, drawing detailing sand-blasting and bush-hammering finishes for 'crow's nest' balconies, 1964. Pei Cobb Freed & Partners**

This drawing shows the precise structural and surface treatments for the towers' concrete exterior, focusing on the compact 'crow's nest' balcony that protrudes from the top floor of each tower. Bush-hammering created vertical striations on the bulk of the facade, while sand-blasting was used to give parapets and overhangs a contrasting smoothness.

OPPOSITE:

4.20 | **Naho Kubota, NCAR's wall texture and irregular forms echoing characteristics of the surrounding landscape, 2021. Photo commissioned by M+**

The reinforced concrete of the NCAR headquarters is composed of reddish-brown stone aggregate extracted from a quarry in Lyons, Colorado, to the north of Boulder. To colour the cement, Pei used sand ground from the same stone. The resulting colour and texture evoke the erosion of rock formations. Varying amounts of light and shadow play against the building's narrow shafts of tinted glass and textured concrete with the movement of the sun and clouds.

4.22.1 | **Diagonal bush-hammering underway on the facade, ca.1967.
Rockwell News Bureau; Everson Museum of Art Archive**

4.21 | **Robert J. Arnold, cantilevered galleries under construction in a developing community plaza in downtown Syracuse, 1967. Everson Museum of Art Archive**

Everson Museum of Art (1961–1968)
Syracuse, New York

In his choice of poured-in-place reinforced concrete as the primary material for the Everson Museum of Art, Pei sought to take advantage of the material's plasticity and to evoke an abstract sculpture set on a civic plaza. Construction began in 1966 after years of fundraising and a thorough investigation of the soil to verify the feasibility of building cantilevered galleries. The floating foundation that Pei proposed required the total weight of the museum structure to equal that of the soil displaced in the excavation of the underground level, thereby eliminating the need for additional anchors to stabilise the structure. Although the four overhanging blocks appear independent of one another, they are tied together by the waffle-slab roof of the central court and a continuous belt of concrete bridges running along the upper-level galleries.

4.22.2 | **Advertisement featuring the Everson Museum of Art's concrete helical staircase, in** *Concrete Construction* **14 (July 1968). Everson Museum of Art Archive**

4.22.3 | **Robert J. Arnold, construction of formwork for sculpture court's staircase, 1967. Everson Museum of Art Archive**

4.22.1–4.22.3

The use of concrete inside and out emphasises the building's sculptural character. When it proved impossible to cast each of the four cantilevered blocks as single entities, mechanical bush-hammering was used on the structure's vertical surfaces to conceal the joints that emerged from each successive concrete pour. After first using the bush-hammering technique on the National Center for Atmospheric Research, Pei introduced guides to increase the uniformity of the striations chiselled onto the surface. However, the slanted grooves made by labourers as they tested their tools led him to decide on a diagonal pattern across the exterior and interior, which softened the rectilinearity of the blocks while keeping a smooth piping along the borders of each plane. Horizontal surfaces were acid-etched to expose the Croghan Red Granite aggregates in the concrete mix and produce a warm hue that harmonised with historical brick structures nearby. Indoors, poured-in-place concrete was used to construct the central court's helix staircase, which the museum's first director, Max W. Sullivan, considered 'our most extravagant piece of sculpture'. Wooden forms reaching five metres in height allowed for casting in one pour.

The Everson Museum of Art is a unique example of Brutalist architecture. Constructed entirely in concrete, it nevertheless eschews the post-war tendency towards over-articulation of elements in favour of a commitment to simple, Platonic forms. In 2019, the museum held a competition for a new restaurant to be constructed in the building's east wing. The competition was motivated by Louise Rosenfield's offer to donate more than three thousand ceramic works from her collection, in addition to funding the project. Her only condition was that the collection had to be somehow used in the restaurant. We came across this photograph after learning we had been selected as finalists for the competition. It became the most important image for us because it shows the way in which the museum's strategies of sculptural massing produce intense contrasts of darkness and light. We can see how the concrete devours sunlight, leaving the deep volumes beyond in almost total darkness. The image reveals a dimension of the project that could no longer be experienced, or at least not without shutting off all the lights.

Our proposal, which went beyond the competition brief for the restaurant, and which was eventually selected, centres on three main strategies. First, because much of the east wing is below ground level, the daylighting conditions produce the chiaroscuro effect that we found so striking. We proposed to offset this with materials and surfaces that multiply the reflection and refraction of natural light. Second, the east wing has always had an ambiguous relationship to the rest of the museum. The upper floor is publicly accessible, but the lower level is accessible only to staff—and yet both are joined, visually and acoustically, by a double-height atrium called Mather Court. By relocating a set of doors separating the east wing from the main ceramics gallery on the lower level, we argued that Mather Court could become a semi-public space for events and exhibitions. Finally, we proposed a series of display elements for the Rosenfield Collection—larger than furniture but smaller than a building—to be delicately inserted into the east wing. In the end, much of our work will recede into the background, materialising daylight without any physical alterations to the existing architecture.

– Zeina Koreitem and John May

Zeina Koreitem and John May are founding partners of MILLIØNS, a Los Angeles–based practice selected for a renovation project at the Everson Museum of Art in 2019.

MATERIAL & STRUCTURAL INNOVATION 189

4.23.1 | **Interior of Mather Court, which housed the members' lounge in the building's east wing, ca.1967. Everson Museum of Art Archive**

4.23.2 | **Iwan Baan, double-height atrium of Mather Court redesigned by MILLIØNS to display the Rosenfield Collection, 2022. MILLIØNS**

4.23.1–4.23.2
The Everson Museum of Art was constructed entirely of reinforced concrete, left exposed in all interiors except for the galleries. For their intervention in the east wing's double-height, lower interior courtyard, MILLIØNS introduced connections to an adjacent gallery and the café above while emphasising the original exposed concrete, rectilinear slabs, and skylights.

4.24.1 | George Cserna, photograph of model of the FAA Air Traffic Control Tower prototype, *Architectural Forum* 119 (November 1963): 112. USModernist

Federal Aviation Administration (FAA) Air Traffic Control Towers (1962–1972)
Multiple locations, United States

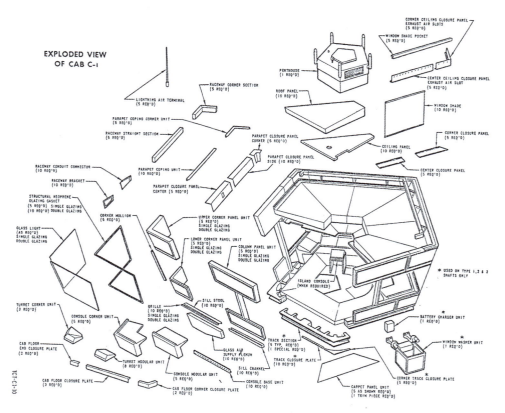

4.24.2 | Exploded view showing components of the FAA towers' pentagonal observation decks, ca.1962. Pei Cobb Freed & Partners

4.24.3 | **George Cserna, America's first forty-metre-tall FAA tower in El Paso, Texas, ca.1968. Avery Architectural and Fine Arts Library, Columbia University**

4.24.1–4.24.3
As part of the Kennedy administration's first initiatives to improve federal buildings, Najeeb Halaby, head of the newly established Federal Aviation Agency (now the Federal Aviation Administration), held a competition for a standardised control tower that could symbolise the reliability of the agency's safety measures. Pei's prototypical design demonstrates a reassessment of the tower's function to enhance its operational efficiency, arranging its components in sleek sculptural forms. A tapered concrete tower is crowned by a pentagonal observation deck enclosed by slanted glass panes and transparent epoxy joints to optimise visibility. Within the seamless glass membrane, Pei also designed a prefabricated console system that consolidated controllers' instruments. While each tower's concrete shaft housed mechanical services, supporting operations are concentrated in the submerged base building. Pei delivered specifications for towers in five different heights with thirteen variations comprising interchangeable components that engineers could adapt to different airport contexts. Of the seventy towers ordered in the original contract, seventeen were built before the FAA's priorities shifted towards lower-cost models; several remain in use today.

4.25.1 | **Thorney Lieberman, front plaza of Dallas City Hall with a sculpture by Henry Moore, ca.1977. Pei Cobb Freed & Partners**

Dallas City Hall (1966–1977)
Dallas

OPPOSITE:
4.25.2 | **Naho Kubota, west elevation of Dallas City Hall showing the inverted pyramid profile, 2021. Photo commissioned by M+**

4.25.1–4.25.2
Pei's design for Dallas City Hall considered the spatial requirements and civic services of different government departments. His approach of concentrating public-facing offices—with relatively small footprints—in easily accessible public spaces at the base of the building resulted in an inverted pyramid form. Expressed with a thirty-four-degree inclined facade, the gravity-defying structure is supported entirely through an innovative post-tensioning system, although structurally independent stair towers appear to prop it up. Distributed across its 183-metre length, the building's fourteen load-bearing walls are arranged in pairs, where vertical tendons run down one wall and are fed up the other to form looped systems, such that each tendon applies compressive forces simultaneously to both walls. On individual floors, each extending 2.8 metres further out than the one below, horizontal tendons are anchored to the angled front facade and extend through the load-bearing walls to the building's opposite end, which transfers the cantilever's over-turning force to the vertical tendons and down into the foundations.

4.26.1 | **Inclined front facade under construction, 1974. Pei Cobb Freed & Partners**

4.26.1–4.26.2
The city's strict budget and need for a large space led Pei to design a structure of exposed concrete. When their own tests of different aggregate mixes did not yield satisfactory results, Pei's team turned to a newly patented shrinkage-compensating concrete. Working with local cement producers Texas Industries, Pei's office developed a buff-coloured Type K cement to imitate local earth tones, achieved by burning a component of the cement in a kiln—an arduous but necessary process at a time when pigments were not yet used to achieve colour consistency across batches. The shrinkage-compensating concrete was cast with durable resin-coated plywood formwork, which was reusable across the building's repetitive structural elements to produce extremely smooth surfaces.

MATERIAL & STRUCTURAL INNOVATION   195

OPPOSITE:
4.26.2 | **Naho Kubota, front facade with a column seemingly supporting the incline, 2021. Photo commissioned by M+**

4.27 | **Typical coarse aggregate sample case, ca.2021. Reginald D. Hough**

These jars contain samples of coarse aggregates from across the United States, collected between 1965 and 1969 for a material library as Pei's office ventured into the use of structural concrete. Reginald D. Hough, who specialised in architectural concrete in Pei's firm, coordinated the collection of twenty-two cases of cement, sand, and aggregates to better understand the impact of these raw materials on the textures and colours of concrete mixtures. By extensively refining a material that is notoriously difficult to control, Pei's firm amassed and developed more technical expertise than most construction contractors in the industry, allowing it to embark on the innovative use of exposed concrete in such projects as Kips Bay Plaza and the Everson Museum of Art. The geographic breadth of the collection also functioned as a reference for locally available materials, something that was essential when considering the logistical and economic needs of a project.

Polaroid Tower (1969; unbuilt)
Cambridge, Massachusetts

4.28 | **Helmut Jacoby, rendering of base entrance and steel latticed exoskeleton of Polaroid Tower, 1968. Pei Cobb Freed & Partners**

Pei conceived of this forty-five-storey high-rise as the Polaroid Corporation's new headquarters, part of a technology hub called Kendall Square near MIT. The design relies on an exterior bracing structure reminiscent of the unbuilt Hyperboloid, combining steel members horizontally and diagonally in a mega-truss system. Presented with glass behind the lattice-bracing found in such structures as gas storage tanks, thin floor plates extend from the perimeter to a central core between column-free interiors. The latticed exoskeleton departs from standard building practices of the 1960s and presents an honest expression of the building's structural system.

National Gallery of Art East Building (1968–1978)
Washington DC

4.29.1 | **Paul Stevenson Oles, early rendering of the East Building atrium with concrete coffered ceiling, 1969. National Gallery of Art, Washington DC, Gallery Archives**

4.29.2 | **Paul Stevenson Oles, perspective study of the skylight in the East Building atrium, 1971. National Gallery of Art, Washington DC, Gallery Archives**

4.29.1–4.29.2
Documented in Paul Stevenson Oles's visualisations, which were critical in helping the project team grasp the complex spatial relationships within the triangular volume of the East Building, the design of the central atrium underwent a major transformation when its initial concept of a coffered concrete ceiling was replaced with a soaring skylight late in the design process. Finding the solid roof too heavy for the windowless atrium enclosure, Pei changed its existing construction plans to introduce natural light and the open quality of an outdoor public plaza—necessarily covered owing to the extreme seasonal variations in temperature in Washington DC.

The exterior form of the expansion of the National Gallery of Art had been determined by two decisions: to physically isolate the new facility from John Russell Pope's West Building, and to maximise the volume of the addition within the zoning and height restrictions. Following those decisions, my role in the development of the triangular spaces of the interior was to produce sketches based primarily on the observations and suggestions of I. M. Pei and his colleagues—that is, to provide ongoing visual feedback to the emerging design consensus. The time and expense required to construct sufficiently illustrative study models discourage their use for early investigation in this type of interior study, which demands rapidity of choice and the suggestion of lighting implications. As Pei himself has written: 'Only drawings can animate. They remain the most effective way of studying the elusive qualities of light and scale.'

– Paul Stevenson Oles

Paul Stevenson Oles is an architectural illustrator who visualised many of I. M. Pei's projects, including the National Gallery of Art East Building and the Grand Louvre, as part of the design process.

4.30.1 | **Prefabricated frame of a skylight unit for the East Building atrium, ca.1976. Pei Cobb Freed & Partners**

4.30.2 | **Construction image documenting the installation of the atrium skylight, 1977. Pei Cobb Freed & Partners**

MATERIAL & STRUCTURAL INNOVATION 199

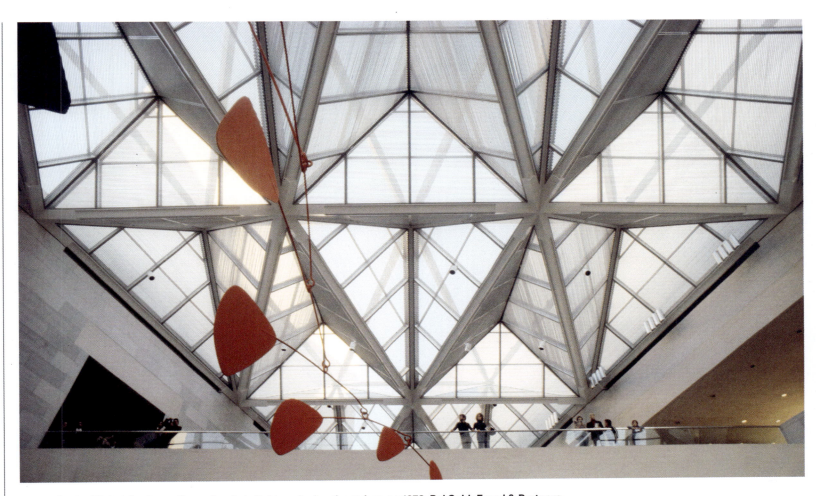

4.30.3 | **John Nicholais, three-dimensional skylight enclosing the atrium, ca.1978. Pei Cobb Freed & Partners**

4.30.1–4.30.3
Making up the atrium skylight are twenty-five tetrahedrons that measure nine metres on one side of the base and thirteen and a half metres on the other two, adhering to the 2:3-ratio isosceles modules that define the building's geometry. Suspended twenty-four metres above the ground, the three-dimensional steel structure spans the 1,550-square-metre opening. Each prefabricated tetrahedron is embedded with electrical systems for lighting and heating, as well as gutters for water run-off, with the whole connected by five-tonne cast-steel nodes. Double-pane insulating glass is fitted onto each facet, with ultraviolet filters to protect artwork, along with tubular aluminium louvres that form a screen to diffuse harsh sunlight into soft illumination.

4.31.1 | **National Gallery of Art Building Committee's visit to marble quarries in Knoxville, Tennessee, 1971. Pei Cobb Freed & Partners**

4.31.2 | **Workers laying out the composition of marble slabs for the East Building's facade, ca.1971. Pei Cobb Freed & Partners**

4.31.1–4.31.2
A design brief that required Pei's addition to the National Gallery of Art to harmonise with John Russell Pope's original building all but mandated the use of identical Tennessee pink marble. Reopening the quarry that supplied the builders of the West Building, Pei elected to use slabs in the same dimensions of 0.6 by 1.5 metres, but as 7-centimetre-thick sheathing on a concrete and brick-wall structure. He did this in order to give the impression of a solid masonry building. Paying careful attention to shape, colour—five gradations were used to mirror the subtle colour shift from the West Building's darker base to its lighter roof—and texture, each piece of stone was strategically positioned within the facade's overall composition before installation. To account for the thermal expansion of the stone, the slabs are individually anchored with stainless-steel plates and the 0.3-centimetre seams between filled with neoprene gaskets, allowing each to float independently in a double-wall construction.

OPPOSITE:
4.32 | **Naho Kubota, coffered concrete ceiling of the Center for Advanced Study in the Visual Arts, 2022. Photo commissioned by M+**

With an emphasis on its moulding process, Pei used architectural concrete at the East Building as a fine finish as much as a structural component. Beyond the bridge and roof, in which the material's strength is fully utilised, it is also employed across the interiors, where concrete surfaces were moulded from Douglas fir formwork that had been precisely crafted to cabinet-making standards. Echoing the rosy hue of the building's cladding, base white cement was mixed with marble dust and then finished with a light acid wash to achieve a smooth, stone-like tone and texture that is complementary yet visually distinct in its monolithic expression.

The East Building of the National Gallery of Art displays a unified range of design concerns, from the urban context to the smallest detail. The trapezoidal site is derived from the diagonal axes of Pierre Charles L'Enfant's 1791 plan for Washington DC. Pei mirrored the diagonal to produce a building made up of triangular figures. The acute triangular geometry informs the gallery spaces, the atrium, the skylights, and the building cores, and manifests itself in the knife-edge prow on the front facade. Like John Russell Pope's West Building, the East Building is clad in Tennessee pink marble, and Pei reveals the thickness of the material at the severe angle of the corner. The knife-edge prow conveys an honest reading of the material and the context of L'Enfant's diagonal, an expression of urban and geometric questions in an architectural detail.

– Eric Höweler

Eric Höweler is principal of Höweler + Yoon and an associate professor at the Harvard Graduate School of Design, where he hastaught courses focusing on contemporary construction and building technologies. He moderated a panel on technology at the 'Rethinking Pei' symposium organised by M+ and the GSD in 2017.

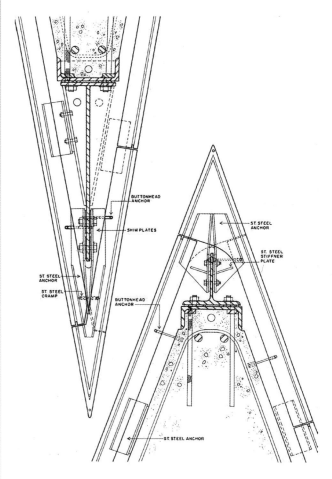

4.33.1 | **Plan detailing steel anchors for the stone cladding on the East Building's corner prows, ca.1973. Pei Cobb Freed & Partners**

OPPOSITE:
4.33.2 | **Naho Kubota, view towards the knife-edge prow at the Center for Advanced Study in the Visual Arts, 2022. Photo commissioned by M+**

4.33.1–4.33.2
Located at the south-west corner of the East Building's Center for Advanced Study in the Visual Arts, the iconic knife-edge prow is defined by its sharp, 19.5-degree angle. To imitate masonry construction, Pei's specifications required that triangular pieces of stone be carved out from behind to articulate the acute angle as if it were a solid block, avoiding joints or bevelled edges. The unconventional form—typically discouraged by stone companies owing to the risk of breakage—was welcomed by the client, whose support convinced industry professionals to realise Pei's vision.

4.34 | **OCBC Centre under construction photographed from six different sites, ca.1974. M+, Hong Kong, Gift of Architects Team 3, 2015**

OCBC's desire for its new headquarters to be built quickly—Singapore's government was awarding significant tax benefits for promptly completed development projects—led Pei to design the building with three stacked units of fifteen floors each, which could be constructed simultaneously in tiers. The fifty-two-storey tower is anchored at either side by two semi-circular concrete cores that house the building's vertical transportation systems. The cores were erected independently with slip-form moulds. Spanning thirty-five metres between the service cores, steel girders were installed on the building's fourth, twentieth, and thirty-fifth floors. Construction of the remaining floors could proceed simultaneously, with each girder transferring its load to the cores.

Oversea-Chinese Banking Corporation (OCBC) Centre (1970–1976)
Singapore

4.35 | **I. M. Pei demonstrating how the tower's tapered form was devised using four triangular-shaped pieces of wood, ca.1982. Pei Cobb Freed & Partners**

The Bank of China Tower's need for structural strength and visual prominence led to a design that tapers as it rises. Pei and his son Sandi generated the design by putting together four triangular wooden sticks with slanted ends to create an obelisk-like form. They then pushed each of the four sticks upwards from the base so that each was higher than the last. This process reminded Pei of the Chinese idiom *jie jie gao sheng*, describing a bamboo trunk that rises higher section by section as a metaphor for taking measured steps in order to excel. Pei and Sandi's concept, which met the need for an imposing banking hall and 130,000 square metres of office space for the bank and its tenants, was translated into buildable reality by engineer Leslie E. Robertson.

MATERIAL & STRUCTURAL INNOVATION

Bank of China Tower (1982–1989)
Hong Kong

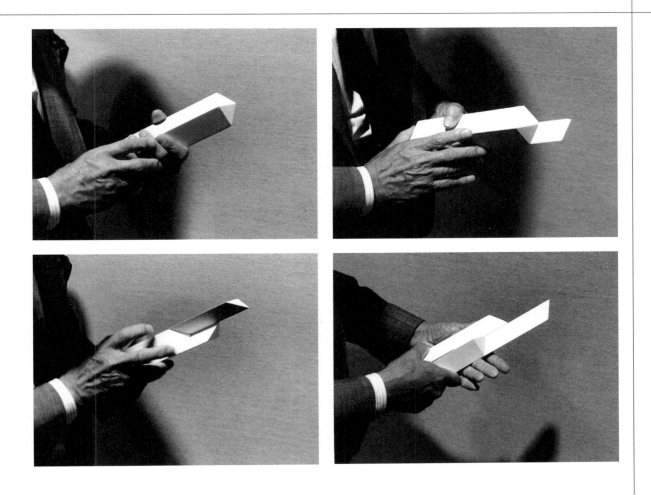

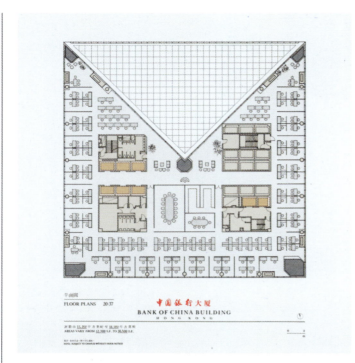

4.36.1 | **Plan of the 20th to 37th floors from a leasing brochure, ca.1988. Sherman Kung & Associates Architects Ltd**

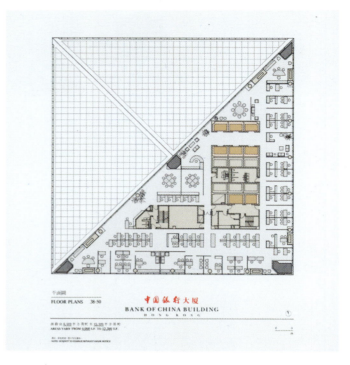

4.36.2 | **Plan of the 38th to 50th floors from a leasing brochure, ca.1988. Sherman Kung & Associates Architects Ltd**

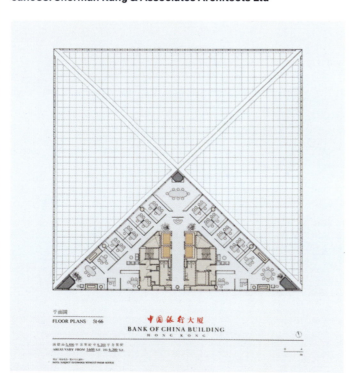

4.36.3 | **Plan of the 51st to 66th floors from a leasing brochure, ca.1988. Sherman Kung & Associates Architects Ltd**

MATERIAL & STRUCTURAL INNOVATION 207

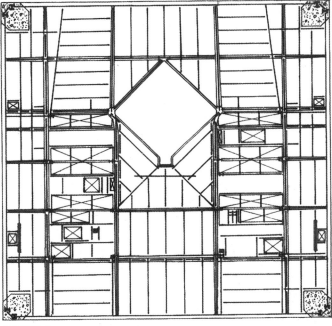

4.37.1 | **Fourth-storey truss plan, ca.1982. Pei Cobb Freed & Partners**

STORY 4

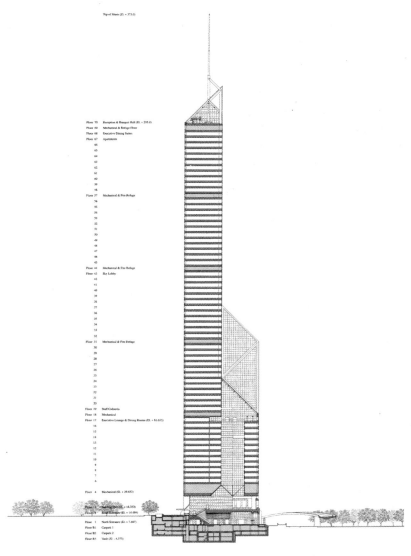

4.36.4 | **Elevation and section of the tower, ca.1982. Pei Cobb Freed & Partners**

4.36.1–4.36.4
The tower's division into four identical triangles, each of a different height, made a single central service core impossible. It also placed the vertical and lateral forces far from the centre of the building's base. Robertson proposed that the lateral force system—which had to meet wind-load requirements twice those of New York and Chicago and earthquake proofing four times that of Los Angeles—be located on the facade through the use of perimeter diagonal bracing, with the diagonals meeting at the building's corners. This led to what Robertson called a 'superframe', a three-dimensional space truss whose members penetrate through the building to unite the vertical planes of the building's four columns through a fifth, central column. Pei's proposal to locate the cross-bracing inside the facade meant that it had to follow the curtain-wall module. The basic module, at 1.333 metres wide, was derived from the minimum width of a Hong Kong office, including false ceiling space to provide flexibility to tenants.

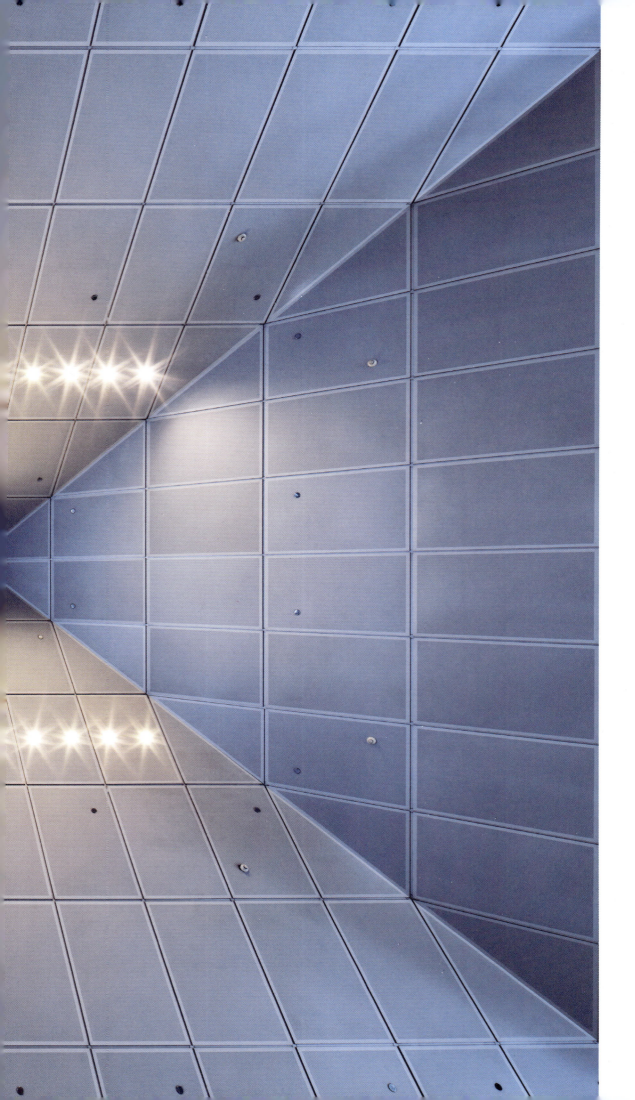

4.37.2 | **South Ho, skylight enclosure as seen from fourth floor, 2021. Photo commissioned by M+**

4.37.1–4.37.2
At the centre of the fourth floor, where the tower meets the granite base of the banking hall, an open square atrium rises fifteen storeys to a skylight enclosure, providing spatial continuity and natural lighting.

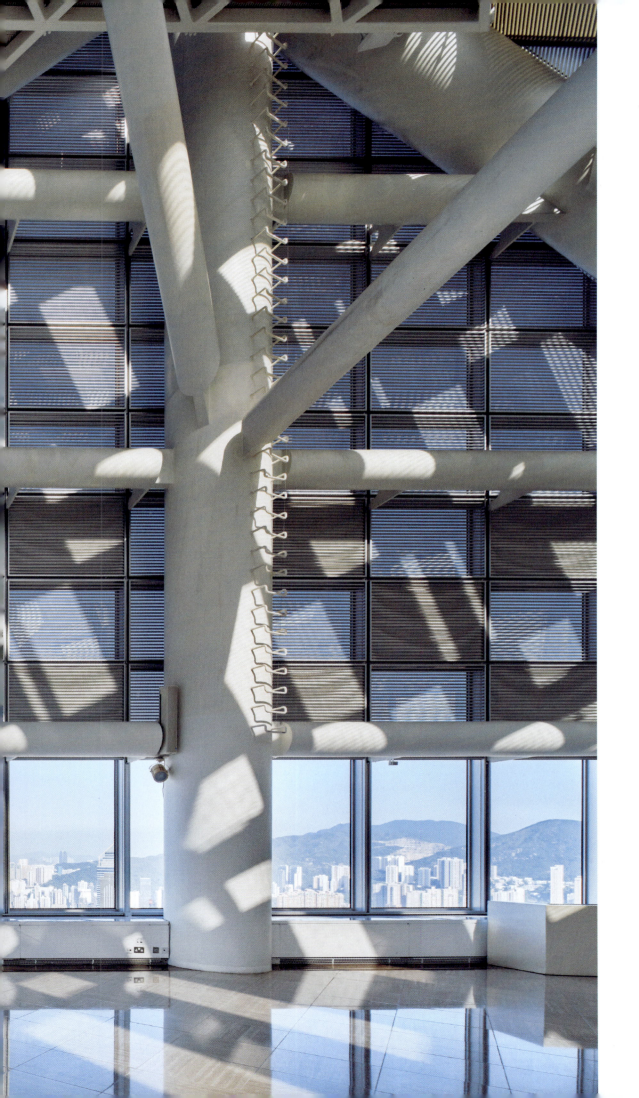

4.38 | **South Ho, seventieth-floor penthouse, 2021. Photo commissioned by M+**

The sloped, screened skylight of the seventieth-floor penthouse lounge offers a vista of the city and Victoria Harbour, framed by the tower's tubular-steel superstructure supporting and bracing two communication antennae, each approximately twelve storeys high.

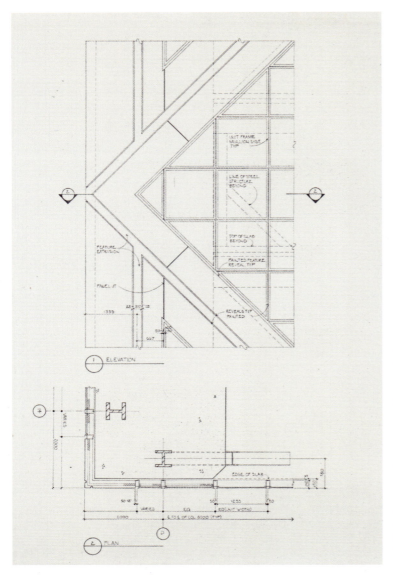

4.39.1 | **I. M. Pei & Partners and Wong/Kung & Lee Associate Architects,** elevation and plan of a typical corner, with curtain wall and column, 1985. Sherman Kung & Associates Architects Ltd

4.39.3 | **John Nye,** construction view of the superstructure and interior fifth column, ca.1987

4.39.2 | **View of construction of a joint for a belt truss,** ca.1985. PEI Architects

OPPOSITE:
4.39.4 | **South Ho,** facade of Bank of China Tower, 2021. Photo commissioned by M+

4.39.1–4.39.4
The tower's space-truss structure consists of flat steel frames bonded at the corners by reinforced concrete. This composite system creates a three-dimensional framework through two-dimensional steel-to-steel connections that eliminate cross-grain tension. This increased structural strength not only halved the amount of steel needed, but also reduced the cost and time of construction. Once construction had begun in 1985, the tower rose at a rate of one floor every four days, with the entire superstructure completed in only sixteen months.

Grand Louvre
Phase I (1983–1989) &
Phase II (1989–1993)
Paris, France

4.40.2 | **Isometric drawing of an early study for the pyramid's steel space frame viewed from within the pyramid, 1986. Pei Cobb Freed & Partners**

4.40.1–4.40.2
For the Grand Louvre, the inherent structural stability of a pyramid emerged as an important starting point as Pei strove to build 'a structure that was as transparent as technology would allow'. With a square base measuring 34.2 metres on each side and reaching 21.6 metres in height, the pyramid is composed of a criss-crossed web of pre-stressed cables and 128 interlocking trusses, aligned diagonally behind the seams of the outer layer's diamond-shaped glass panes. This steel space frame utilises a relationship of tensegrity—simultaneous tension and compression—that ensures the structure's stability while minimising visual obstructions. The pyramid's structural system is enclosed by non-weight-bearing glass that is supported entirely by the steel members.

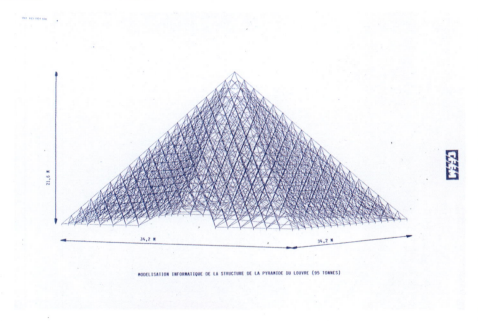

4.40.1 | **Modelling of the Louvre pyramid's steel structure, ca.1986. Pei Cobb Freed & Partners**

MATERIAL & STRUCTURAL INNOVATION 215

4.41.1 | **Half-section drawing of early joint design for the pyramid, ca.1984.
Pei Cobb Freed & Partners**

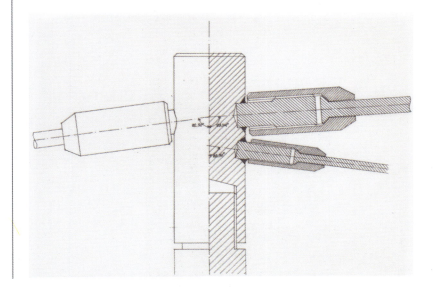

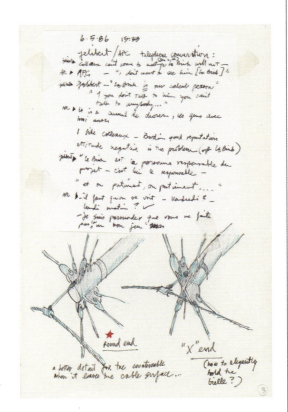

4.41.2 | **Yann Weymouth, sketches of round- and X-end nodes, 1985. Yann Weymouth Collection, Frances Loeb Library, Harvard University Graduate School of Design**

4.41.3 | **Close-up of a node during construction, viewed against the Cour Napoléon, ca.1988.
Pei Cobb Freed & Partners**

4.41.1–4.41.3
Finding that the technology required to develop the Louvre pyramid's tensegrity space frame was not yet available in the building industry, Pei turned to yacht manufacturers to realise what closely resembled a rigging system. Customised joints were produced by Navtec—an American rigging company specialising in racing yachts—to fasten the complex intersections of rods and pre-stressed chords that make up the pyramid's structure. Based on designs by Yann Weymouth, a designer working for Pei, the X-shaped cast-steel nodes were developed to accommodate up to nine chords that converge between diagonal trusses. Each truss was fitted with adjustable parts for fine-tuning. The nodes also attach from behind to the non-structural curtain wall, where lateral stresses are transferred to the steel frame.

4.42.1 | **Mock-up of the glass pyramid using high-iron glass with its characteristic greenish tint, ca.1985. Pei Cobb Freed & Partners**

4.42.2 | **Attachment of glass panels to the pyramid's steel structure, ca.1988. Pei Cobb Freed & Partners**

OPPOSITE:
4.42.3 | **Giovanna Silva, Richelieu wing as viewed from within the glass pyramid, 2021. Photo commissioned by M+**

4.42.1–4.42.3
Wary of the greenish tint characteristic of commercially available glass, Pei insisted on using a completely clear alternative for the Louvre's pyramid. Along with President Mitterrand's intervention, this led France's largest glass manufacturer, Saint-Gobain, to devise an entirely new production process for large-scale manufacturing. Beginning by sourcing pure white sand from Fontainebleau, Saint-Gobain proceeded to develop a specialised furnace that reduces the amount of the naturally occurring iron oxide in the glass formula, eliminating the source of the green hue. The 675 diamond and 118 triangular panes were transported to a factory in the United Kingdom that was able to polish their surfaces to perfect planarity, achieving flawless results with optical properties close to those of crystal.

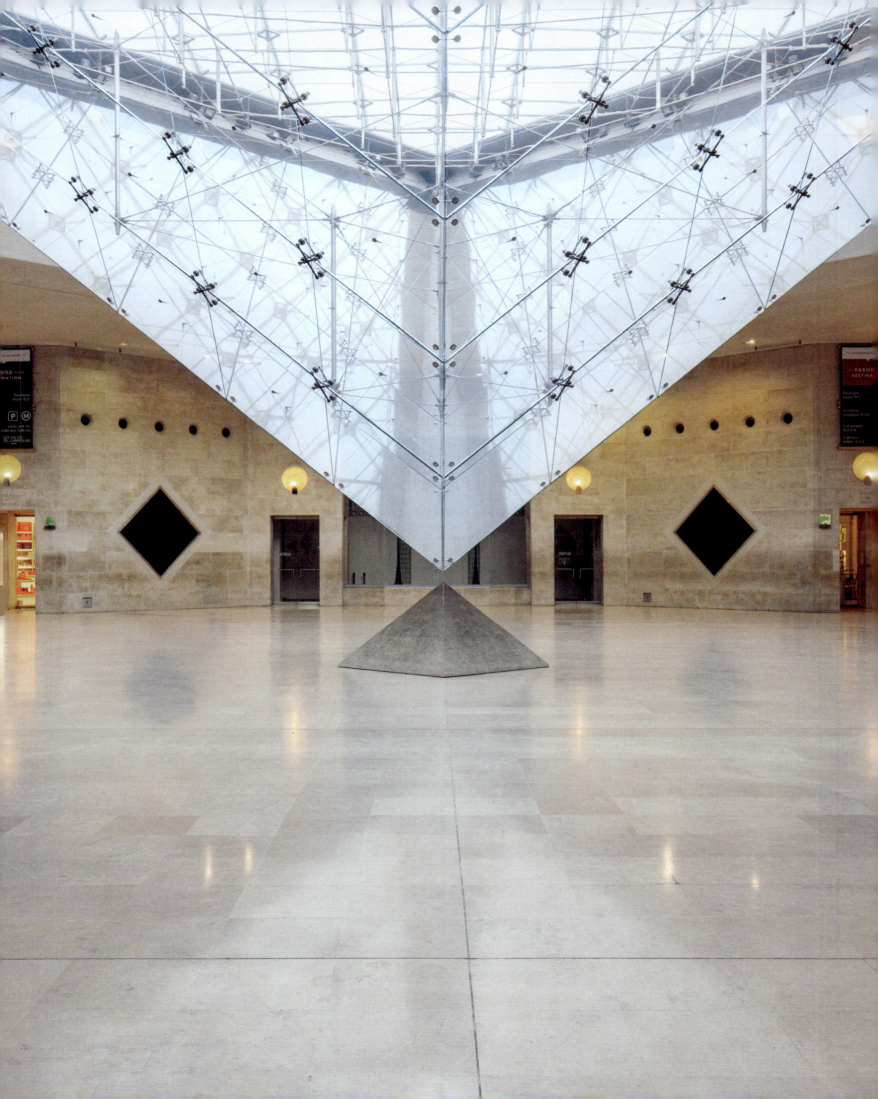

Unlike the main pyramid, which is in a courtyard the size of a football field, the inverted pyramid is in a relatively small stone chamber underground. There is a skylight above it, so I didn't have to worry about joint sealants to keep out the rain, but I did have one significant concern: how do you clean it? The solution was in the configuration of the inverted pyramid and the small pyramidal stone below it. By shifting the stone aside and removing the pyramid's bottom four lights of glass, a worker can step inside and easily clean the inner surfaces, as the pyramid's interior is a void with no cross-cables or other obstructions. The inverted pyramid is like a chandelier. Because its glass has bevelled edges (inspired by the cut glass on the front door of my house), sunlight is refracted in a prism of rainbow colours on the floor and walls. I had considered this for the main pyramid but didn't pursue it because of dimensional considerations: there was a conflict in trying to fit both the bevels and the sealant required for weather protection into the narrow space between the glass edge and the steel frame; it could get messy. But in the inverted pyramid, where weather was not an issue, the joints could be completely open, so I thought to give it a try. In cases that didn't conflict with his design intention, I. M. gave me free rein. It was about trust. In all the years I worked with him, our conversations were few and very short.

– Michael D. Flynn

Michael D. Flynn is one of the world's leading authorities on curtain-wall design and technology and has been responsible for overseeing building enclosures at Pei Cobb Freed & Partners since 1962.

4.43 | **Giovanna Silva, inverted pyramid at the Carrousel du Louvre, 2021. Photo commissioned by M+**

Designed to bring light into the underground passage between the Louvre's entrance and a new subterranean shopping plaza, the geometry of the inverted pyramid is derived from the main pyramid but employs glass as a structural element rather than a non-load-bearing skin. While its structurally independent base acts as the skylight, individual glass panes forming the pyramid's triangular facets are suspended by a web of cables and rods anchored to heavy steel beams that surround the roof opening, eliminating the need for mullions. With all structural components contained within the glass void, the pyramid appears to float.

4.44.1 | **Model showing an early design for the suspension bridge traversing a ravine to reach the Miho Museum's entrance, ca.1991. Papers of I. M. Pei, Library of Congress, Washington DC**

Miho Museum (1991–1997)
Shigaraki, Shiga

MATERIAL & STRUCTURAL INNOVATION　　221

4.44.2 | **Kawasaki Heavy Industry, plan and section of Miho Museum bridge, ca.1991. Shimizu Corporation**

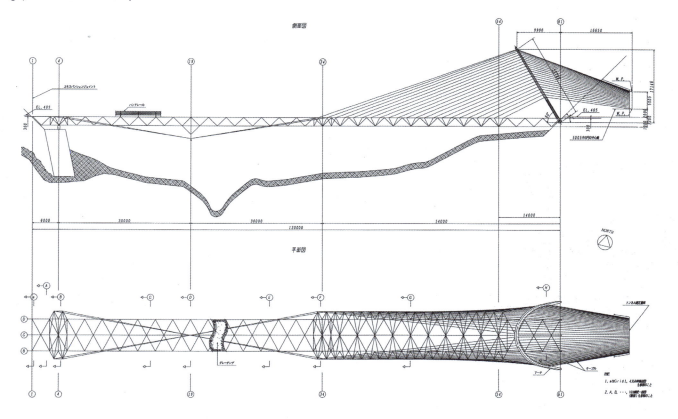

4.44.3 | **Higashide Kiyohiko, Miho Museum bridge cantilevered without vertical supports, ca.1997. Pei Cobb Freed & Partners**

4.44.1–4.44.3
Late in his career, Pei was commissioned by Shinji Shumeikai to design a series of structures that would represent the Japanese religious organisation's promotion of the power of beauty. The Miho Museum is located near a cluster of the group's buildings in the mountains of Shigaraki, to the south-east of Kyoto. A pedestrian bridge spans a 120-metre ravine to arrive at the museum's entrance. Designed with Leslie E. Robertson, the bridge is supported by a total of ninety-six post-tensioned steel cables anchored from the opening of a tunnel to a tilted arch pylon. Following the curvature of the arch, the cables increase in size from base to crown, reaching forty-eight metres in length and sixty millimetres in diameter. The bridge cantilevers without vertical supports, which makes the thin structure appear to float and prevents it from intruding onto the nature preserve below. Visitors step onto the bridge's ceramic-infilled deck—designed to drain water while avoiding soil erosion below—and are engulfed in the splay of cables, which flare towards the museum's grand entrance.

Miho Institute of Aesthetics Chapel (2008–2012)
Shigaraki, Shiga

4.45.1 | **Aslıhan Demirtaş, sequence of photographs showing how the chapel's conical form was devised, ca.2010**

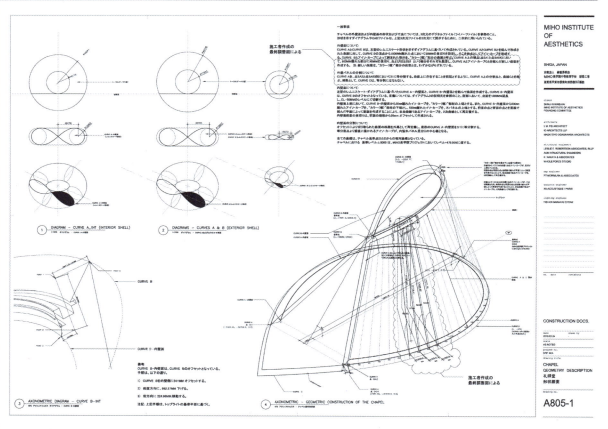

4.45.2 | I. M. Pei Architect and io Architects, diagram of geometrically generated lemniscate curve for the chapel's plan, 2010. io Architects

4.45.1–4.45.2
As part of a larger commission from Shinji Shumeikai to design a campus for religious studies, Pei sought to make the school's chapel its focal point. Beginning with a simple gesture, Pei conceived the shape of the Miho Institute of Aesthetics Chapel by bending a fan-shaped piece of paper to meet at a single point. However, transferring this conical form into a mathematical or structural model proved challenging until project designer Aslıhan Demirtaş was able to generate it geometrically. The teardrop-shaped plan is defined with a lemniscate (infinity) curve, which is achieved by creating a cross-section of a torus tangential to its inner circle. With its variables adjusted to achieve Pei's desired form, the lofted surface connecting two stacked curves produces the chapel's structural concrete shell, while its openings become the chapel's front entrance and skylight.

MATERIAL & STRUCTURAL INNOVATION   223

4.46.1 | **Study model of early chapel design showing a metal-clad interior, ca 2010. io Architects**

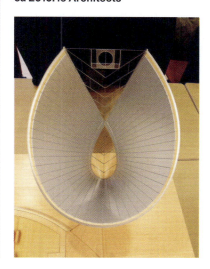

4.46.2 | **Aslıhan Demirtaş, section model of an early study of the chapel, ca.2010**

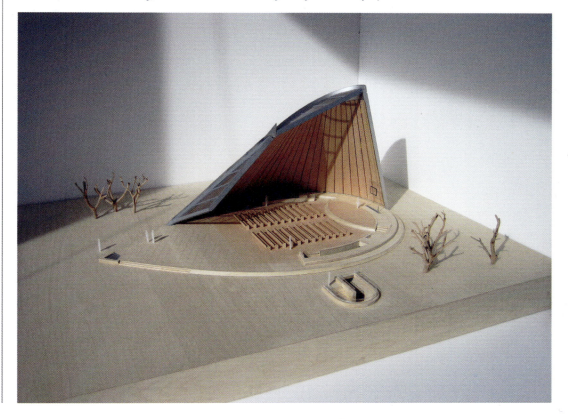

4.46.3 | **Higashide Photo Studio, exterior view of the chapel, ca.2012. io Architects**

4.46.1–4.46.3

Pei's original intention was for the Miho Institute of Aesthetics Chapel to be built entirely in metal, but the insulation and acoustic requirements of a space meant for prayer and congregation necessitated the use of reinforced concrete. To achieve the desired sculptural effect of a wrapped metallic exterior, Pei sheathed the building in fifty-one stainless-steel panels. Crafted with a pressing technique developed expressly for the chapel by Japanese manufacturer Kikukawa, which produces steel panels for Apple shops globally, each of the 18.5-metre trapezoidal panels is custom warped to form the building's complex curved shell. Inside, slats of Yoshino Japanese red cedar wood mask the structural shell, strategically spaced with gaps that increase with height so sound can be absorbed by the concrete, which produces an environment suitable for contemplation.

I. M. Pei and the Tools of Invention

Janet Adams Strong

In 1985, while working on my PhD, I was asked through a friend to write a few short texts for I. M. Pei & Partners. From this casual introduction came an engagement of more than twenty-five years as the firm's full-time writer and editor, historian, documentarist, director of communications, sometime archivist, and curator. Amid busy daily activities and seemingly endless charrettes, I realised that I was not following the traditional architectural historian's route of piecing together the past primary sources but experiencing the making of history from a privileged inside perch. In preparation for writing a monograph on the practice in the 2000s, I studied original documents and conducted scores of interviews with members of the firm, which averaged about two hundred people. I recorded lengthy conversations with the partners and their teams, including architects, planners, resource specialists, technologists, graphic designers, and model makers, as well as engineers and other outside consultants.

Pei was remarkably generous with his time. In numerous unhurried meetings we discussed far-ranging aspects of his architecture, often sharing an insight, some of long-term resonance. On one such occasion I. M. allowed that he was a 'practical dreamer'; he didn't dream things that couldn't be built. Underlying this casual revelation was the storied role of his firm. From the beginning, as the architectural division of Webb & Knapp and then in independent practice as I. M. Pei & Associates (later Partners), and subsequently Pei Cobb Freed & Partners, it was the firm that materialised Pei's dreams. Arguably his greatest creation, it combined the careful artistry of a small atelier with the sophisticated apparatus of a large architectural office dedicated to solving complex urban problems. The quantity, size, and scope of the firm's work was as remarkable in its broad scale as in its widely recognised precision detailing at the other, fine end of the spectrum.

From the outset, Pei was the driving force towards the implicitly understood goal to be 'the best, not the first'.[1] Under his leadership, the firm became a laboratory of creative ferment and technical prowess, always pushing the building industry forward. And because architects tended to stay with Pei for years, many for their entire career, the firm's depth of expertise constantly grew. Indeed, a significant factor in Pei gaining the commission to redesign the Louvre lay in his assurance to French president François Mitterrand that most of his colleagues had been with him for more than three decades.[2]

Pei's approach to design was cultivated during his studies in architectural engineering at the Massachusetts Institute of Technology. For his senior thesis, he investigated the potential of steel, wood, and bamboo for use in portable structures that would circuit the Chinese countryside to bring news and entertainment to refugees from the civil war. In 1941, on a scholarship, Pei zigzagged 13,000 kilometres across the United States to visit manufacturers of cement, Masonite, Celotex, and other prefab materials, all of which he intended to introduce to China.[3] His interest in materials and technology was solidified at the Harvard Graduate School of Design, where Walter Gropius inculcated the tenets of industrialisation that he had developed at the Bauhaus, as well as a commitment to collaboration.

By the time Pei graduated from Harvard, the underpinnings of his architecture were firmly in place: an interest in concrete, the embrace of research and technology, collaborative practice, working directly with industry, and the pursuit of excellence in both design and execution. Stylistically, it was perhaps Le Corbusier and his world of sculptural possibilities that left the strongest mark. Also influential were Pei's friend Marcel Breuer, who taught architecture as a reflection of life; Frank Lloyd Wright's embrace of rich building materials and balance with nature; and Mies van der Rohe's commitment to precision detailing and an economy of means. As Pei later recalled, these influences were 'very foreign to those of us brought up on Beaux-Arts symmetry. It was like walking into a candy store: which one to buy? In the end, you buy them all and make something out of it that is your own.'[4] Pei's personal amalgam was notable for advancing technology, whereas his forbears used technology but did not push it forward. He also respected history when architects typically eschewed it. Both qualities were foundational in his work.

In 1948, two years after graduation, Pei was engaged as an 'ideas man' by William Zeckendorf, the big-thinking New York developer at the real-estate corporation of Webb & Knapp. Pei hired former students from classes he had taught at Harvard and gradually brought in other Bauhaus-trained designers from Yale University and Black Mountain College, and then from elsewhere. In what was effectively a continuation of graduate school, he created a close-knit community—more a lifestyle than a job—with a culture of sophistication and mutual respect. This was unusual at a time when most architectural practices were rigorously hierarchical. Pei was among the first architects to incorporate an in-house planning department. Projects were viewed within their larger context, with considerations given to how they would relate to the neighbourhood and be seen from afar, and to how people would move around and within them. Pei included full-time graphic designers on staff, another innovation. As a result, street furniture, signage, and wayfinding evolved with the architecture, rather than being added at the end. The office was also exceptional in its inclusion of interior specialists with deep resourcing expertise, and in having its own fully fledged model shop.

Perhaps most remarkable, however, was the seamless integration of staff. At Webb & Knapp and subsequently as an independent firm, the office was not so much a collection of different departments as a group of different teams with diverse, complementary skills. Each team started small and grew as needed until a project's drawings went out for construction. Importantly, the teams stayed together, ensuring there was follow-through from start to finish, rather than a passing of projects from one department to the next. If not the most efficient operation from the perspective of management and profitability, the method was a profound investment in the firm, as it allowed team members to experience the entirety of the architectural process. Implicit in the organisation was the secondary role of business to the primacy of design.

Pei's first few years with Webb & Knapp were mostly spent on large-scale planning projects and designs that remained unexecuted. This changed in the late 1950s, when Zeckendorf took advantage of post-war government subsidies and became the unchallenged leader of urban renewal in the United States. As Pei knew nothing about public housing, Zeckendorf directed him to learn. In a way that seems unimaginable—developers typically being loath to accept the idea of eventual profitability—Zeckendorf gave Pei the time and the resources to explore.

Standard 1950s housing projects were brick with punched windows. Zeckendorf owned such properties and anticipated the same for Kips Bay Plaza in New York. But Pei convinced him that the practice of building a structural frame and then covering it in brick was extravagant when compared with the economical one-step process of pouring concrete into a form. Once hardened, the form would be removed to reveal the finished building in which structure, fireproofing, window framing, and facade were combined in an honest whole of such quality that no exterior cladding or interior finishes were required. Le Corbusier and others had made assets of the dark grey colour and rough texture of *béton brut*. Pei's vision, in contrast, called for the transformation of raw concrete into a building material more akin in colour and quality to limestone. The problem was that no one had experience with this new material; technology and process alike had to be invented. Pei therefore turned his office into a research and development centre. He was undermined by Zeckendorf's associates at Webb & Knapp, more traditional developers who wanted only formulaic, reliably profitable housing and were uninterested in innovative architecture. Risk-averse construction contractors were also opposed to Pei's explorations. Asked for estimates, two major builders conspired in projecting USD18–19 per square foot, roughly twice the prevailing rate for low-cost housing. The inflated price quashed any hope of construction—until Zeckendorf gamely purchased a concrete company.

In the end, Kips Bay cost only slightly more to build than standard housing projects. It showed that low-income housing and public space could be created at a competitive price, and that urban renewal could achieve distinction through thoughtful design. Instead of the six identical buildings originally envisioned, Pei consolidated 1,120 apartments in two twenty-one-storey slabs, leaving open more than half of the 40,000-square-metre site as a park. In marked contrast to the dense accretion of unrelated buildings on surrounding streets, Kips Bay presented a cohesive planned environment. Now, sixty years later, it remains a prized New York address. Pei built his firm on the success of Kips Bay. It inspired six other large-scale housing projects, each designed for a particular site and programme,[5] and informed dozens of corporate, institutional, and civic buildings, most heroically Dallas City Hall, a colossus of three-way post-tensioned architectural concrete completed in 1977.

In 1968, when Pei received the commission for the National Gallery of Art East Building, Paul Mellon, the museum's benefactor, insisted on using the same Tennessee pink marble that his father had chosen for the existing museum, built in 1941. Pei thus restricted architectural concrete to strategic tensile elements, such as long-span exterior lintels and interior bridges, headers, and ceiling coffers. All of the concrete was carefully blended to complement the colour of the masonry walls—but not to match it exactly, so that the two materials would retain their integrity and individual identities. Never before had Pei been able to so completely apply his firm's mastery of architectural concrete. It was in the East Building, and later at the Louvre, that he came closest to realising the material's potential as liquid limestone.

In the late 1950s, concrete essentially consisted of aggregate (sand, gravel, or crushed rock), water, and cement, the binding agent. It was the least predictable of building materials because, unlike brick or metal and glass curtain walls, which are produced in factory-controlled conditions, concrete was produced on-site, with raw materials, by local labour, according to loosely defined standards. Structural-concrete workers had no experience with the high-quality results Pei desired, so his office conducted its own research and trial-and-error testing. With ready help from the industry, it investigated various mixes, colours, and material sources before discovering that Saylor cement, through specialised firing, could produce a warm light-beige alternative to the cold grey-green typical of structural concrete. Pei encouraged its commercial production. The firm tested various sand and aggregate blends for colour consistency, different setting times, pouring and vibrating techniques, air entrainment, and surface treatments. They studied cracking, ageing, the effects of weather, pollution and mould, erosion, spalling, shrinkage, and 'creep', all to achieve enduring quality. Expansion and pour joints received special attention to ensure Pei's sculptural vision of the monumental whole.

Experimentation continued with different formwork materials and methods of assembly to prevent leakage and discoloration; mistakes in exposed architectural concrete are almost impossible to hide. The office developed gasketing, clamping, and bracing systems; easy-release techniques so the forms could be reused; and new ways to protect corners and crisp edges. Team members visited an automobile manufacturer in Michigan to learn about fibreglass coatings and applied that knowledge to prevent wood graining from telescoping onto the concrete walls of Kips Bay Plaza. Such reconnaissance typified Pei's informed approach to design. Rather than simply meeting with sales representatives in the office, team members engaged the industry on its own turf, visiting factories, speaking to the people involved in production, and learning industry problems and limitations to better understand what could be achieved architecturally. For Kips Bay, Pei ultimately hired a cabinet-maker to fabricate the wooden forms, like fine furniture. He was perhaps the first architect to provide specifications in working drawings for construction formwork.

Beyond such labour-intensive explorations were significant issues of documentation and oversight, of translating design intent into drawings for construction and the creation of essential specifications that did not previously exist. Multiple discrete but fundamentally related operations were involved. The quality of materials was critical, but even more important was the process, which had to be developed step by step. Paramount was Pei's insistence on a full-scale mock-up in which the typical and most difficult conditions could be tested. Owners and contractors balked at the expense, but this dress-rehearsal allowed problems to be discovered and resolved before the actual building was begun.

In time, Pei's firm came to know more about concrete than many other firms, occasionally to the consternation of contractors. Some refused to work with the firm, deterred by its exacting standards. More often, however, they benefitted from the challenge. For significant buildings like the National Gallery of Art and the Louvre, work crews were invited to view building models and hear the architects explain design intent. Offered this level of involvement, labourers invariably delivered their best work, sometimes exceeding expectations.

Pei's innate technical abilities and geometrical design strategies informed virtually everything his firm did. He set the tone, and like-minded architects followed. He understood that the continuity of senior staff was a major attribute and inspired loyalty with respect and trust, allowing architects the freedom to follow their inclinations to arrive at a result that was consistent with his vision. Charming and diplomatic, Pei was extremely adept at securing new work, which enabled the firm's expansion and ever-deepening expertise in supporting the kind of difficult, high-profile projects he attracted.

A full complement of technical resources—which became tools of invention—distinguished the firm from all others. A few of them are listed below.

The Cement Collection
While developing architectural concrete, the office built a collection of raw materials from across the United States so that, for each new building, concrete colours and costs could be reliably determined. Shipping was expensive so it was important to know the location of raw materials relative to a building site. In the 1960s and 1970s, the collection contained samples from every cement-producing plant, every sand deposit, every crushed stone quarry, and every natural stone deposit in the country (see 4.27, page 195). In later years, technological advances, new production methods, and overnight delivery of material samples made the in-house collection less critical. In addition, after the completion of the National Gallery of Art East Building, Pei began designing in other materials, in large part because the extreme refinement of architectural concrete effectively priced it out of the market.

An I. M. Pei & Associates staff member relates to the human scale of a 1.5-storey mock-up for Kips Bay Plaza, ca.1958. Pei Cobb Freed & Partners

Partial view of the stone library with samples, ca.1980s. Pei Cobb Freed & Partners

The Stone Library

Pei's office assembled the largest collection of stone samples in the United States, perhaps in the world. In 2012, the library housed around nine thousand pieces—mostly twelve-by-twelve-inch panels. Samples were organised by type, size, name, colour, and finish, and titled and stored on industrial shelving, like books in a library. Each sample was assigned a unique accession number and codified in a master log with the stone's specifics, including official and generic names, fabricator, distributor, agent, colour, finish, size, date acquired, and which of the firm's buildings, if any, had incorporated the stone. A special display area showcased unique, especially beautiful, or otherwise noteworthy samples together with dimensional stone and corner elements.

Like browsing in a bookshop, perusing the stone library invited ideas that might not otherwise come to mind and enabled the firm to benefit from decades of past research. It was a place where comparisons could be made, practical matters calculated, and palettes assembled—an open forum where architects could learn about subjects that had not formed part of their training, such as the appropriateness of different materials for horizontal, vertical, or wearing surfaces, and differences in hardness, durability, and water absorption. The library was also a resource for clients, who could see and feel a range of material possibilities and thus clearly identify what they did or did not like. The stone library brought design issues into sharp focus and was a major resource for the firm's approach to design. Sadly, it was destroyed during Hurricane Sandy in 2012.

The Model Shop

From its earliest days, the firm distinguished itself by having its own model shop. A full complement of twelve to fifteen skilled technicians produced the large table models that Zeckendorf used to sell his ideas, including not just a single building or group of buildings but multiple city blocks or entire districts. It was all part of the larger vision that Pei developed at Webb & Knapp and carried forward. When he left for independent practice, he took the model shop with him. Staffed by perfectionists with different specialisations, the shop purchased only raw materials, nothing readymade, using durable plastics and metals to create buildings, people, light fixtures, water textures, and different kinds of trees. It experimented with paints and adhesives, created its own mixes, and developed tools not commercially available, using photo etching—a distant predecessor of laser cutting—to achieve an especially fine level of detail. In a way that far surpassed the capabilities of other offices, the shop milled its own machinery to more accurately create buildings in miniature. The head model maker credited Pei with keeping up morale and inspiring the shop's unwavering quality, stating simply, 'I. M. liked precision.'[6]

One of Pei's greatest strengths was his ability to identify the talents of each member of staff and then challenge them to do their best. He put enormous trust in young people, and they often rose to the occasion, developing great expertise on the job. Some grew beyond the firm to achieve international prominence. For example, Michael D. Flynn, a young architect and urban designer, learned about metals while working on the Federal Aviation Administration Air Traffic Control Towers project; he went on to become the firm's technology partner and one of the world's leading experts on curtain walls. Reginald D. Hough built the firm's cement collection as a junior architect and later became an international authority on architectural concrete. Others became respected experts on metals, glass, hardware, and stone, or specialists in such exacting fields as elevator cores.

Over four decades, from the beginning of Pei's career at Webb & Knapp in 1948 until his retirement from Pei Cobb Freed & Partners in 1990, some 2,300 people worked in his firm. Many went on to share their knowledge of architecture, design, and planning in different parts of the world. All left having experienced an unflagging commitment to architectural excellence, an exceptionally informed approach to design, a truly collaborative culture based on mutual respect, and—likely never to be encountered again—ready access to the tremendous in-house expertise and tools of invention that made I. M. Pei & Partners unique.

Model shop of I. M. Pei & Partners, ca.1980s. Pei Cobb Freed & Partners

Bob Adelman, I. M. Pei (second from right) constructing a model of Fragrant Hill Hotel with the model making team, 1979. Bob Adelman Estate

Power, Politics & Patronage

5

'I had a client from beginning to end'

PAGE 228:
Eddie Hausner, Pei with Jacqueline Kennedy and Robert Kennedy at a press conference announcing Pei's selection as architect for the John Fitzgerald Kennedy Presidential Library, 14 December 1964. New York Times

Pei's selection to design the John F. Kennedy Presidential Library—in an announcement that made headlines across the United States—brought a great deal of prestige to his newly established independent practice. Yet the project proved to be a difficult one, dragging on for fifteen years through multiple changes in site and design, unexpected shifts in politics, and disruptions to the relationship with the client.

The year 1989 was such a prolific one for Pei that *New York Times* architecture critic Paul Goldberger anointed it the 'year of I. M. Pei'.[1] Completing the Grand Louvre in Paris would have been enough. That same year, however, Pei also completed the Bank of China Tower in Hong Kong, the Morton H. Meyerson Symphony Center in Dallas, and a new headquarters for the Creative Artists Agency in Beverly Hills. Once again, Pei had demonstrated his finesse in working with clients across politics, culture, finance, and entertainment to become an architect whose influence spanned the globe.

By then seventy-two years old, Pei had built his success and stature over decades. As early as 1976, a cartoon by Al Hirschfeld, also in the *New York Times*, placed the architect within a popular culture pantheon that included musician Stevie Wonder, dancer Mikhail Baryshnikov, and actor Robert Redford. Pei had become something of a household name, a figure who circulated among the American and global elite in a way that cannot be separated from his architecture.

Throughout his career, only the masterfulness of Pei's buildings was remarked upon more than his affability and gifts of persuasion. Pei was a charmer. His talent and charisma, combined with his patrician background and pedigreed education, gave him near-immediate entrée into the upper echelons of American society, despite being an immigrant facing the prejudices of his era. When Jacqueline Kennedy chose a then relatively unknown Pei to design the John F. Kennedy Presidential Library and Museum—over the far more established Mies van der Rohe, Louis Kahn, John Carl Warnecke, and others—it was because, she later recalled, 'I marshaled all these rational reasons to pick I. M., but it was really an emotional decision. He was so full of promise, like Jack; they were born in the same year. I decided it would be fun to take a great leap with him.'[2]

For Pei, architecture was an art, although one manifested through not just forms and volumes but also negotiation. In the same way that he saw his physical spaces as being simultaneously social, civic, and urban ones, his buildings were realised through personal dynamics, especially with his clients. Starting with his success at convincing a marble company to sponsor his first built project, the Gulf Oil office building, completed in 1952, Pei's ability to coax and persuade was legendary. 'It's a mutual challenge,' he said. 'I challenge the client, of course. You have to. But they challenge me … If I count all the projects I have a fondness for, behind them are great clients.'[3]

Indeed, as an architect, Pei was not of the tormented artist genre, and neither did he play the infallible genius. This, along with his relative disengagement with academia (unlike many of his peers who were active in teaching and publishing), led some architects and others to think that Pei had little design or theoretical influence.[4] And yet the commissions to remake institutions and cities kept coming his way, fuelled by both his architectural abilities and his knack for earning clients' trust as a collaborator sensitive to their needs. As journalist Michael Cannell notes in his unofficial biography of Pei, the architect inspired 'in [his clients] a collaborative pursuit of something finer and more ambitious than was originally imagined, no matter the cost'.[5]

Walter Orr Roberts, founding director of the National Center for Atmospheric Research and one of Pei's earliest patrons, granted the architect his first large commission outside the urban context. Roberts was impressed by Pei's willingness to work closely with him and the centre's scientists to develop a unique laboratory environment. More broadly, Pei's comfort with power was inextricable from his understanding of architecture's relationship with it. In addition to the Kennedys, he skilfully cultivated relationships with such clients as the mayor of a then booming Dallas (for the commission to design a new Dallas City Hall), the philanthropist Paul Mellon and museum director J. Carter Brown (the National Gallery of Art East Building in Washington DC), French president François Mitterrand (the Grand Louvre)—and later, Singapore developer Tao Shing Pee (Gateway), Hong Kong–based investor Yang Yuan-loong and the Chinese government (Fragrant Hill Hotel), and Sheikh Hamad bin Khalifa Al-Thani of Qatar (Museum of Islamic Art), as these regions rose in global prominence. Pei later reminisced, 'What I enjoy the most is recalling the process of overcoming the difficulties, all the problems I had to face, and all the help I got from various people, especially from project collaborators and my clients.'[6]

Pei's high-flying commissions invited a high level of scrutiny and, sometimes, controversy. The more-than-a-decade-long public dispute over the location of the John F. Kennedy Presidential Library and Museum, which required numerous redesigns on multiple sites, left Pei so disheartened that, with unusual candour, he eventually admitted he was fed up and turned his attentions elsewhere. 'The whole project was for me tragic,' he said. 'It could have been so great.'[7] In 1972, the glass windows fell out of the newly built John Hancock Tower, designed by Pei's partner Henry N. Cobb, bringing major disrepute to Pei's office. Of course, the controversies surrounding the library and the tower would later pale in comparison to the uproar in France around the plans to revamp the hallowed ground of the Louvre—and by a Chinese American corporate architect, no less.

In 1990, Pei announced his retirement, yet he continued to work. A request from Koyama Mihoko, founder of the Japanese religious organisation Shinji Shumeikai, proved too difficult to resist. When Koyama came to New York expressly to ask Pei to design a bell tower for the group's compound outside Kyoto, he dismissed the job as being too small, but agreed to visit the site the following year. Mesmerised by what he saw on that trip, he agreed to the commission, which led to him also designing for Koyama the Miho Museum and the Miho Institute of Aesthetics Chapel. These would be his final projects, fitting capstones to an all-encompassing, career-long engagement with clients and patrons who had a willingness to accompany the architect on his journey of developing the design. 'I had a client from beginning to end,' Pei said.[8]

— Aric Chen

5.1 | **Naho Kubota, NCAR complex on the mesa, 2021. Photo commissioned by M+**

After more than fifty years, the imposing presence of the Mesa Laboratory, as it is called by NCAR's community, continues to hold its own against the massive rock formations known as the Flatirons. As Pei once said: 'The shapes [of NCAR] have been cribbed time and again. But the spirit of the NCAR building is in the context, in the site. That you cannot copy.'

5.2 | **Walter Orr Roberts and I. M. Pei at the dedication of the building, 11 May 1967. University Corporation for Atmospheric Research**

As an architect who had never designed large-scale projects outside an urban setting, Pei was not an obvious choice for the NCAR commission. But founding director Walter Orr Roberts considered his lack of experience with this kind of site an advantage, something that would allow him to immerse himself in the project. Pei was also chosen for his reputation of working well with clients and dealing with tight budget constraints, especially in the use of structural concrete.

National Center for Atmospheric Research (NCAR) (1961–1967)
Boulder, Colorado

5.3 | **Topographic site plan, 1967. Pei Cobb Freed & Partners**

NCAR's design resulted from a close collaboration between Pei, Roberts, and a group of scientists who had a clear idea for a workplace that could facilitate both research and theoretical contemplation on atmospheric science. The clustering of scientists into smaller groups and settings, as well as the complex floor plan—which provided flexible outdoor areas, a mix of private and semi-private spaces, and spaces for meetings—emerged from Pei's understanding of the staff's desire for spontaneous encounters.

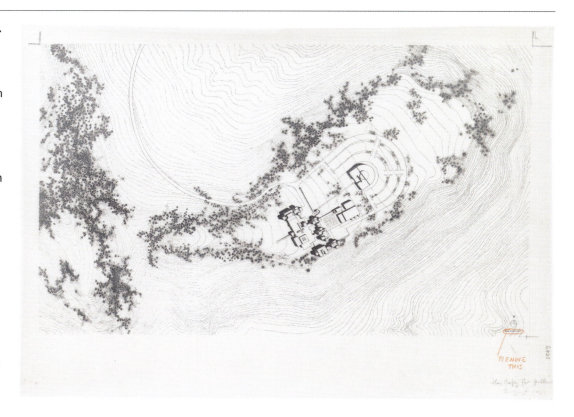

5.4 | **Aerial view of the road leading to the NCAR complex during its construction, 1964. University Corporation for Atmospheric Research**

Working in collaboration with landscape architect Dan Kiley, Pei designed NCAR's access road as a gently curving path through the surrounding meadowland, creating views of the mountains between trees before the NCAR complex finally presents itself. He described the effect as a sense of 'conquering the top of the mesa'.

5.5 | **Naho Kubota, interior view of a 'crow's nest' balcony, 2021. Photo commissioned by M+**

Pei designed more than thirty balconies of various sizes for public areas and offices. The most peculiar form part of the six 'crow's nests'—temporary retreats rather than permanently assigned offices— and are accessible only from a spiral staircase on the floor below or from an outdoor ramp. The narrow balconies are offset by the large windows framing the surrounding mountains and evergreen mesa. In response to the harsh sun and wind on the mesa, Pei designed the majority of the NCAR complex to be windowless, and these apertures make the crow's nest spaces stand out.

John F. Kennedy Presidential Library and Museum (1964–1979)
Dorchester, Massachusetts

5.6 | **Voting tally showing consulting architects' nominations for commission candidates, 1964. William Walton Personal Papers, John F. Kennedy Presidential Library and Museum**

5.7.1 | **Model showing a revised version of Pei's initial 1965 scheme featuring circular masses that occupy the bulk of the site, 1970. I. M. Pei Papers, Library of Congress, Washington DC**

After the death of John F. Kennedy, his widow, Jacqueline Kennedy, and brother Robert Kennedy began the search for an architect to design his presidential library, which would be combined with a museum, archive, and school for politics. Aiding their search was William Walton, chairman of the United States Commission of Fine Arts, who invited eighteen of the world's leading architects to consult and advise. From the tally of the architects' own nominations, Pei—at that time relatively less established than his peers—prevailed as one of the shortlisted candidates. An ability to work well with the family was a priority alongside professional qualifications, and it was the immediate rapport between Jacqueline Kennedy and Pei, in addition to the potential he exhibited, that made a deep impression on the clients.

POWER, POLITICS & PATRONAGE   241

5.7.2 | **Model of the first publicised scheme, which features a semi-circular building and a pyramid-shaped glass atrium, 1973. I. M. Pei Papers, Library of Congress, Washington DC**

5.7.3 | **Model of revised scheme, reduced in size, with the museum and archives separated from the school in two triangular masses, 1974. I. M. Pei Papers, Library of Congress, Washington DC**

5.7.4 | **Model of revised scheme featuring a long horizontal building to house the Kennedy archives, 1975. I. M. Pei Papers, Library of Congress, Washington DC**

5.7.1–5.7.4
It was President Kennedy's hope that his presidential library would be erected near Harvard University, his alma mater, on a site then occupied by a depot belonging to the Massachusetts Bay Transportation Authority. The weight of his legacy won his family the five-hectare plot, which sat on the north bank of the Charles River in Cambridge, Massachusetts. These models document the transformation of Pei's scheme on this site between 1970 and 1975. First envisioned as a set of semi-circular masses occupying almost the entire site, the project was gradually scaled down over multiple revisions to a narrow orthogonal brick structure buffered by green space. The museum portion was eliminated in this configuration and relocated off-site amid locals' growing reluctance towards having a crowd-attracting monument in their small community. After 1968, the assassination of Robert Kennedy and the remarriage of Jacqueline Kennedy left Pei without a public champion and vulnerable to public pressure. The project was ultimately moved twelve kilometres away from Cambridge, to Dorchester, with a site secured after more than a decade of planning.

5.8 | Ada Louise Huxtable, 'What's a Tourist Attraction Like the Kennedy Library Doing in a Nice Neighborhood Like This?', *New York Times*, 16 June 1974. I. M. Pei Papers, Library of Congress, Washington DC

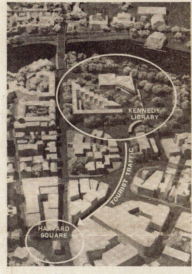

Pei's monumental proposals for the library faced vicious opposition from the Cambridge community. Local residents were quick to criticise each iteration for its massive scale and stark modernity, which they saw as fundamentally out of step with the historic neighbourhood. Locals also feared that the influx of tourists attracted by the new institution would detrimentally affect the urban environment. Spurred on by the formation of civic groups to voice resistance, government-implemented zoning and design reviews played a large part in delaying, and eventually averting, the project's realisation near Harvard Square. The lengthy debate captured the attention of *New York Times* architectural critic Ada Louise Huxtable.

5.9 | Bob Dean, aerial view of the presidential library (top left) on an isolated site adjacent to the University of Massachusetts Boston and a housing estate, 1982. *The Boston Globe* via Getty Images

The drawn-out process of planning the Kennedy presidential library for its original site had all but compromised the original concept and architectural expression of Pei's vision. While a new site offered by the University of Massachusetts Boston presented a blank slate, Pei was unhappy with the decision on the part of the client, the Kennedy Library Corporation, to relocate the project to Columbia Point in Dorchester, where clusters of low-income housing and disused landfills contrasted with well-heeled Cambridge. On the other hand, Jacqueline Kennedy Onassis, as she was now known, embraced the four-hectare lot overlooking Boston Harbor because it paid homage to President Kennedy's love of the ocean. In collaboration with Design Architect Theodore Musho, Pei conceived a sculptural composition combining a circle, triangle, and square, raised four and a half metres above ground level to make the most of the vast waters and open skies.

POWER, POLITICS & PATRONAGE 243

5.10.1 | **Mona Zamdmer, thirty-three-metre-high space frame glass atrium, ca.1979. Pei Cobb Freed & Partners**

5.10.2 | **Thorney Lieberman, nine-storey triangular tower and glass pavilion structure facing Dorchester Bay, ca.1979. Pei Cobb Freed & Partners**

5.10.1–5.10.2
After fifteen years of controversy and changes in programme, the building opened as an effective repository, museum, and memorial. A thirty-three-metre-high space-frame glass pavilion—contiguous to a nine-storey precast concrete tower housing the library—opens to the sky and Dorchester Bay, inviting contemplation for visitors as they emerge from the darkened exhibition space below ground.

PAGES 244–245:

5.11.1 | **Naho Kubota, view of Dallas City Hall from the front of the building, 2021. Photo commissioned by M+**

5.11.2 | **Model of Dallas City Hall and surrounding buildings with the adjoining public plaza to the north and the unrealised extension to the south, ca.1967. Pei Cobb Freed & Partners**

Dallas City Hall (1966–1977)
Dallas

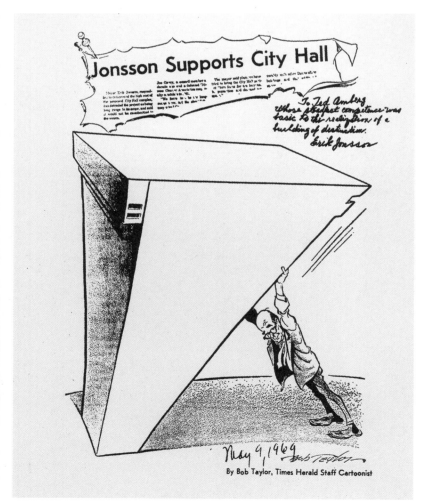

5.11.3 | **Bob Taylor, 'Jonsson Supports City Hall',** *Dallas Times Herald*, **9 May 1969. Pei Cobb Freed & Partners**

5.11.1–5.11.3
Pei's inverted-pyramid design for Dallas City Hall embodies the forward-thinking spirit behind interim mayor Erik Jonsson's master plan to reinvent the city's image following the assassination of President John F. Kennedy in 1963. Jonsson raised the possibility of Pei designing the building when the two men first met at the opening of the Center for Earth Sciences at the Massachusetts Institute of Technology, a project that had been sponsored by Cecil Green, co-founder, along with Jonsson, of Texas Instruments. Pei earned the commission with a design informed by a thorough environmental study, which came to include, in addition to the main building, an adjoining public plaza and plans for future expansion. Despite their reluctance, Pei pressed city leaders to purchase adjacent lots for his plan, securing a 2.4-hectare lot in front of the site. The project languished well beyond Jonsson's term owing to high construction costs, coming to completion only through an innovative bond offering and the addition of a revenue-generating underground car park below the public plaza.

POWER, POLITICS & PATRONAGE   247

5.12.1 | **Robert Lautman, interior atrium of Dallas City Hall, ca.1977. National Building Museum**

5.13 | **A scene from *RoboCop* (1987) by Paul Verhoeven, featuring Dallas City Hall altered by special effects, 93:51. MGM**

Director Paul Verhoeven created Dallas City Hall's evil doppelganger for his dystopian science-fiction film *RoboCop* (1987). Pei developed the geometric form of the city hall as part of a project to ennoble public service in a city with progressive aspirations. In Verhoeven's bleak vision, Pei's concrete-and-glass structure has been enveloped by the headquarters of Omni Consumer Products, an unscrupulous private conglomerate presiding over a fictional Detroit's demise. Notably, the *RoboCop* production designers reworked Pei's horizontal building, with its sharp geometry, as a looming monolith.

5.12.2 | Naho Kubota, Dallas City Hall and the adjoining public plaza, 2021. Photo commissioned by M+

5.12.1–5.12.2
Having been given a 2.8-hectare lot in a dilapidated area just south of the city's growing central district, Pei was careful to consider the broader urban positioning of Dallas City Hall to create an environment fit for a significant civic space. His scheme transformed an adjacent lot into a plaza with a park—the first public space in the heart of the city—to enforce a spatial buffer between the impressive municipal building and surrounding run-down structures. The plaza even featured a Henry Moore sculpture and indigenous trees. The city hall itself, a top-heavy, exposed-concrete form that slopes outward at a thirty-four-degree angle, is at once monolithic and welcoming. The dramatic overhang acts as a civic-scale front porch, while the interior plan concentrates public services on the ground floor for easy access.

5.14 | **Al Hirschfeld, 'Major Cultural Figures',** *New York Times,* **26 December 1976. Al Hirschfeld Foundation**

With high-profile commissions underway in the late 1970s, Pei joined the pantheon of cultural figures of the period in this illustration by Al Hirschfeld. The inclusion of Pei's caricature alongside those of Stevie Wonder, Mikhail Baryshnikov, Robert Redford, and other luminaries suggests that the architect had achieved household-name status, at least among readers of the *New York Times.* Although clearly meant to celebrate diverse figures in American life, Hirschfeld's drawings also rely on well-worn racial stereotypes.

National Gallery of Art East Building (1968–1978)
Washington DC

5.15 | **Robert Lautman, aerial view of the National Gallery of Art East and West buildings, where Pennsylvania Avenue meets the National Mall, ca.1978. National Building Museum**

For Pei, the National Gallery of Art's location on the National Mall was 'the most sensitive site in the United States'. The relationship of his design for the gallery's East Building with the surrounding structures—particularly its adherence to set-back regulations and the differing historic height limits on Pennsylvania Avenue and Constitution Avenue—was crucial to its success with the United States Commission of Fine Arts, the body responsible for approval. The building's completion in 1978 was a welcome relief, especially after the disastrous case of windowpanes falling out of the John Hancock Tower designed by his firm. It also cemented his position in the upper echelon of international architects and led to the commission for the Grand Louvre.

POWER, POLITICS & PATRONAGE 251

5.16 | **From left: Paul Mellon (President, National Gallery of Art), Chief Justice Warren Burger (Chairman, National Gallery of Art), and J. Carter Brown (Director, National Gallery of Art) at the East Building groundbreaking ceremony, 6 May 1971. National Gallery of Art, Washington DC, Gallery Archives**

Built on land secured by industrialist and philanthropist Andrew Mellon when the National Gallery of Art was established in 1937, the East Building owed much of its success to the support of the gallery's president, Paul Mellon (son of Andrew), and its director, J. Carter Brown. The building's cost of around USD95 million was funded by Paul Mellon and his sister, Ailsa Mellon Bruce, with additional funding from the Andrew W. Mellon Foundation. Brown provided a clear programme for the project and also advocated for Pei's approach. For Brown, Pei's design had a clear relationship with Pierre Charles L'Enfant's 1791 plan for Washington DC, as well as a Cubist interlocking of spaces, something he considered to be suitable for a modern art museum with an eye to the future.

5.17.1 | Eileen (left) and I. M. Pei (seated, second from right) meeting with Chinese vice premier Gu Mu (far right) at the Great Hall of the People in Beijing, 1978. I. M. Pei Papers, Library of Congress, Washington DC

Fragrant Hill Hotel (1979–1982)
Beijing

5.17.2 | **No. 225 Contract for Hotel Construction and Reconstruction between Beijing First Service Bureau (now the Beijing Municipal Bureau of Culture and Tourism) and YTT Tourism, which includes the Fragrant Hill Hotel, Mingzu Hotel, and Xinqiao Hotel, 1979. Esquel Group**

OPPOSITE:
5.17.3 | **Tian Fangfang, main garden of the Fragrant Hill Hotel set against surrounding mountains, 2021. Photo commissioned by M+**

5.17.1–5.17.3
Following the implementation of its Four Modernisations policy in 1978, the People's Republic of China invited Pei to participate in a large-scale tourism development project in Beijing, with the idea of projecting an image of an émigré Chinese architect contributing to the construction of a new China. Pei was unconvinced by the idea of building a high-rise hotel near the city centre. The client, Beijing First Service Bureau, ultimately agreed on a project for a low-lying hotel in the former imperial hunting grounds of Fragrant Hill, thirty kilometres to the north-west of the city. Financing for the hotel's design and construction was secured through the involvement of Hong Kong–based YTT Tourism, a group co-founded by Yang Yuan-loong, who, like Pei, was an alumnus of St John's University in Shanghai. In the context of China's era of reform, this was an important early collaboration between a domestic municipality and an overseas enterprise.

I. M. Pei selected a site for the Fragrant Hill Hotel in a government-owned wooded preserve outside Beijing. The area was otherwise deforested; all trees were valued. How to build without clearing? You start by distinguishing healthy trees from dying ones and old growth from new, and then zigzag the future guest rooms through the site. It would have been more efficient to stack the rooms vertically, but that would have overpowered the natural setting; we set the maximum height at two to three storeys.

As no drawings existed, I created a field plan with symbols to indicate the different tree species and later had them surveyed. There were some rare white-bark pines and a precious gnarled specimen I called the '#1 pine'. I worked out from the centre, staying a safe distance from the trees and creating a separate courtyard for the #1 pine.

On a trip back from Singapore, with a very tight schedule that allowed me to attend my daughter's graduation, I. M. instructed me to stop in Beijing. 'They claim your site plan is killing two hundred trees,' he said. I went there and walked the building's footprint (traced in ashes on the ground in preparation for construction). It appeared to be true: most of the trees I tried to preserve were indeed endangered! Long story short, an on-site miscalculation had shifted the project's centreline by ten feet. I worked through the night to rectify the discrepancy and flew home the next morning. Several years later, when I returned for the hotel's opening, I was greeted as 'Mr Wong, saviour of trees'.

– Kellogg Wong

Kellogg Wong was a member of I. M. Pei's team for more than fifty years and worked on the planning and site-selection phase of the Fragrant Hill Hotel.

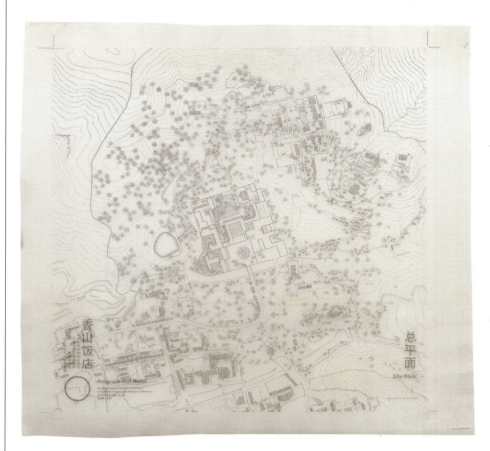

5.18.1 | **Early site plan of the hotel based on Kellogg Wong's detailed arboreal survey, 1979. Pei Cobb Freed & Partners**

5.18.2 | **Fragrant Hill Hotel gift portfolio for Chinese officials, designed by Tracy Turner with indigo fabric and a title printed in Chinese calligraphy with silver foil stamping, ca.1979. Tracy Turner**

5.18.3 | **Calvin Tsao, promotional collage composed of an axonometric representation of the Fragrant Hill Hotel set within a reproduction of a landscape painting by Zheng Zhong, ca.1979. Tracy Turner**

5.18.4 | **Aerial photo of the hotel, ca.1979. Calvin Tsao**

5.18.1–5.18.4

The hotel's rural setting and the need to preserve trees led Pei to look to the vernacular architecture of Jiangnan region as a reference. Counter to the prevailing approaches of either mimicking traditional forms or importing Euro-American ones, Pei attempted to develop a nationally and regionally relevant form through the reinterpretation and abstraction of spatial and formal archetypes. To gain support for his proposal, Pei gave officials a portfolio in indigo fabric with loose sheets of model shots, plans, elevations, and axonometric drawings. The documents included a collage of the hotel in a landscape painting by the late seventeenth-century artist Zheng Zhong. The hotel is represented as a four-storey flat-roofed structure in white stucco, accented by grey-tiled latticework and diamond-shaped windows, in a meandering composition of guest-room wings intertwined with interior courtyards and gardens. The meticulously produced presentation model of the hotel further demonstrates Pei's enthusiasm for the project's smallest details.

5.19.1 | Calvin Tsao, hundred-kilogram model used to facilitate discussion with officials in Beijing, 1979

5.19.2 | Paul Goldberger, 'Winning Ways of I. M. Pei', *New York Times*, 20 May 1979. New York Times

5.19.3 | **Marc Riboud, view of hotel's atrium lobby (Four Seasons Courtyard) from an opening on the upper floor, ca.1982. Association Les amis de Marc Riboud**

5.19.1–5.19.3
Although Fragrant Hill Hotel was celebrated as a triumph in the American media, the reality of its development was much more fraught. While as many as three thousand construction workers were on-site and capable of digging a foundation by hand, they lacked the experience and technology to build to Pei's standards. Apart from the atrium space frame, which was fabricated in the United States, materials and methods were sourced locally. Pei was faced with the challenge of navigating a deeply entrenched bureaucratic apparatus, with construction and landscaping teams reporting separately to the mayor of Beijing. Launching a campaign of cajoling officials, Pei's team made important gains, such as permission to import weathered limestone pillars from the Shilin stone forest of Yunnan for the hotel's gardens and courtyard.

5.20.1 | **Liu Heung Shing, I. M. Pei with Jacqueline Kennedy Onassis and guests at the hotel's opening, 17 October 1982**

5.20.2 | **Tian Fangfang, stairwell and newly carpeted corridor in the Fragrant Hill Hotel, 2021. Photo commissioned by M+**

5.20.1–5.20.2
As the building's construction came to an end, Beijing First Service Bureau decided not to engage Hyatt to manage the hotel, despite what had been agreed with YTT Tourism. Simultaneously, the bureau repaid YTT Tourism's investment, thereby gaining full control of the hotel. This resulted in a net loss for the investor, as well as a totally inexperienced hotel staff. Pei and his team were involved in preparing for the soft opening, whose guests included Jacqueline Kennedy Onassis and Thomas Hoving, former director of the Metropolitan Museum of Art. Far from grasping Pei's design intention, the majority of the local media assessed the hotel in terms of its functionality, cost, and relationship to the site. Among architects in China, the project stirred a debate on the place of history in contemporary design, influencing a generation of architects who sought to integrate heritage with progressive modernisation.

Grand Louvre
Phase I (1983–1989) & Phase II (1989–1993)
Paris

In the spring of 1983, I. M. invited me to lunch to discuss something he had shared only with Eileen, not even his partners in the office. The French president, François Mitterrand, had asked him to redesign the Louvre. 'You can't change the Louvre,' I. M. said. 'It's sacred!' Still, at Mitterrand's request, he visited the Louvre for days, finding it in a sad state. It had been designed as a palace, and it was not equipped to meet the needs of a modern museum. As a young bureaucrat working in the Ministry of Finance in the Louvre's Richelieu wing, Mitterrand had wondered why the building was broken up; he felt the whole should become a single museum.

I. M.'s thought was to preserve the historic palace, transform the ministry's offices into exhibition galleries, and construct the required expansion space and all the necessary facilities underground. (We had used the underground connection concept successfully at the National Gallery of Art.)

The entrance, I. M explained, needed to be at the centre of the U-shaped building for easy access to all three wings. But how to keep the underground space from feeling like a subway station? His solution was that it needed 'volume and light'; he wanted the palace to be seen from below ground, so the entrance required a skylight, square in plan to complement the Louvre's orthogonal footprint. A glass pyramid would provide the greatest amount of natural light, its sloped and transparent walls minimising obstruction of the surrounding palace. All of this he explained over lunch with words and a quick line sketch.

– Yann Weymouth

Yann Weymouth was design architect for the Grand Louvre and the National Gallery of Art East Building.

5.21.1 | **I. M. Pei, early sketch of the proposed entrance in line with the historical urban axis at the Cour Napoléon, ca.1983. Pei Cobb Freed & Partners**

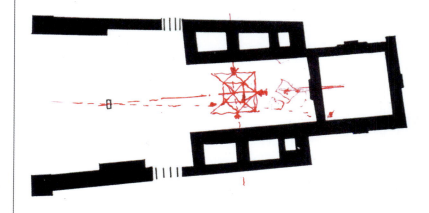

POWER, POLITICS & PATRONAGE 261

5.21.2 | **Cour Napoléon as a car park for the Ministry of Finance prior to the Grand Louvre renovation, ca.1983.** Pei Cobb Freed & Partners

5.21.3 | **Workers remove a Ministry of Finance sign following the ministry's departure from the Richelieu wing, 1988.** Pei Cobb Freed & Partners

5.21.1–5.21.3
French president François Mitterrand announced the transformation of the Louvre as one of his large-scale cultural projects by setting up the Établissement public du Grand Louvre in 1983, with Émile Biasini—who was strategically involved in the Ministry of Culture—as its president. Impressed by the East Building of the National Gallery of Art in Washington DC, Biasini strongly recommended Pei to Mitterrand for a direct commission, bypassing the architectural competition required under French law. While Pei was honoured by Mitterrand's invitation, he accepted the undertaking only after four months of on-site study, leading to a design that satisfied Mitterrand's ambition to unify the palace into a single museum complex. This would involve moving the Ministry of Finance out of the Louvre's Richelieu wing. Pei's proposal was to excavate the Cour Napoléon, then a car park, to the level of the Seine to create two underground levels for new infrastructure, as well as an entrance at the centre of the court.

I. M. Pei began his project to expand and modernise the Louvre with a painstaking investigation of options and constraints. He ultimately determined that a new entrance should be constructed in the parking lot occupying the centre of the museum's three wings. The question then became one of character, material, and, most importantly, shape of the new entry structure. The glazed pyramid was adopted as a single solution to address all the structural and historic criteria and the requirement of light-admitting transparency. The series of decisions that followed involved determining the exact size and shape of the proposed structure, including its base, height, and slope.

That is the point at which I became involved, producing precise visual representations of the various choices being assessed. As it happened, the field of computer representation was coming of age at the time, and a major computing firm volunteered to aid in the task of accurately visualising the proposed structure in the context of the three surrounding pavilions. The challenge for me was to produce—by way of traditional hand-constructed perspectives—a drawing that precisely verified the images made objectively by machine. That verification was achieved, providing Pei's office with confidence that their prospective representation of the pyramid would ultimately correspond exactly with the built structure.

– Paul Stevenson Oles

Paul Stevenson Oles is an architectural illustrator who visualised many of I. M. Pei's projects, including the National Gallery of Art East Building and the Grand Louvre, as part of the design process.

5.22.1 | **Paul Stevenson Oles, early visualisation of the pyramid in the Cour Napoléon as seen from street level, 1983. Pei Cobb Freed & Partners**

5.22.2 | **CAD drawing of the Louvre and the pyramid as seen from street level, 1983. Archives nationales de France**

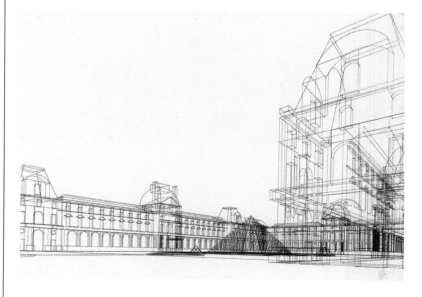

5.22.3 | **François Mitterrand, letter to I. M. Pei expressing his approval of Pei's proposal with emphasis on the need for careful studies of the pyramid's design and its effect on the historic site, 1 December 1983. Papers of I. M. Pei, Library of Congress, Washington DC**

5.22.1–5.22.3
Pei's proposal hinged on a glass-and-steel pyramid structure as a grand entrance into the underground complex. To convince President Mitterrand of this approach, Pei presented a precise and realistic visualisation of its presence in the Cour Napoléon from the perspective of a pedestrian. The president gave Pei his full support, but urged him to refine the design, with particular focus on the pyramid's height, slope, base layout, and relationship with the perspective from the Carrousel du Louvre to the Arc de Triomphe. Mitterrand was anxious for the project to progress to an irreversible stage before the end of his seven-year presidential term. To reduce the constraints of French bureaucracy, Pei's firm was given unprecedented final contractual responsibilities, which were usually under the purview of engineers and the client. This gave Pei full control of the project, from developing the design in consultation with museum curators to determining on-site construction details.

LE PRÉSIDENT DE LA RÉPUBLIQUE

Paris, le 1er décembre 1983

Cher Monsieur,

Je tiens à vous dire combien votre proposition pour le Grand Louvre m'a séduit.

Je demande donc au Ministre de la Culture qu'il mette en place tous les moyens pour que votre mission se poursuive dans les meilleures conditions.

Il me paraît nécessaire que vous étudiez, dès maintenant, diverses variantes de cette construction pyramidale, en fonction notamment de sa hauteur, de la pente de ses faces, de l'aménagement de sa base et de son insertion dans ce site historique. Vous savez en particulier combien je suis soucieux de la perspective du Carrousel à l'Arc de Triomphe et de la perception qu'aura le promeneur de ce nouvel édifice.

Je serais heureux que vous puissiez veiller avec l'Etablissement Public du Grand Louvre, à une exécution rapide des travaux.

En vous renouvelant ma confiance, je vous prie d'agréer, Cher Monsieur, l'assurance de ma haute considération, *et de mon meilleur souvenir*

F. Mitterrand

François MITTERRAND

Monsieur I.M. PEI
600 Madison Avenue
NEW YORK 10022

5.23.1 | André Fermigier, 'La maison des morts' (The House of the Dead), *Le Monde*, 26 January 1984. Le Monde

5.23.2 | Jean Pattou, 'L'hyper Louvre', 1984

POWER, POLITICS & PATRONAGE

5.23.3 | **Gabriel Macé, 'Mitterramsès Ier et sa pyramide' (Mitterramses the First and His Pyramid), *Le Canard enchaîné*, 1 February 1984. Archives nationales de France. Le Canard enchaîné**

5.23.4 | **Association pour le renouveau du Louvre et SOS Paris (Union for the Revitalisation of the Louvre and SOS Paris), 'Au secours le Louvre!' (Help the Louvre!), ca.1985. Archives nationales de France**

5.23.1–5.23.4
As soon as Mitterrand's endorsement of Pei's vision for the Louvre was made public, the architect's proposal was met with intense criticism that made a mockery of the glass pyramid and characterised Pei's intervention as a hyper-commercialisation of French cultural heritage. Public vitriol peaked between 1984 and 1985, with media headlines fuelling the controversy. *Le Monde* called the Louvre 'the house of the dead' for its underground access. Cartoonists and critics denounced the project as a Disneyland-like development. The pyramid was considered tasteless, and Mitterrand was compared to a megalomaniacal pharaoh. An association founded by former minister of culture Michel Guy, in alliance with such art critics as André Fermigier, mobilised opposition in the name of 'rescuing' Paris. The 'Battle of the Pyramid' also became as much about politics—with the right wing using the pyramid as a tool against Mitterrand's Socialist Party—as architecture and French identity.

5.24.1 | **Jacques Chirac introducing the Louvre scheme to the press, 1985.** Alamy

Pei made a very intelligent proposal to the public, one that allowed people to visualise the space. As you know, there was a lot of controversy, and the project was attacked by the press, by public opinion, and by writers. But most of all I wanted to avoid opposition from Jacques Chirac, who was then the mayor of Paris. Chirac was against all our projects: against the Opéra Bastille, against Christo and Jeanne-Claude's *empaquetage* of the Pont Neuf, against everything we did. His support wasn't necessary, but in the battle of public opinion over the Grand Louvre I felt it would be strategically important for us to have it. I asked Madame Pompidou, Jean Prouvé—who had been president of the jury for the Centre Pompidou competition—and Pierre Boulez to speak with Chirac, to ask him not to make a decision immediately. I knew that if he had to decide right away, he would say no. Instead, I asked them to request a meeting. Pei and the three of them met with Chirac, and Pei presented the model. It worked; Chirac was seduced. This was the only time we got his support.

– Jack Lang

Jack Lang served as minister of culture in the French government between 1981 and 1986, and between 1988 and 1993.

**5.24.2 | A full-sized mock-up of the pyramid at the Cour Napoléon, 1985.
Pei Cobb Freed & Partners**

5.24.1–5.24.2
After hearing Pei explain his thinking behind the Grand Louvre scheme and viewing the maquette, Jacques Chirac, mayor of Paris, expressed support for the design, with particular emphasis on how the plan would benefit Paris from an urbanistic point of view. However, he expressed uncertainty over the pyramid's size and proportions and demanded to see a full-scale mock-up. In May 1985, four carbon-fibre cables were suspended from a crane to simulate the pyramid's final form, at its exact proposed location in the Cour Napoléon. The volume was left as a void to communicate the transparency of the glass design. The exercise led Mitterrand and Chirac to approve the design and was witnessed by sixty thousand Parisians. It marked a critical turning point in public opinion regarding the Louvre project.

I think my father would say that the Louvre was his most challenging and personally rewarding project because the result was so widely acclaimed. Projects can progress smoothly: the architect is hired, does the design, and then builds it. But because the Louvre is the building dearest to the French people, the experience was very different.

We read the newspapers and knew about the raging controversy, but that was not our concern. We knew what our job was, and we were convinced of the solution. Our client, Émile Biasini, understood French bureaucracy and had a 'bulldog' reputation for getting things done. He'd say the French don't like your design now, but they'll love it once it's built; the same thing happened with the Eiffel Tower and the Arc de Triomphe. He was very encouraging. Beyond that, we knew we had the initial support of President Mitterrand. All this sustained us and, although we didn't win every battle, we did win the war.

– Chien Chung (Didi) Pei

Chien Chung (Didi) Pei was associate partner for design and administration for the Grand Louvre project.

5.25.1 | **Interview with I. M. Pei and Didi Pei on a French public national news programme during work on the Grand Louvre project, Antenne 2, 1987. Institut national de l'audiovisuel**

5.25.2 | **New year's greeting card from l'Établissement public du Grand Louvre, 1989. Pei Cobb Freed & Partners**

OPPOSITE:

5.25.3 | **Giovanna Silva, spiral staircase leading to the museum's entrance under the pyramid, 2021. Photo commissioned by M+**

5.25.1–5.25.3
As the tide of public opinion turned, media outlets began to express genuine curiosity about the design concept behind the remodelling of the Louvre and monitored construction progress in anticipation of its completion. Even the daily newspaper *Le Figaro*, which had led the campaign against Pei's pyramid, celebrated the new landmark as it came to be embraced as the new centre of the complex, further elevating it as a prominent icon of the city. The Grand Louvre was inaugurated in 1989 and the renovation of the Richelieu wing was completed in 1993, creating a new source of cultural pride for the city of Paris.

Joy of Angels Bell Tower (1988–1990)
Shigaraki, Shiga

5.26 | **View of Shinji Shumeikai's Misono sanctuary with the Joy of Angels Bell Tower (right) designed by I. M. Pei, Meishusama Hall (left) designed by Minoru Yamasaki, and the Miho Museum visible in the distance, ca.1997. Shinji Shumeikai**

Founded by Koyama Mihoko, heiress of the Toyobo textiles business, Shinji Shumeikai is a religious organisation devoted to the belief that enlightenment can be achieved through the contemplation of beauty in art and nature. When Koyama approached Pei in 1987 to design a bell tower to complete the organisation's sanctuary outside Kyoto, Pei was initially hesitant owing to the project's small scale. After a visit to the site, which features an ablutions fountain—a water feature used for ritual washing before prayers—by Nagare Masayuki and a hall of worship by Minoru Yamasaki set amid a forest, he accepted the commission as an individual, independent of his firm. He modelled the tower after a *bachi* (a type of plectrum used to play Japanese stringed instruments), translating its form into a tower that flares outward from a narrow base, with the curvature of its shaft the inverse of the sloped roof of Yamasaki's hall. Realising that the client's proposed cladding in pinkish Korean granite would not complement the white ribs of the hall, Pei proposed the use of white granite from Vermont. The client was convinced despite the enormous shipping costs. The bell tower commission marked the beginning of an enduring partnership with Shinji Shumeikai.

5.27.1 | **I. M. Pei (third from right) reviewing the Miho Museum model with Koyama Mihoko (second from left), her daughter Koyama Hiroko (far left), and board members of Shinji Shumeikai, ca.1991. Shinji Shumeikai, io Architects**

Miho Museum (1991–1997)
Shigaraki, Shiga

PAGES 272–273:
5.27.2 | **Yoneda Tomoko, view from the Miho Museum's main hall, with the top of the Joy of Angels Bell Tower visible at far left, 2021. Photo commissioned by M+**

OPPOSITE:
5.27.3 | **Yoneda Tomoko, view of suspension bridge leading to the Miho Museum, 2021. Photo commissioned by M+**

5.27.1–5.27.3
Influenced by Church of World Messianity founder Okada Mokichi, who had established an art museum to nurture the public's appreciation of beauty, Koyama sought to build a museum for her growing collection of objects relating to the Japanese tea ceremony. She invited Pei to build the museum, and the two eventually decided on a mountainous site. Instead of building a road up the side of the mountain, Pei proposed a more dramatic approach to the museum inspired by the classical Chinese legend 'The Peach Blossom Spring', which recounts the discovery of a paradise through a passageway in a grotto. Koyama's commitment to this vision endured through difficult negotiations with local and national governments, and she succeeded in purchasing additional land in order to build a tunnel and suspension bridge across the valley.

5.28.1 | **Documentation of site excavation with the caption 'hill to be retained—dirt to be replaced, hill replanted', ca.1995. Papers of I. M. Pei, Library of Congress, Washington DC**

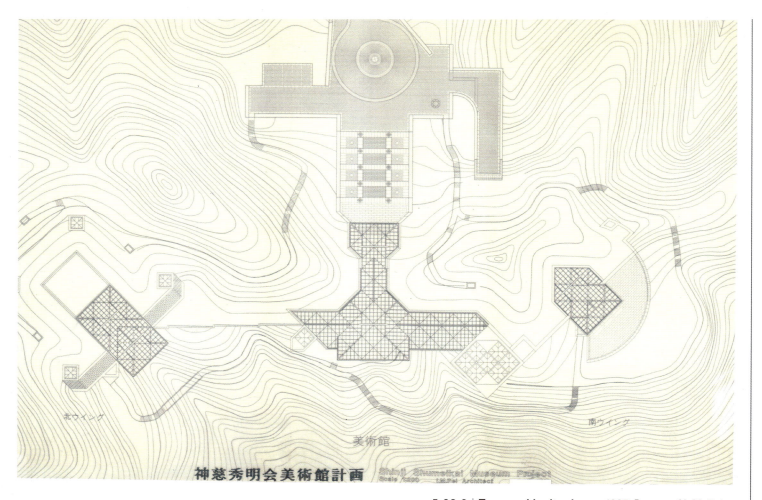

5.28.2 | **Topographic site plan, ca.1995. Papers of I. M. Pei, Library of Congress, Washington DC**

POWER, POLITICS & PATRONAGE 277

5.28.3 | **Construction of the museum's seismic cavity wall and foundation, ca.1995. Miho Museum**

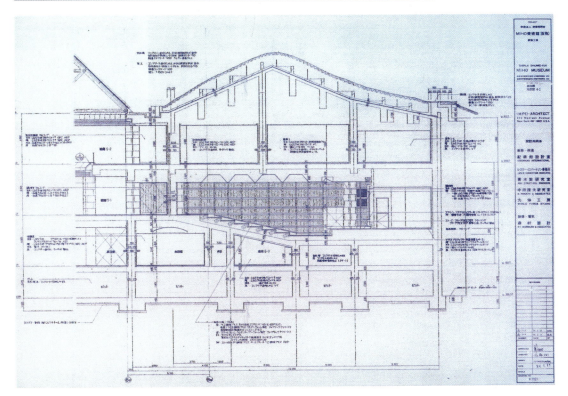

5.28.4 | **Kibowkan International, section showing the museum's structure beneath the surface of the mountain, 1994. io Architects**

5.28.1–5.28.4
Building on a hilly nature reserve with dense vegetation, traditionally considered to be sacred land, Pei faced a restriction on the extent to which exposed structures could be built, as well as a height limitation of thirteen metres above ground. In response, most of the museum was built underground. The contractor recommended replacing the earth following the completion of construction, and the prefecture approved, providing that similar trees and plantings were introduced. Koyama fully supported Pei's vision and also acted on his recommendation to expand her collection by acquiring objects from cultures along the Silk Road.

5.29.1 | **I. M. Pei Architect, io Architects, and Masatoyo Ogasawara Architects, transverse section of the chapel, 2010. io Architects**

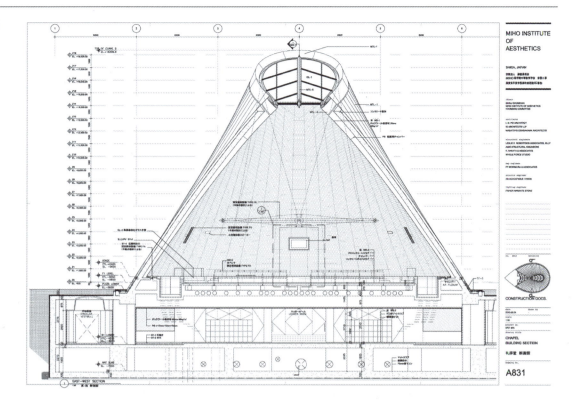

Miho Institute of Aesthetics Chapel (2008–2012)
Shigaraki, Shiga

5.29.2 | **Higashide Photo Studio, interior of the chapel clad in Yoshino Japanese red cedar, ca.2012. io Architects**

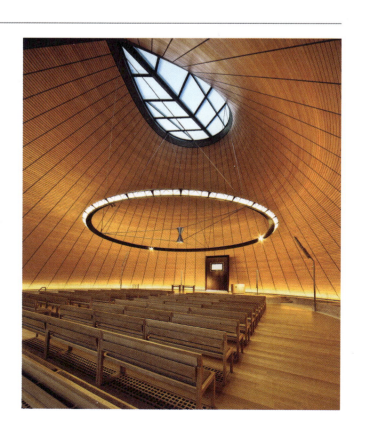

5.29.3 | **Aerial view of the chapel at the centre of the campus, ca.2012.
Shinji Shumeikai, io Architects**

5.29.1–5.29.3
A decade after the Miho Museum's completion, Pei was asked to design a chapel for the Miho Institute of Aesthetics, a private boarding school, and collaborate with io Architects on the institution's master plan. Angled towards the sanctuary at Misono on the other side of the mountain, the chapel was originally going to be placed on the highest point of the eight-hectare site. Instead, Pei proposed to locate it in the middle of the school's campus, making it more accessible to students and reinforcing the notion of the chapel as the school's physical and spiritual centre. To protect the site and introduce a sculptural gesture of the chapel rising from the ground, principal access was defined through two underground tunnels.

Museum of Islamic Art (2000–2008)
Doha

5.30.1 | **Paul Stevenson Oles, early drawing of the museum's tree-lined entrance path with a cascade running through the fountain plaza, ca.2000. Museum of Islamic Art**

5.30.1–5.30.2
Conceived in the late 1990s, the Museum of Islamic Art was a cornerstone of Qatar's ambition, initiated by the then emir, Sheikh Hamad bin Khalifa Al-Thani, to diversify its activities beyond the creation of wealth from petrochemical reserves. The museum would be the first of many planned by the Qatar Museums Authority to make the country a regional and global cultural centre. Pei's commission followed a 1997 architectural competition organised by the Aga Khan Trust for Culture. The winning design by Jordanian architect Rasem Badran was ultimately not pursued for the reason that it did not sufficiently represent the museum's vision of presenting Islamic art as regional and universal heritage. Inspired by the formal logic of the ninth-century Mosque of Ibn Tulun in Cairo, Pei's design, the massing of which is a Cubist progression from an octagon to a square and finally a circle, was seen to manifest a regionally specific yet universal aspiration.

5.31.1 | **Composite photograph showing the newly reclaimed site for the museum, at left, sixty metres from the south side of Doha's Corniche, ca.2001. Museum of Islamic Art**

5.30.2 | **Keiichi Tahara, I. M. Pei and Sheikh Hamad bin Khalifa Al-Thani, ca.2000**

When my father, His Highness Sheikh Hamad bin Khalifa Al-Thani, decided that I. M. Pei should be the one to design the Museum of Islamic Art (MIA), the architect was retired. The decision came on the heels of an international competition that had not resulted in any submissions matching the ambitious vision. The objective was not simply to build a museum that would house Qatar's prodigious collection of Islamic art, but to create an architectural masterpiece that would convey the historical magnificence of Islamic civilisation.

Some years later, when I asked Pei what it was about this commission that made him come out of retirement, he told me that he was curious about the Islamic world—a world he had never visited, a religion he knew little about. He travelled to Africa, Asia, Europe, and the Gulf to learn about our culture, religion, and history. He ultimately imbued the MIA with a perfection born out of a profound understanding of the premise of Islamic architecture: beauty, achieved through geometric harmony. The space intimately envelops the collection and, most importantly, celebrates Islamic culture in its purest form.

I sat next to Pei on his one-hundredth birthday and watched him blow out the candles on his cake, which was baked in the shape of our museum. I wondered why, of all his many projects, he had chosen the MIA to celebrate his centennial. He responded that it had been a fascinating, rejuvenating experience during which he became a student again. For him, a continuous quest for knowledge was an engine of life. It is my hope that, in time, all of humanity will share the passion for learning and understanding that Pei possessed and expressed through this icon on Doha's skyline.

– Sheikha Al-Mayassa bint Hamad bin Khalifa Al-Thani

Sheikha Al-Mayassa bint Hamad bin Khalifa Al-Thani is the chairperson of Qatar Museums.

5.31.2 | **Mohamed Somji,** the museum seen from the public promenade that circles its eastern side, 2022. Photo commissioned by M+

5.31.3 | **Model of the museum on an artificial island, ca.2001. Jock Pottle, Aslıhan Demirtaş**

5.31.1–5.31.3
Aware of plans to develop Doha as a major commercial centre through intense construction and land reclamation, Pei declined to build along the city's Corniche. Instead, he requested an artificial island that would be linked to the mainland, to ensure that the museum would not be overshadowed by future developments. Sited on a 260,000-square-metre island 60 metres off the south side of the Corniche, the cream-coloured, limestone-clad museum—composed of a five-storey main building and an expansive two-storey education centre connected across a courtyard—was protected from the Gulf to the north and industrial buildings to the east by a crescent-shaped peninsula, and made visible from all around the city.

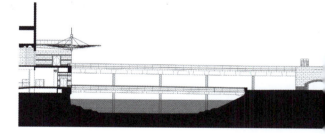

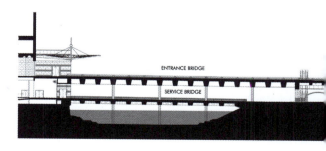

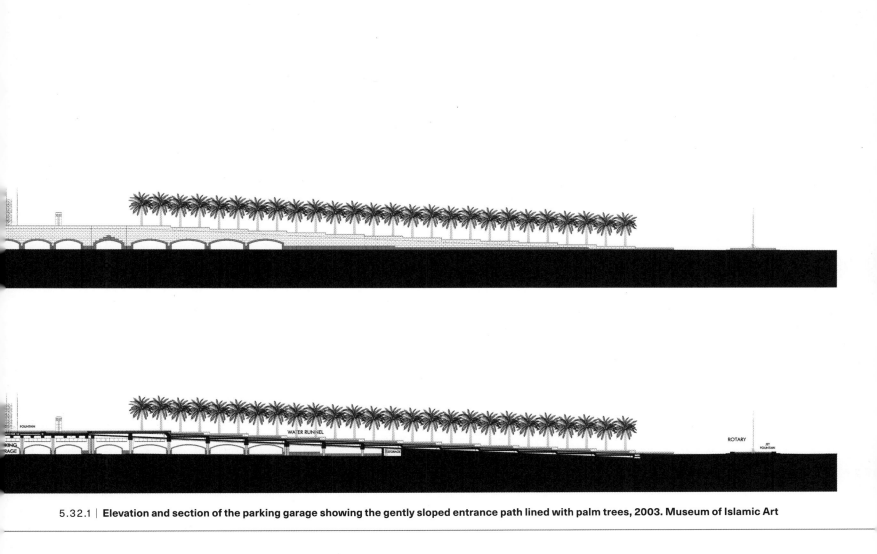

5.32.1 | **Elevation and section of the parking garage showing the gently sloped entrance path lined with palm trees, 2003. Museum of Islamic Art**

5.32.2 | Mohamed Somji, men at *maghrib* (dusk) prayers beside the museum's entrance path, 2022. Photo commissioned by M+

5.32.1–5.32.2
The museum's design incorporated an adjoining park of approximately twenty-six hectares of gently sloping landscaped gardens and small bodies of water along the Corniche. The park provides the building with a scenic backdrop and direct public access via two bridges. One is part of a path lined with palm trees carefully selected to correspond with the museum's height, which sets the stage for the museum as it gently ascends onto a causeway that leads to the plaza, a fountain, and the entrance. A boat dock intended for the emir's use is set at a ninety-degree angle to this main entrance. The other entry is at the beginning of the C-shaped peninsula and the park, which further opens the museum to the city and community. The park's area was eventually expanded to twenty-eight hectares by Pei Partnership Architects (now PEI Architects), providing much-needed public space.

OCBC Centre
The Iconic Turn of the Singapore Model of Asian Global Capitalism

Jiat-Hwee Chang

On 1 October 1976, the Oversea-Chinese Banking Corporation (OCBC) Centre—I. M. Pei's first built project in Singapore—opened after six years of planning, design, and construction.[1] The project has not been considered significant in Pei's body of work, receiving only a passing mention in Michael Cannell's 1995 biography. But it merits a closer look. At 100 million Singapore dollars, the OCBC Centre was at the time the most expensive urban redevelopment project in Singapore. Rising 198 metres, it was also the tallest building in Asia outside Japan. Unsurprisingly for a bank headquarters, its banking hall was a key feature. A largely column-free space of 1,200 square metres in floor area and 12 metres in height, it gave a sense of vastness, which was further accentuated by the treatment of the enclosing surfaces. Separating the hall from the outside was a glass facade that allowed for visual continuity. On the inside, the remaining three walls were covered with large stainless-steel panels polished to a mirror-like finish. The ceiling featured thirty-six stainless-steel coffers lit by 500-watt halogen bulbs. The floor was covered by an enormous 372-square-metre gold carpet. All these elements came together to create an optical illusion, giving, in the words of a local journalist, 'a sensation of depth and width stretching beyond the reach of the eye of the beholder'.[2]

The sense of spatial infinity in the light and bright banking hall was both enabled and counter-balanced by the two massive semi-circular concrete cores flanking it. Contained in the two cores are twenty-seven elevators, staircases, toilets, and other services. Three sets of post-tensioned concrete-encased steel transfer girders span the fourth, twentieth, and thirty-fifth floors. Each set of these girders in turn supports the fourteen floors of office space above it. This structural system enabled an innovative construction process. First, the two structural and service cores were built using the slip-form method. Once the levels of the transfer girders were reached, the girders, which had been fabricated off-site, were hoisted into position and the construction of the floors above could commence. This method allowed for the simultaneous construction of the three building sections, thus speeding up the process.[3] The OCBC Centre combines the openness and transparency of the banking hall with the mass and solidity of the structural and service cores. It has elements of both the 'closed' design of pre-war banks and the 'open' design of post-war banks in North America and Europe.

How should we read the monumental architecture of the OCBC Centre? Existing literature sees it as a translation of the design brief given to Pei by the then chairman of the OCBC, Tan Chin Tuan.

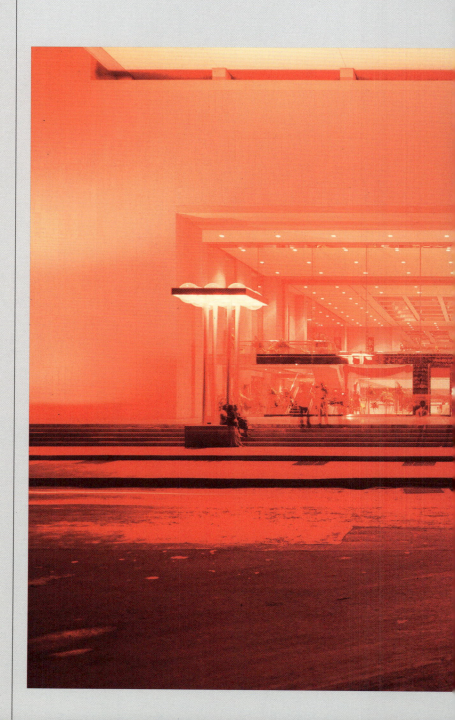

Tan asked Pei—who came from a family of Chinese bankers and was a family friend of Tan's—to design a building that reflected the philosophy of the bank: 'solid as a rock, conservative yet modern, dynamic, progressive in a calculated and stable manner and of course efficient in service while being prestigious in image'.[4] Broadly speaking, we know that a bank purveys no tangible product, deals in trust, and depends on the confidence of its customers. The architecture of a bank serves as a tangible artefact that materially and symbolically communicates the bank's dependency and reliability to its customers and the general public. The design brief's emphasis on 'solid as a rock' is thus understandable, especially when OCBC was rated the largest bank in Singapore and the fourth largest in Southeast Asia in 1976, the year the building was completed.[5] However, the rock-solid corporate monument should also be seen in the context of the broader socio-economic and political transformations of Singapore.

The economy of colonial Singapore was largely dominated by three British banks—the Hongkong and Shanghai Bank; the Chartered Bank of India, Australia, and China; and the Mercantile Bank of India, London, and China—that were focused on financing trade between Malaya (of which Singapore was the financial centre) and the metropolitan countries and dominions of the British Empire. They served as exchange banks, with the local Chinese banks relying on them for foreign-exchange transactions. These Chinese institutions were based on Singapore's language groups. The Hokkiens, as the largest group, had three: the Chinese Commercial Bank, Ho Hong Bank, and Oversea-Chinese Bank. Formed from the merger of these three Hokkien banks in 1932, OCBC expanded rapidly in the post-war and post-independence periods under the chairmanship first of Lee Kong Chian and then of Tan Chin Tuan. One of Tan's early ambitions was to emulate the British agency houses and establish a network of companies linked to OCBC. In 1944, he wrote: 'I am afraid I am always dreaming of building bigger and stronger business organisations with Chinese management and capital in Malaya … Why can't we have a Chinese "Sime Darby" or "Cold Storage"?'[6] Sime Darby was the largest of the agency houses, with complex and many-sided enterprises, each of which owned a network of companies through interlocking directorship and managerial arrangements. They dominated British Malaya's economy in the mid-twentieth century.[7]

The confluence of two major historical events in the post-war era allowed Tan to realise his dream. The Korean War led to a surge in demand for rubber, creating a tremendous amount of wealth for a number of OCBC's major shareholders. At around the same time, Malaya, including Singapore, was preparing for independence. The shareholders of the British agency houses felt uncertain about their post-colonial future and began to sell their shares and withdraw their capital. These conditions allowed Tan to acquire stakes in large colonial companies on behalf of OCBC from the 1950s onwards. With these acquisitions, the OCBC group became a large conglomerate with companies in fields as diverse as banking, insurance, tin mining, smelting, rubber plantations, trading, hotels, properties, manufacturing, and management services.[8]

When Singapore attained self-government in 1959 and then independence in 1965, the government planned to complement the country's entrepôt economy with an industrial economy. The new industrialisation programme required significant capital, which provided the local banks with opportunities to offer loans and grow. The government also sought to develop the city-state into a regional financial centre by introducing the Asia dollar, bond, and gold markets. OCBC was one of the main local banks to benefit from these political developments and economic policies. The expansion of Singapore's financial sector was reflected in urban and architectural changes, particularly the planning of the Golden Shoe area as part of an urban renewal programme to house both the newly arrived international financial institutions and local institutions with

Kouo Shang-Wei, nighttime view of OCBC Centre banking hall, 1976. Kouo Shang-Wei Collection, National Library Board, Singapore

new, larger headquarters.⁹ The OCBC Centre was one of three local bank headquarters to be completed in the mid-1970s. The other two were the United Overseas Bank (UOB) building and the Development Bank of Singapore (DBS) building, both designed by Architects Team 3, a leading local firm. All three projects were part of the state-led urban renewal initiative. Before he was involved in the OCBC Centre, Pei had been commissioned to design the new headquarters of Chung Khiaw Bank in the late 1960s.¹⁰ That project was aborted when the bank was merged into UOB.

As both the UOB building and the OCBC Centre were located on Chulia Street, with fairly similar urban contexts, a comparison of the ways in which they addressed their surroundings is revealing. The UOB building (completed in 1974 and extensively renovated in 1995) occupied a corner site, with three sides facing Chulia Street, Bonham Street, and Boat Quay.¹¹ It consisted of a thirty-storey octagonal tower and a four-storey podium block. The podium was conceived by Architects Team 3 as a way to mediate between the tower and the extant shophouses and colonial buildings around it. In the words of firm principal Lim Chong Keat, it was an attempt to 'agree with the scale and tone of the business centre, Raffles Place, [and] relate pleasantly to the historical Singapore River along whose banks the building is disposed'.¹²

In Singapore, the podium-and-tower typology was prescribed by the state planning authority for new buildings in the city centre, as part of the urban renewal programme in the 1960s and 1970s. Furthermore, all such buildings were expected to have a uniform podium height with connected covered walkways at the ground-level perimeter to ensure that a 'harmonious streetscape' with the old shophouses would be maintained.¹³ Given this context, the absence of a visible podium in the OCBC Centre is unusual. With the podium block tucked behind the tower and hidden from view, there was nothing to mediate between the horizontality of the low-lying shophouses that form the urban setting and the verticality of the two solid cores flanking the fifty-two-storey tower. The only urban gesture in the design of the OCBC Centre was the setting-back of the tower from the edge of the street, creating a small square, in which a Henry Moore sculpture was subsequently placed. This accentuated the perception of the building as a free-standing object.

The OCBC Centre was undoubtedly a simpler and clearer design scheme compared to the UOB building. The latter sat on a smaller and more challenging site surrounded by three streets. Its design attempted to respond to the streets by placing the entrance to the banking hall on one and the entrance to the tower on another. In contrast, the OCBC Centre has only one frontage and entrance, facing Chulia Street. Unencumbered by a visible podium, the OCBC Centre was volumetrically articulated as a monolithic structure with three cantilevered office volumes and an opening at ground level framing the vast banking hall. If an iconic building is about 'a single uncomplicated idea, an architectural one-liner', and often an acontextual design that seeks to stand out and be different from its surroundings, then the OCBC Centre is probably the first iconic modern building in Singapore.¹⁴ Nicknamed 'the calculator' by the public, it was probably also one of the first modern buildings in

Model of proposed Collyer Quay/Raffles Square Development project commissioned by the Singapore River Association featuring the about-to-be-completed OCBC Centre, ca.1975. Pei Cobb Freed & Partners

POWER, POLITICS & PATRONAGE 291

View of OCBC Centre against existing skyscrapers in Singapore's financial district, ca.1976. M+, Hong Kong. Gift of BEP Akitek, 2019

Singapore to possess what architectural historian Charles Jencks regards as another important attribute of an iconic building: to stir the imagination of the general public and create suggestive overtones.[15] Many of those writing about iconic architecture by so-called starchitects in the 1990s and 2000s have argued that iconic architecture should be understood as cultural objects of transnational capitalism.[16] Although the OCBC Centre was from an earlier era, it was also inextricably linked to incipient forces of transnational capitalism in Singapore, particularly the rise of OCBC as a major international bank and the emergence of Singapore as a regional financial centre.

The OCBC Centre marked an important moment in the architectural history of Singapore. It denoted the end of an era of allocating the most prestigious architectural projects to local architects. Singapore's transition to self-government in 1959 also began a process of nationalisation of the architectural profession. In the public sector, expatriate architects were replaced with local architects. The state awarded commissions of national importance to local firms. In the private sector, new local practices were founded while many expatriate offices from the colonial era were localised. Young architects were entrusted with major commissions to design corporate towers, hotels, mixed-use complexes, and condominiums in the 1960s and early 1970s. Even the most prestigious commercial projects, such as the DBS and UOB headquarters, were given to local architectural firms. Alfred Wong, one of Singapore's pioneer architects, characterises this time as the 'heroic period' for the local architectural profession. He also sees this short period as having been succeeded by what he calls the 'iconic era', when

> our entrepreneurs … felt the compulsion to make certain their own buildings which personify their economic power and success, should be represented by models which have already been demonstrated in other cities of the developed world. No chances were to be taken with anything less than major renowned architects who have completed such edifices … and which are already being held in high esteem and admiration.[17]

The building of the OCBC Centre represents this pivotal change from the heroic to the iconic. The design was originally awarded to BEP Akitek, a local firm helmed by Ong Eng Hung, after a limited design competition. However, Pei was brought on board as the main design consultant, working with BEP throughout the process.[18] After the completion of the building, more and more projects were given to international offices. Pei, for instance, went on to design the mega-development Raffles City (completed in 1986), a 'city within a city' that includes two office towers, a hotel, a conference centre, and a large shopping centre, grouped around a huge atrium with a 'glass-enclosed garden'.[19] Subsequent developments that dominated Singapore's urban landscape were almost always the work of internationally renowned architectural firms—such as Marina Square (1986) by John Portman & Associates, Suntec City (1995) by Tsao & McKown, UOB Plaza (1995) by Kenzo Tange Associates, and Marina Bay Sands (2010) by Moshe Safdie.

Regenerating Cultural & Historical Archetypes

6

'Like embedded rocks and rooted trees'

PAGE 292:
Li Chung Pei, I. M. Pei noting the white walls of a garden house in Yangzhou during a research trip to Jiangnan region, 1978. Pei Cobb Freed & Partners

Asked by Chinese journalists in 1982 for his thoughts on the meaning of 'root', Pei responded that architecture was 'the crystallisation of history, culture, and material production', in which 'modernisation is indispensable'. This photograph was taken during his trip to historical sites in Jiangsu and Zhejiang provinces prior to starting work on the Fragrant Hill Hotel in Beijing.

Philip Johnson—architect and gadfly of architectural theory—once proclaimed the headquarters of the National Center for Atmospheric Research (NCAR) in Boulder, Colorado, which Pei designed in the 1960s, to be the first post-modernist building.[1] However, the hooded tops and irregularly set keyhole windows of its concrete towers, which were informed by the geometries of cliff dwellings at Mesa Verde in south-west Colorado, built between the twelfth and fourteenth centuries, preceded the 1970s and 1980s discourse of post-modern historicism. NCAR's elemental forms and reddish-brown surfaces, composed of stone aggregate extracted from a nearby quarry, did not result from a semiotic exercise involving the use of historical architectural elements for a modern-day pastiche. Rather, the design stemmed from a conviction that the complex should merge with but also stand against the majestic rock formations of the Flatirons as effectively as the Mesa Verde dwellings themselves, which Pei described as being 'like embedded rocks and rooted trees'.[2]

While Johnson's comment on NCAR may have been one of his many provocations, it points to the need to reappraise Pei's engagement with culture and history as two fundamentally intertwined questions. Leaving aside the often-repeated rhetoric of Pei's weaving-together of essential cultural-historical traits, this chapter examines his design decisions as part of his broader commitment to situating modern architecture within diverse, pluralistic programmes and geographies. Considering the effect of Pei's émigré Chinese American background on his long-held aspiration to develop a modern vernacular for 'a new China', this chapter also traces his evolving interpretation of historical precedents of Chinese architecture and garden design in projects set in contexts related to his birthplace.

While Pei often attempted to discern the essence of a cultural or historical archetype, he did so not as part of a reductive and essentialist view of culture, but to derive from it a formal or spatial characteristic that informs a design strategy suited to a specific context. The choice of the Mosque of Ibn Tulun in Cairo as a model for the design of the Museum of Islamic Art in Doha is a clear example of this approach. Pei was drawn to the geometric progression of the dome structure of the mosque's *sebil* (ablution fountain)—from an octagon to a square, and from a square to a circle. For him, it offered a specific yet universally relatable geometry that was appropriate for the conditions in Qatar, a place with few examples of a local architectural language for buildings of a large scale. The *sebil*'s strong presence in the void of the mosque's quadrilateral courtyard also inspired the siting of the museum on a newly constructed island, set apart from the rapid urban development taking place along Doha's Corniche. Similarly, Pei's understanding of the architectural and urban histories of the Louvre and the city of Paris, coupled with a grasp of institutional goals and practical needs, cemented a proposal that unified and modernised the museum. The excavation of the Cour Napoléon, the transformation of the Richelieu wing, and the placement of the pyramid as a gravitational centre turned the Louvre into a single U-shaped complex with more space for display, new infrastructure for public accessibility, and a visual and symbolic alignment with the historical axis of the Champs-Élysées—all without demolishing the original structure. In Pei's projects for the National Gallery of Art East Building in Washington DC and the Deutsches Historisches Museum in Berlin, deference to a historical precedent intersects with other concerns to create a productive tension.

The tension that results from applying and transforming historical archetypes is clearly present in Pei's projects in Chinese cultural and geographical contexts. In addition to the widely documented 'homecoming' projects for the Fragrant Hill Hotel and the Suzhou Museum, this chapter considers work built before the social and economic reform of the late 1970s in mainland China and the beginning of post-modernist discourse. Taking this longer historical view is crucial in order to transcend the typical understanding of Pei's work in China, which solidified in the late 1970s, as an integration of elements of vernacular Chinese architecture into a nostalgic re-reading of the past. Pei's projects for a museum of Chinese art in Shanghai, a campus design for Huatung University in the same city, and Tunghai University in Taichung demonstrate a consistent application of visual and experiential dialectics in elements of both modern architecture and Chinese architectural precedents. For example, each project carefully incorporates the salient features of the Chinese garden in rocks, plantings, pavilions, and bridges as part of a picturesque composition and spatial structure to emphasise the interweaving of interior and exterior, and of the built and natural environments. Pei's intention with these elements was emphatically not to argue for an unchanging Chinese architectural tradition, but rather to make the social and technological progressiveness of modern architecture relevant to specific climates, histories, cultures, and lives.

While Pei's Shanghai museum concept evokes the intimate experience of art in nature offered by a scholar's garden, his insertion of a central garden with a pavilion connected to the upper and lower floors casts the museum as a space for social encounter, and not just for display. On the marshy site of Huatung University, the interweaving of structures on stilts—designed to be built with such modern materials as glass and reinforced concrete—over pools within landscaped gardens is culturally sensitive as much as it is economical and functional. And although the Tunghai campus is characterised by clusters of buildings around a courtyard with covered walkways and canted-roof structures influenced by Chinese vernacular architecture, the master plan includes an axial avenue cutting through the campus, typical of an American university, while the design employs inventive use of prefabricated reinforced concrete and timber-frame construction.

Pei's involvement in the design of a pavilion for Taiwan at Expo '70 in Osaka and the rock landscape he designed for the Suzhou Museum also demonstrate his ability to reinterpret and manifest subtle spatial–philosophical traits of historical Chinese architecture and garden design. Composed of two triangular concrete volumes connected by tubular bridges around a four-storey central space with a concrete ceiling of triangular coffers, the Expo '70 pavilion was accepted by the Taiwanese authorities as a result of Pei's argument that its exterior simplicity and interior complexity, multiple and shifting perspectives through an unfolding sequence of spaces, and the coexistence of solids and voids are inherent in the traditional Chinese courtyard garden. This acceptance signalled a shift in the government's definition of what constituted 'Chinese architecture', which it had previously framed as an application of formal elements that are immediately identifiable as Chinese.[3] At the Suzhou Museum, Pei applied an intertextual approach to Chinese garden design by composing a low-lying stone relief made of thirty sliced rocks as a three-dimensional interpretation of *Cloudy Mountains*, a landscape painting by the Song dynasty painter Mi Youren, thereby integrating rock work as a key sculptural component within the spatial constraints of the garden.

Pei was committed to enriching plurality through 'fruitfully imaginative developments' between past and present and across different 'cultural soils'.[4] For Pei, tradition—a term that could refer to Chinese garden typologies or the modern movement—was a time-tested, dynamic, and compelling model that called for the architect to reorganise the heterogeneous realities of society and the built environment, aside from any preconceived definition of style.[5] In the landscape of 1980s Euro-American architectural discourse, reference to the past signalled a form of post-modernist theoretical gesturing. But seen against rapid urban redevelopment in China, it becomes clear that Pei's engagement with historical archetypes had real implications for architecture and urban design. Fragrant Hill Hotel, for example, had precipitated a wave of contextual regionalism and urban renewal that respected the existing fabric of the city, moving both discourse and practice beyond the binary of tradition and modernity across China.[6]

— Shirley Surya

6.1 | **I. M. Pei, A Patio, third-year project in architectural design at the Massachusetts Institute of Technology, 1938. MIT Museum**

This design for a patio as part of a studio brief is possibly Pei's earliest exercise in Chinese cultural specificity, with its use of a semi-enclosed quadrangle, auspicious red on its columns and ceiling, patterns of ornamental tiles, bamboo planting, and a scroll-like mural along the arcades. Yet its strictly planar and orthogonal cantilevered structure on pilotis is a clear nod to modern architecture.

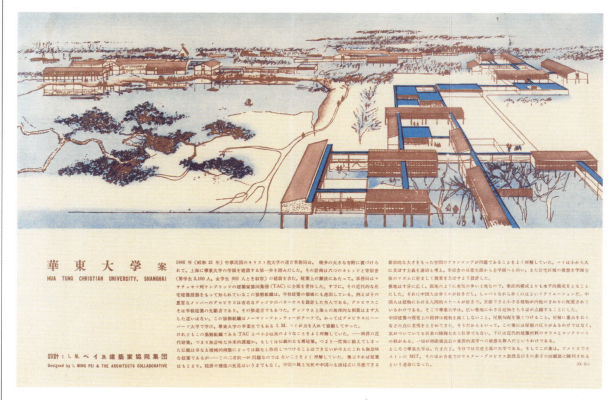

6.2.1 | **'Hua Tung Christian University, Shanghai—Proposal; Designed by I. Ming Pei & The Architects Collaborative'**, *International Architecture: Kokusai-Kentiku—A Monthly Journal for Contemporary Architecture* 19 (July 1952): 25. Papers of I. M. Pei, Library of Congress, Washington DC

Huatung University (1946–1948; unbuilt)
Shanghai

6.2.2 | 'Hua Tung Christian University—Dormitories', *International Architecture: Kokusai-Kentiku— A Monthly Journal for Contemporary Architecture* 19 (July 1952): 34–35. Papers of I. M. Pei, Library of Congress, Washington DC

6.2.1–6.2.2
The design for Huatung University was neither an imitation of an extinct tradition nor a wholesale importation of a Euro-American style. The interweaving of structures on stilts over bodies of water in landscaped gardens was an economical, functional, and culturally sensitive response to campus life that also reflected the intimacy with the natural environment characteristic of traditional Chinese landscape designs. While the structures are orthogonally planned and built with modern materials, the project's formal and spatial solutions are grounded in tradition. Low-lying academic buildings and dormitories spread across the campus are designed at the scale of the human body, with the width of a building encompassing the size of a single classroom and an external corridor. Sloped tiled roofs, covered corridors, courtyard gardens, and glass and reinforced-concrete columns that function as partitions between indoors and outdoors emphasise harmony with nature and facilitate natural cooling in the hot, humid summers.

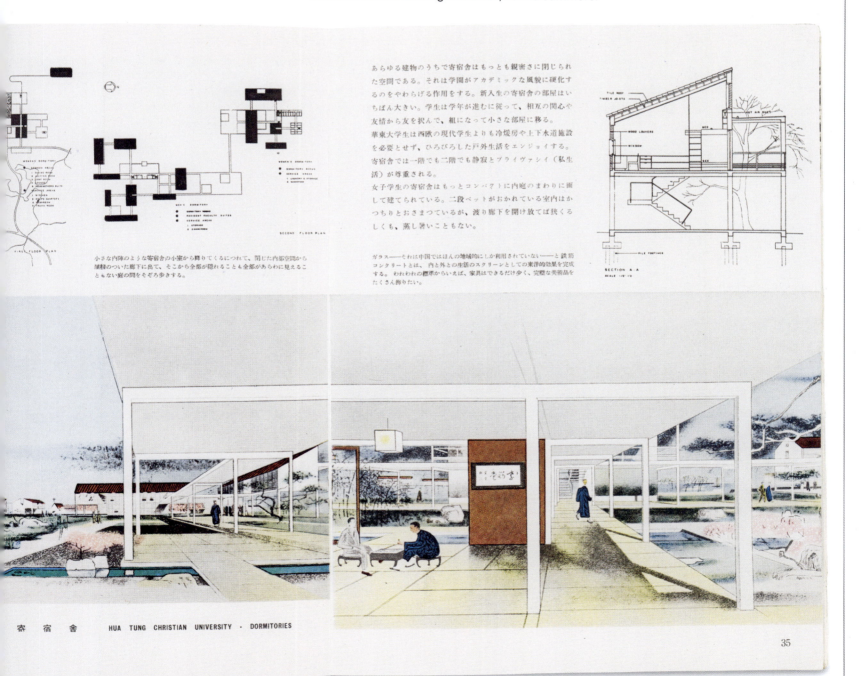

6.3 | **I. M. Pei Architect and Chen Chi-kwan, ink drawing of concept master plan for Tunghai University, 1954. Family of Chen Chi-kwan**

After 1949, the United Board for Christian Colleges in China (UBCCC) sought to establish universities outside mainland China. Under the direction of the board's general secretary, William P. Fenn, who was also responsible for commissioning the Huatung University project, Tunghai University was founded in Taiwan in 1955. Fenn, in his vision statement, sought to ensure that the design of Tunghai could model 'the right modern architecture for Formosa [Taiwan]'. Unsatisfactory proposals from an open call, for which Pei was a member of the jury, led Fenn to commission Pei to design the 140-hectare campus himself. Pei, who remained committed to his work with Webb & Knapp in New York, enlisted Chang Chao-kang and Chen Chi-kwan—two Chinese architects who had worked and studied with Walter Gropius—to manage the details of design and construction. Chen's aerial drawing, rendered in ink, expresses the 'Chinese vision' that underpinned Tunghai's design, characterised by an asymmetrical layout of structures clustered around a semi-enclosed courtyard. A chapel slides away from the axis of Wen-li Boulevard, embedded in the landscape of Taichung's Dadu Mountain.

Tunghai University (1954–1963)
Taichung

6.4.1 | **Early study of courtyard-house massing in the campus layout, ca.1954. Pei Cobb Freed & Partners**

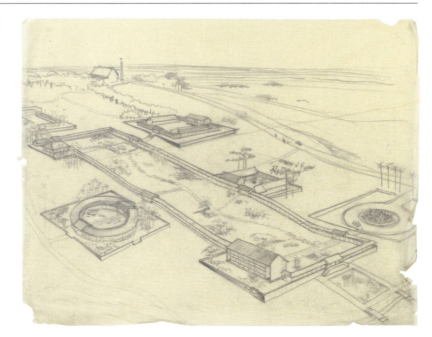

6.4.2 | Mary E. Ferguson, letter from the UBCCC requesting Chang Chao-kang's application for US permanent residency to enable his trip to Taiwan, written on behalf of I. M. Pei, 13 June 1955. Papers of I. M. Pei, Library of Congress, Washington DC

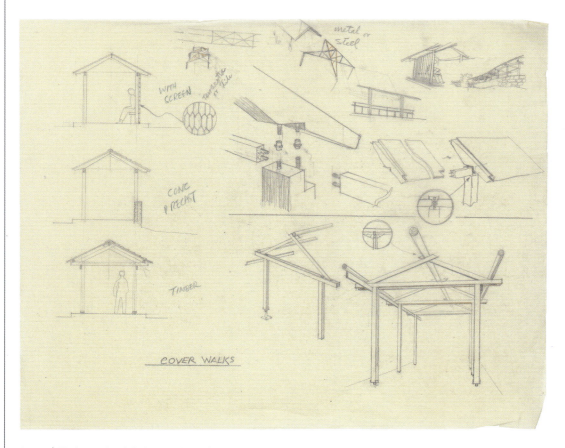

6.4.3 | Early study of timber-and-reinforced-concrete framework for covered walkways, ca.1954. Pei Cobb Freed & Partners

OPPOSITE:
6.4.4 | Lee Kuo-Min, one of the covered walkways connecting buildings within a courtyard compound, 2021. Photo commissioned by M+

6.4.5 | Chen Chi-kwan, early drawing of Luce Memorial Chapel at Tunghai University, ca.1956. Family of Chen Chi-kwan

6.4.1–6.4.5
In April 1954, Pei began to supervise the development of the preliminary design for Tunghai from New York. It was not until 1956 that Chang and Chen visited Taiwan. Early massing studies of the semi-enclosed courtyard house and gabled roofs reveal attempts at an articulation of elements of traditional Chinese architecture. These attempts include drawing from Beijing's *siheyuan* quadrangle courtyard residences and the enclosed circular *tulou* courtyard of Hakka vernacular architecture, as well as the introduction of the structural framework of gable-roofed walkways between buildings. Methods of contemporary construction and other cultural associations coexist with these references. Tunghai's central avenue, for example, recalls the university malls in America, while pre-cast concrete was used alongside traditional timber construction.

6.5.1 | **Chang Chao-kang, the College of Science on an elevated base with a view of the three-storey library along Wen-li Boulevard, ca.1957. Family of Chang Chao-kang**

6.5.2 | **Chang Chao-kang, the Administrative Building located at the beginning of Wen-li Boulevard, ca.1957. Family of Chang Chao-kang**

OPPOSITE:
6.5.3 | **Lee Kuo-Min, the back of the old three-storey library, now an academic building, 2021. Photo commissioned by M+**

6.5.1–6.5.3
The design of Tunghai reflects a desire for harmony between humankind and nature, a touchstone in the history of Chinese art and architecture. The placement of the buildings maintains vistas of the neighbouring acacia forest and mountain range, whose silhouette is complemented by the buildings' gabled roofs. Traditional Chinese structural and spatial elements can be seen in the buildings' central bay entrance with an elevated base with steps, and in the simulation of traditional timber construction in the reinforced-concrete frame for clay-tiled wooden gabled roofs. This allowed for the introduction of non-load-bearing walls with decorative, ventilating, and sun-shading functions. The old library's openwork walls use ceramic tubes and coin-shaped tiles, structurally reinforced with hidden rebar. The exposed gable roof beams and articulated rectangular eaves and rafters have been likened to Japan's *shoin-zukuri* model, while the triangular louvred ventilation under the gables and modular construction method have even been compared to the American ranch house.

```
                    Comments and Suggestions after Conference -II.
                         between C. K. Chang and I. M. Pei

        Dining-hall
            A.   The dining area seems rather dark, and the seating a bit congest-
                 ed; the hip roof connection and short core are difficult to work
                 clearly, structurally and architecturally.  It is accordingly
                 suggested

                 1.  that the seating be rearranged parallel to the longitudi-
                     nal axis.

                 2.  that the pantry core be enlarged, making a flat roof,
                     and raising the eaves of the dining and kitchen blocks.

            B.   With regard to the working conditions in the rice cooking area,
                 as well as the fuel storage location and the architectural re-
                 lation with the main building, it would be appropriate to

                 1.  Have a bay on each end of the kitchen block and make the
                     plan symmetrical.  These bays would be used for workers'
                     quarters and fuel storage, with an enlarged cooking area.

            C.   The location of the dining hall on the proposed plan is archi-
                 tectually desirable, but attention will need to be paid to
                 landscaping, and to terracing the contour drop.

            D.   Overhangs are suggested on the gable end walls to balance the
                 big cantilevered eaves on the sides, thus providing covering
                 at the corners and to avoid the feeling of a sudden cut-off
                 between the side and end walls.

        Gymnasium
                 I.M. Pei prefers the outside open staircase at the back, or
                 if the special door is necessary, just one door on the gable
                 end wall which faces the men's dormitory, with a canopy over
                 the door and steps going to the back without crossing the
                 stone wall.

                 Tiles for the terrace

                 With reference to the special floor tile manufactured by Tung-
                 Yang of which Mr. Chen has sent photographs, Mr. Pei thinks
                 these could be used for the gymnasium only, but not on the tai
                 and other buildings.  He would like to know the material of
                 which these new tiles are made.  It may be worthwhile consider-
                 ing putting a test strip on the main campus thoroughfare, so as
                 to observe the durability of the grooves, whether it collects
                 dust easily, and if it is easy to clean after it is muddy.  The
                 results of the above observations would decide whether or not
                 to use the tile.

                               - - -oOo- - -
```

6.6.1 | **List of I. M. Pei's comments and suggestions for the design of the university's dining hall and gymnasium after a conference call with Chang Chao-kang, ca.1958. Papers of I. M. Pei, Library of Congress, Washington DC**

6.6.2 | **Chang Chao-kang, entrance of the gymnasium, ca.1958. Family of Chang Chao-kang**

6.6.1–6.6.2
Pei was deeply involved in the design process for Tunghai, even from New York. In this document, he expresses the need for a better structural relationship between the hip roof connection and its short core, for overhangs on the gable end walls to balance the large, cantilevered eaves, and for a durability test before determining the use of certain floor tiles for terraces. Designed by Chang, the gymnasium's entrance features projecting rafters underneath the overhang, an exposed concrete framework that allowed for non-load-bearing walls—which were divided by contrasting bands of wooden lattice for ventilation—and a low gate made of hollow ceramic tubes.

REGENERATING CULTURAL & HISTORICAL ARCHETYPES

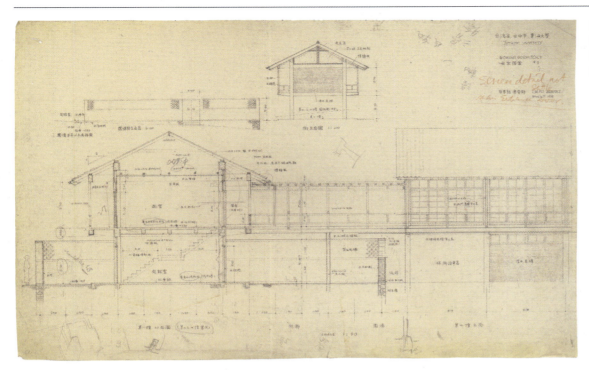

6.7.1 | **I. M. Pei Architect and Chang Chao-kang, elevation and section of the Women's Dormitory, 1955. Pei Cobb Freed & Partners**

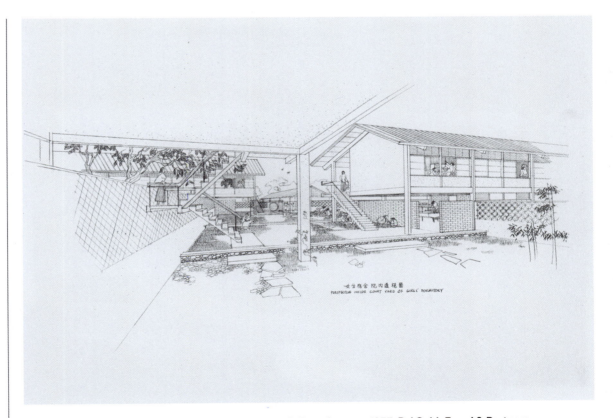

6.7.2 | **Chen Chi-kwan, courtyard view of the Women's Dormitory, ca.1955. Pei Cobb Freed & Partners**

PAGES 310–311:
6.7.3 | **Lee Kuo-Min, Women's Dormitory, 2021. Photo commissioned by M+**

6.7.1–6.7.3
The Women's Dormitory was designed as part of a series of courtyards meant to resemble a traditional Chinese garden, with irregular stone-stepped paths and a moon gate. Built in reinforced concrete and with a gabled roof in clay tile, the dormitory's bedrooms connect to an open corridor on the second floor, while the ground floor contains the lounge and bicycle parking.

6.8.1 | **The pavilion seen from the Festival Plaza, in 'Brochure of the Japan World Exposition '70 Republic of China Pavilion' by the Committee of Tourism of Ministry of Transportation and Communications, ROC, 1970.**
Lee Chu-yuan

Expo '70 Taiwan Pavilion (1969–1970)
Osaka

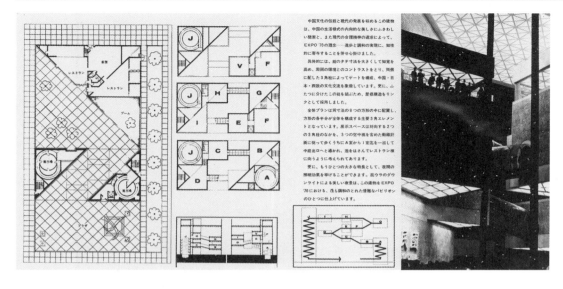

6.8.2 | **Plans and section showing the pavilion designed on an eight-square grid, in 'Brochure of the Japan World Exposition '70 Republic of China Pavilion' by the Committee of Tourism of Ministry of Transportation and Communications, ROC, 1970. Lee Chu-yuan**

6.8.3 | **Chen Yong-kui, Taiwan Pavilion at the Expo '70 grounds, between the South Korean Pavilion on the left and the New Zealand Pavilion on the right, 1970. Central News Agency**

6.8.1–6.8.3

The government of Taiwan's nationalistic claim to be the true custodian of Chinese culture led to the Kuomintang's preference for buildings with identifiably traditional Chinese features, like the upturned eaves of palatial structures. However, under the direction of Minister of Economics and Finance Li Kwoh-ting, the commission for the Taiwan Pavilion at Expo '70 called for a more progressive agenda. Pei, who was first invited to be a member of the jury for the pavilion's design competition, was asked to 'curate' and further develop the winning proposal. Pei simplified its geometry and raised it to a thirty-two-metre structure composed of two triangular concrete volumes of galleries, connected by criss-crossing tubular bridges around a four-storey atrium. The authorities accepted the design based on Pei's argument that it reflected the spatiality of traditional Chinese courtyard gardens, in the form of its exterior simplicity and interior complexity, the coexistence of solids and voids, and the shifting perspectives through an unfolding sequence of spaces, which ended with visitors descending a four-hundred-metre circular ramp while watching a film projected at the bottom.

Fragrant Hill Hotel (1979–1982)
Beijing

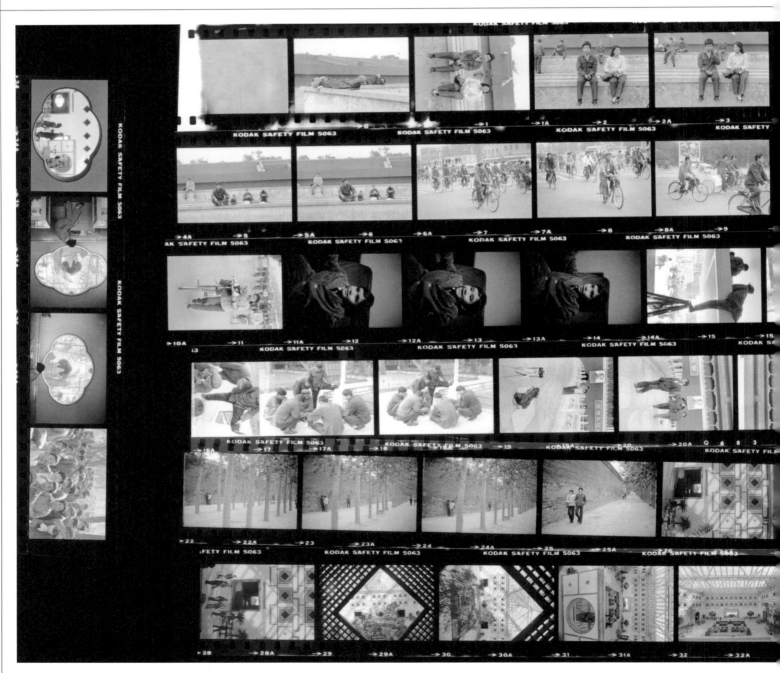

6.9.1 | **Marc Riboud, contact sheet of photographs of Beijing and the Fragrant Hill Hotel around the time of the hotel's soft opening, ca.1982. Association Les amis de Marc Riboud**

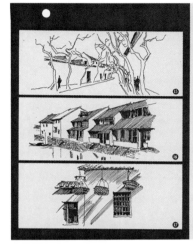

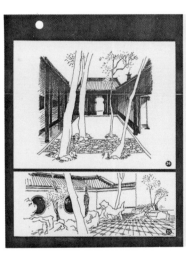
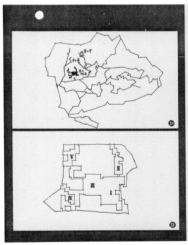

6.9.2 | **I. M. Pei and Wang Tianxi, illustrations of features found in vernacular housing in southern China that informed the design of the Fragrant Hill Hotel, from Pei's lecture 'Urban Planning in Beijing and the Problem of the Nationalisation of Architectural Creation in China', delivered to Beijing's Tsinghua University delegates as part of the Tsinghua Alumni Association of Greater New York, 30 May 1980. Papers of I. M. Pei, Library of Congress, Washington DC**

6.9.1–6.9.2

The Fragrant Hill project was conceived against the backdrop of China's transition towards social and cultural openness. In a lecture in New York for delegates from Tsinghua University, Pei described features that could distinguish China's vernacular housing from that of other parts of the world: a material vocabulary of white walls, black terracotta titles, and grey bricks; delicate gardens with a visual relationship to landscape paintings; screens and windows that frame views between homes and gardens; and an intimate connection between buildings and gardens. By reinterpreting the use of these features, Pei advocated a modern architecture specific to China.

PAGES 316–317:

6.10.1 | **Tian Fangfang, view of the Four Seasons Courtyard through a circular opening in a spirit screen, 2021. Photo commissioned by M+**

6.10.2 | **First-floor plan of Fragrant Hill Hotel, 1979. Pei Cobb Freed & Partners**

6.10.1–6.10.2
Pei's intention of weaving the landscape into the hotel resulted in a floor plan that evokes the unfolding visual and spatial experience of the classical Chinese garden. Upon entering the complex via an austere forecourt, guests are confronted with a strong north-to-south axiality, typical of traditional Chinese architecture, from the reception up through the four-storey lobby. Pei introduced a spirit screen with a moon gate–like aperture framing a view of the lobby towards the back entrance and main garden beyond. From the courtyard, one can enter the corridors and guest rooms, carefully arranged with views onto eleven smaller gardens with ancient trees set against white walls.

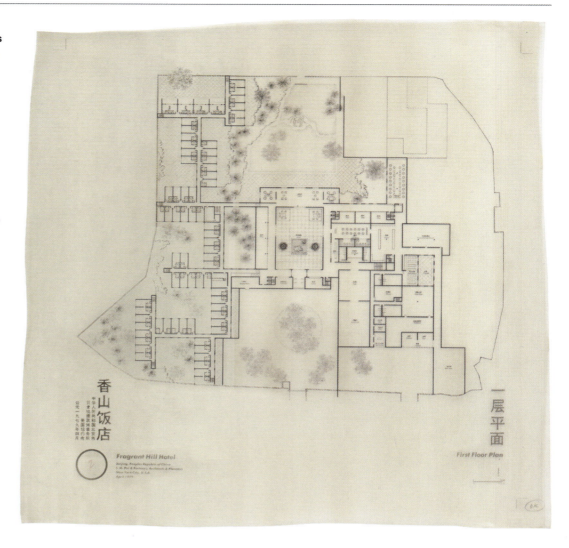

6.11.1 | **Drawing of the facade and space truss for the roof of Fragrant Hill Hotel's Four Seasons Courtyard, ca.1979. Pei Cobb Freed & Partners**

6.11.2 | **Grey tiles and trelliswork on Fragrant Hill Hotel's stucco facade. Pei Cobb Freed & Partners**

6.11.1–6.11.2
At a time when post-modern historicism was dominating Euro-American architectural discourse, American architects saw Fragrant Hill Hotel, with its grey tiles and trelliswork set in geometrical openings on a bone-white stucco facade, as marking Pei's post-modern turn. However, his reference to the vernacular and historical was a crucial part of his effort to read these elements on their own terms and to position them as components of a modern Chinese architecture. Instead of mimicking the upturned roof and intricate brackets of Chinese palatial structures, Pei abstracted traditional forms, applied old construction materials in new ways, and brought the spatial experience of Chinese gardens indoors. Grey tiles, traditionally used on Beijing's city walls to prevent cracking, were set into square lattice frames alongside the hotel's windows. The tiles were no longer produced locally, but Pei's team found an artisan who was willing to use an old kiln to make them. Windows of various shapes offer views onto the courtyards, creating a carefully calibrated relationship between indoors and outdoors. Plum blossom–shaped openings line the main ceremonial spaces, diamond-shaped lattice openings line the corridors, and lattice side panels are present in the guest rooms.

This lamp was designed for the atrium lobby of the Fragrant Hill Hotel. Lighting this vast space was a challenge. There was a need for general illumination as well as a sense of warmth and intimacy for guests. John Morford—the lead interior designer—and I determined that lamps for this space should not directly light faces. Instead, light should be pointed down onto the carpet, and then reflected up to the guests.

We decided on the lamp's round shape for its non-directionality, and metal for its potential for attenuation. The European—and specifically Bauhaus—resonance of this form and material led us to employ cloisonné enamel and a cracked-ice pattern for the surface, elements that have strong associations with design history in China. The cloisonné technique allowed us to apply colour to the metal structure, which lightened the form. We brought the cracked-ice pattern from paving and screens in the hotel to the scale of the lamp, introducing a continuity in that sense. Each lamp was fabricated by hand, which allowed us to soften the strict, minimal form with rounded edges and pitched planes.

– Calvin Tsao

Calvin Tsao joined I. M. Pei & Partners in the early 1980s as one of the architects working on the Fragrant Hill Hotel, before co-founding the New York–based practice Tsao & McKown in 1985.

6.12 | **Calvin Tsao and John Morford, lamp for the Fragrant Hill Hotel, ca.1982. M+, Hong Kong**

Pei oversaw Fragrant Hill as a total design project, from landscaping to interior furnishings. A result of his attempt to locally source and manufacture as many of the hotel's elements as possible, this lamp was produced by the Beijing Enamel Factory, whose use of cloisonné enamelling was normally applied to historically derivative souvenirs for tourists. By contrast, this lamp consists of a streamlined form made according to traditional craft techniques. The understated cream enamel highlights the bronze wiring around each enclosure, which forms a tessellation resembling the crackle glaze of traditional ceramic ware, as well as the cracked-ice pattern in the lattice design around the hotel's windows.

REGENERATING CULTURAL & HISTORICAL ARCHETYPES　　321

6.13.1 | **Calvin Tsao, workers constructing a replica of a damaged *qu shui liu shang*, ca.1980**

6.13.2 | **The hotel's main garden with the replica *qu shui liu shang* in the foreground, ca.1982. Pei Cobb Freed & Partners**

PAGES 322–323:

6.13.3 | **Tian Fangfang, the main garden with one of the trees placed to form a composition against the end wall of a hotel wing, 2021. Photo commissioned by M+**

6.13.1–6.13.3
For his design of Fragrant Hill's landscape architecture, Pei collaborated with Chen Congzhou, a leading expert on Chinese garden design. Both Chen and Pei were interested in applying and adapting traditional garden design to contemporary contexts. Chen favoured the southern Jiangnan gardens over northern alternatives for their open, airy designs and their privileging of the interdependence of the natural and hand-crafted in water, rocks, plantings, and built structures. Pei introduced a large body of water into the main garden of Fragrant Hill by reopening a stream. At its centre, he placed a replica of a *qu shui liu shang* (water maze)—a marble block, carved with a serpentine pattern, that had been found on-site. Rock formations from Yunnan were installed to introduce a balance integral to the *shanshui* (mountain and water) aesthetic of painting and garden design.

Some people labelled Fragrant Hill as a post-modern building, but my father totally rejected this notion. No, he would say, this building does not borrow historical elements for decoration but rather incorporates traditional elements in a way that is true to their original use. He was looking for a living vernacular that would be applicable anywhere in China. The project generated quite a bit of debate in our office as it was a complete departure, at least stylistically, from anything we had ever done.

– Chien Chung (Didi) Pei

Chien Chung (Didi) Pei is the second son of Eileen and I. M. Pei. He joined I. M. Pei & Partners in 1972 before establishing Pei Partnership Architects (now PEI Architects) in 1990. He was the design architect for the Fragrant Hill Hotel.

6.14 | **Advertisement for *Connoisseur* magazine featuring Chen Congzhou and I. M. Pei against an image of the Fragrant Hill Hotel's entrance under construction, *New Yorker*, 14 February 1983. Condé Nast**

Thomas Hoving, a former director of the Metropolitan Museum of Art in New York and editor of *Connoisseur* from 1981 to 1991, attended the opening of the Fragrant Hill Hotel in 1982. The headline of this advertisement for *Connoisseur* reflects fundamental questions on the impact of Pei's participation in the Fragrant Hill commission.

6.15.1 | **Drawing of the revised facade design without horizontal bands, ca.1983. Pei Cobb Freed & Partners**

6.15.1–6.15.2
Pei and Bank of China officials were keenly aware of the importance of feng shui in architectural and urban design in Hong Kong. Following the announcement of the tower's design, local geomancers decried the inauspicious giant boxed 'X's on the building's facade, which resulted from a structural expression of the lateral diagonal bracing. In response, having sought structural engineer Leslie E. Robertson's assurance that minimising the structural expression would not affect the design's integrity, Pei concealed the heavy horizontals of the transfer trusses and described the result as a pattern of interlocking diamonds.

Bank of China Tower (1982–1989)
Hong Kong

6.15.2 | **Model of the tower's early design with structural expression of boxed 'X' bracing on the facade, ca.1983. Pei Cobb Freed & Partners**

The Bank of China Tower marks the skyline of Hong Kong with a distinctive faceted form that marries structure and sculpture. Pei's design for the tower consists of four triangular quadrants that set back at different heights, allowing only one quadrant to reach its full height. All quadrants are cut on a forty-five-degree slope, which gives the tower its distinctive profile. Leslie Robertson's structural design places the primary structure at the perimeter in a triangulated multistorey frame. The triangulation of the braced frame gives the tower its faceted geometry, diminishing as it rises. The frame is also expressed on the facade as bright aluminium cladding that connects from corner to corner, creating the expression of an auspicious diamond pattern. The surrounding site is landscaped as an abstracted series of cascading gardens and water features. The angular stone hardscape incorporates koi ponds and sculptural scholar stones. The abstraction of the shaft of the tower gives way to a far more site-specific design for the way it meets the ground. The base of the tower reflects Pei's own struggle to reconcile his Bauhaus education with the particularities of place; and in this case, it is particularly resonant with his own departure from China, its distance and proximity. Pei's Bank of China speaks to the demands of the tall building—as an urban artefact, a broadcast medium, the forces that it is subjected to, and the placelessness/placeedness of the building type.

– Eric Höweler

Eric Höweler is principal of Höweler + Yoon and designed many high-rise structures in Hong Kong while at Kohn Pedersen Fox Associates.

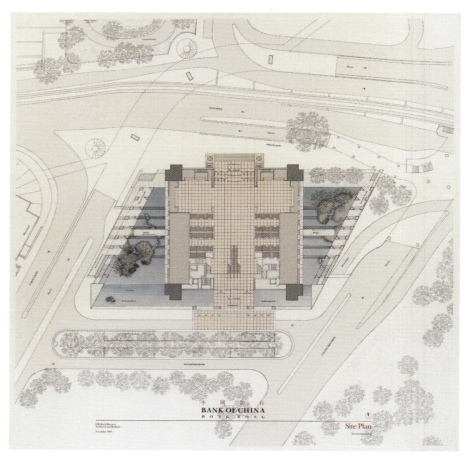

6.16 | **Site plan, ca.1984. Pei Cobb Freed & Partners**

Financial losses by corporations whose headquarters are located around the Bank of China Tower have been attributed to the *sat hei*, or 'killing energy', of the building's sharp-angled design, said to bring misfortune. The tower's rock-and-water gardens were considered as a means of collecting or diverting this inauspicious energy. The two triangular gardens were also meant to form a dignified setting and a promenade for the building's difficult site. They presented a continuous landscape, beginning with the pool at the upper southern entrance and continuing with the two angular, terraced basins on opposite sides of the building, whose waterfalls muffled traffic noise.

REGENERATING CULTURAL & HISTORICAL ARCHETYPES 327

6.17.1 | **Sandi Pei on a rock-scavenging expedition near the Shilin stone forest in Yunnan, ca.1989. Pei Cobb Freed & Partners**

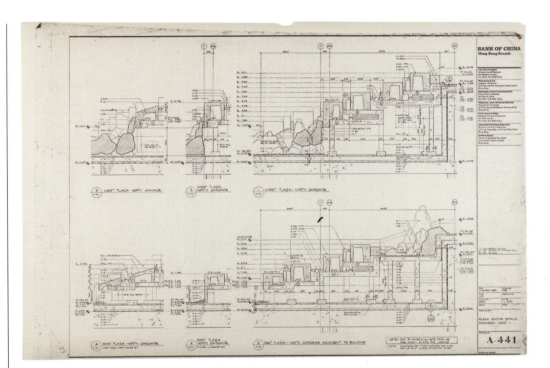

6.17.3 | **I. M. Pei & Partners and Wong/Kung & Lee Associate Architects, section of garden plaza, 1985. Sherman Kung & Associates Architects**

6.17.1–6.17.3
The details of the 1,300-square-metre garden plaza show Pei's application of principles of Chinese garden design. His approach followed the philosophy of open, contextual design espoused by Chen Congzhou, with whom he collaborated on the landscape design of Fragrant Hill Hotel. Elements such as trees and rock work were organised on cascading slabs on the steep slope, whose triangular geometry reflects the building's angled profile and granite base. These elements demonstrate the classical method of embracing a site's topography and features, as well as the contrast between and interdependence of hills, water, and rocks.

6.17.2 | **Sandi Pei (left), Kellogg Wong (second from right), and I. M. Pei (right) overseeing the setting of stones on the tower's garden plaza, ca.1989. Pei Cobb Freed & Partners**

6.18 | **South Ho, garden plaza of the Bank of China Tower, 2021. Photo commissioned by M+**

The Bank of China Tower's natural granite base rises to the level of the banking hall on the third floor, where it is articulated with a series of square openings reminiscent of the walls of ancient Chinese watchtowers. This could seem incongruous with the building's glass-and-steel portion, but the choice of an age-old material was intended to symbolise the solid base on which the towering skyscraper rests, and from which it might seem to have been excavated. It was also conceived as part of a dialogue with the tower's site and its masonry-built neighbours, such as the old Bank of China tower.

Grand Louvre
Phase I (1983–1989) & Phase II (1989–1993)
Paris

I. M. Pei was faced with a great challenge when the French state approached him to modernise the Musée du Louvre. He had never undertaken a project with this kind of visibility: a heritage building at the heart of one of the best-known cities in the world. He began by studying the history of Paris and the palaces of Versailles and Vaux-le-Vicomte and then convinced the state to create a very precise three-dimensional model of the site. This would allow him to demonstrate the importance of the new entrance hall he intended to construct in the context of the complexity of the Louvre's architecture and urban setting. Pei understood that the renovation of the Louvre had to be integrated into the east–west axis of the urban master plan, a plan that also comprised the architectural projects for the Grande Arche de la Défense by Johan Otto von Spreckelsen, the Opéra Bastille by Carlos Ott, and the new Bibliothèque nationale by Dominique Perrault. The model was presented to President François Mitterrand in February 1984. When the president asked about the large empty space in the Cour Napoléon, Pei took out of his pocket a Plexiglas pyramid and placed it at the centre. Following this dramatic flourish, the acceptance of the project was immediate. The battle of the pyramid could begin.

– Françoise Mardrus

Françoise Mardrus is an art historian who joined the management of the Louvre during the conception of the Grand Louvre project in 1988. In 2013, she founded the Louvre's Dominique-Vivant Denon Centre, dedicated to the history of the institution.

6.19.1 | **Marc Riboud, I. M. Pei with a model of the Grand Louvre, ca.1984. Association Les amis de Marc Riboud**

6.19.2 | **Giovanna Silva, Louvre pyramid as seen from the first-floor terrace of the Denon wing, 2021. Photo commissioned by M+**

6.19.3.1 | **Model of the Louvre fortress in the thirteenth century, ca.1989. Pei Cobb Freed & Partners**

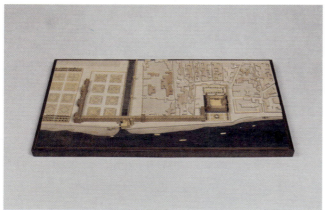

6.19.3.2 | **Model of the Louvre palace extending into the Jardin des Tuileries in the late fourteenth century, ca.1989. Pei Cobb Freed & Partners**

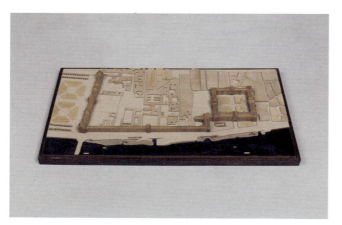

6.19.3.3 | **Model of the Louvre palace extending along the Seine and into the Jardin des Tuileries in the late seventeenth century, ca.1989. Pei Cobb Freed & Partners**

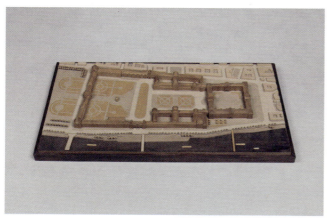

6.19.3.4 | **Model of the Louvre enclosing the Jardin des Tuileries in the mid-nineteenth century, ca.1989. Pei Cobb Freed & Partners**

6.19.1–6.19.3.4
Pei prepared this series of exhibition models documenting the Louvre's evolution for the opening of the Grand Louvre in March 1989. The models demonstrate his deep familiarity with the palace's eight-hundred-year history, from which he derived a scheme of reorganisation and modernisation even before accepting the commission. From its origins as a fortress in the twelfth century to a royal residence from the fourteenth to the eighteenth centuries and a public museum under Napoleon, the Louvre has remained a centrepiece of French state power and public culture. Pei excavated the Cour Napoléon and the Cour Carrée to create an underground network of spaces necessary for an up-to-date museum infrastructure, while preserving the buildings and unifying them in a single complex. The transparent glass-and-steel pyramid, a central point of entry, simultaneously expressed continuity and signalled a visual break with the past.

6.20.1 | Israël Silvestre, plan of Vaux-le-Vicomte by André Le Nôtre, ca.1660. Alamy

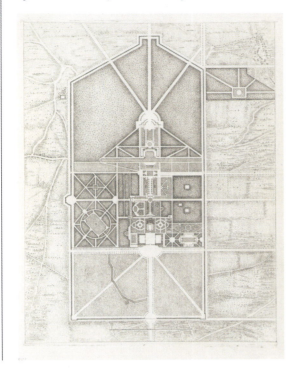

6.20.2 | Aerial photograph of the Louvre looking west, showing the urban axis running through the Jardin des Tuileries and the Champs-Élysées, ca.2021. Getty Images

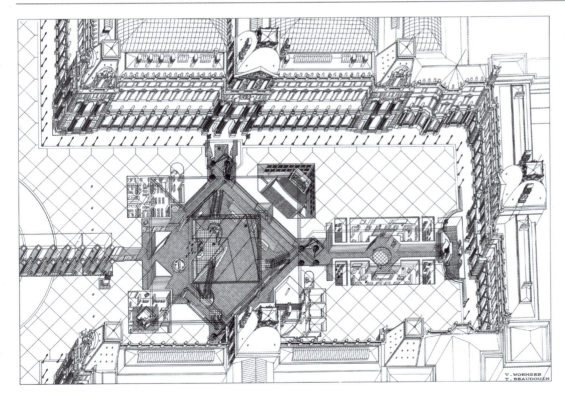

6.20.3 | Axonometric drawing of the underground network extending from the pyramid entrance, ca.1983. Pei Cobb Freed & Partners

PAGE 334:
6.20.4 | Giovanna Silva, a bride's photoshoot captured from Passage Richelieu, 2021. Photo commissioned by M+

6.20.1–6.20.4
Pei's project sought to address the Louvre's relationship with Paris's urban grid. He turned to formal French garden design for inspiration, particularly the geometrical landscapes of André Le Nôtre, who redesigned the Jardin des Tuileries in the 1660s. Responding to the Tuileries scheme, as well as looking to Le Nôtre's gardens at Vaux-le-Vicomte for inspiration, Pei defined an axial order for the Louvre's entrance through the pyramid and its arteries, reinforcing the palace's symmetry. His intervention also aligned the complex with the historic east–west axis of Paris's Voie triomphale, which extends through the Tuileries, the Place de la Concorde, the Avenue des Champs-Élysées, and the Arc de Triomphe, all the way to La Défense.

6.21 | **Higashide Kiyohiko, south-west facade of the Musée d'Art Moderne with the old walls of Fort Thüngen in the foreground, ca.2006. io Architects**

After receiving a commission for a new art museum for the city of Luxembourg, Pei chose the unfrequented hillside grounds of the eighteenth-century Fort Thüngen as a site. The tension of building something new on the foundations of a fortress appealed to him. The project also offered the potential to link Luxembourg's historic city centre with the newer district of Kirchberg. Requiring careful consideration of the historic site, the project took seventeen years to complete. In plan, the museum follows the fort's arrow-like layout; however, preservationists opposed Pei's initial proposal to place the main entrance through the fort itself and move the entryway to the rear of the complex. The challenge of building new foundations inside the old walls resulted in one side of the V-shaped building cantilevering over the ruins. The museum's glass facades, open central spaces, and glass bridge crossing the ruins allow direct views onto the fort as well as the city centre below.

Musée d'Art Moderne Grand-Duc Jean (MUDAM) (1989–2006)
Luxembourg City

6.22 | **Werner Huthmacher, view from the top floor of the new museum wing's spiral stair tower towards (from left) the Zeughaus, the Neue Wache, and the Palais am Festungsgraben, 2003. Papers of I.M. Pei, Library of Congress, Washington DC**

Following Germany's reunification, Pei was commissioned to design an extension to the Deutsches Historisches Museum in Berlin. The Zeughaus, the museum's pre-existing building, is a former armoury located on a small plot near the dense, historically rich Museumsinsel. The new wing was conceived to be barely visible from the grand boulevard of Unter den Linden, from which visitors would pass Karl Friedrich Schinkel's Neue Wache memorial before reaching Museumsinsel. To heighten the presence of the new structure while reinforcing its relationship with the site's distinguished past, Pei designed a three-storey triangular building in limestone and a glass-and-steel hall punctuated by a wide, cantilevered, glazed spiral staircase. Seen from without, transparency, light, and movement emanate from the stair tower. From inside, the addition brings the Neue Wache and its surrounding chestnut grove into focus and offers views of the Zeughaus and the Palais am Festungsgraben. To maintain the character of the historic alleyways and passages around Museumsinsel, Pei introduced a below-ground connection between the Zeughaus and the new wing.

Deutsches Historisches Museum (1996–2003)
Berlin

Joy of Angels Bell Tower (1988–1990)
Shigaraki, Shiga

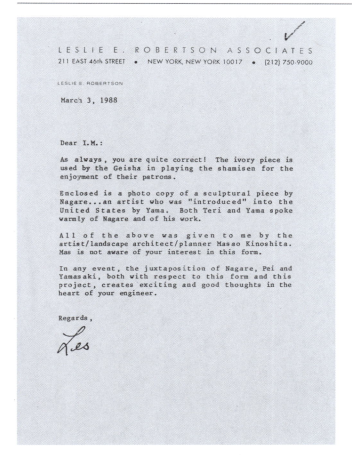

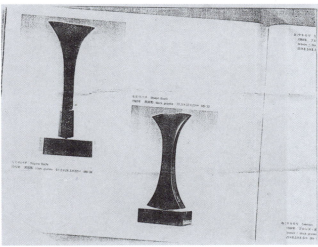

6.23.1 | **Leslie E. Robertson, letter to I. M. Pei with a photocopied page of Nagare Masayuki's granite sculptures affirming Pei's choice of the** *bachi* **for the tower's form, 3 March 1988. Papers of I. M. Pei, Library of Congress, Washington DC**

6.23.2 | **The Joy of Angels Bell Tower, located at the head of the plaza at Misono sanctuary, ca.1990. Pei Cobb Freed & Partners**

6.23.1–6.23.2
For his first project in Japan, a bell tower for the grounds of Shinji Shumeikai's Misono sanctuary outside Kyoto, Pei looked for a form that would resonate with Japanese tradition, and which would suit the hilly, forested site. Having recently found an ivory *bachi* (a type of plectrum used to play the three-stringed shamisen) he had bought in Kyoto in the 1950s, Pei decided to model the bell tower's form on the musical device. Nagare Masayuki, who had created an ablutions fountain for the sanctuary, also used this form in his work. Designed with the assistance of Design Architect Christopher Rand, the sixty-metre bell tower, clad in white Vermont granite, rises from a seven-metre-high square base before flaring out at the top. An elevator and a spiral staircase terminate at an observation deck, housing fifty bronze bells cast in the Netherlands.

Miho Museum (1991–1997)
Shigaraki, Shiga

6.24.1 | I. M. Pei, letter to Koyama Hiroko, daughter of Koyama Mihoko, with a copy of 'The Peach Blossom Spring' by Tao Yuanming, a scholar and official from the Six Dynasties period, 1997. Papers of I. M. Pei, Library of Congress, Washington DC

6.24.2 | **Model of the tunnel with a view of the suspension bridge and the museum beyond, ca.1991. Papers of I. M. Pei, Library of Congress, Washington DC**

PAGE 340:
6.24.3 | **Yoneda Tomoko, curved aluminium-clad tunnel, 2021. Photo commissioned by M+**

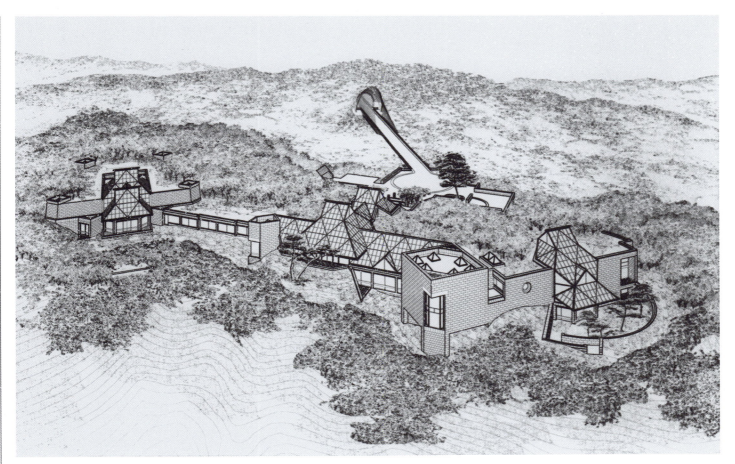

6.24.4 | **Drawing of the museum complex, bridge, and tunnel looking east, ca.1991. Pei Cobb Freed & Partners**

6.24.1–6.24.4
Pei's proposal to create an approach for the museum via a tunnel and a bridge was instantly supported by Koyama Mihoko, founder of Shinji Shumeikai, for its minimal disturbance of the natural environment. The proposal was inspired by the Chinese fable 'The Peach Blossom Spring' from the Six Dynasties period, which tells of a fisherman's discovery of an idyllic land through a narrow cavern. The path towards the museum is a carefully orchestrated sequence of concealment and unveiling. From the reception pavilion, visitors make their way through a curved tunnel burrowed into a mountain ridge. The tunnel is lined with aluminium, which reflects the surroundings. A view of the museum's skyline emerges only at the end of the tunnel, framed by the cables of a 120-metre post-tensioned bridge spanning a ravine. The bridge ends at a paved plaza and stairway leading to the museum's entrance.

REGENERATING CULTURAL & HISTORICAL ARCHETYPES

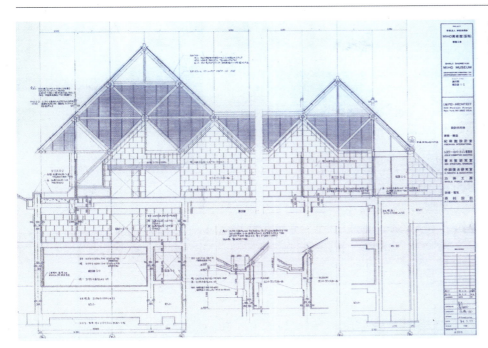

6.25.1 | **I. M. Pei Architect and Maehara Hitoshi, section of the museum's roof structure and gallery, 1994. Kibowkan International**

6.25.2 | **A typical *minka* (farmhouse) from the Edo period in Kyoto prefecture. Alamy**

6.25.3 | **Koyama Hiroko on a raised platform next to the tetrahedral carbon-steel tube roof truss at the museum's 'golden bolt' ceremony, ca.1996. Shinji Shumeikai**

PAGES 342–343:
6.25.4 | **Yoneda Tomoko, glazed roof with the steel space frame composed of tessellated tetrahedrons and finely slated sunscreens, 2021. Photo commissioned by M+**

6.25.1–6.25.4
With the majority of the museum built underground, the roof design brings filtered natural light into the double-height hallways through aluminium sunscreens painted to look like wood. The glazed roof structure, a tetrahedral space frame composed of carbon-steel tubes, produces a silhouette of peaks and valleys rising out of the landscape. This ensemble evokes the profile of the steep gabled roofs of the nearby Edo-period *minka*, or farmhouses. The roof doubles as a facade as it rises from the museum's boundary walls, as well as framing views of the hills and valleys to the west.

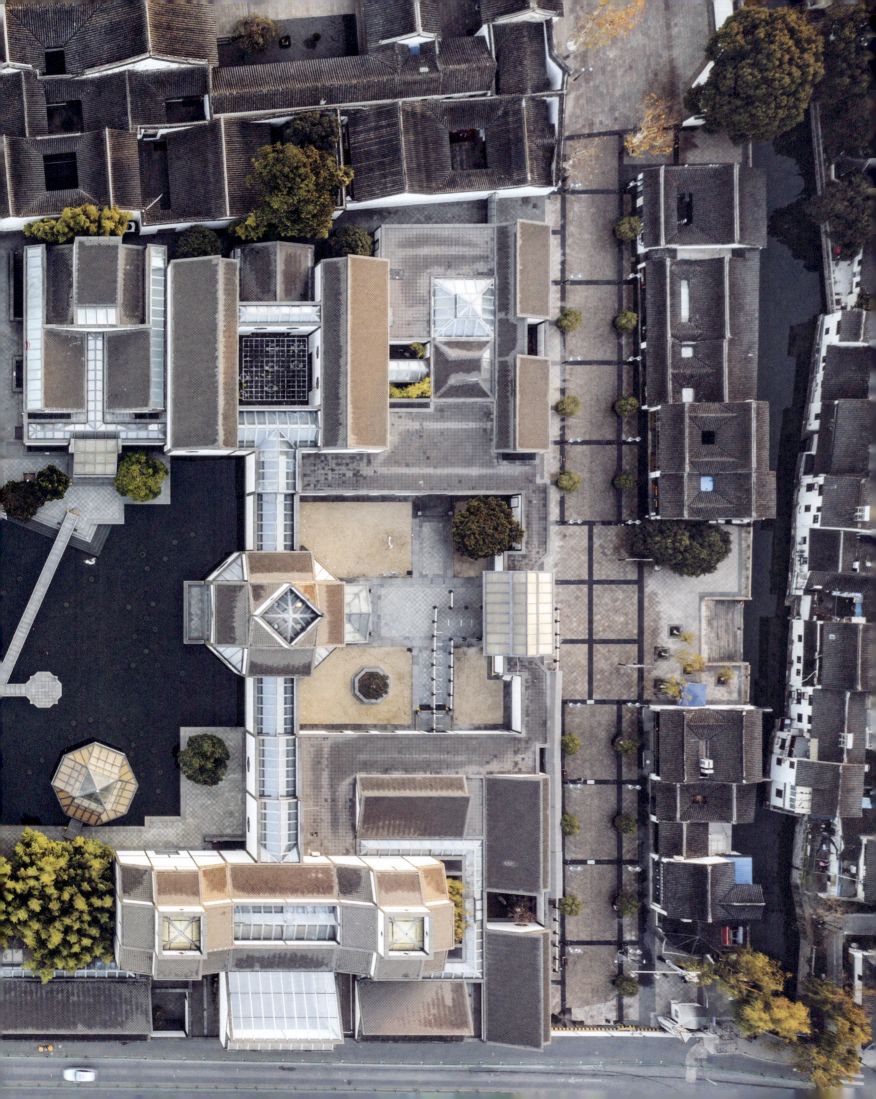

PAGES 344–345:

6.26 | **Tian Fangfang, view of the Suzhou Museum (centre) with the Humble Administrator's Garden (at left) and the Prince Zhong Mansion (at top), 2021. Photo commissioned by M+**

Since the 1990s, Suzhou city officials had repeatedly invited Pei to build in his ancestral home. The architect consistently rejected their offers, replying that the city was not in need of modern architecture but a plan for historical preservation and the cleaning of its waterways. In 2000, when Pei accepted the offer to design a new home for the Suzhou Museum, preservation guidelines were in place—partly owing to an urban revitalisation workshop led by his son T'ing Chung Pei in 1996—and the canals had been decontaminated. Located in Suzhou's historic district, adjacent to the sixteenth-century Humble Administrator's Garden, the project incorporated a mansion on the compound of the nineteenth-century Palace of Prince Zhong, the museum's home since 1960. Pei's careful intervention drew from the surrounding urban fabric in form, scale, and materiality. This view shows the museum framing a large pond with a bridge and octagonal pavilion, as well as water flowing through the wall that the complex shares with the Humble Administrator's Garden.

Suzhou Museum (2000–2006)
Suzhou

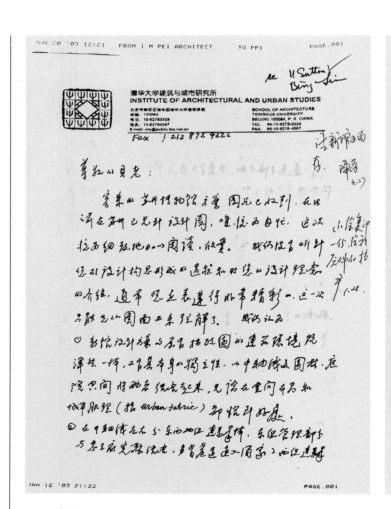
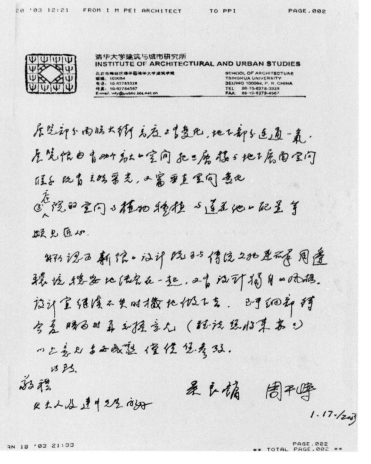

6.27.1 | **Wu Liang-yong and Zhou Gan-shi, letter to I. M. Pei on the effective integration of the design of the Suzhou Museum with the Humble Administrator's Garden and the city's urban fabric, 17 January 2003. Suzhou Museum**

6.27.2 | **Basement construction of the museum's West Wing, ca.2003. Suzhou Museum**

6.27.1–6.27.2
Pei's design for the Suzhou Museum was placed under greater scrutiny than Fragrant Hill Hotel had been owing to concerns that it would disrupt the continuity between the Humble Administrator's Garden and the Palace of Prince Zhong. To address these concerns, Pei consulted architects and academics from Beijing, Nanjing, and Suzhou, including Wu Liang-yong and Zhou Gan-shi, architects and champions of historic preservation and urban rehabilitation. The final design consists of a complex of whitewashed plaster walls and tiled roofs in black granite. To ensure most of the museum remained lower than the existing structures, the two-storey complex was placed half underground, with a maximum height of four metres, while the three-storey Central Hall and West Wing do not exceed sixteen metres.

Some have noticed stylistic similarities between the Suzhou Museum and the Museum of Islamic Art in Doha, built around the same time. But the architecture of I. M. Pei is not about style. The scale, materials, and colour of the Suzhou Museum are derived from its surroundings. Pei focused on how buildings and nature come together in Suzhou and studied how gardens have marked the city's landscape over the centuries. During his first trip to Suzhou for the project, he visited the Humble Administrator's Garden and spoke with experts on the city's history. His aim was to build a modern garden, in his own language. The scale of the Suzhou Museum references the human scale of the city, as well as the scale of the artefacts in the museum's collection, to bring together the vernacular with a contemporary public in an institutional setting. Responding to historical private gardens, Pei designed a public garden with an unconventional rock composition that introduces the abstraction of Chinese painting into landscape design. In China today, there are many museums built at important historical sites, yet few speak to the long history of their place. The Suzhou Museum is a reflection on historical context as well as a perspective directed towards the future.

– Lin Bing

Lin Bing is a Shanghai-based partner at OLI Architecture. He was part of Pei Partnership Architects between 1998 and 2010, and served as field architect for the Suzhou Museum.

6.28.1 | **Li Chung Pei, steel roof structure of the museum's two-storey buildings with the same profile as neighbouring grey-tiled roofs, ca.2005. PEI Architects**

PAGES 348–349:
6.28.2 | **Tian Fangfang, view of the main garden, 2021. Photo commissioned by M+**

6.28.1–6.28.2
The then governor of Suzhou strongly advocated the use of traditional clay-tiled roofs, but Pei insisted on constructing a steel-roofed structure in dark-grey granite. Doing away with traditional decorations on the eaves, he designed a monochrome roof to correspond with the profile of the sloped, charcoal-coloured roofs of surrounding buildings. This distinctive formal language was also translated onto the design of gates, windows, and stairs. The steel structure enabled the construction of a volumetric roof and allowed for an interweaving of cubes, squares, and triangles in continuity with the walls. The trapezoidal facades achieve a crisp geometric outline, trimmed with the same black granite. Inside, slender wood-clad metallic sunscreens bring shadows and natural lighting into the display spaces.

6.29.1 | **I. M. Pei, composition sketch of sliced rocks for the stone landscape, ca.2000. PEI Architects**

6.29.2 | **Li Chung Pei, the main garden under construction, with a view of I. M. Pei's stone landscape, the pond's cobblestone bottom, the bridge, and one of the first transplanted trees, ca.2005. PEI Architects**

PAGES 352–353:
6.29.3 | **Tian Fangfang, the Central Hall's framed views of the garden's key features, including the pavilion, the stone landscape, and trees, 2021. Photo commissioned by M+**

6.29.1–6.29.3
In his design for the Suzhou Museum, Pei responded to the challenge of deferring to but differing from historical Chinese gardens. He created his version of a scholar's microcosm of the natural world by including the indispensable *shanshui* elements of water, rocks, and plants within one fifth of the museum's plot. Framed by the museum's galleries, the northern wall bordering the Humble Administrator's Garden features a stone landscape and trees with fluid outlines, as well as an octagonal open pavilion and a bridge designed to encourage multiple viewpoints. Traditional scholar's gardens include ensembles of rocks formed naturally into distinctive shapes. Pei's intervention in the landscape of the Suzhou Museum instead consists of painstakingly worked stones grouped in a silhouette-like composition, inspired by *Pian Shi Shan Fang* (Mountain Studio of Rock Fragments) by the early Qing painter and monk Shitao, and by *Cloudy Mountains* (1130) by the Song dynasty painter Mi Youren. Granite from Shandong was sliced with steel wire, arranged from dark to light, and treated with a blowtorch to imitate a painterly vision of depth.

Museum of Islamic Art (2000–2008)
Doha

6.30.1 | **Mohamed Somji, view of the faceted central structure, 2022. Photo commissioned by M+**

The architectural programme of the Museum of Islamic Art necessitated that the building be an inclusive container for a collection comprised of diverse works from across Islamic cultures. At the same time, the context of the museum in the relatively new city of Doha did not present examples of built heritage that could ground the design. I. M. therefore made himself familiar with the distinct architectural cultures and vocabularies of the geographies of Islam. He searched for a building that he could relate to, and whose formal logic could be a reference point. He wanted a kind of emotional connection with an element of Islamic architecture that he could then interpret in Doha. The Mosque of Ibn Tulun in Cairo captivated him because of its spatial and formal clarity in addition to its history. It is an early mosque—commissioned by Ahmad ibn Tulun, who broke away from the Abbasid caliphate and established his own dynasty—and predates the city of Cairo. The mosque is austere in terms of its material and spatial organisation. It is made entirely with red brick faced in carved stucco. The mosque is a rectangular building surrounding a courtyard with a *sebil* (ablution fountain) at its centre, which casts strong shadows on the stone paving. I. M. really became attached to the *sebil*. By choosing this building, and particularly its water element, as an anchor, he distanced the design process from the building traditions of the major Islamic empires. Like the *sebil* positioned in the midst of a void, the Museum of Islamic Art is pushed out into the water, away from the city and the intensity of construction happening nearby. This was also a way to make sure that the museum wouldn't be lost in the rapidly changing urban texture.

– Aslıhan Demirtaş

Aslıhan Demirtaş was lead project designer for the Museum of Islamic Art in Doha, and lead project designer and collaborator for the Miho Institute of Aesthetics Chapel in Shigaraki.

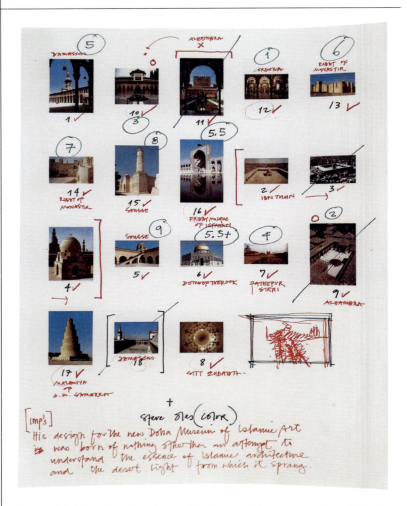

6.30.2 | **Aslıhan Demirtaş, index of Islamic architecture used by I. M. Pei in his search for a reference to ground the museum's design, compiled for the exhibition *From Córdoba to Samarkand* held at the Grand Louvre, 2006**

6.30.1–6.30.2
The Museum of Islamic Art presented Pei with the challenge of finding an anchor for the design that would reflect the museum's collection, which spans three continents and thirteen centuries. Project designer Aslıhan Demirtaş produced an index of photographs, sketches, and models of examples of Islamic architecture for Pei to review, organising them according to geography, historical period, materiality, and other categories. Pei was drawn to the Mosque of Ibn Tulun in Cairo, particularly its domed *sebil* (ablution fountain), which offered a geometry—a progression from octagon to square and finally to circle—that was culturally and historically specific yet could also be read as universal. Its formal, spatial, and material simplicity was appropriate for the context of Qatar, which did not have a particular architectural tradition for a building of this scale.

6.31.1 | **Model of the museum on an artificial island connected to Doha's Corniche via two causeways, ca.2003. Jock Pottle, Aslıhan Demirtaş**

PAGES 358–359:
6.31.2 | **Mohamed Somji, central courtyard connecting the main building with the education wing, 2022. Photo commissioned by M+**

6.31.1–6.31.2
References to specific elements of Islamic architecture can be seen throughout the museum's design. The angular volumes, which progressively step back as the central tower rises to a height of nearly twenty metres, refer to the spare ornamentation and geometry of the *sebil* of the Mosque of Ibn Tulun. The two main buildings and connecting courtyard are framed within a rectangular walled enclosure with covered hallways and arched openings, recalling the *ribat* (fortification) at Sousse in Tunisia. The central courtyard with a pavilion, divided into four parts by walkways and flowing shallow water, is akin to the *charbagh*, a traditional Persian quadrilateral garden.

360 LIFE IS ARCHITECTURE

6.32.1 | **Section model of the atrium, ca.2003.**
Jock Pottle, Aslıhan Demirtaş

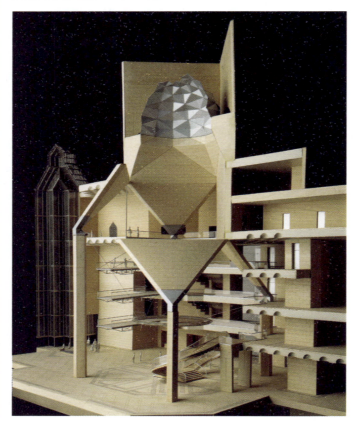

6.32.2 | **I. M. Pei Architect, detailed drawing of double-shelled dome, 2003.** Aslıhan Demirtaş

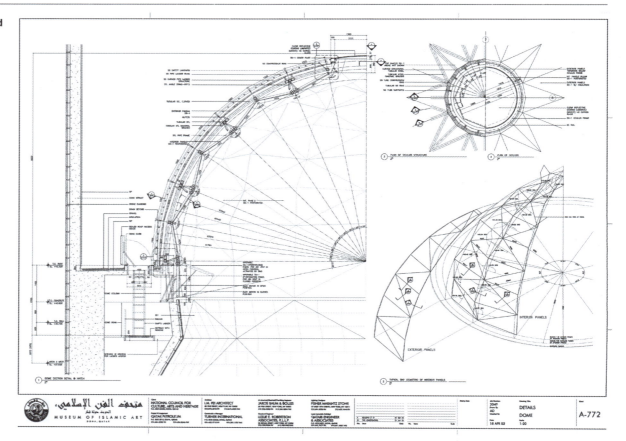

REGENERATING CULTURAL & HISTORICAL ARCHETYPES   361

6.32.3 | **Morley von Sternberg**, view of the central atrium from below the centre of the dome, with its chandelier, four pilasters, and coffered ceiling rising towards the oculus, ca.2012

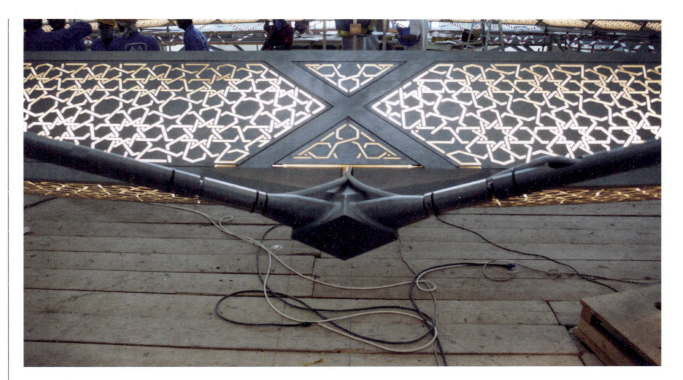

6.32.4 | Close-up view of the chandelier's lattice pattern derived from a computer programme developed by Craig Kaplan, ca.2008. Museum of Islamic Art

6.32.1–6.32.4
The museum's design reinforces the shift from austere exterior to interior ornamentation, characteristic of much Islamic architecture. Seen from the central stair, the atrium resolves into a circular oculus of a stainless-steel dome whose multiple facets capture the changing light. It is a homage to *muqarnas*, intricate honeycomb vaults traditionally used in the construction of domes and arches. The dome evolves as the structure descends, with the perimeter becoming an octagon and then a square, before being transformed into four triangular column supports. A chandelier, meant to give the space a more intimate scale, refers to the ring lamp of the Süleymaniye Mosque in Istanbul.

6.33 | Part of I. M. Pei's library, photographed before the sale of 11 Sutton Place in New York, his residence of forty-seven years, 2021. Estate of I. M. Pei

Pei's library reflects his diverse interests, cosmopolitan spirit, and wide travels. A representative selection of the volumes he kept at hand includes monographs on Zao Wou-Ki, Francesco Borromini, and Henri Matisse, as well as books on Chinese painting, Mexican murals, and Italian garden design.

I. M. Pei and Chinese Spatiality at Expo '70

Wu Kwang-tyng

On 15 March 1970, the first world exposition hosted by a country in Asia opened in Osaka. In past editions, the Taiwan pavilion had focused exclusively on exhibitions and spatial designs that showcased 'traditional Chinese culture with palace-style building', ignoring the concerns of modernity at the heart of the expositions.[1] In 1970, at the invitation of the Taiwanese government, I. M. Pei demonstrated the possibility of Chinese architecture expressed in modern forms. The pavilion is largely excluded from discussions of Pei's body of work, but it deserves to be considered not only in terms of the transformative effect it had on architecture in Taiwan and the discussion of modern Chinese design taking place there, but also for its significance in the architect's practice.

Between 1951 and 1965, the United States carried out a programme of aid for the government of the Republic of China (ROC), which was dominated by the Kuomintang. The US aid allowed Taiwan to rebuild and modernise its economy. Li Kwoh-ting, minister of economics and later of finance between 1965 and 1976, first proposed the idea of inviting Pei to supervise the Taiwan pavilion at Expo '70. He believed that cultural initiatives were just as important as economic policy for the project of modernisation, and that unwavering adherence to tradition could be an obstacle to this project.[2] Li's conviction reflects the central tension in architecture in Taiwan in the second half of the twentieth century. On the one hand, ROC president Chiang Kai-shek insisted on a conservative, identifiably 'Chinese' style for public projects. Palace-style designs were instruments of the nationalist political agenda. On the other hand, architects in Taiwan were deeply concerned with a modern language of design that could be Chinese without resorting to traditionalist imagery. Both sides of the debate strove to define an architectural language for a 'new China'.

In May 1968, the Ministry of Economic Affairs began preparations for Taiwan's participation in Expo '70. Meanwhile, in New York, Pei was quickly becoming one of the most prominent architects of his generation. Projects such as the National Center for Atmospheric Research in Boulder, Colorado, and the Everson Museum of Art in Syracuse, New York, demonstrated his increasingly important position. For Li, Pei was the only architect who could introduce a new approach to space in the pavilion and make a clear statement on the future of modern Chinese architecture. His role was envisioned as that of an advisor or project overseer, rather than a designer. Pei intended to decline the invitation, owing to the demands of ongoing projects in the United States and the inconvenience of the travel that would be involved, but his father, Tsuyee Pei, who was living in

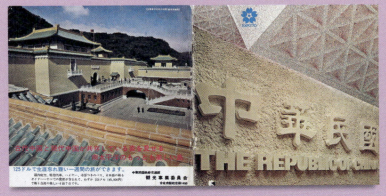

Front and back cover, 'Brochure of the Japan World Exposition '70 Republic of China Pavilion' by the Committee of Tourism of Ministry of Transportation and Communications, ROC, 1970. Lee Chu-yuan

Taiwan, intervened and encouraged him to accept.³ In July 1968, he arrived in Taiwan to review the results of the open call for design proposals.⁴

Pei chaired the jury for the open call, which also included one of his Harvard Graduate School of Design (GSD) classmates, Wang Da-hong, and three government representatives. A proposal by Atelier Cambridge, led by Hsiung Chi-wei, was selected as the winning project.⁵ The architects were all alumni of the Department of Architecture at National Cheng Kung University in Tainan and had studied and worked in Boston and New York. However, serious doubts about the quality of the project and the ability of the young architects led the government to announce that Pei himself would design the pavilion. Pei quickly countered that he would instead consult with Atelier Cambridge on the development of the project, adopting a 'team + team' model of working that would ensure that the design met the desires of the government. In effect, Pei acted as the curator of the pavilion. Lee Chu-yuan of Atelier Cambridge and Peng Yin-Hsuan of I. M. Pei & Partners were named as lead designers.

Between July and October 1968, working from Pei's office in New York, the design team refined the preliminary proposal with a similar triangular plan. When it was published, government officials and members of the public expressed concern over the absence of an obviously 'Chinese' character in the architectural form and decorative features. Pressure on the architects to articulate a national image in the pavilion only increased. Pei's solution was to reorganise the basic geometry of the original design and raise it from a one-storey pavilion to a thirty-two-metre structure for greater visibility. He developed the exhibition space as two triangular concrete volumes connected by tubular bridges, a form he described as resembling 'a city gate from the front, fully showcasing the magnificence of ancient Chinese architecture'.⁶ Discussing the approach after the pavilion was completed, Lee cited Pei's conviction that 'we did not intentionally express the traditional Chinese style, for we have all been cultivated in the Chinese culture for many years and have naturally injected the Chinese spirit and features into the work'.⁷ The team drew on traditional Chinese garden design for inspiration, creating a contrast between a simple exterior and rich interior as well as constructing a sequence of spaces by moving visitors over bridges and along a circular ramp. Adamant about avoiding the 'vulgar and festive' palace style, they instead sought to convey Chinese-ness as an idea rather than an immediately identifiable aesthetic: something almost intangible that is expressed as much in literature and philosophy as in architecture.⁸

Pei's engagement with the question of how modern architecture can coexist with history in a Chinese cultural context began during his years as a student at the GSD, at the prompting of one of his professors, Walter Gropius. His 1946 thesis project, Museum of Chinese Art for Shanghai, expressed a relationship to the past not through superficial ornament or references to historical forms, but through a spatial strategy derived from garden design. He conceived the museum as a sequence of galleries with an open courtyard and perforations in the roof that create contrasts between interior and exterior. A similar concern with solids and voids, exterior and

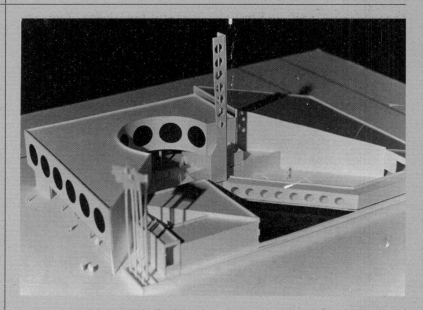

Atelier Cambridge, model of winning design for the Expo '70 Taiwan Pavilion, Wu Kwang-tyng

Project credits, in 'Brochure of the Japan World Exposition '70 Republic of China Pavilion' by the Committee of Tourism of Ministry of Transportation and Communications, ROC, 1970. Lee Chu-yuan

REGENERATING CULTURAL & HISTORICAL ARCHETYPES

Semi-outdoor plaza underneath the enclosed bridges connecting the two triangular volumes of the pavilion, 1970. Papers of I. M. Pei, Library of Congress, Washington DC

interior, and a narrative sequence of space is fundamental to Pei's design for the Everson Museum of Art, completed in 1968. The museum is defined by a multilayered sequence of concrete volumes housing the galleries, punctuated by openings, elevated walkways, and outdoor plazas. Its plan had been compared to 'traditional quadrangle houses in China', with 'separate living units around a central courtyard that is the core of family life'.[9] In plan, both the Museum of Chinese Art for Shanghai and the Everson Museum of Art can be read as interpretations of the garden-and-courtyard-house design in traditional Chinese architecture. When placed within the trajectory of Pei's practice, the Taiwan Pavilion at Expo '70—with its rhythm of voids and concrete solids, multiple viewpoints, covered atrium, and knife-edge corners—appears almost as a forerunner to the design of the National Gallery of Art East Building in Washington DC, developed in the same period. It also suggests Pei's continued exploration to define a modern architecture that is universal yet specific to China.

The pavilion ultimately symbolised the strategy of porousness that was allowed to supersede the palace-style form in architecture in Taiwan. In the context of Li's vision for a globalised economy, this can be considered as a materialisation of the desire to engage in the international conversation on modern architecture while at the same time asserting a national identity. Despite its ephemeral context, the pavilion was a clear articulation of an alternative for an official architecture in Taiwan. For Pei, it was a possible solution to a problem with which he had long been preoccupied. Cultural subjectivity offered a way for him to reconcile history with modernity. Through the specificity of a Chinese cultural context and a space for the display of this culture, Pei broke free from the formal dialectic of traditional and modern to arrive at a spatiality that is distinctly Chinese.

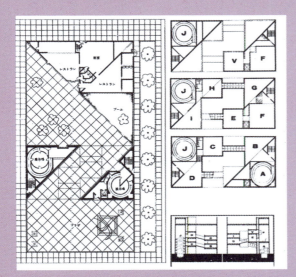

Plans and section showing the pavilion's three levels, in 'Brochure of the Japan World Exposition '70 Republic of China Pavilion' by the Committee of Tourism of Ministry of Transportation and Communications, ROC, 1970. Lee Chu-yuan

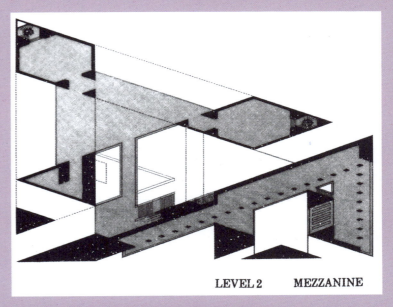

Plan of the Level 2 mezzanine in the National Gallery of Art East Building, ca.1979. Pei Cobb Freed & Partners

I. M. Pei's Pictorial Vision of Space

Liu Linfan

In a 2009 documentary released after the completion of one of I. M. Pei's final projects, the Museum of Islamic Art in Doha, the architect defines the idea of place as the most important consideration in architecture.[1] For Pei, place is a thread that weaves through his design philosophy. There are profound links between place and culture, place and site, and place and the experience of space in his work. Considering his work in the cultural context of East Asia sharpens our understanding of his view of place, which often finds its expression in a pictorial, even painterly, vision.[2]

Pei is well known for rigorous geometric and sculptural expression in his designs, but what is less recognised is his exploration of the pictorial quality of space, a quality that is fundamentally tied to his reading of architectural space. Nowhere is this more evident than in two projects in China: Fragrant Hill Hotel in Beijing and the Suzhou Museum. In both the design of the buildings themselves and the construction of rock landscapes for the projects, Pei borrowed from pictorial compositions and orchestrated the experience of moving in a way that is informed by encounters with traditional Chinese landscape paintings.

Rocks play an important role in classical Chinese garden design, and they take a prominent position at both Fragrant Hill and the Suzhou Museum. Pei's childhood experiences at Shizi Lin in Suzhou, most famous for *taihu shi*, the 'great lake rock', can be read in the adult architect's attention to the formal and cultural significance of rocks:

> Rock farmers [had] a sense of accountability to time. They usually worked with a porous volcanic rock ... Then they chiseled them most carefully ... yet the rock would still be very raw, not unlike the perforations and imperfections implanted by time when the farmer found it. Then he would find, also most carefully, a spot near the edge of a lake or a stream. And he would place the rock, just so, into the water, which, over a generation, or sometimes over two or three, would erode the shape. The farmer himself, or his son or grandson, would later harvest the rock, incorporating it into the composition of the garden. This sense of connection, of continuity, is an extremely telling aspect of Chinese culture.[3]

Pei articulated a sensitivity to two crucial aspects of rocks: the perceptual and metaphorical expression of time revealed through their physical presence, and the classical aesthetic criteria of leanness, surface texture, and the structure of perforations (*shou, zhou, tou*).[4] For Pei, the act of integrating rocks into a spatial design embodied a sense of cultural continuity.[5] After arriving in Beijing in 1979 to work on Fragrant Hill, he quickly determined that rocks would be a key component of the landscape design. To articulate this vision, Calvin Tsao, an architect working with Pei, produced a montage depicting the hotel complex within a Ming dynasty handscroll, Zheng Zhong's *Viewing the Wonderful Sceneries of Rivers and Mountains*.[6] Tsao carefully placed an axonometric view of the hotel among the dramatic peaks of Zheng's painting, while in reality the site is characterised by gently rolling hills (see 5.18.3, page 255).[7] This painterly expression is an attempt to situate the hotel in a long aesthetic tradition for the client.

Pei's anchoring of Fragrant Hill on traditional landscape aesthetics extends beyond conceptual expression to construction. He selected limestone from the Shilin stone forest in Yunnan for a landscape feature in the main garden and the indoor atrium—both the sculptural forms and the ensemble refer to typical elements of a classical Chinese garden. Claiming that the limestone had a distinctively 'natural' appearance, Pei rigorously followed established aesthetic criteria and crafted a coherent vision across the languages of painting, rock art, and modern landscape design.[8]

For the garden at the Suzhou Museum, Pei used *Cloudy Mountains* (1130), a Song dynasty painting by Mi Youren, as the primary design reference.[9] Granite from Shandong province was sliced into thin pieces and shipped to the site, where the pieces were arranged on a three-tiered platform. The tiers simulate the vertical composition of

REGENERATING CULTURAL & HISTORICAL ARCHETYPES

Liu Linfan, rock landscape in Shizi Lin, ca.2016

Mi Youren, *Cloudy Mountains*, ink and colour on silk, 1130. Cleveland Museum of Art

Chinese landscape painting to represent depth. The simple triangular shapes are direct references to Mi's depiction of mountains, and the design team used a blowtorch to mimic the 'Mi dot', a brushstroke invented by the painter. As a result, the completed sculptural ensemble appears as a painted landscape when viewed from the museum's Central Hall. In this design, Pei collapsed the mediums of rock art and painting, emphasising the aesthetic continuity across the two.

The two artists referenced at Fragrant Hill and the Suzhou Museum, Zheng Zhong and Mi Youren respectively, are markedly different: the former was a professional painter of the Northern School who strove for technical excellence and visual intricacy in his compositions, while the latter was a literati painter of the Southern School who favoured more subjective depictions.[10] The shift in references signals a shift in design intent. The emphasis on veracity and formal language at Fragrant Hill gives way to an expressive sensibility at the Suzhou Museum, particularly in the design of the rock landscape. The distinction between these two projects reflects a refinement of the architect's reading of cultural tradition. Moving from direct reference to formal language, to conceptual accordance, Pei presents two very different views in the gardens. The symbolic elements at Fragrant Hill are replaced at the Suzhou Museum by a cohesive picture. The dialogue with landscape painting encourages a heightened aesthetic sensitivity on the part of the viewer while also allowing for open interpretation.

The logic and refinement reflected in Pei's rock landscapes are also guiding principles of the design of the built forms themselves. At Fragrant Hill, the architect selected a vernacular clay tile along with white stucco as the principal building materials to express the idea of a continuous building tradition, albeit one that has its origins in southern China. The materials created a black-and-white motif, which recalls images of traditional dwellings—in Pei's view, a way of life that has continued for generations.[11] The introduction of black and white and the selection of specific construction materials constitute a pictorial strategy to create an image of a building steeped in its context and history. However, it was for this quality that most critics dismissed Fragrant Hill as superficial post-modernist posturing, and Pei himself admitted that the tiles were simply decorative and that this was a shortcoming of the project. His response to the criticism of Fragrant Hill can be seen in the design of Suzhou Museum. The museum is clad in white stucco and black granite, recalling the earlier project, but the granite at Suzhou expresses a structural logic, rather than serving as pure decoration. In addition to tiling the roof, which is a building tradition in China, black granite is used for edge trims, including all openings, corners, and transitions between levels and walls of different heights. The granite tiles trace the edges and joints of the facades, maintaining a sensitivity to place without symbolic expression.

Chinese scroll painting, while in sections largely presenting a direct visual experience, in its entirety follows the logic of a glance without a point of focus.[12] There are essentially two ways of seeing in a landscape painting: a stationary view of a fragment of nature, and a wandering glance of an expansive landscape. At both Fragrant Hill and the Suzhou Museum, Pei translated this pictorial mode of seeing into architectural experience.

Spatial transitions created by windows and doorways in both projects offer opportunities for intimate views. Pei was familiar with the pictorial function of a window in Chinese architectural history, as well as the notion of the 'framed view' coined by Ming dynasty garden designer Ji Cheng.[13] At Fragrant Hill, windows in the guest rooms are orientated towards the eleven courtyards, where old trees have been carefully preserved. In public spaces, elaborate frames and views of certain landscape compositions are situated to introduce 'paintings', or sections of paintings, into the indoor spaces. Both the articulated frames and the landscape views are a direct reference to traditional gardens. Framed views are also an important element at the Suzhou Museum, but the frames are simpler than their historical antecedents, in step with the geometric rhythm of the building. These views simultaneously punctuate and expand the spatial experience of the museum.

Beyond the specificity of the frames and the pictures, Pei also paid careful attention to the positions of all the 'landscape paintings' seen through the windows in the rooms. Often, they echo one another as a frame within a frame to increase spatial depth. More importantly, they appear as frontal views following the anticipated travelling route within the building complex. At Suzhou Museum, the moon gates and the framed landscapes are precisely aligned on the axes of the main hall to create moments of intensified focus. In this way, the pictorial views are presented as a sequence as people move through the hall, inviting them to explore.

Pei also recognised the importance of water in Chinese culture and the associated experience of meandering in a garden.[14] At Fragrant Hill, an elevated stone passage was modified to break a straightforward connection between the main building and the replica of a damaged *qu shui liu shang*, or water maze.[15] The final path was placed parallel to the main building so that people would be led through the garden before reaching the sculpture. A similar concept formed part of the design of the central pond at the Suzhou Museum, where a zigzag pedestrian passage was built across the water to connect the east and west sections of the museum without giving direct access to the main hall. Along the path, a bamboo grove grows to the west, a tea pavilion stands at the south-west corner, a terrace faces south towards the main hall, and the rock landscape is placed against the north wall. In this way, the central pond provides an expansive view that loosely ties all these features together, while views in each direction anticipate wandering without a central focus. Considering Pei's pictorial mode of seeing, the central pond is an organising structure that enables an ambulatory viewing experience.

While the emphasis in this essay has been on two projects in China, a continuity of pictorial vision can be found throughout Pei's career. Whether it was in the form of presenting a sequence of perspectives in the East Building of the National Gallery of Art in Washington DC or creating an expansive view in the central atrium of the Louvre in Paris, he consistently designed spaces with a choreographed visual sensibility. For Pei, this aspiration was not bounded by tradition but was a breathing force that informed his work.

Liu Linfan, stone landscape designed by I. M. Pei in the grounds of the Suzhou Museum, 2016

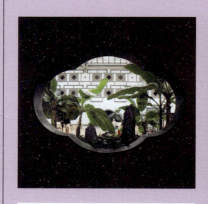 

Liu Linfan, framed views through the windows at Fragrant Hill Hotel (left column) and at the Suzhou Museum (right column), 2016

This timeline is an attempt to provide a comprehensive list of the architectural and urban planning projects, built and unbuilt, undertaken by I. M. Pei as a student; as head of Webb & Knapp, I. M. Pei & Associates, I. M. Pei & Partners, and Pei Cobb Freed & Partners (up until his retirement from the office in 1990); and as an individual in collaboration with various architects. The timeline also includes specific events that formed the social, political, and economic milieu that shaped the trajectory of Pei's life and practice. Pei was involved in every project to a greater or lesser degree up to and including the John F. Kennedy Presidential Library and Museum. This high-profile commission led to an influx of major projects, which required Pei to assign responsibility for certain projects to partners in his firm, such as Henry N. Cobb (HNC) and Araldo Cossutta (AC). As the firm evolved, other partners included Harold Fredenburgh (HF) and James Ingo Freed (JIF), each assuming full responsibility for a particular building while Pei remained instrumental in securing commissions. Pei cultivated a shared design ethos and sensibility that drew on the firm's deep pool of design expertise, technical resources, and trusted external consultants.

Compiled by Janet Adams Strong

KEY: | LIFE : WORLD EVENTS | WORK

Timeline of I. M. Pei's Life and Work

1910

1920

1912

The Republic of China (ROC) is established with Sun Yat-sen as the provisional president. The country remains divided between the republic and regional warlords.

1921

The Chinese Communist Party (CCP) is founded.

1923

Attends St Paul's College Primary School in Hong Kong.

1927

To defeat regional warlords and reunify the country, Chiang Kai-shek leads the Northern Expedition to conquer southern and central China. KMT successfully concludes the war and brings the country under its control the following year.

1919

The Kuomintang (KMT), or the Chinese Nationalist Party, is formally established in Shanghai.

Nationwide anti-imperialist May Fourth Movement begins in Beijing.

1918

Tsuyee Pei moves to Hong Kong to establish the Hong Kong main branch of the Bank of China.

Pei's family relocates to Hong Kong.

1917

I. M. Pei is born on 26 April in Canton (Guangzhou).

Father, Tsuyee Pei, becomes manager of the Canton branch of the Bank of China.

1927

Tsuyee Pei becomes manager of the Bank of China's headquarters in Shanghai.

Pei's family relocates to Shanghai.

Attends YMCA Middle School.

1930

1940

1931

Japan's invasion of China begins in Manchuria.

1937

Full-scale Sino-Japanese War begins in Beijing, Shanghai, and Nanjing.

1942

Marries Eileen Loo.

Begins his master's degree at the Harvard Graduate School of Design (GSD).

1945

The Second World War ends. Japan surrenders Taiwan to the Republic of China.

1931

Attends St John's Middle School.

1930

Mother, Chuang Lien Kwun, dies.

1935

Sails to the United States aboard the SS President Coolidge.

Briefly attends the University of Pennsylvania before transferring to the Massachusetts Institute of Technology (MIT).

1940

Graduates from MIT (BArch).

1940

Undergraduate thesis: 'Standardized Propaganda Units for War Time and Peace Time China'

1943

Pauses graduate studies to join the National Defense Research Committee in Princeton, New Jersey.

1945

Resumes graduate school at the GSD.

First son, T'ing Chung, is born.

1950

1948

Joins William Zeckendorf to head the architectural division of Webb & Knapp.

1951

Uses the Harvard GSD Wheelwright Fellowship to visit Europe for the first time.

1946

Master's thesis: Museum of Chinese Art for Shanghai

Huatung University (1946–1948; unbuilt), Shanghai (consultant for The Architects Collaborative)

1948

Helix (1948–1949; unbuilt), multiple locations

1950

Gulf Oil Building (1950–1952), Atlanta, Georgia

Roosevelt Field Planning (1950), Garden City, New York

1952

Mile High Center (1952–1956), Denver, Colorado

Pei Residence (1952), Katonah, New York

Denver Urban Renewal (1952), Denver, Colorado

1946

Graduates from the GSD (MArch).

Hired as an instructor and then as an assistant professor at the GSD.

Second son, Chien Chung 'Didi', is born.

1949

The CCP declares victory over the KMT and establishes the People's Republic of China.

The KMT retreats from the mainland to establish rule over Taiwan.

1951

Roosevelt Field Shopping Center (1951–1956), Garden City, New York

Franklin National Bank (1951–1957), Garden City, New York

1946

Chinese Civil War recommences between the CCP and the KMT.

1949

Third son, Li Chung 'Sandi', is born.

1949

Webb & Knapp Headquarters (1949–1952), New York

1954

Tunghai University and Luce Memorial Chapel (1954–1963), Taichung

Hyperboloid (1954–1955; unbuilt), New York

Palace of Progress (1954–1955; unbuilt), New York

Courthouse Square (1954–1960), Denver, Colorado (HNC, AC)

1955

I. M. Pei & Associates is established. The firm works exclusively for William Zeckendorf.

1956

University Gardens, Hyde Park (1956–1961), Chicago (AC)

1958

Pittsburgh Redevelopment (1958), Pittsburgh, Pennsylvania

Washington Plaza (1958–1964), Pittsburgh, Pennsylvania

Slayton House (1958–1960), Washington DC

1953

Southwest Washington Urban Redevelopment (1953–1959), Washington DC

Town Center Plaza (1953–1961), Washington DC

1954

US Civil Rights Movement gains momentum with the *Brown v. Board of Education* decision.

1955

Place Ville Marie (1955–1962), Montreal (HNC)

1955

United States guarantees Taiwan's defence.

1954

Receives architectural licence.

Becomes a naturalised US citizen.

1957

Kips Bay Plaza (1957–1962), New York

Society Hill (1957–1964), Philadelphia

Hartford Redevelopment Plan (1957–1958), Hartford, Connecticut

1960

1960

East-West Center (1960–1963), Honolulu (AC)

National Airlines Terminal, Idlewild Airport (now JFK International Airport) (1960–1970), New York

Erieview Master Plan (1960–1961), Cleveland, Ohio

University Plaza (1960–1966), New York University, New York (JIF)

Pan Pacific Metropolitan Tower (1960; unbuilt), Honolulu

1961

Century City Apartments (1961–1965), Los Angeles (with Webb & Knapp)

National Center for Atmospheric Research (NCAR) (1961–1967), Boulder, Colorado

Everson Museum of Art (1961–1968), Syracuse, New York

S. I. Newhouse Communications Center (1961–1964), Syracuse University, New York

Bushnell Plaza (1961–1970), Hartford, Connecticut

L'Enfant Plaza (1961–1968), Washington DC (AC)

Downtown North General Neighborhood Renewal Plan (1961–1962), Boston

Government Center Urban Renewal Plan (1961–1963), Boston

Weybosset Hill Development Plan (1961–1962), Providence, Rhode Island

Hamedina/Nordia Development Plans (1961–1962), Tel Aviv

Inter-American University Chapel (1961; unbuilt), San Germán

1960

Fourth child, Liane, is born.

I. M. Pei & Associates separates from Webb & Knapp.

1959

Cecil and Ida Green Center for Earth Sciences (1959–1964), MIT, Cambridge, Massachusetts

Chancellery for the United States Embassy (1959–1969), Montevideo

1962

State University of New York (1962–1971), Fredonia, New York (HNC)

Federal Aviation Administration Air Traffic Control Towers (1962–1972), multiple locations, United States (JIF)

1963

US president John F. Kennedy is assassinated.

1963

Cleo Rogers Memorial County Library (1963–1971), Columbus, Indiana

Hoffman Hall, University of Southern California (1963–1967), Los Angeles

New College (1963–1967), Sarasota, Florida

ALICO/Wilmington Tower (1963–1971), Wilmington, Delaware (AC)

Central Business District General Neighborhood Renewal Plan (1963–1964), Oklahoma City, Oklahoma

State Street Redevelopment, Government Plaza (1963–1964), Hartford, Connecticut

1964

Becomes a fellow of the American Institute of Architects (AIA).

1965

Tandy Residence (1965–1969), Fort Worth, Texas

Canadian Imperial Bank of Commerce (1965–1973), Toronto

Polaroid Office & Manufacturing Complex (1965–1970), Waltham, Massachusetts

Des Moines Art Center Addition (1965–1968), Des Moines, Iowa

Washington Post (1965–1969; unbuilt), Washington DC

Polaroid Site Selection Study (1965–1967), Cambridge, Massachusetts

1966

I. M. Pei & Associates is renamed I. M. Pei & Partners.

Pei's office moves to 600 Madison Avenue, New York.

1967

John Hancock Tower (1967–1976), Boston (HNC)

Third Church of Christ, Scientist (1967–1971), Washington DC (AC)

1968

US senator Robert F. Kennedy is assassinated.

Jacqueline Kennedy marries Aristotle Onassis.

1968

I. M. Pei & Partners receives the AIA Firm Award.

1965

Zeckendorf files for bankruptcy.

Singapore gains independence.

1964

Camille Edouard Dreyfus Chemistry Building (1964–1970), MIT, Cambridge, Massachusetts

John F. Kennedy Presidential Library and Museum (1964–1979), Dorchester, Massachusetts

Christian Science Center (1964–1973), Boston (AC)

Harbor Towers (1964–1971), Boston (HNC)

1966

Fleischmann Building (1966–1968), NCAR, Boulder, Colorado

Dallas City Hall (1966–1977), Dallas

Bedford-Stuyvesant Superblock (1966–1969), New York

Baltimore World Trade Center (1966–1977), Baltimore (HNC)

Kiryat Sir Isaac Wolfson, Development Plan (1966–1967), Jerusalem

John Hancock Property, Development Plan (1966), Boston

1968

Paul Mellon Center for the Arts (1968–1973), the Choate School, Wallingford, Connecticut

National Gallery of Art East Building (1968–1978), Washington DC

Herbert F. Johnson Museum of Art (1968–1973), Cornell University, Ithaca, New York

Robert F. Kennedy Gravesite (1968–1971), Arlington National Cemetery, Arlington, Virginia

Columbia University Master Plan (1968–1969), New York

Wilson Commons (1968–1976), University of Rochester, New York (HNC)

88 Pine Street (1968–1973), New York (JIF)

1970

1969

Expo '70 Republic of China Pavilion (1969–1970), Osaka

Chung Khiaw Bank (1969; unbuilt), Singapore

Raffles International Center Redevelopment (1969–1972)

Polaroid Tower (1969; unbuilt), Cambridge, Massachusetts

1971

Laura Spelman Rockefeller Halls (1971–1973), Princeton University, Princeton, New Jersey

1972

Ralph Landau Chemical Engineering Building (1972–1976), MIT, Cambridge, Massachusetts

National Bank of Commerce (1972–1976), Lincoln, Nebraska (JIF)

1972

US president Richard Nixon visits China.

1969

IBM Office Tower (1969; unbuilt), New York

1970

Expo '70 is held in Osaka, the first world exposition in Asia.

1972

Chien Chung Pei joins I. M. Pei & Partners.

1971

United Nations (UN) General Assembly recognises the People's Republic of China over Taiwan's government as the legitimate holder of China's seat in the UN.

1970

Tête de la Défense (1970–1971; unbuilt), Paris (AC)

Oversea-Chinese Banking Corporation (OCBC) Centre (1970–1976), Singapore

Collins Place (1970–1981), Melbourne (HNC)

1973

An oil crisis caused by a Saudi Arabia–led embargo results in a price surge and fuel shortage in the US.

Glass facade fails and windows shatter at the John Hancock Tower in Boston.

1973

University Village, Excellence in Education Study (1973–1974), Dallas

Honiron Development Plan (1973–1974), Honolulu

Raffles City (1973–1986), Singapore

1974

Returns to China after four decades as part of a cultural exchange delegation organised by the AIA.

1975

Kapsad Development (1975–1978; unbuilt), Tehran

Nathan Road Development Plan (1975–1976), Singapore

Singapore River Development (1975–1976), Singapore

Orchard Road Development Plan (1975), Singapore

Augusta/Richmond County Civic Center (1975–1980), Augusta, Georgia (HNC)

1976

Li Chung Pei joins I. M. Pei & Partners.

1977

Museum of Fine Arts, West Wing (1977–1981), Boston

IBM Corporate Office Building (1977–1984), Purchase, New York

Akzona Corporate Headquarters (1977–1981), Ashville, North Carolina

Sunning Plaza (1977–1982), Hong Kong

One Dallas Center (1977–1979), Dallas (HNC)

499 Park Avenue (1977–1981), New York (JIF)

Gem City Plaza (1977–1981), Dayton, Ohio (JIF)

One West Loop Plaza (1977–1980), Houston, Texas (JIF)

1978

Joint Communiqué establishes Sino-US diplomatic relations.

1974

Art Museum and Academic Building (1974–1982), University of Indiana, Bloomington, Indiana

Long Beach Museum (1974–1979; unbuilt), Long Beach, California

Asia House (1974; unbuilt), New York

Augusta Chamber of Commerce (1974–1977), Augusta, Georgia (HNC)

Broad Street Mall (1974–1977), Augusta, Georgia (HNC)

Collyer Quay/Raffles Square Development Study (1974–1975), Singapore

1976

Industrial Credit Bank (1976; unbuilt), Tehran

Al Salaam (1976–1979; unbuilt), Kuwait City

Johnson & Johnson World Headquarters (1976–1982), New Brunswick, New Jersey (HNC)

Johnson & Johnson Baby Products Headquarters Complex (1976–1981), Montgomery Township, New Jersey (HNC)

Commercial Plaza II (1976–1979), New Brunswick, New Jersey (HNC)

1976

Mao Zedong dies.

1978

Wiesner Building/Center for Arts & Media Technology (1978–1984), MIT, Cambridge, Massachusetts

Texas Commerce Tower (1978–1982), Houston, Texas (HF)

MIT Northwest Area Development Framework Plan (1978), Cambridge, Massachusetts

ARCO Tower (1978–1983), Dallas (HNC)

16th Street Transitway Mall (1978–1982), Denver, Colorado (HNC)

Mobil Research & Development Center (1978–1983), Dallas (HNC)

Charles Shipman Payson Building (1978–1983), Portland Museum of Art, Portland, Maine (HNC)

One Galleria Tower (1978–1981), Oklahoma City, Oklahoma (JIF)

1980

1981

The Morton H. Meyerson Symphony Center (1981–1989), Dallas

Guggenheim Pavilion (1981–1992), Mount Sinai Medical Center, New York

Gateway (1981–1990), Singapore

Immobiliaria Refotib (1981; unbuilt), Mexico City

United States Embassy Land Use Requirements Proposal (1981), Beijing

Columbia Square (1981–1987), Washington DC (HNC)

1979

The shah of Iran is overthrown in the Islamic Revolution.

Deng Xiaoping ushers in the Four Modernisations.

1982

François Mitterrand initiates his *grands projets* programme following his election as president of France.

1979

Wins the AIA Gold Medal.

1983

Receives the Pritzker Prize.

1980

Austral Lineas (1980; unbuilt), Buenos Aires

United Engineers/Robertson Quay Development Concept (1980), Singapore

CenTrust/Miami Tower (1980–1986), Miami (HF)

East Cove Development (1980–1981; unbuilt), New York

1982

Tsuyee Pei dies.

1983

Grand Louvre Phase I (1983–1989), Paris

IBM Office Campus (1983–1989), Somers, New York

First Interstate Tower/ Library Tower (1983–1989), Los Angeles (HNC)

Regent (1983–1985; unbuilt), Costa Mesa, California

1979

Fragrant Hill Hotel (1979–1982), Beijing

Jacob K. Javits Convention Center (1979–1986), New York (JIF)

Warwick Post Oak Hotel (1979–1982), Houston, Texas (JIF)

Pitney Bowes World Headquarters (1979–1986), Stamford, Connecticut (HNC)

1982

Bank of China Tower (1982–1989), Hong Kong

IBM Headquarters Entrance Pavilion (1982–1985), Armonk, New York

Marina South Development Plan (1982–1983), Singapore

Allied Bank Tower (1982–1986), Dallas (HNC)

1984

Commerce Square (1984–1993), Philadelphia (HNC)

Central Terminal Complex, JFK International Airport (1984–1990; unbuilt), New York (HNC)

1985

Choate Rosemary Hall Science Center (1985–1989), Wallingford, Connecticut

Potomac Tower (1985–1988), Rosslyn, Virginia (JIF)

1986

Credit Suisse First Boston (1986–1991), London (HNC)

Creative Artists Agency (1986–1989), Beverly Hills

United States Holocaust Memorial Museum (1986–1993), Washington DC (JIF)

Los Angeles Convention Center Expansion (1986–1993), Los Angeles (JIF)

1987

John F. Kennedy Presidential Library and Museum Extension (1987–1990), Dorchester, Massachusetts

Rock and Roll Hall of Fame and Museum (1987–1995), Cleveland, Ohio

1988

Joy of Angels Bell Tower (1988–1990), Shigaraki, Shiga

Four Seasons Hotel (1988–1993), New York

World Trade Center (1988–1999), Barcelona (HNC)

Grand Marina Hotel (1988–1999), Barcelona (HNC)

Crown Center (1988–1991), Kansas City, Missouri (HNC)

Johnson & Johnson World Headquarters Child Development Center (1988–1990), New Brunswick, New Jersey

First Bank Place (1988–1992), Minneapolis, Minnesota (JIF)

Kirklin Clinic (1988–1992), University of Alabama, Birmingham, Alabama

1299 Pennsylvania Avenue (1988–1991), Washington DC (JIF)

1988

François Mitterrand is re-elected as president of France.

1989

The fall of the Berlin Wall marks the beginning of German reunification.

1989

I. M. Pei & Partners is restructured as Pei Cobb Freed & Partners.

New York Times critic Paul Goldberger declares 1989 'the year of Pei' for the completion of five major projects, including the Grand Louvre Phase I, the Bank of China Tower, and the Morton H. Meyerson Symphony Center.

1989

Grand Louvre Phase II (1989–1993), Paris

Buck Institute for Age Research (1989–1999), Novato, California

Musée d'Art Moderne Grand-Duc Jean (MUDAM) (1989–2006), Luxembourg City (with Pei Cobb Freed & Partners)

1990

1991

Miho Museum (1991–1997), Shigaraki, Shiga

1992

Sentra BDNI (1992–1998; incomplete), Jakarta (with Pei Partnership Architects)

1995

Sheikh Hamad bin Khalifa Al-Thani, emir of Qatar, begins an extensive programme of economic reform.

1995

Republic of Korea Permanent Mission to the UN (1995–1999), New York (with Pei Cobb Freed & Partners)

1992

Supports his sons in the formation of Pei Partnership Architects, renamed PEI Architects in 2019.

1994

Bank of China Head Office Building (1994–2001), Beijing (with Pei Partnership Architects)

1993

La Caixa Bank Headquarters (1993–1998; unbuilt), Barcelona (with Pei Cobb Freed & Partners)

Basil & Elise Goulandris Museum of Modern Art (1993–1997; unbuilt), Athens

1999

Oare Pavilion (1999–2003), Wiltshire

Ronald Reagan UCLA Medical Center (1999–2008), Los Angeles (with Pei Partnership Architects)

1996

Deutsches Historisches Museum (1996–2003), Berlin

1990

Retires from his firm for independent practice.

1990

Bilbao Emblematic Building (1990–1992; unbuilt), Bilbao (with Pei Cobb Freed & Partners)

2000

2001

Beijing is chosen to host the 2008 Summer Olympics.

2000

Suzhou Museum (2000–2006), Suzhou (with Pei Partnership Architects)

Museum of Islamic Art (2000–2008), Doha

Embassy of the People's Republic of China, Chancery Building (2000–2008), Washington DC (with Pei Partnership Architects)

2002

Macau Science Center (2002–2009), Macau (with Pei Partnership Architects)

2003

T'ing Chung Pei dies.

2010

2010

Receives the Royal Gold Medal of the Royal Institute of British Architects.

2014

Eileen Pei dies.

2008

Miho Institute of Aesthetics Chapel (2008–2012) Shigaraki, Shiga

2017

Hundredth birthday.

2019

Dies on 16 May.

NOTES

Introduction: Architecture Is Life

1. Michael Cannell, *I. M. Pei: Mandarin of Modernism* (New York: Carol Southern Books, 1995), 369.
2. I. M. Pei, quoted in Gero von Boehm, *Conversations with I. M. Pei: Light Is the Key* (Munich: Prestel, 2000), 18.
3. Von Boehm, *Conversations with I. M. Pei*, 57.

Chapter 1: Transcultural Foundations

Introduction

1. The term 'cosmopolitan nationalism', as it describes Tsuyee and I. M. Pei's disposition, most closely aligns with its definition in Miri Yemini *et al.*, 'Cosmopolitan Nationalism and Global Citizenship Rhetoric: Analysis of Policies and Curricula in South Korea, Israel and the United States', in Daniel Tröhler, Nelli Piattoeva, and William F. Pinar, eds, *World Yearbook of Education 2022: Education, Schooling and the Global Universalization of Nationalism* (London: Routledge, 2021), 219–234.
2. Tsuyee Pei, letter to the president and vice-president of the Bank of China, 1918, Bank of China (Hong Kong).
3. See Pei's letter to Frederick G. Roth (1946), Papers of I. M. Pei, Library of Congress, Washington DC, and Gero von Boehm, *Conversations with I. M. Pei: Light Is the Key* (Munich: Prestel, 2000), 42–43.
4. See Henry N. Cobb's and Pei's descriptions of the Harvard curriculum in Michael Cannell, *I. M. Pei: Mandarin of Modernism* (New York: Carol Southern Books, 1995), 77, and Von Boehm, *Conversations with I. M. Pei*, 87.

The American Education of I. M. Pei

1. Joseph Hudnut, 'The Education of an Architect', *Architectural Record* (May 1931): 412.
2. Henry N. Cobb, quoted in 'The GSD Celebrates the Centennial Birthday of I. M. Pei MArch '46 with Special Events and Exhibition', *GSD News*, 25 April 2017, https://alumni.gsd.harvard.edu/gsd_news/centennial-birthday-of-i-m-pei/, accessed 15 December 2022.
3. Naomi Elegant, 'The Story of Liang and Lin', *Pennsylvania Gazette*, 23 October 2019, https://thepenngazette.com/21167-2/, accessed 15 December 2022.
4. Michael Cannell, *I. M. Pei: Mandarin of Modernism* (New York: Carol Southern Books, 1995), 64.
5. Peter Lemos, 'The Stylish Artistry of I. M. Pei', *Pan Am Clipper* (November 1984): 96, cited in Cannell, *I. M. Pei: Mandarin of Modernism*, 65.
6. William Emerson to George H. Edgell, 4 June 1935, Harvard University Archives, cited in Mardges Bacon, *Le Corbusier in America: Travels in the Land of the Timid* (Cambridge, MA: MIT Press, 2001), 95.
7. See 'Ultramodern Cities on Stilts Pictured by French Architect', *Christian Science Monitor*, 8 November 1935, cited in Bacon, *Le Corbusier in America*, 96.
8. Le Corbusier, *When the Cathedrals Were White: A Journey to the Country of Timid People* (New York: Reynal & Hitchcock, 1947), 142.
9. Gero von Boehm, *Conversations with I. M. Pei: Light Is the Key* (Munich: Prestel, 2000), 36.
10. I. M. Pei, lecture delivered at MIT, 1 March 1985, cited in Bacon, *Le Corbusier in America*, 97.
11. See John E. Burchard, '[Report of] Director of the Albert Farwell Bemis Foundation', *Massachusetts Institute of Technology Bulletin* 77, no. 1 (October 1941): 72.
12. I. M. Pei, 'Standardized Propaganda Units for War Time and Peace Time China', BArch diss., Massachusetts Institute of Technology, 1940, 1–2.
13. Pei, 'Standardized Propaganda Units for War Time and Peace Time China', 1–3, 20.
14. 'A Magazine for the Younger Generation in Architecture', *TASK* 2 (Summer 1941): 3.
15. As Pei told an interviewer, 'The school was then full of women and foreigners, aliens like myself, and Philip Johnson, who was a little bit older than the others, so he didn't have to go to war. Plus many, many South Americans.' Quoted in Barbaralee Diamonstein, 'I. M. Pei: "The Modern Movement Is Now Wide Open"', *ARTNews* (Summer 1978): 66, cited in Cannell, *I. M. Pei: Mandarin of Modernism*, 79. The real reason Philip Johnson was not serving in the military had nothing to do with

his age, of course, but with his activities as a fascist sympathiser in the late 1930s. On the diversity of the GSD at this time, see my essay in a monograph on Ira Rakatansky, a Jewish student who also entered the GSD in 1943 and got to know Pei there: Joan Ockman, 'Why Is a Modern House', in John Caserta and Lynnette Widder, eds, *Ira Rakatansky: As Modern as Tomorrow* (Richmond, CA: William Stout Publishers, 2010), esp. 18–22.

16   'Variety of Houses from Identical Prefabricated Units of General Panel Corp. designed by Harvard Students', *New Pencil Points* (December 1943): 76–81; Pei's project on page 81.

17   On this fascinating yet little-known subject of modernist architects working for the NDRC during the Second World War, with mention of Pei's part in it, see Karen J. Weitze, 'In the Shadows of Dresden: Modernism and the War Landscape', *Journal of the Society of Architectural Historians* 72 (September 2013): 322–357.

18   I. M. Pei, quoted in 'Art: Flagpole in the Square', *Time*, 22 August 1960, cited in Cannell, *I. M. Pei: Mandarin of Modernism*, 76.

19   'Winning Design – Second Prize, I. M. Pei and E. H. Duhart', *California Arts & Architecture* (August 1943): 34.

20   I. M. Pei and E. H. Duhart, 'House for the Post War Worker', *California Arts & Architecture* (January 1944): 32–33.

21   See '5 Designs Awarded Honorable Mention in *Arts & Architecture*'s Second Annual Competition Sponsored by the United States Plywood Corporation', *Arts & Architecture* (March 1945): 31–41; Pei's project on pages 38–39. Previously titled *California Arts & Architecture*, the Los Angeles–based magazine changed its name in 1944 under the editorial direction of John Entenza, who sought to pitch it to a wider audience. Entenza would be one of the strongest promoters of the prefabricated house during the war years and afterwards, launching the famous Case Study House Program in January 1945.

22   The first-prize winners in the 'House for Cheerful Living' competition were Jean Bodman Fletcher and Norman Fletcher, two of the founding partners of The Architects Collaborative (TAC), established the same year, 1945, with Walter Gropius; between 1946 and 1948, Pei would collaborate with TAC as an associated architect on an unrealised project for Huatung University in Shanghai. Pei and Roth also won third prize in 1944 in a competition for 'dealer establishments', sponsored by General Motors. Another competition, sponsored by *Progressive Architecture* and Rich's Department Store in Atlanta, was for 'A Realistic House for Georgia'; Pei received a mention and his project appeared in *Progressive Architecture* in April 1946. Taken together, the plethora of competitions during the war years—and the repetitive winners, among them Pei—afford a vivid picture of the architectural preoccupations of the period and the aspirational ties between the profession and American manufacturers and retailers.

23   I. M. Pei, quoted in Andrea O. Dean, 'Conversations: I. M. Pei', *AIA Journal* (June 1979): 63.

24   On the feud between Hudnut and Gropius, see Jill Pearlman, *Inventing American Modernism: Joseph Hudnut, Walter Gropius, and the Bauhaus Legacy at Harvard* (Charlottesville: University of Virginia Press, 2007); phrase quoted, 195.

25   Pei may also have been influenced somewhat by Alexander Dorner's concept of the 'Living Museum'. Dorner, an émigré art historian and director of a pioneering museum in Hanover, Germany, during the Weimar Republic, introduced this concept to GSD students as a lecturer and guest professor at the school in the late 1930s and 1940s. A polemical personality, Dorner asserted that art museums should not be mausoleums and should instead stay in close contact with everyday life and the new currents of their time. Dorner gave the 'Living Museum' as a studio brief for at least two years at the GSD on Gropius's invitation; after he left, Gropius took over the project. Examples of student work under both Dorner and Gropius appear on pages 11 and 80–83 in the same special issue of *L'architecture d'aujourd'hui* as Pei's museum (see note 28). For more on Dorner and his ideas, see Samuel Cauman, *The Living Museum: Experiences of an Art Historian and Museum Director— Alexander Dorner* (New York: New York University Press, 1958); and Joan Ockman, 'The Road Not Taken: Alexander Dorner's Way Beyond Art', in Robert Somol, ed., *Autonomy and Ideology: Positioning an Avant-Garde in America* (New York: Monacelli Press, 1997), 81–120.

26   'Museum for Chinese Art, Shanghai, China', *Progressive Architecture* 29 (February 1948): 52.

27   For a statement reflecting Giedion's shift in thinking, see his essay 'The New Regionalism', in Sigfried Giedion, *Architecture You and Me: The Diary of a Development* (Cambridge, MA: Harvard University Press, 1958), 138–151. Giedion writes: 'Experience is slowly showing us that the rationalist and exclusively materialist attitude, upon which the latest phase of Western civilization has been grounded, is insufficient. Full realization of this fact can lead us slowly toward a new hybrid development—a cross between Western and Eastern civilizations', 141.

28   'Walter Gropius et son école/The Spread of an Idea', special issue, *L'architecture d'aujourd'hui* 28 (February 1950): 1–116; Pei's project occupies pages 76–77.

29   Henry N. Cobb, 'The School of Gropius', *Henry N. Cobb: Words & Works 1948–2018: Scenes from a Life in Architecture* (New York: Monacelli Press, 2018), 30.

30   Including in Carter Wiseman's monograph *I. M. Pei: A Profile in American Architecture* (New York: Harry N. Abrams, 1990); see page 41.

Chapter 2: Real Estate & Urban Redevelopment

Introduction

1   William Zeckendorf, 'Baked Buildings', *Atlantic Monthly* 188 (December 1951): 46–49.

2   Henry N. Cobb, *Henry N. Cobb: Words & Works 1948–2018: Scenes from a Life in Architecture* (New York: Monacelli Press, 2018), 49.

3   Cobb, *Words & Works 1948–2018*, 103.

4   William Zeckendorf and Edward A. McCreary, *Zeckendorf: The Autobiography of William Zeckendorf* (New York: Holt, Rinehart & Winston, 1970), 266–267.

5   Carter Wiseman, *I. M. Pei: A Profile in American Architecture* (New York: Harry N. Abrams, 2001), 59.

6   I. M. Pei, 'Urban Renewal in Southwest Washington', *AIA Journal* 39, no. 1 (January 1963): 65–69.

7   I. M. Pei, quoted in Michael Cannell, *I. M. Pei: Mandarin of Modernism* (New York: Carol Southern Books, 1995), 120.

I. M. Pei and Urbanism in North America, 1948–1960

1   Eric Mumford, *Defining Urban Design: CIAM Architects and the Formation of a Discipline, 1937–69* (New Haven and London: Yale University Press, 2009), 64–79.

2   'I. M. Pei—Words for the Future', special issue, *A+U* (August 2008): 75–77.

3   Sara Stevens, *Developing Expertise: Architecture and Real Estate in Metropolitan America* (New Haven: Yale University Press, 2016), 187–234.

4   Joan Ockman and Edward Eigen, *Architecture Culture 1943–1968: A Documentary Anthology* (New York: Columbia Books of Architecture/ Rizzoli, 1993), 55–63.

5   Mumford, *Defining Urban Design*, 80–121.

6   Josep Lluís Sert, quoted in Eric Mumford, ed., *The Writings of Josep Lluís Sert* (New Haven and London: Yale University Press; Cambridge, MA: Harvard Graduate School of Design, 2015), 34.

7   Stevens, *Developing Expertise*, 205–234.

8   Josep Lluís Sert, quoted in Mumford, *The Writings of Josep Lluís Sert*, 40.

9   Mumford, *The Writings of Josep Lluís Sert*, 2–10.

10   Martha Biondi, 'Robert Moses, Race, and the Limits of an Activist State', in Hilary Ballon and Kenneth T. Jackson, eds, *Robert Moses and the Modern City: The Transformation of New York* (New York: W. W. Norton & Co., 2007), 116–121.

11   Edmund N. Bacon, *Design of Cities* (New York: Viking Press, 1967).

12   'I. M. Pei': 77–83; and Ballon and Jackson, *Robert Moses and the Modern City*, 271–273.

13   Mumford, *Defining Urban Design*, 146–151; and Graduate School of Design, Harvard University, 'General Report of Proceedings Third Urban Design Conference', *Ekistics* 8, no. 46 (August 1959): 112–129.

14   Graduate School of Design, Harvard University, 'General Report of Proceedings Third Urban Design Conference', 112.

15. Graduate School of Design, Harvard University, 'General Report of Proceedings Third Urban Design Conference', 129.
16. Graduate School of Design, Harvard University, 'General Report of Proceedings Third Urban Design Conference', 115.
17. Graduate School of Design, Harvard University, 'General Report of Proceedings Third Urban Design Conference', 118.

Chapter 3: Art & Civic Form

Introduction

1. Ada Louise Huxtable, 'Mr. Pei Comes to Washington', *New York Times*, 11 July 1971.
2. Ada Louise Huxtable, 'A Capital Art Palace', *New York Times*, 7 May 1978.
3. I. M. Pei, quoted in 'Museum for Chinese Art, Shanghai, China', *Progressive Architecture* 29 (February 1948): 51.
4. 'Museum for Chinese Art, Shanghai, China': 52.
5. Gero von Boehm, *Conversations with I. M. Pei: Light Is the Key* (Munich: Prestel, 2000), 45.
6. I. M. Pei, quoted in Von Boehm, *Conversations with I. M. Pei*, 45.
7. Von Boehm, *Conversations with I. M. Pei*, 65.

I. M. Pei's Museum of Chinese Art, Shanghai: Modernism between East and West

1. 'Museum for Chinese Art, Shanghai, China', *Progressive Architecture* 29 (February 1948): 50–52; and 'Chinese Art Museum in Shanghai', *L'architecture d'aujourd'hui* 20 (February 1950): 76–77.
2. Le Corbusier's 1935 trip to the United States had an enormous impact on Pei, who recalled the Swiss architect's visit to Cambridge as 'the two most important days in my professional life'. See Gero von Boehm, *Conversations with I. M. Pei: Light Is the Key* (Munich: Prestel, 2000), 36.
3. I. M. Pei, 'Standardized Propaganda Units for War Time and Peace Time China', BArch diss., Massachusetts Institute of Technology, 1940.
4. Franklin D. Roosevelt's speech was reprinted in full in the *Herald Tribune* (New York) on 11 May 1939, and can be found on the website of the Museum of Modern Art: https://www.moma.org/research-and-learning/archives/archives-highlights-04-1939, accessed 7 September 2021.
5. *New York Times*, 10 July 1945, quoted in Hilary Ballon et al., *The Guggenheim: Frank Lloyd Wright and the Making of the Modern Museum* (New York: Guggenheim Museum, 2009), 156.
6. 'New Buildings for 194X', *Architectural Forum* (May 1943): 69–189. See also Andrew M. Shanken, *194X: Architecture, Planning, and Consumer Culture on the American Home Front* (Minneapolis: University of Minnesota Press, 2000); and Barry Bergdoll, 'Architecture of 194X', in Mark Robbins, ed., *American City "X": Syracuse after the Master Plan* (New York: Princeton Architectural Press with Syracuse Univeristy School of Architecture, 2014), 18–25.
7. 'Index of Projects and Contributing Architects', *Architectural Forum* (May 1943): 72.
8. On the Everson Museum of Art, see Barry Bergdoll, 'I. M. Pei, Marcel Breuer, Edward Larrabee Barnes, and the New American Museum Design of the 1960s', in Anthony Alofsin, ed., *A Modernist Museum in Perspective: The East Building, National Gallery of Art* (Washington DC: National Gallery of Art, 2009), 106–123.
9. Ludwig Mies van der Rohe, quoted in 'Museum, Mies Van Der Rohe, Architect, Chicago, Ill.', in 'New Buildings for 194X': 84.
10. Mies van der Rohe, 'New Buildings for 194X': 84.
11. 'Museum for Chinese Art, Shanghai, China': 50–51.
12. 'Museum for Chinese Art, Shanghai, China': 52.
13. 'Museum for Chinese Art, Shanghai, China': 50–51.
14. I. M. Pei, quoted in 'Museum for Chinese Art, Shanghai, China': 51.
15. 'Museum for Chinese Art, Shanghai, China': 52.
16. The winning project responding to Dorner's brief to the Harvard students was by Victor Lundy, for a 'Living Art Museum', a design that clearly drew on Pei's earlier project in its interweaving of a landscape garden under and through the spaces of a museum and its development of a partially sunken section.

Chapter 4: Material Life & Structural Innovation

Introduction

1. Gordon Bunshaft, quoted in Carter Wiseman, *The Architecture of I. M. Pei* (London: Thames & Hudson, 2001), 62.
2. Janet Adams Strong, 'Continuity and Change: Fine-Face Concrete in Physical Manifestation of I. M. Pei's Approach to Architecture', paper presented at 'Rethinking Pei: A Centenary Symposium', Harvard Graduate School of Design, on 13 October 2017, https://www.gsd.harvard.edu/event/rethinking-pei-a-centenary-symposium/.
3. 'Small Office Buildings—1. Marble Curtain Walls Hung from the Inside of Pre-fab Framing Cut Costs but Preserve Quality', *Architectural Forum* 96 (February 1952): 108–110.
4. Henry N. Cobb, *Henry N. Cobb: Words & Works 1948–2018: Scenes from a Life in Architecture* (New York: Monacelli Press, 2018), 103.
5. Strong, 'Continuity and Change'.
6. I. M. Pei, interview with Lucy Warner, 14 May 1985, UCAR/NCAR Oral History Collection, tape no. 16, https://voices.nmfs.noaa.gov/sites/default/files/2021-12/Pei_IM.pdf, accessed 15 December 2022.

I. M. Pei and the Tools of Invention

1. I. M. Pei, conversation with the author, May 1995.
2. I. M. Pei, conversation with the author, January 1999.
3. I. M. Pei, conversation with the author, April 1995.
4. I. M. Pei, conversation with the author, June 1996.
5. Society Hill, Philadelphia (1957–1964); Washington Plaza, Pittsburgh (1958–1964); Century City Apartments, Los Angeles (1961–1965); University Plaza, New York (1960–1966); Bushnell Plaza, Hartford (1961–1970); and Harbor Towers, Boston (1964–1971).
6. George Gabriel, head model maker, conversation with the author, October 1995.

Chapter 5: Power, Politics & Patronage

Introduction

1. Paul Goldberger, 'Architecture View: A Year of Years for the High Priest of Modernism', *New York Times*, 17 September 1989.
2. Jacqueline Kennedy, quoted in Carter Wiseman, *The Architecture of I. M. Pei* (London: Thames & Hudson, 2001), 99.
3. I. M. Pei, quoted in Michael Cannell, *I. M. Pei: Mandarin of Modernism* (New York: Carol Southern Books, 1995), 352.
4. Cannell, *I. M. Pei: Mandarin of Modernism*, 368.
5. Cannell, *I. M. Pei: Mandarin of Modernism*, 351.
6. I. M. Pei, quoted in Gero von Boehm, *Conversations with I. M. Pei: Light Is the Key* (Munich: 2000), 57.
7. I. M. Pei, quoted in Philip Jodidio and Janet Adams Strong, *I. M. Pei: Complete Works* (New York: Rizzoli, 2008), 107.
8. I. M. Pei, quoted in Wiseman, *The Architecture of I. M. Pei*, 323.

OCBC Centre: The Iconic Turn of the Singapore Model of Asian Global Capitalism

1. The research for this essay was supported by a Ministry of Education Academic Research Fund (Tier 1) for 'Agents of Modernity: Pioneer Builders, Architecture and Independence in Singapore, 1890s–1970s', WBS no. R-295-000-127-112.
2. 'Biggest Banking Hall in Se-A', *Straits Times*, 1 October 1976.
3. 'A Great Leap Skywards', *Building Materials & Equipment* (September 1976): 27–75.
4. 'Chairman Followed Development of Project Closely', *Straits Times*, 1 October 1976.
5. 'OCBC Is Still No. 1 in Local Banking', *The Business Times*, 20 October 1977; and 'OCBC and DBS Are among Top 10 in ASEAN', *The Business Times*, 20 November 1976.
6. Tan Chin Tuan, quoted in Lee Su Yin, *Rock Solid: The Corporate Career of Tan Chin Tuan* (Singapore: Landmark Books, 2006), 87.
7. J. H. Drabble and P. J. Drake, 'The British Agency Houses in Malaysia: Survival in a Changing World', *Journal of Southeast Asian Studies* 12, no. 2 (1981): 306. It was estimated that in the 1950s, the twelve largest agency houses' share of Malaya's trade ranged from a third to a half.

See James J. Puthucheary, *Ownership and Control in the Malayan Economy* (Singapore: Eastern Universities Press, 1960).
8   Lim Mah Hui, *Ownership and Control of the One Hundred Largest Corporations in Malaysia* (Kuala Lumpur: Oxford University Press, 1981), 91. John Tan, 'OCBC's Power Goes Beyond Banking', *The Business Times*, 14 October 1976.
9   'Business Centre Springs Up on Shenton Way, Singapore', *Asian Building & Construction* (May 1972); and Chua Beng Huat, *The Golden Shoe: Building Singapore's Financial District* (Singapore: Urban Redevelopment Authority, 1989), 76.
10 Anthony Ramasamy, 'Exclusive Interview with I. M. Pei', *Building Materials & Equipment* (March/April 1975): 6–7. I am grateful to Shirley Surya for alerting me to this interview.
11 The UOB building was extensively renovated and extended with the addition of a new podium block and a second, sixty-seven-storey tower by the Japanese architectural firm of Kenzo Tange Associates in 1995. The complex was renamed UOB Plaza.
12 Lim Chong Keat, quoted in 'UOB Building Sets the Scale for Further Re-development of the Riverfront', *Building Materials & Equipment* (September 1974): 5, 7.
13 Lee Kah-Wee, 'Regulating Design in Singapore: A Survey of the Government Land Sales (GLS) Programme', *Environment and Planning C: Government and Policy* 28, no. 1 (2010).
14 Graham Morrison, 'Look at Me!', *The Guardian*, 12 July 2004.
15 Charles Jencks, 'The Iconic Building Is Here to Stay', *City* 10, no. 1 (2006).
16 Maria Kaika, 'Architecture and Crisis: Re-inventing the Icon, Re-imag(in)ing London and Re-branding the City', *Transactions of the Institute of British Geographers* 35, no. 4 (October 2010); and Leslie Sklair, 'Iconic Architecture and Capitalist Globalization', *City* 10, no. 1 (2006).
17 Alfred H. K. Wong, 'A Brief Review of Our Recent Architectural History', in Singapore Institute of Architects, ed., *Contemporary Singapore Architecture* (Singapore: Singapore Institute of Architects, 1998), 252.
18 This was revealed to me by Yvonne Leong, the archivist of the Malaysia office of BEP Akitek, in an email correspondence dated 8 September 2017. BEP Akitek was behind quite a number of important industrial, religious, and commercial buildings in the 1960s and 1970s. These include Tien Wah Press Building (1961), St Matthew's Church (1963), the Hilton Singapore (1969), McGraw-Hill Far Eastern Publishers (1969), Plaza Singapura (1974), and Comcentre (1979).
19 Florence Tan, 'Raffles Centre Man Speaks', *New Nation*, 3 March 1976.

Chapter 6: Regenerating Cultural & Historical Archetypes

Introduction

1   I. M. Pei, interview with Lucy Warner, 14 May 1985, tape no. 16, transcript, UCAR/NCAR Oral History Collection, University Corporation for Atmospheric Research, https://voices.nmfs.noaa.gov/sites/default/files/2021-12/Pei_IM.pdf, accessed 15 December 2022.
2   I. M. Pei, quoted in Gero von Boehm, *Conversations with I. M. Pei: Light Is the Key* (Munich: Prestel, 2000), 59–60.
3   Lee Chu-yuan, 'Recalling the Design of the Republic of China Expo '70 Pavilion', *Jianzhu yu jihua* (*Architecture & Planning*) (July 1970): 38–43.
4   'Interview with I. M. Pei', *Christian Science Monitor*, 16 March 1978, 33.
5   I. M. Pei, Pritzker Prize Laureate Ceremony Acceptance Speech, 1983, https://www.pritzkerprize.com/sites/default/files/inline-files/IM_Pei_Acceptance_Speech_1983.pdf, accessed 15 December 2022.
6   Zhu Jianfei, 'Beyond Revolution: Notes on Contemporary Chinese Architecture', *AA Files* 35 (Spring 1998): 3–14.

I. M. Pei and Chinese Spatiality at Expo '70

1   'Architecture News', *Jianzhu yu jihua* (*Architecture & Planning*) (January 1969): 10.
2   Chao Chi-Chang, *The Utilization of the US Aid* (Taipei: Linking Publishing, 1985), 2.
3   Interview with Chen Mai, one of the members of Atelier Cambridge, in 2017. As governor of the Central Bank of China between 1946 and 1947, Tsuyee Pei was part of the country's Nationalist government, which established the Republic of China in Taiwan.
4   Lee Chu-yuan, interviews with the author, 12 and 27 September 2017.
5   Along with Hsiung Chi-wei and Lee Chu-yuan, Atelier Cambridge consisted of Chen Mai, Chu Chun, Fei Chung-cheng, Hua Chang-yi, and Pai Chin.
6   I. M. Pei, quoted in *Jianzhu yu jihua* (*Architecture & Planning*) (July 1970): 39.
7   Lee Chu-yuan, 'Designing the Republic of China Pavilion', *Jianzhu yu jihua* (*Architecture & Planning*) 9 (1970): 40–41.
8   Lee Chu-yuan, 'Designing the Republic of China Pavilion', 40.
9   I. M. Pei, quoted in Philip Jodidio and Janet Adams Strong, *I. M. Pei: Complete Works* (New York: Rizzoli, 2008), 90.

I. M. Pei's Pictorial Vision of Space

1   *Learning from Light: The Vision of I. M. Pei* (2009), directed by Bo Landin and Sterling Van Wagenen, 84 mins.
2   Philip Jodidio and Janet Adams Strong write that 'unlike most of Pei's buildings, freestanding sculptural forms, Fragrant Hill is more *painterly* since indoors and outdoors unfold together, a garden in a park, as in a Chinese scroll.' Philip Jodidio and Janet Adams Strong, 'Fragrant Hill Hotel', in *I. M. Pei: Complete Works* (New York: Rizzoli, 2008), 183.
3   I. M. Pei, quoted in Michael Cannell, *I. M. Pei: Mandarin of Modernism* (New York: Carol Southern Books, 1995), 57.
4   For a discussion of classical aesthetic criteria, see John Hay, 'Structure and Aesthetic Criteria in Chinese Rocks and Art', *RES: Anthropology and Aesthetics* 13 (Spring 1987): 5–22.
5   Cannell, *I. M. Pei: Mandarin of Modernism*, 58.
6   For a study of this painting, see Elizabeth Fulder, 'Professional Painters in Fukien and Nanking', in James Cahill, ed., *The Restless Landscape: Chinese Painting of the Late Ming Period* (Berkeley: University Art Museum, University of Berkeley, 1971), 105–107.
7   Conversation with Calvin Tsao, 19 April 2016.
8   I. M. Pei and Lin Bing, 'Appendix: The Chinese Sentiment of I. M. Pei', in I. M. Pei and Gero von Boehm, eds, *Conversations with I. M. Pei: Light Is the Key*, trans. Lin Bing (Taipei: Lian Jing Press, 2003), 184.
9   Pei misidentified Mi Fu, the father of Mi Youren, as the painter and used him as the reference. This painting was discovered in the Suzhou Museum project archive at Pei Partnership Architects. I have drawn the conclusion that this painting was the reference for the rock landscape at the museum owing to the formal resemblance between the painting and the landscape, and the fact that it was the only painting in the project folder.
10 Although their development is complex, these two great lineages in the history of Chinese painting offer an insight into the appropriation of landscape aesthetics in other art forms.
11 Cannell, *I. M. Pei: Mandarin of Modernism*, 305.
12 There is a large body of literature on this issue, and here I give only a few representative examples. For the logic of glance, see Norman Bryson, 'The Gaze and the Glance', in *Vision and Painting: The Logic of the Gaze* (New Haven: Yale University Press, 1983), 87–131. For realism, see Wen Fong, *Beyond Representation: Chinese Painting and Calligraphy, 8th–14th Century* (New York: Metropolitan Museum of Art; New Haven: Yale University Press, 1992); and Richard Edwards, *The World around the Chinese Artist: Aspects of Realism in Chinese Painting* (Ann Arbor: LSA Checkpoint, College of Literature, Science, and the Arts, University of Michigan, 1987).
13 Louise Chipley Slavicek, *I. M. Pei* (New York: Chelsea House, 2010), 80–81.
14 Jodidio and Strong, *I. M. Pei: Complete Works*, 317.
15 This design change is documented in a series of sketches in the archive of Pei Cobb Freed & Partners.

SELECTED BIBLIOGRAPHY

Books

Primary

Chen Congzhou. *On Chinese Gardens* (Shanghai: Tongji University Press, 1984).

Cobb, Henry N. *Henry N. Cobb: Words & Works 1948–2018: Scenes from a Life in Architecture* (New York: Monacelli Press, 2018).

Fenn, William P. *Ever New Horizons: The Story of the United Board for Christian Higher Education in Asia, 1922–1975* (New York: United Board for Christian Higher Education in Asia, 1980).

Hough, Reginald D., with Janet Adams Strong. *Soft Mud, Hard Beauty: A Personal Story of Architectural Concrete* (New York: Primedia eLaunch LLC, 2021).

Mardrus, Françoise. *La pyramide du Louvre* (Paris: Éditions El Viso, 2019).

Robertson, Leslie E., and Janet Adams Strong. *The Structure of Design: An Engineer's Extraordinary Life in Architecture* (New York: Monacelli Press, 2017).

von Boehm, Gero, and I. M. Pei. *Conversations with I. M. Pei: Light Is the Key* (Munich: Prestel, 2000).

Zao Wou-Ki. *Couleurs et mots: entretiens avec Zao Wou-Ki* [Colours and Words: Conversations with Zao Wou-Ki] (Paris: Le Cherche Midi, 2013).

Zeckendorf, William, and Edward A. McCreary. *The Autobiography of William Zeckendorf* (New York: Holt, Rinehart & Winston, 1970).

Secondary

Alofsin, Anthony. *A Modernist Museum in Perspective: The East Building, National Gallery of Art* (Washington DC: National Gallery of Art, 2009).

Auger, Timothy. *A River Transformed: Singapore River and Marina Bay* (Singapore: Editions Didier Millet, 2015).

Cannell, Michael. *I. M. Pei: Mandarin of Modernism* (New York: Carol Southern Books, 1995).

Chua Beng Huat. *The Golden Shoe: Building Singapore's Financial District* (Singapore: Urban Redevelopment Authority, 1989).

Cody, Jeffrey W., Nancy S. Steinhardt, and Tony Atkin, eds. *Chinese Architecture and the Beaux-Arts* (Honolulu: University of Hawai'i Press, 2011).

Desmoulins, Christine. *Michel Macary Architecte* (Levallois-Perret: Éditions PC, 2014).

Fierro, Annette. *The Glass State: The Technology of the Spectacle, Paris, 1981–1998* (Cambridge, MA: MIT Press, 2006).

Harris, Neil. *Capital Culture: J. Carter Brown, the National Gallery of Art, and the Reinvention of the Museum Experience* (Chicago: University of Chicago Press, 2013).

Hellerman, D. J., and Steffi Chappell. *The Everson at 50* (Syracuse: Everson Museum of Art, 2019).

Hendgen, Yann, and Françoise Marquet, eds. *Zao Wou-Ki: 1935–2010* (New York: Abbeville Press, 2018).

Herbert F. Johnson Museum of Art. *A Handbook of the Collection* (Ithaca: Herbert F. Johnson Museum of Art, Cornell University, 1998).

Hong Ming-shui. *Tunghai Feng: Tunghaidaxue chuangxiao sishizhounian tekan* [Tunghai Magazine: Tunghai University 40th Anniversary Special Issue] (Taichung: Tunghai University Press, 1995).

Jodidio, Philip. *Museum of Islamic Art: Doha, Qatar* (Munich: Prestel, 2008).

Jodidio, Philip. *I. M. Pei: The Louvre Pyramid* (Munich: Prestel, 2009).

Jodidio, Philip, and Janet Adams Strong. *I. M. Pei: Complete Works* (New York: Rizzoli, 2008).

Keswick, Maggie, Alison Hardie, and Charles Jencks. *The Chinese Garden: History, Art and Architecture* (London: Frances Lincoln, 2003).

Knowles, Scott Gabriel. *Imagining Philadelphia: Edmund Bacon and the Future of the City* (Philadelphia: University of Pennsylvania Press, 2009).

Laubier, Marie de. *Saint-Gobain 1665–2015: The History of the Future* (Paris: Albin Michel, 2015).

Liu Dunzhen. *Suzhou gudian yuanlin* [Classical Gardens of Suzhou] (Beijing: China Architecture & Building Press, 1979).

Poy, Vivienne. *Building Bridges: The Life & Times of Richard Charles Lee—Hong Kong, 1905–1983* (Scarborough, Ontario: Calyan Publishing, 1998).

Prentice, Helaine Kaplan. *Suzhou: Shaping an Ancient City for the New China* (Washington DC: Spacemaker Press, 1998).

Stevens, Sara. *Developing Expertise: Architecture and Real Estate in Metropolitan America* (New Haven: Yale University Press, 2016).

Urban Redevelopment Authority. *Living the Next Lap: Towards a Tropical City of Excellence* (Singapore: Urban Redevelopment Authority, 1991).

Warner, Lucy. *The National Center for Atmospheric Research: An Architectural Masterpiece* (Boulder, CO: University Corporation for Atmospheric Research, 1985).

Wiseman, Carter. *The Architecture of I. M. Pei* (London: Thames & Hudson, 2001).

Wiseman, Carter. *I. M. Pei: A Profile in American Architecture* (New York: Harry N. Abrams, 2001).

Zhang Xin. *Suzhou Museum* (Beijing: Great Wall Publishing House, 2008).

Zheng Huimei. *Kongjian, zaojing, Chen Chi-kwan* [Space, Environment, Chen Chi-kwan] (Taiwan: Lion Art Books, 2004).

Journals and Articles
Primary
Bacon, Edmund N. 'A Case Study in Urban Design', *Ekistics* 10, no. 62 (1960): 368–373.

Brown, J. Carter. 'The Designing of the National Gallery of Art's East Building', *Studies in the History of Art* 30 (1991): 278–295.

Fenn, Dan H., Jr. 'Launching the John F. Kennedy Library', *The American Archivist* 42, no. 4 (October 1979): 429–442, http://www.jstor.org/stable/40292863, accessed 15 December 2022.

Friedman, Edward L. 'Cast-in-Place Technique Restudied', *Progressive Architecture* 41 (October 1960): 158–175.

Glynn, Thomas. '"Buildings Are Not That Important ... Social Fabric Is More Important": An Interview with I. M. Pei', *Challenge!* 10, no. 12 (December 1979): 2–11.

Gropius, Walter. 'Chinese Art Museum in Shanghai', *L'architecture d'aujourd'hui* 28 (February 1950): 76–77.

Gropius, Walter. 'Université de Hua-tung', *L'architecture d'aujourd'hui* 28 (February 1950): 26–29.

'Interview with I. M. Pei, 2004', *Architectural Record*, 25 April 2017, https://www.architecturalrecord.com/articles/12628-interview-with-i-m-pei-2004, accessed 15 December 2022.

Mellon, Paul. 'The National Gallery of Art: An American Experiment', *Proceedings of the American Philosophical Society* 119, no. 5 (1975): 349–352.

'Museum for Chinese Art, Shanghai, China', *Progressive Architecture* 29 (February 1948): 50–52.

Pei, I. M. 'Standardized Propaganda Units for the Chinese Government', *TASK* 2 (Summer 1941): 13–16.

Pei, I. M., and E. H. Duhart. 'House for the Post War Worker', *California Arts & Architecture* (January 1944): 32–33.

Pei, I. M. 'Community-Share-Use Plan', *Arts & Architecture* 62 (March 1945): 38–39.

Pei, I. M. 'Urban Renewal in Southwest Washington', *AIA Journal* 39, no. 1 (January 1963): 65–69.

Wong, Kellogg. 'The Bank of China Tower—From the Architect's Perspective', *ARCH* 1, no. 2 (1988): 34–52.

Zeckendorf, William. 'Baked Buildings', *The Atlantic Monthly* 188, no. 6 (May 1951): 46–49.

Secondary
Alraouf, Ali A. 'The Role of Museum's Architecture in Islamic Community: Museum of Islamic Art, Doha', *Journal of Islamic Architecture* 1, no. 2 (2010), https://doi.org/10.18860/jia.v1i2.1721, accessed 15 December 2022.

'Apartment Helix Spirals Wedge-Shaped Floors around a Slim Utility Core, Achieves a New Flexibility of Living Space and Rentals', *Architectural Forum* 92, no. 1 (January 1950): 90–96.

Bailey, James. 'RFK's Favorite Ghetto', *Architectural Forum* 128, no. 3 (April 1968): 46–53.

Bailey, James. 'Concrete Frames for Works of Art', *Architectural Forum* 130, no. 5 (June 1969): 54–67.

Baker, James. 'The Making of a Civic Space', *Architectural Forum* 135, no. 4 (November 1971): 40–45.

Ballon, Hilary. 'Robert Moses and Urban Renewal: The Title I Program', in Hilary Ballon and Kenneth T. Jackson, eds, *Robert Moses and the Modern City: The Transformation of New York* (New York: W. W. Norton & Co., 2007), 94–115.

'Beijing Xiangshan Fandian jianzhu sheji zuotanhui' [Discussions on Xiangshan Hotel], *Jianzhu xuebao* (*Architectural Journal*) 3 (1983): 57–63.

Blake, Peter. 'I. M. Pei & Partners', *Architecture Plus* 1, no. 1 (February 1973): 52–59.

Blake, Peter. 'I. M. Pei & Partners', *Architecture Plus* 1, no. 2 (March 1973): 20–25.

Blake, Peter. 'Cornell—On an Old and Venerable Campus, a Radical and Visible Departure', *Architecture Plus* 2, no. 1 (January/February 1974): 52–59.

Blake, Peter. 'Scaling New Heights', *Architectural Record* 179, no. 1 (January 1991): 76–83.

Campbell, Barbara Ann. 'Design Review: Light Periscope', *The Architectural Review*, January 1994.

Campbell, Robert, and Jeffrey Cruikshank. 'Art in Architecture', *Places* 3 (1986): 3–20.

Chang Dawei. '"He, jie, tou, jing" ji qita' [Interior Design of Xiangshan Hotel], *Jianzhu xuebao* (*Architectural Journal*) 3 (1983): 75–78.

'Chapel for China', *Architectural Forum* 106, no. 3 (March 1957): 118–119.

Clunas, Craig. 'Nature and Ideology in Western Descriptions of the Chinese Garden', *Extrême-Orient Extrême-Occident* 22 (2000): 153–166.

Dean, Andrea O. 'Conversations with I. M. Pei', *AIA Journal* 68 (June 1979): 61–67.

Dickinson, Elizabeth Evitts. 'Louvre Pyramid: The Folly that Became a Triumph', *ARCHITECT*, 19 April 2017, https://www.architectmagazine.com/awards/aia-awards/louvre-pyramid-the-folly-that-became-a-triumph_o, accessed 15 December 2022.

Dixon, John Morris. 'Connoisseurs of Cast-in-Place', *Progressive Architecture* 55 (September 1974): 90–93.

Flener, Ryan. 'A Conversation with George Schrader', *AIA Dallas*, 15 July 2016, https://www.aiadallas.org/v/blog-detail/A-Conversation-with-George-Schrader/oh/, accessed 15 December 2022.

Frutiger, Kimbro. 'Calculated Risk: I. M. Pei's Everson Museum of Art', *Mod* 1 (2014): 8–12.

Glover, Daniel. 'I. M. Pei's Imprint on the FAA', *Medium*, 19 May 2020, https://medium.com/faa/i-m-peis-imprint-on-the-faa-d4c77b656399, accessed 15 December 2022.

Gu Liyuan. 'Trends in Chinese Garden-Making', *Garden History* 46 (Winter 2018): 184–195.

Gu Mengchao. 'A Chinese View of Fragrant Hill', *AIA Journal* 72 (November 1983): 88–89.

Guo Ying. 'Cong jingying jiaodu kan Xiangshan Fandian' [Management of Xiangshan Hotel], *Jianzhu xuebao* (*Architectural Journal*) 3 (1983): 64–69.

Helleiner, Eric. 'International Policy Coordination for Development: The Forgotten Legacy of Bretton Woods', *UNCTAD Discussion Papers* 221 (May 2015): 7.

Hsiao, Leah. 'I. M. Pei's Unbuilt 1948 Shanghai Museum', *The Architectural Review*, 19 May 2015, https://www.architectural-review.com/buildings/museum/im-peis-unbuilt-1948-shanghai-museum, accessed 15 December 2022.

'Hua Tung Christian University, Shanghai—Proposal; Designed by I. Ming Pei & The Architects Collaborative', *International Architecture: Kokusai-Kentiku* 19 (July 1952): 26–35.

Jiang Bo-Hong, and Wu Kwang-tyng. 'Localizing of Modernity Transplanting from Modern Western Architecture in 60s Taiwan: In the Case of Luce Chapel', *Japanese Society of Architectural History*, December 2006, https://tkuir.lib.tku.edu.tw/dspace/handle/987654321/59373.

Ju, Sam. 'Modernist Masterwork: Luce Memorial Chapel at 50', trans. Jonathan Barnard, *Taiwan Panorama* 103, no. 1 (January 2014): 50–56.

Karnik, Pranjali. 'Hudec's Art Deco Park Hotel by László Hudec: Asia Meets Europe', *Rethinking the Future*, 8 January 2021, https://www.re-thinkingthefuture.com/2021/01/08/a2722-hudecs-art-deco-park-hotel-by-laszlo-hudec-asia-meets-europe/, accessed 15 December 2022.

King, Amy. 'Power, Shared Ideas and Order Transition: China, the United States, and the Creation of the Bretton Woods Order', *European Journal of International Relations* 28, no. 4 (2022): 910–933.

Kögel, Eduard. 'Modern Vernacular—Walter Gropius and Chinese Architecture', trans. Rebecca Philipps Williams, *bauhaus imaginista*, 29 March 2018, https://www.bauhaus-imaginista.org/articles/343/modern-vernacular, accessed 15 December 2022.

Lee Chu-yuan. 'Recalling the Design of the Republic of China Expo '70 Pavilion', *Jianzhu yu jihua* (*Architecture & Planning*) (July 1970): 38–43.

Leslie, Stuart W. '"A Different Kind of Beauty": Scientific and Architectural Style in I. M. Pei's Mesa Laboratory and Louis Kahn's Salk Institute', *Historical Studies in the Natural Sciences* 38, no. 2 (May 2008): 173–221, https://doi.org/10.1525/hsns.2008.38.2.173, accessed 15 December 2022.

Liu Pinghao and Zhu Wenyi. 'A Study on the First Public Gymnasium in China—Shanghai YMCA Sichuan Rd Club', *International Journal of Culture and History* 1, no. 2 (December 2015): 122–128, http://www.ijch.net/vol1/023-D006.pdf, accessed 15 December 2022.

Luo Xiaowei. 'Beiyuming xiansheng jianzhu chuangzuo sixiang chutan' [I. M. Pei's Early Reflections on Architecture], *Shidai jianzhu* (*Time + Architecture*) 1 (1984): 4–7.

McQuade, Walter. 'Pei's Apartments round the Corner,' *Architectural Forum* 115, no. 2 (August 1961): 106–114.

Marlin, William. 'Mr. Pei Goes to Washington', *Architectural Record* 164, no. 2 (August 1978): 79–92.

Miller, Steven H. 'Engineering a Pei Cantilever—Dallas City Hall', *Architecture Week*, 29 July 2009, http://www.architectureweek.com/2009/0729/building_2-1.html, accessed 15 December 2022.

'Museum of Art', *Progressive Architecture* 43 (November 1962): 126–131.

'New Tower to Grace Airports', *Architectural Forum* 119, no. 11 (November 1963): 112–114.

'The 1959 National Honor Awards Report of the Jury', *AIA Journal* 31 (June 1959): 83.

Osborn, Robert. 'Calder's International Monuments', *Art in America* 57, no. 2 (March–April 1969): 32–49.

Ouyang Can. 'Xiangshan Fandian chufang' [Visiting Xiangshan Hotel], *Jianzhu xuebao* (*Architectural Journal*) 3 (1983): 70–74.

Owen, Christopher. 'Exploring a New Vernacular: I. M. Pei & Partners' Fragrant Hill Hotel near Beijing', *AIA Journal* 72, no. 9 (September 1983): 34–42.

Papademetriou, Peter. 'Angling for a Civic Monument', *Progressive Architecture* 60 (May 1979): 102–105.

'The Park Hotel, Shanghai—and Its Automatic Sprinkler Installation', *The Sprinkler Bulletin* 151 (30 June 1935): 1354–1356.

Pastier, John. 'Bold Symbol of a City's Image of Its Future', *AIA Journal* 67, no. 6 (Mid-May 1978): 112–117.

'Picasso's Prestressed Sculpture', *Engineering News-Record* 181, no. 6 (8 August 1968): 20–21.

Potts, Alex. 'Henry Moore's Public Sculpture in the US: The Collaborations with I. M. Pei', *British Art Studies* 3 (18 July 2016), https://doi.org/10.17658/issn.2058-5462/issue-03/apotts, accessed 15 December 2022.

Qiao Zhengyue. 'Park Hotel Represents Hudec's Crowning Achievement', *Shine*, 17 July 2017, https://www.shine.cn/feature/art-culture/1707170787/, accessed 15 December 2022.

'Report of the Jury: Pencil Points—Pittsburgh Architectural Competition', *Pencil Points, Progressive Architecture* 26 (May 1945): 52–92.

Robinson, Cervin. 'Bright Landmark on a Changing Urban Scene', *Architectural Forum* 125, no. 5 (December 1966): 21–29.

'Roosevelt Field Shopping Center: A Webb & Knapp Project', *Progressive Architecture* 36, no. 9 (September 1955): 91–97.

Russell, James S. 'The Profession: Glazing Systems—Evanescent Architecture', *Architectural Record* 183, no. 6 (June 1995): 36–39.

'Sculpture in the Plaza', *North Carolina Architect* 11, no. 11 (October 1968): 17.

'Shells Soar in Formosa', *Architectural Forum* 121, no. 2 (August/September 1964): 136–139.

'Small-House Perfection', *Vogue* 138 (15 January 1961): 86–93.

'Small Office Buildings—1. Marble Curtain Walls Hung from the Inside of Pre-fab Framing Cut Costs but Preserve Quality', *Architectural Forum* 96, no. 2 (February 1952): 108–110.

Sokol, David. 'Pei's Addition to the German Historical Museum Nears Completion', *Architectural Record* 190, no. 6 (June 2002): 24.

Stephens, Suzanne. 'The Adventures of Harry Barber in OPEC Land', *Progressive Architecture* 57, no. 10 (October 1976): 56–65.

Surya, Shirley. 'Building Dreams Are Made of These ...—Pei's Unbuilt Projects in Singapore', *The Singapore Architect* 16 (2019): 146–154.

Tepest, Eva-Maria. '"Temporary Until Further Notice": The Museum of Islamic Art and the Discursive Endeavour of Displaying Islamic Art in Qatar', *Museum and Society* 17, no. 2 (2019): 157–172, https://doi.org/10.29311/mas.v17i2.3043, accessed 15 December 2022.

Thompson, Peter. 'The OCBC Centre Singapore', *The Arup Journal* 11 (October 1976): 3–11.

Wakeman, Rosemary. 'Shanghai and New York: Mid-century Urban Avant-Gardes', *Built Heritage* 3 (2019): 49–61, https://doi.org/10.1186/BF03545743, accessed 15 December 2022.

Watanabe Yasumitsu. 'Miho Museum Bridge, Shigaraki, Japan', *Structural Engineering International* 12 (2002): 245–247, https://doi.org/10.2749/101686602777965054, accessed 15 December 2022.

Yemini, Miri, Laura Engel, Moosung Lee, and Claire Maxwell. 'Cosmopolitan Nationalism and Global Citizenship Rhetoric: Analysis of Policies and Curricula in South Korea, Israel and the United States', in Daniel Tröhler, Nelli Piattoeva, and William F. Pinar, eds, *World Yearbook of Education 2022: Education, Schooling and the Global Universalization of Nationalism* (London: Routledge, 2021), 219–234.

Yu Kongjian and Peter Del Tredici. 'Infinity in a Bottle Gourd: Understanding the Chinese Garden', *Arnoldia* 53 (Spring 1993): 2–7.

Zhu Jianfei. 'Beyond Revolution: Notes on Contemporary Chinese Architecture', *AA Files* 35 (Spring 1998): 3–14.

Zhu Zixuan. 'Dui Xiangshan Fandian sheji de liangdian kanfa' [Views Towards Xiangshan Hotel], *Jianzhu xuebao* (*Architectural Journal*) 3 (1983): 78–79.

Newspapers

'Air Tower Plan Accepted by F.A.A.', *New York Times*, 7 November 1962.

Amon, Rhoda. 'A Shopping Giant Arrives: Developer's Idea Produces a Mighty Mall at Roosevelt Field', *Newsday*, 17 August 2019.

Baker, Russell. 'Capital Planning City Within a City', *New York Times*, 2 January 1956.

'Big Operator's Base: Realty Tycoon Bill Zeckendorf Dreams Up Far-Flung Deals in a Dream of an Office', *New York Sunday News*, 22 May 1955.

Chua, K. Y. 'Raffles City Project a Different Concept', *Straits Times*, 4 October 1979.

Fermigier, André. 'La maison des morts' [The House of the Dead], *Le Monde*, 26 January 1984.

'Founder of Bank of China Hong Kong Tsuyee Pei', *Ta Kung Pao*, 23 August 2017.

'Going On in Real Estate—Pei Joins Webb & Knapp', *New York Herald Tribune*, 12 September 1948.

Goldberger, Paul. 'Winning Ways of I. M. Pei', *New York Times*, 20 May 1979.

Goldberger, Paul. 'Architecture View: A Year of Years for the High Priest of Modernism', *New York Times*, 17 September 1989.

Hervaux, Yves. 'Au petit matin. Les essais secrets de la pyramide du Louvre' [In the Early Morning: The Secret Tests of the Louvre Pyramid], *Le Quotidien de Paris*, 20/21 April 1985.

Huxtable, Ada Louise. 'Kennedy Family Announces the Selection of Pei to Design Library', *New York Times*, 14 December 1964.

Huxtable, Ada Louise. 'Architecture: Object Lesson in Art and Museology', *New York Times*, 29 October 1968.

Huxtable, Ada Louise. 'Mr. Pei Comes to Washington', *New York Times*, 11 July 1971.

Huxtable, Ada Louise. 'What's a Tourist Attraction Like the Kennedy Library Doing in a Nice Neighborhood Like This?', *New York Times*, 16 June 1974.

Huxtable, Ada Louise. 'A Capital Art Palace', *New York Times*, 7 May 1978.

'Interview with I. M. Pei', *Christian Science Monitor*, 16 March 1978.

Keegan, Matthew. 'Hong Kong: The City Still Shaped by Feng Shui', *The Guardian*, 19 July 2018.

Macé, Gabriel. 'Mitterramsès Ier et sa pyramide' [Mitterramses the First and His Pyramid], *Le Canard enchaîné*, 1 February 1984.

'New $200 Million "Heart" for City', *Straits Times*, 17 October 1969.

Prial, Frank J. 'Tsuyee Pei, Banker in China for Years', *New York Times*, 29 December 1982.

Schneider, Pierre. 'Paris: Clouds in a Changing Skyline', *New York Times*, 18 September 1972.
Scott, Lael. 'Man With a Plan to Beautify the Ghetto', *New York Post*, 20 May 1967.
'Shopping Center Accents Parking', *New York Times*, 22 July 1956.
Stetson, Damon. 'World's Loftiest Tower May Rise on Site of Grand Central Terminal', *New York Times*, 8 September 1954.
Turek, Diana. 'Johnson Museum to Open', *Cornell Daily Sun*, 4 May 1973.
Wen, Patricia. 'The Lost Liberal Arts University of China', *Boston Globe*, 3 March 2012.

Other Printed Matter
Primary
Andrews, Mary L. 'Summary of Meeting between Dr. Roberts and I. M. Pei in Boulder', 26 June 1961, NCAR Archives, Mesa Laboratory Construction Records, folder: Building File 1960–69, https://opensky.ucar.edu/islandora/object/archives%3A1810/datastream/OBJ/view, accessed 15 December 2022.
Association pour le renouveau du Louvre et SOS Paris [Union for the Revitalisation of the Louvre and SOS Paris], 'Au secours le Louvre!' ['Help the Louvre!'], 1985, Archives nationales de France.
Beijing No. 1 Municipal Service Bureau and YTT Tourism. 'Jianshe he gaizao fandian hetong 225 hao' [No. 225 Contract for Hotels Construction and Reconstruction], 25 February 1979.
Chang Chao-kang and I. M. Pei. 'Comments and Suggestions after Conference -II. Between C. K. Chang and I. M. Pei', 1958, Papers of I. M. Pei, Library of Congress, Washington DC.
Chen Chi-kwan. Letter to H. S. Fong, 14 December 1959, the Getty Foundation, 2018, https://www.getty.edu/foundation/pdfs/kim/luce_chapel.pdf, accessed 15 December 2022.
Chen Chi-kwan. Memo to I. M. Pei, 9 April 1960.
Commemorative Booklet for Yang Yuan-loong (Hong Kong: Esquel, 2004).
Development Bank of Singapore Ltd, *First Annual Report 1968* (Singapore: Development Bank of Singapore Ltd, 1969), 4.
Ferguson, Mary E. Letter from the United Board for Christian Colleges in China, 13 June 1955, Papers of I. M. Pei, Library of Congress, Washington DC.
Hunter, Eileen. Letter to I. M. Pei, 26 July 1993, Papers of I. M. Pei, Library of Congress, Washington DC.
I. M. Pei & Associates. *The Hyperboloid—A Webb & Knapp Project for the Grand Central Terminal* (New York: I. M. Pei & Associates, 1956).
I. M. Pei & Partners. *Xiangshan Fandian sheji jianjie* [Design of the Fragrant Hill Hotel] (New York: I. M. Pei & Partners, 1979).
I. M. Pei & Partners. *Gateway—Office Development Proposal for Land Parcel 8* (Singapore: Singapore Land Ltd, 1981).
I. M. Pei & Partners. *Bank of China Building Hong Kong leasing brochure* (Hong Kong: Bank of China, 1987).
I. M. Pei & Partners and W. Szeto & Partners. *Sunning Plaza leasing brochure* (Hong Kong: Hysan Development Company Ltd, 1981).
Mitterrand, François. Letter to I. M. Pei, 1 December 1983, Papers of I. M. Pei, Library of Congress, Washington DC.
Morris, Frederick K. Letter to William Emerson, 2 October 1936, Papers of I. M. Pei, Library of Congress, Washington DC.
'National Gallery of Art East Building Fact Sheet', National Gallery of Art, https://www.nga.gov/content/dam/ngaweb/press/assets/2016/eastbuildingkit/eastbuildingarchitecture-factsheet.pdf, accessed 15 December 2022.
An Oriental Skyscraper: The New J. S. S. Building (Shanghai: Millington Ltd, 1934), László Hudec Collection, University of Victoria (BC) Special Collections.
Pei, I. M. Letter to his parents, 12 October 1935, Shanghai Municipal Archives.
Pei, I. M. Letter to Tsuyee Pei, 13 May 1939, Second Historical Archives of China.
Pei, I. M. 'Standardized Propaganda Units for War Time and Peace Time China', BArch diss., Massachusetts Institute of Technology, 1940.
Pei, I. M. Letter to Frederick G. Roth, 1946, Papers of I. M. Pei, Library of Congress, Washington DC.
Pei, I. M. Letter to Walter Gropius, 25 October 1948, Bauhaus-Archiv Berlin.
Pei, I. M. Telegram to Max W. Sullivan, 19 April 1965, Everson Museum of Art Archive.
Pei, I. M. Letter to Koyama Hiroko, 14 July 1997, Papers of I. M. Pei, Library of Congress, Washington DC.
Pei, I. M., and Wang Tianxi. 'Urban Planning in Beijing and the Problem of the Nationalisation of Architectural Creation in China', unpublished presentation notes, Tsinghua Alumni Association of Greater New York, 30 May 1980, Papers of I. M. Pei, Library of Congress, Washington DC.
Pei, Tsuyee. Letter to I. M. Pei, 17 December 1962, Patricia Pei.
Robertson, Leslie E. Letter to I. M. Pei, 3 March 1988, Papers of I. M. Pei, Library of Congress, Washington DC.
St. Paul's College School Prospectus 2021–2022 (Hong Kong: St Paul's College, 2022): 26, http://spc.edu.hk/upload_files/editor_image/school_prospectus_2021-2022.pdf, accessed 15 December 2022.
Webb & Knapp, Inc. 'Urban Renewal Plan—Southwest Urban Renewal Project Area C: A Report of Existing Conditions and a Plan for Urban Renewal', United States National Capital Planning Commission, 1956.
Wu Liang-yong and Zhou Gan-shi. Letter to I. M. Pei, 20 January 2003, Suzhou Museum.
Zeckendorf, William, and I. M. Pei. 'Multistory Building Structure', US Patent 2,698,973, 11 January 1955, https://patents.google.com/patent/US2698973A/, accessed 15 December 2022.

Secondary
'Bei shi jiazu he shizilin de yuanyuan' [The Origins of the Pei Family and Shizilin], Suzhou Gardens and Virescence Management Bureau, 23 December 2017, http://ylj.suzhou.gov.cn/szsylj/ryyl/201712/8462ac013ff44d79837d976e150db55c.shtml, accessed 15 December 2022.
'Conservation Management Plan: Luce Memorial Chapel', the Getty Foundation, 2018, https://www.getty.edu/foundation/pdfs/kim/luce_chapel.pdf, accessed 15 December 2022.
Krugier, Jan, and Maria Gaetana Matisse. *Zao Wou-Ki: encres de Chine 1982–1996* (New York: Jan Krugier Gallery, 1996).
Poncellini, Luca. 'Laszlo Hudec in Shanghai (1919–1947): The Brilliant Trajectory of a Hungarian Architect in the Process of Modernization of the Greatest City of the East', PhD thesis, Technical University Torino, 2007, http://www.hudecproject.com/files/l_poncellini_article.pdf, accessed 15 December 2022.
Zao Wou-Ki: Paintings & Drawings, 1976–80 (New York: Pierre Matisse Gallery, 1980).

Other Non-printed Matter
Primary
Cai Guo-Qiang. Email correspondence, 7 December 2021.
Cheng Kai Chor. Personal interview, 10 February 2022.
Demirtaş, Aslıhan. Personal interview, 15 February 2022.
Hsu, Simon. Personal interview, 11 January 2022.
Kung, Sherman. Personal interview, 24 May 2022.
Lang, Jack. Personal interview, 25 November 2021.
Lee Chu-yuan. Personal interview, 31 March 2021.
Lin Bing. Personal interview, 30 August 2021.
Liu Thai Ker. Personal interview, 30 June 2017.
Mardrus, Françoise. Personal interview, 3 September 2019.
Oles, Paul Stevenson. Email correspondence, 20 June 2021.
Pei, Chien Chung. Personal interview, 29 July 2021.
Pei, I. M. Pritzker Prize Laureate Ceremony Acceptance Speech, 1983, https://www.pritzkerprize.com/sites/default/files/inline-files/IM_Pei_Acceptance_Speech_1983.pdf, accessed 15 December 2022.
Pei, I. M. Interview with Lucy Warner, 14 May 1985, UCAR/NCAR Oral History Collection, tape no. 16, https://voices.nmfs.noaa.gov/sites/default/files/2021-12/Pei_IM.pdf, accessed 15 December 2022.
Pei, I. M., and Robert Campbell. 'A Conversation with I. M. Pei', forum at John F. Kennedy Presidential Library and Museum, 26 September 2004, https://www.jfklibrary.org/events-and-awards/forums/past-forums/transcripts/a-conversation-with-im-pei, accessed 15 December 2022.
Pei, Li Chung. Personal interview, 22 July 2021.
Pei, Liane. Personal interview, 20 July 2021.
Pei, Patty. Personal interview, 29 June 2021.
Robertson, Leslie E. 'Bank of China, Miho Museum and Bridge, and Other

Projects', paper presented at 'Rethinking Pei: A Centenary Symposium', Harvard Graduate School of Design, 13 October 2017.
Strong, Janet Adams. Email correspondence, 1 September 2022.
Tsao, Calvin. Personal interview, 11 January 2022.
Turner, Tracy. Email correspondence, 31 May 2022.
Weymouth, Yann. Personal interview, 5 July 2022.
Weymouth, Yann. Personal interview, 11 July 2022.
Wong, Kellogg. Personal interview, 7 August 2017.
Wong, Kellogg. 'I. M. Pei & Partners, the Pei Team, and Singapore', paper presented at 'Rethinking Pei: A Centenary Symposium', Harvard Graduate School of Design, 13 October 2017.

Secondary

Abramson, Daniel M. 'Vexing Government Center', paper presented at 'Rethinking Pei: A Centenary Symposium', Harvard Graduate School of Design, 13 October 2017.
A Better Tomorrow. Directed by John Woo, Fortune Star Media, 1986.
Bideau, André. 'Between the Superblock and the Pyramid: I. M. Pei and Araldo Cossutta at La Défense', paper presented at 'Rethinking Pei: A Centenary Symposium', Harvard Graduate School of Design, 13 October 2017.
Chang Chin-Wei. 'High Modernists at Harvard University GSD: I. M. Pei, Walter Gropius, and TAC's Huatung/Tunghai University', paper presented at 'Rethinking Pei: A Centenary Symposium', University of Hong Kong, 14 December 2017.
Daniell, Thomas. 'Divine Light', paper presented at 'Rethinking Pei: A Centenary Symposium', University of Hong Kong, 15 December 2017.
Du, Juan. 'A Tower for "Modern China"', paper presented at 'Rethinking Pei: A Centenary Symposium', University of Hong Kong, 14 December 2017.
Eigen, Edward. 'I. M. Pei and the "Big Plan": The Several Lives of the John F. Kennedy Presidential Library & Museum', paper presented at 'Rethinking Pei: A Centenary Symposium', Harvard Graduate School of Design, 13 October 2017.
Fierro, Annette. 'Effective Depths: Transparent Domains', paper presented at 'Rethinking Pei: A Centenary Symposium', Harvard Graduate School of Design, 13 October 2017.
'I. M. Pei on Sculpture'. Interview conducted for *American Masters: Alexander Calder*, directed by Roger Sherman, Public Broadcasting Service, 24 July 1997, https://www.youtube.com/watch?v=5ofmkeLZl08, accessed 15 December 2022.
Kuan, Seng. 'Sculpture as Architecture and Architecture as Sculpture', paper presented at 'Rethinking Pei: A Centenary Symposium', University of Hong Kong, 14 December 2017.
Lai Delin. 'Defining the Present Perfect Tense of I. M. Pei's Space', paper presented at 'Rethinking Pei: A Centenary Symposium', Harvard Graduate School of Design, 13 October 2017.
'Large Reclining Figure'. Henry Moore Foundation, https://catalogue.henry-moore.org/objects/14059/large-reclining-figure?ctx=aa9f735a-10d1-4c54-9f82-627da530c62c, accessed 15 December 2022.
Leslie, Stuart W. 'I. M. Pei's Modern Monastery: The NCAR Mesa Laboratory', paper presented at 'Rethinking Pei: A Centenary Symposium', Harvard Graduate School of Design, 13 October 2017.
Leslie, Thomas. 'Brutal Grace: I. M. Pei's Early Art Centers', paper presented at 'Rethinking Pei: A Centenary Symposium', Harvard Graduate School of Design, 13 October 2017.
'Lot Essay, Harry Bertoia (1915–1978), Dandelion from the Hilton Hotel, Denver, Colorado', Christie's, https://www.christies.com/en/lot/lot-5653055, accessed 15 December 2022.
'MIHO Chapel', Kikukawa, https://www.kikukawa.com/en/product/miho-chapel/, accessed 15 December 2022.
Naderi, Kamran Afshar. 'Pei's Planning for Changing the Downtown of Tehran', paper presented at 'Rethinking Pei: A Centenary Symposium', University of Hong Kong, 15 December 2017.
RoboCop. Directed by Paul Verhoeven, MGM, 1987.
Roskam, Cole. 'The Fragrant Hill Hotel: Reassessing the Politics of Tradition and Abstraction in China's Early Reform Era', paper presented at 'Rethinking Pei: A Centenary Symposium', Harvard Graduate School of Design, 13 October 2017.
Schneider, Brett. 'Early Tall Structures in Context', paper presented at 'Rethinking Pei: A Centenary Symposium', Harvard Graduate School of Design, 13 October 2017.
Stevens, Sara. 'Designing Development: The Architectural Division of Webb & Knapp', paper presented at 'Rethinking Pei: A Centenary Symposium', University of Hong Kong, 15 December 2017.
Strong, Janet Adams. 'Continuity and Change: Fine-Face Concrete in the Physical Manifestation of I. M. Pei's Approach to Architecture', paper presented at 'Rethinking Pei: A Centenary Symposium', Harvard Graduate School of Design, 13 October 2017.
Su Meng-Tsun. 'Construing the Other: The Architecture of Hybridity at Tunghai University in Postwar Taiwan', paper presented at the 'International Conference on East Asian Architectural Culture: Reassessing East Asia in the Light of Urban and Architectural History', Kyoto University, Kyoto, 2006.
Surya, Shirley. 'Pei's Office and Singapore's Urban Core: Corporate Architecture, Symbolic Aestheticization and Economic Pragmatism', paper presented at 'Rethinking Pei: A Centenary Symposium', Harvard Graduate School of Design, 13 October 2017.

CONTRIBUTORS

Barry Bergdoll is Meyer Schapiro Professor of Art History at Columbia University. His research interests centre on modern architectural history. He was Philip Johnson Chief Curator of Architecture and Design at the Museum of Modern Art, New York, between 2007 and 2014. His numerous publications include *Marcel Breuer: Building Global Institutions* (2018) and *European Architecture, 1750–1890* (2000).

Jiat-Hwee Chang is Associate Professor in the Department of Architecture and Asia Research Institute at the National University of Singapore. His publications include *Everyday Modernism: Architecture and Society in Singapore* (2022) and *A Genealogy of Tropical Architecture: Colonial Networks, Nature and Technoscience* (2016).

Aric Chen is General and Artistic Director of Het Nieuwe Instituut in Rotterdam. He was formerly the first lead curator for design and architecture at M+ before becoming the first curatorial director for the Design Miami fairs. He is a widely published author, has curated numerous exhibitions and biennials, and has served as professor and founding director of the Curatorial Lab at the College of Design and Innovation at Tongji University, Shanghai.

South Ho is a Hong Kong–based photographer and artist. His photographs capture everyday observations of the built environment and are often informed by the socio-political conditions of the city. Ho photographed the Bank of China Tower in Hong Kong.

Naho Kubota is a New York–based artist and architectural photographer. Her approach highlights the traces of habitation in built spaces. Kubota photographed Kips Bay Plaza in New York, the National Center for Atmospheric Research in Boulder, Dallas City Hall, and the National Gallery of Art East Building in Washington DC.

Lee Kuo-Min is a Taipei-based photographer whose practice encompasses context-specific approaches towards capturing the spatiality of architecture and its surroundings. He photographed the Tunghai University campus and Luce Memorial Chapel in Taichung.

Liu Linfan is an architect at DIGSAU in Philadelphia and overseas editor of China-based interior design magazine *id+c*. She received her architectural training in China and the United States before completing her PhD in architectural history and theory at the University of Pennsylvania.

Eric Mumford is the Rebecca and John Voyles Professor of Architecture at the Sam Fox School of Design and Visual Arts at Washington University in St Louis. He is a historian focusing on modern architecture and urbanism, and his publications include *Designing the Modern City: Urbanism Since 1850* (2018) and *The CIAM Discourse on Urbanism, 1928–1960* (2000).

Joan Ockman is Vincent Scully Visiting Professor in Architectural History at the Yale School of Architecture and a senior lecturer at the University of Pennsylvania. Her numerous publications on the history, theory, and criticism of architecture include *Architecture School: Three Centuries of Educating Architects in North America* (2012) and *Architecture Culture 1943–1968: A Documentary Anthology* (1993).

Giovanna Silva is a Milan-based photographer and publisher. She originally trained as an architect, and her practice and numerous photographic books seek to examine cities and their narratives and histories. She is the co-founder of *San Rocco* magazine and the founder and editor-in-chief of Humboldt Books. Silva photographed the Louvre in Paris.

Mohamed Somji is a Dubai-based editorial and architectural photographer. He is the director of Gulf Photo Plus, a gallery and community organisation cultivating visual practices in photography in the United Arab Emirates. Somji photographed the Museum of Islamic Art in Doha.

Janet Adams Strong is an architectural historian and architectural media consultant. She was engaged to write for I. M. Pei & Partners (later Pei Cobb Freed & Partners) before becoming the firm's director of communications. As a writer and editor, she has contributed to numerous publications related to architecture and I. M. Pei, including *I. M. Pei: Complete Works* (2008).

Shirley Surya is Curator of Design and Architecture at M+. Her research and writings on architectural and design developments in greater China and Southeast Asia have contributed to shaping the M+ collections and exhibitions, including *Hong Kong: Here and Beyond* (2021), *Things, Spaces, Interactions* (2021), and *In Search of Southeast Asia through the M+ Collections* (2018).

Tian Fangfang is a Shanghai-based photographer with a background in architecture. He is the founder of Studio FF, which specialises in architectural photography and videography. Tian photographed Fragrant Hill Hotel in Beijing and the Suzhou Museum.

Wu Kwang-tyng has been a professor at the General Education Center of National Tsing Hua University in Taiwan since 2021. Between 2013 and 2021, he was head of the Department of Architecture at the National Cheng Kung University. He has contributed to numerous publications on Taiwan's modern architectural and urban history after 1945, including *Unexpected Modernity: Essays on Modern Architecture in Taiwan* (2015).

Yoneda Tomoko is a London-based artist whose practice centres on photographing landscapes, sites, and interiors. She photographed the Miho Museum in Shiga prefecture, Japan.

ACKNOWLEDGEMENTS

This first major institutional retrospective of I. M. Pei's life and work, in the form of an exhibition and this publication, would not have been possible without the generosity and trust of the late I. M. Pei, his family, and the firm he co-founded, Pei Cobb Freed & Partners. The project was carried out thanks to the essential participation of Senior Researcher and Advisor Janet Adams Strong, the team at M+, and numerous contributors and advisors.

We are particularly grateful to Li Chung (Sandi) Pei, who welcomed the possibility of M+ holding this retrospective when we proposed it in 2014. We also want to thank Calvin Tsao, who opened many doors for us to gain such support from the beginning. Our conversations eventually led to I. M. Pei granting us permission to launch a re-examination of his career in the form of 'Rethinking Pei: A Centenary Symposium' in 2017, co-organised with the Harvard Graduate School of Design (GSD) and the University of Hong Kong (HKU) Faculty of Architecture, and to his seeking the support of Pei Cobb Freed & Partners to collaborate with M+ in organising this exhibition in 2018. We are thankful to former Harvard GSD dean Mohsen Mostafavi, former HKU head of architecture Nasrine Seraji, and fellow symposium conveners Seng Kuan and Cole Roskam for co-organising the transcontinental discussions in Cambridge, Massachusetts, and Hong Kong, which were formative in framing this retrospective. We want to thank the scholars and architects who took part in the symposium and whose contributions, in the form of essays and anecdotes, are included in this publication: Barry Bergdoll, André Bideau, Cai Guo-Qiang, Jiat-Hwee Chang, Aslıhan Demirtaş, Michael D. Flynn, Eric Höweler, Zeina Koreitem, Sherman Kung, Jack Lang, Lin Bing, Jing Liu, Liu Linfan, Liu Thai Ker, Françoise Mardrus, John May, Eric Mumford, Joan Ockman, Paul Stevenson Oles, Chien Chung (Didi) Pei, Li Chung (Sandi) Pei, Liane Pei, Seng Kuan, Janet Adams Strong, Al-Mayassa bint Hamad bin Khalifa Al-Thani, Calvin Tsao, Kellogg Wong, Yenn Weymouth, and Wu Kwang-tyng. We also want to acknowledge Lin Bing for organising the first exhibition on Pei, titled *I. M. Pei Documents*, at the Suzhou Art Museum in 2017, a reference for this project.

The exhibition and publication, as a reappraisal of I. M. Pei's work, were contingent on unearthing a new set of visual and material evidence. We are therefore indebted to the support of the late Henry N. Cobb, one of the three co-founding partners of Pei Cobb Freed & Partners, and current partner José Bruguera in granting us access to the firm's archive. The extensive investigation of this archive was only possible through the conscientious work of Emma Cobb, senior editor at Pei Cobb Freed & Partners, and Janet Adams Strong, this project's senior researcher and advisor and former director of communications at Pei Cobb Freed & Partners. We are also grateful to our past and present colleagues at M+, in particular Olatz Irijalba Claramunt and Sonia So, who—with the support of Emma Cobb and Janet Adams Strong—completed the challenging task of digitising selected materials.

In attempting to uncover more documentation to elaborate on the contexts of I. M. Pei's practice, we are grateful for the oral histories, photographs, printed documentation, essays, anecdotes, and other references provided by Pei's former colleagues and collaborators, as well as to those who have directly or indirectly engaged with Pei's work. These include Barbara Bair, Cai Guo-Qiang, the family of Chang Chao-kang, Steffi Chappell, the family of Chen Chi-kwan, the family of Chen Congzhou, Cheng Kai Chor, Rosaline Cheng, Aslıhan Demirtaş, Jonathan Duval, Michael D. Flynn, Julia Gonnella, Yann Hendgen, Reginald D. Hough, Simon Hsu, Inagaki Hajime, Sanjay Kanvinde, Zeina Koreitem, Sherman Kung, Jack Lang, Chien Lee, Lee Chu-yuan, Jing Liu, Lesley Ma, Maehara Hitoshi, Françoise Mardrus, John May, Kamran Naderi, Nakahara Mari, Joan Ockman, Okamoto Hiroshi, Paul Stevenson Oles, Ong Ker-Shing, Chien Chung (Didi) Pei, Liane Pei, Marc Pelletreau, Allen Poon, Katie Porter, Pascal Riviale, Mildred Tao, Al-Mayassa bint Hamad bin Khalifa Al-Thani, Calvin Tsao, Tracy Turner, Queenie Wang, Watanabe Yasumitsu, Yann Weymouth, Kathleen Williams, Marjorie Yang, Ines Zalduendo, Gary van Zante, and Zhou Hongjun.

Our deep gratitude goes to the seven photographers who accepted the commission to capture I. M. Pei's built work across geographies through a contextual lens, amid the challenges of venue closures owing to renovations or the Covid-19 pandemic: South Ho, Naho Kubota, Lee Kuo-Min, Giovanna Silva, Mohamed Somji, Tian Fangfang, and Yoneda Tomoko. We also thank Abdulla Al Dosari, Nanxi Cheng, Kiso Keiichiro, Scott Laine, Wei Tseng, and Susan B. Wertheim, who provided access and permission to photograph the sites.

As a project that required a vast amount of institutional resources for research, digitisation, and editorial support, we thank Suhanya Raffel, Veronica Castillo, Doryun Chong, Pauline J. Yao, and Ikko Yokoyama for their unwavering support and guidance in enabling colleagues from various teams to contribute to this publication.

We are grateful to those who were directly involved in conceiving and realising this publication. The project would not have been possible without Naomi Altman, whose insightful research and meticulous project coordination ensured its success. She was assisted by other members of the curatorial team, including Fei Tse, Victor Chan, Tanja Cunz, Christine Lee, Tommy Chow, Iris Ng, Spencer Lam, and Natalie Kung. As the pandemic prevented us from travelling to mainland China for research, we thank Shanghai-based Wang Xuerui and Ye Zi for their resourcefulness in gathering key materials, especially archives in Shanghai and Nanjing. We are deeply grateful to Andrew Goodhouse, whose reflective and critical engagement with the book's content, coupled with his editorial rigour, made his contributions exceed those of a project editor. We benefitted greatly from the incisive critique of the manuscript offered by Greg Barton, Jayne Kelley, and Alisa Kotmair. We thank the editorial team of William Smith, Jacqueline Leung, Juliet Cheung, Lam Lap Wai, Zhong Yuling, and Or Ka Uen for their support and feedback in refining the English manuscript and its Chinese translation by Charles Lai Chun Wai and Joanna Wong. We also thank Jacqueline Chan, Crystal Yu, and Tom Morgan, who managed the process of sourcing more than five hundred images with care and precision. We thank Dustin Cosentino and Sasha Anderson for shepherding the book through the production process, and our publishing partner, Thames & Hudson—in particular Lucas Dietrich and Julian Honer—for supporting the vision of this book from design to production, and for ensuring its global reach. Lastly, we thank Johanne Lian Olsen for weaving together the varied and complex documents featured in this book in an elegant relationship between text and image.

Shirley Surya and Aric Chen

IMAGE CREDITS

Every effort has been made to appropriately credit the images included in this publication.

Page numbers are given in **bold**.

l = left; r = right; t = top;
b = bottom; c = centre

Cover: © Arnold Newman/Arnold Newman Collection via Getty Images; **12, 13l, 13r**: © Estate of I. M. Pei. Courtesy of The Second Historical Archives of China; **14, 30t, 30b, 32t, 32c, 32b, 33t, 110t, 110b, 299**: © MIT Museum. Courtesy MIT Museum; **20t**: Courtesy of The Estate of I. M. Pei; **20b, 21**: Courtesy of Patricia Pei; **22, 23t**: © All rights reserved. Courtesy of the University of Victoria Special Collections and University Archives; **23b**: © Kautz Family YMCA Archives, University of Minnesota Libraries; **24t**: Special Collections, Yale Divinity School Library; **24bl, 160lt, 160lb**: © Estate of I. M. Pei. Courtesy of The Estate of I. M. Pei; **24br**: Courtesy of The Estate of I. M. Pei. Library of Congress, Prints & Photographs Division, LC-DIG-ds-15081; **25t**: Image courtesy of National Diet Library, Japan; **25b, 339b**: © Estate of I. M. Pei. Courtesy of Pei Cobb Freed & Partners; **26t, 26b**: © Liu Dunzhen. Image courtesy of Liu Qi; **27**: Courtesy of The Estate of I. M. Pei. Library of Congress, Prints & Photographs Division, LC-DIG-ds-14835; **28**: © Estate of I. M. Pei. Courtesy of Shanghai Municipal Archives; **29t**: © All rights reserved. Library of Congress, Prints & Photographs Division, LC-DIG-ds-15079; **29b**: © All rights reserved. Container 460 Folder 3, I. M. Pei Papers, Manuscript Division, Library of Congress, Washington DC; **31tl, 31tc, 31tr, 154tl, 154tr, 154b**: © All rights reserved. Pei, I. M., 'Standardized Propaganda Units for War Time and Peace Time China, MIT thesis, 1940', Bachelor of Architecture, Department of Architecture. Department of Distinctive Collections, MIT Libraries, Cambridge, Massachusetts. Available at https://dspace.mit.edu/handle/1721.1/29220; **31b**: © All rights reserved. Courtesy MIT Museum; **33b**: Courtesy of the Frances Loeb Library. Harvard University Graduate School of Design; **34t, 34b, 35t, 35b, 37t, 37b, 38t, 38b, 144**: © Estate of I. M. Pei. Courtesy of the Frances Loeb Library. Harvard University Graduate School of Design; **36**: Jerry Cooke Photographic Archive, camh-dob-013521, The Dolph Briscoe Center for American History, The University of Texas at Austin; **39, 40**: © All rights reserved. Image source: portaildocumentaire.citedelarchitecture.fr / Bibliothèque d'architecture contemporaine – Cité de l'architecture et du patrimoine; **41l, 41r**: Image courtesy of Bauhaus-Archiv Berlin; **45t**: © All rights reserved. Reinhold Publishing Corporation. Image courtesy of Family of Wang Dahong; **45b, 59l, 59r, 111, 122l, 178bl, 178br**: © All rights reserved. Image source: USModernist®; **46t, 46b**: *Arts + Architecture*, March 1945; © Travers Family Trust. Used with permission; **47**: © All rights reserved. Courtesy of Kanvinde Rai & Chowdhury Archives; **48**: © The Oklahoman – USA TODAY NETWORK; **54t**: From the *New York Times*. © 1948 The New York Times Company. All rights reserved. Used under licence. Container 444 Folder 3, I. M. Pei Papers, Manuscript Division, Library of Congress, Washington DC; **54b, 60b, 63l, 68b, 76, 96, 137, 169b, 183b, 215b, 261t, 261b, 319**: © All rights reserved. Courtesy of Pei Cobb Freed & Partners; **55**: © Daily News, L.P. (New York). Used with permission; **56**: X2010.7.1.13492 Museum of the City of New York; **57tl, 62t, 62bl, 62br, 65, 118r, 119b, 127b**: © Ezra Stoller/Esto; **57tr, 57b, 58l, 58r, 61, 68t, 72l, 72r, 73, 78r, 80, 81t, 81b, 82, 83, 84r, 85r, 88, 93t, 95r, 100–101, 102t, 102b, 115t, 116t, 117t, 118l, 119t, 120, 121t, 123t, 123b, 135t, 138t, 138bl, 156, 157t, 157b, 162, 163l, 163r, 165, 168tl, 168tr, 168bl, 168br, 169t, 170b, 176, 178t, 181r, 184, 190b, 192b, 196, 198t, 198b, 200l, 200r, 202, 205cl, 205cr, 205bl, 205br, 207l, 207r, 214l, 214r, 215tl, 216t, 216b, 236b, 246t, 254t, 255t, 260, 262t, 267, 302b, 304t, 309t, 309b, 318t, 318b, 321b, 325t, 325b, 326, 327t, 327bl, 332t, 332ct, 332cb, 332b, 333b, 365br**: © Pei Cobb Freed & Partners. Courtesy of Pei Cobb Freed & Partners; **60t**: © Lionel Freedman Archives. All rights reserved. Photo by Lionel Freedman, Courtesy of Pei Cobb Freed & Partners; **63r, 69t, 180, 191**: George Cserna photographs and papers, 1937–1978, Avery Architectural & Fine Arts Library © Columbia University in the City of New York; **64–65**: © Pei Cobb Freed & Partners. Courtesy of Avery Architectural and Fine Arts Library, Columbia University; **66–67, 70–71, 128–129, 130–131, 177, 179, 182, 185, 193, 194, 201, 203, 234–235, 238–239, 244–245, 248–249**: © Naho Kubota; **69b**: © All rights reserved. Container 347 Folder 1, I. M. Pei Papers, Manuscript Division, Library of Congress, Washington DC; **74**: Courtesy National Building Museum. Image courtesy of the Architectural Archives, University of Pennsylvania; **75l, 116b, 147, 161**: Photo: Robert Damora © Damora Archive, all rights reserved; **75r**: Special Collections Research Center, Temple University Libraries, Philadelphia, PA; **77t**: © Norman McGrath; **77b**: © Dennis Brack. Library of Congress, Prints & Photographs Division, LC-DIG-ds-15078; **78l**: Text and layout © NYP Holdings Inc. I. M. Pei's photo: © McCarten. Use of the *New York Post* courtesy of NYP Holdings Inc.; **79**: Photo by Gil Amiaga. Used with permission, Amiaga Photographers Inc., 2022; **84l**: © KOUO SHANG-WEI;

IMAGE CREDITS

85l: © Sazeh Consultants. Courtesy of Kamran Afshar Naderi; **86l, 86r, 87t**: © 1981 Hysan Development Company Limited. Photo: M+, Hong Kong; **87b**: © Golden Princess Amusement Co. Ltd/Fortune Star Media Ltd (Subject to licensed territory); **89**: © Pei Cobb Freed & Partners. Courtesy of Tao Shing Pee and Singapore Land Limited; **90t**: © Kellogg Wong. Image courtesy of Kellogg Wong; **90b**: © Architectural Journal Publishing Co. Ltd; **91tl, 91tr, 91bl, 91br, 315tl, 315tr, 315bl, 315br**: © Pei Cobb Freed & Partners. Container 139 Folder 2, I. M. Pei Papers, Manuscript Division, Library of Congress, Washington DC; **92l, 114, 255b, 312, 313t, 363, 364b, 365bl**: © All rights reserved; **92r, 252b**: Image courtesy of Marjorie Yang, Chairman of Esquel Group; **93b, 212tr**: Photo: John Nye © John Nye; **94–95, 208–209, 210–211, 213, 328–329**: © South Ho; **97**: © Tracy Turner. Image courtesy of Tracy Turner; **98–99, 253, 258–259, 316–317, 322–323, 344–345, 348–349, 352–353**: © Tian Fangfang; **104, 126b, 148, 257t, 314, 330**: © Marc Riboud/Fonds Marc Riboud au MNAAG; **112l**: © All rights reserved. Photo by Frank Lerner. Courtesy of Pei Cobb Freed & Partners; **112r**: © All rights reserved. Library of Congress, Prints & Photographs Division, LC-DIG-ds-14838; **113**: Reprinted courtesy of Engineering News-Record, copyright BNP Media, August 8, 1968, all rights reserved. Courtesy of Pei Cobb Freed & Partners; **115b, 117b, 122r, 186t, 186b, 187b, 189t**: © Collection of Everson Museum of Art. Image courtesy of Everson Museum of Art; **121b, 192t, 243b**: Photo: © Thorney Lieberman. Photo by Thorney Lieberman. Courtesy of Pei Cobb Free & Partners; **124**: © All rights reserved. Courtesy of National Gallery of Art, Washington DC, Gallery Archives; **125t, 125bl, 125br, 126t, 127t, 197l, 197r, 251t**: Courtesy of National Gallery of Art, Washington DC, Gallery Archives; **132l**: Reproduced by permission of The Henry Moore Foundation. Library of Congress, Prints & Photographs Division, LC-DIG-ds-15075; **132r**: © Pei Cobb Freed & Partners. Library of Congress, Prints & Photographs Division, LC-DIG-ds-14839; **133**: © Ogawa Taisuke. Courtesy of Pei Cobb Freed & Partners; **134**: © Pei Cobb Freed & Partners. Photo by Li Chung Pei. Courtesy of Library of Congress; **135b**: Photo by Steve Rosenthal © Historic New England, from the Steve Rosenthal Collection of Commissioned Work at Historic New England, all rights reserved; **136**: © Archives nationales (France), 20080657/59; **138br**: © Stéphane Couturier. Courtesy of Pei Cobb Freed & Partners; **139**: © Archives nationales (France), 20140450/17; **140–141, 217, 218, 269, 331, 334**: © Giovanna Silva; **142l**: Photo by Tatsumi Masatoshi. Courtesy Cai Studio; **142t–143t**: Photo by Hiro Ihara. Courtesy Cai Studio; **143b**: Still frames courtesy of Cai Studio; **146**: © Ludwig Mies van der Rohe/VG Bild-Kunst – SACK, Seoul, 2024. Digital Image © The Museum of Modern Art/Licensed by SCALA/Art Resource, NY; **155**: © Estate of I. M. Pei. Container 488 Folder 7, I. M. Pei Papers, Manuscript Division, Library of Congress, Washington DC; **158t**: © Pei Cobb Freed & Partners. Library of Congress, Prints & Photographs Division, LC-DIG-ds-15072; **158b**: © Pei Cobb Freed & Partners. Digitisation of original photomontage by M+, Hong Kong. Courtesy of Pei Cobb Freed & Partners; **159l**: *Architectural Forum* © All rights reserved. Courtesy of Pei Cobb Freed & Partners; **159r**: © All rights reserved. Photo by Edgar Orr. Courtesy of Pei Cobb Freed & Partners; **160r**: Robert Damora, *Vogue* © Condé Nast; **164, 170t, 172, 175t**: © Family of Chen Chi-kwan. Image courtesy of Family of Chen Chi-kwan; **166–167, 171, 173, 305, 306, 310–311**: © Lee Kuo-Min; **174**: © Pei Cobb Freed & Partners. Container 373 Folder 8, I. M. Pei Papers, Manuscript Division, Library of Congress, Washington DC; **175b, 223b, 278b**: © Higashide Photo Studio. Image courtesy of io Architects LLP; **181l**: Amar and Isabelle Guillen – Guillen Photo LLC/Alamy Stock Photo; **183t, 236t**: © 2022 UCAR; **187t**: Layout and text: © All rights reserved. Photo: © Collection of Everson Museum of Art. Image courtesy of Everson Museum of Art; **189b**: © Iwan Baan; **190t**: George Cserna photographs and papers, 1937–1978, Avery Architectural & Fine Arts Library, © Columbia University in the City of New York. Image source: USModernist®; **195**: © All rights reserved. Courtesy of Reginald D. Hough; **199**: © All rights reserved. Photo by John Nicholais. Courtesy of Pei Cobb Freed & Partners; **204–205t**: © Architects Team 3 Pte Ltd, Singapore. Photo: M+, Hong Kong; **206tl, 206tr, 206b, 212tl, 327br**: © Pei Cobb Freed & Partners. Courtesy of Sherman Kung; **212b**: © Pei Cobb Freed & Partners. Courtesy of PEI Architects LLP; **215tr**: © Yann Weymouth. Courtesy of the Frances Loeb Library, Harvard University Graduate School of Design; **220, 276t, 339t**: © Estate of I. M. Pei. Container 459 Folder 6, I. M. Pei Papers, Manuscript Division, Library of Congress, Washington DC; **221t**: © I. M. Pei Architect. All rights reserved. Courtesy of Shimizu Corporation; **221b, 335**: © Kiyohiko Higashide; **222l, 223tr, 284, 356, 357, 360t**: © All rights reserved. Image courtesy of Aslıhan Demirtaş; **222r, 223tl, 278t**: © I. M. Pei Architect + io Architects. Image courtesy of io Architects LLP; **226t, 226b, 227t**: © Pei Cobb Freed & Partners. Courtesy of Janet Adams Strong; **227b**: © Bob Adelman; **228**: Eddie Hausner/The New York Times/IC photo; **237**: © Pei Cobb Freed & Partners. Courtesy of UCAR; **240l**: © All rights reserved. Image courtesy of John F. Kennedy Presidential Library; **240r, 241l, 241c, 241r**: © Pei Cobb Freed & Partners. Container 146 Folder 5, I. M. Pei Papers, Manuscript Division, Library of Congress, Washington DC; **242t**: From the *New York Times*. © 1974 The New York Times Company. All rights reserved. Used under licence. Container 457 Folder 4, I. M. Pei Papers, Manuscript Division, Library of Congress, Washington DC; **242b**: The *Boston Globe* via Getty Images; **243t**: © Mona Zamdmer. Photo by Mona Zamdmer. Courtesy of Pei Cobb Freed & Partners; **246b**: © Bob Taylor, reprinted from the *Dallas Times Herald*. Courtesy of Pei Cobb Freed & Partners; **247t**: © Robert Lautman Photography, National Building Museum; **247b**: ROBOCOP©1987 Orion Pictures Corporation. All Rights Reserved. Courtesy of MGM Media Licensing; **250**: © The Al Hirschfeld Foundation. www.AlHirschfeldFoundation.org; **251b**: © Robert Lautman Photography, National Building Museum. Courtesy of Pei Cobb Freed & Partners; **252t**: © All rights reserved. Library of Congress, Prints & Photographs Division, LC-DIG-ds-14842; **254b**: © Tracy Turner. Courtesy of Pei Cobb Freed & Partners; **256t, 321t**: Photo: © Calvin Tsao; **256b**: From the *New York Times*. © 1979 The New York Times Company. All rights reserved. Used under licence. Photo: © Inge Morath/Magnum Photos/IC photo; **257b**: © Liu Heung Shing; **262b, 265r**: © Archives nationales (France); **263**: © All rights reserved. Container 460 Folder 1, I. M. Pei Papers, Manuscript Division, Library of Congress, Washington DC; **264l**: Une pyramide dans la cour Napoléon – J.M. – Le Monde, 26/01/1984; **264r**: © Jean Pattou; **265l**: © Roland Moisan/ADAGP, Paris – SACK, Seoul, 2024; **266**: © Keystone Press Agency/ZUMA Press; **268t**: Le Grand Louvre, Antenne 2 Midi, 10/04/1987 © INA 1987; **268b**: © pyramide du Louvre, architecte I. M. Pei, musée du Louvre. Courtesy of Pei Cobb Freed & Partners; **270–271, 274, 279, 341b**: © Shumei. Image courtesy of io Architects LLP; **272–273, 275, 340, 342–343**: © MIHO MUSEUM. Photo: © Tomoko Yoneda; **276b**: © Estate of I. M. Pei. Library of Congress, Prints & Photographs Division, LC-DIG-ds-15082; **277t**: © MIHO MUSEUM; **277b, 341t**: © Kibowkan International. Image courtesy of io Architects LLP; **280, 285**: © Estate of I. M. Pei. Image courtesy of Museum of Islamic Art; **281t, 361b**: © All rights reserved. Image courtesy of Museum of Islamic Art; **281b**: © Estate of Keiichi Tahara; **282–283, 286–287, 354–355, 358–359**: © Mohamed Somji; **288–289**: Kouo Shang-Wei collection, National Library, Singapore; **290**: © Pei Cobb Freed & Partners. Courtesy of Kellogg Wong; **291**: © BEP Akitek. Image courtesy of BEP Akitek; **292**: © Pei Cobb Freed & Partners. Photo by Li Chung Pei. Courtesy of Pei Cobb Freed & Partners; **300, 301**: © Bijuku Shuppan-Sha Co. Ltd Container 440 Folder 6, I. M. Pei Papers, Manuscript Division, Library of Congress, Washington DC; **302–303t, 304b**: © Pei Cobb Freed & Partners. Image Courtesy of Family of Chen Chi-kwan; **303b**: © All rights reserved. Container 2 Folder 18, I. M. Pei Papers, Manuscript Division, Library of Congress, Washington DC; **307l, 307r, 308b**: Courtesy of Family of Chang Chao-kang; **308t**: © Pei Cobb Freed & Partners. Container 373 Folder 5, I. M. Pei Papers, Manuscript Division, Library of Congress, Washington DC; **313b**: © The Central News Agency; **320**: © All rights reserved. Photo: M+, Hong Kong; **324**: Image courtesy of Condé Nast; **333tl**: Topographical Collection/Alamy Stock Photo; **333tr**: Nisian Hughes via Getty Images; **336**: © All rights reserved. Library of Congress, Prints & Photographs Division, LC-DIG-ds-14844; **337tl, 337bl**: © All rights reserved. Container 459 Folder 6, I. M. Pei Papers, Manuscript Division, Library of Congress, Washington DC; **337r**: © All rights reserved. Photo by Shuichi Fujita. Courtesy of Pei Cobb Freed & Partners; **338l, 338r**: © Estate of I. M. Pei. Container 459 Folder 8, I. M. Pei Papers, Manuscript Division, Library of Congress, Washington DC; **341c**: Osaze Cuomo/Alamy Stock Photo; **346, 347**: Courtesy of Suzhou Museum; **350t, 350b, 351**: © PEI Architects LLP. Courtesy of PEI Architects LLP; **360b**: © Estate of I. M. Pei. Image courtesy of Aslıhan Demirtas; **361t**: Photo: Morley von Sternberg; **362**: © Dan Bigelow/© PEI Architects LLP. Photo: © Dan Bigelow. Courtesy of PEI Architects LLP; **364t**: © All rights reserved. Image courtesy of National Taiwan Museum; **365t**: © Estate of I. M. Pei. Library of Congress, Prints & Photographs Division, LC-DIG-ds-15073; **366–367b**: Courtesy of The Cleveland Museum of Art; **367t, 368t, 368tl, 368cl, 368bl, 368tr, 368cr, 368br**: © Liu Linfan.

INDEX

Page numbers in *italic* refer to the illustrations.

A

Aalto, Alvar 43
Abbott, Richard 57
Abrams, Charles 103
abstraction 19, 29, 255, 326, 347
Aga Khan Trust for Culture 280
Akzona Corporate Headquarters, Ashville 377
Al-Mayassa bint Hamad bin Khalifa Al-Thani, Sheikha 281
Al Salaam (unbuilt), Kuwait City 377
Albert Farwell Bemis Foundation 43, 44
Algar & Beesley 23
ALICO/Wilmington Tower, Wilmington 21, *21*, 374
Allied Bank Tower, Dallas 378
American Institute of Architects (AIA) 44, 52, 101, 375, 377, 378
Anderson, Lawrence 43
Andrade, Preston 103
Architects Team 3 290
Architectural Forum 115, 145, 152, *159*, 190
ARCO Tower, Dallas 377
Arlington National Cemetery 375
Asia House (unbuilt), New York 377
Atelier Cambridge 364, *364*
Atkinson, Brennan 24
Austral Lineas (unbuilt), Buenos Aires 378

B

Bacon, Edmund 73, 100, 103
Badran, Rasem 280
Baltimore World Trade Center 375
Bank of China 18, 20, 21, 370
Bank of China Head Office Building, Beijing 380
Bank of China Tower, Hong Kong 6, *92–95*, 92–95, 153, 204–213, *205–213*, 231, 325–329, *325–329*, 378
'A Bankers' Club in Hong Kong' (student project) *14*, 16
Basil & Elise Goulandris Museum of Modern Art (unbuilt), Athens 380
Bauhaus 36, 42, 110, 145, 146, 224, 225, 320, 326
Beaux-Arts architecture 28–29, 37, 42, 43, 224
Beckwith, Herbert 43
Bedford-Stuyvesant Superblock, New York 52–53, 78–79, *78–79*, 88, 375
Bei Li-tai (Pei's grandfather) *24*
Bei Runsheng (Pei's grand-uncle) 25, 26
Beijing *91*, 381
    Bank of China Head Office Building 380
    Beijing Enamel Factory 320
    Forbidden City 53, 90–91, *90–91*
    Fragrant Hill Hotel 90–91, *90*, 92, 97, 109, 133, *133*, 227, 232, 252, *252–259*, 254–258, 294, 296, 298, *314–324*, 315–324, 327, 347, 366–368, *368*, 378
    Tsinghua University 315
    United States Embassy Land Use Requirements Proposal 378
BEP Akitek 291
Bertoia, Harry 63
A Better Tomorrow (film) 87, *87*
Biasini, Émile 261, *267*
Bideau, André 82
Bilbao Emblematic Building (unbuilt) 380
Black Mountain College 225
Boston, Massachusetts 43, 44, 242, 374, 375, 376, 377
    Christian Science Center 375
    Government Center Urban Renewal Plan 374
    Harbor Towers 375
    John F. Kennedy Presidential Library and Museum 78, 231, 232–233, *240–243*, 240–243, 375, 379
    Museum of Fine Arts, West Wing 377
Boullée, Étienne-Louis 46
Bretton Woods Monetary Conference (1944) 20, *20–21*, 21
Breuer, Marcel 35, 36, 46, 100, 102, 224
Broad Street Mall, Augusta 377
Brown, J. Carter 124, 126, 232, 251, *251*
Bruce, Ailsa Mellon 251
Buck Institute for Age Research, Novato 379
Bunshaft, Gordon 151
Burchard, John 44
Burger, Warren *251*
Burton, Scott 134–135, *134*, *135*
Bushnell Plaza, Hartford 374

C

Cai Guo-Qiang 109, 142–143, *142–143*
Calder, Alexander *104*, 106, 108, 112, *112*
Cambridge, Massachusetts 17, 42, 43, 44, 47, 241, 242
    Harvard Graduate School of Design (GSD) 18–19, 33, 35–36, 42–47, 100, 101, 103, 107, 144, 145, 147, 224, 364, 371, 372
    Polaroid Site Selection Study 375
    Polaroid Tower (unbuilt) 196, *196*, 376
    see also Massachusetts Institute of Technology
Camille Edouard Dreyfus Chemistry Building, MIT 375
Canadian Imperial Bank of Commerce, Toronto 375
Cannell, Michael 232, 288
Cecil and Ida Green Center for Earth Sciences, MIT 108, 112, *112*, 246, 374
'A Centre of Research for Creative Art' (student project) 110, *110*
CenTrust/Miami Tower, Miami 378
Century City Apartments, Los Angeles 374
Chang Chao-kang 302, *303*, *307*, 308, *308*
Chen Chi-kwan 153, *164*, 165, *168–169*, 169, 302, 302–303, 304, *304*, 309
Chen Congzhou 321, *324*, 327
Chiang, T. T. *170*, 172
Chiang Kai-shek 42, 363, 370
Chinese architecture 39, 143, 144, 146–147, 295, 296–297, 307, 313, 315, 318–319, 363–365
Chinese Civil War (1946–1949) 147, 224, 372
Chinese garden design 19, 25, 26, 39, 107, 145–147, 295–297, 318, 321, 327, 347, 351, 364, 366–368
Chinese paintings 123, 347, 366–368
Chirac, Jacques 266–267, *266*
Choate Rosemary Hall Science Center, Wallingford 379
Christian Science Center, Boston 375
Chuang Lien Kwun (Pei's mother) *20*, *24*, 371
Chung Khiaw Bank (unbuilt), Singapore 290, 376
CIAM *see* Congrès internationaux d'architecture moderne
Cleo Rogers Memorial County Library, Columbus 114, *114*, 374
Cobb, Henry N. 42, 47, 56, *57*, 63, 76, 77, 152, 153, *158*, 233, 369, 373, 374, 375, 376, 377, 378, 379
Collins Place, Melbourne 376
Collyer Quay/Raffles Square Development Study, Singapore 377

Columbia Square, Washington DC 378
Columbia University Master Plan, New York 375
Commerce Square, Philadelphia 379
Commercial Plaza II, New Brunswick 377
Congrès internationaux d'architecture moderne (CIAM) 47, 51, 100, 101–102, 103
Cornell University 120–121, 120–121, 375
cosmopolitanism 18, 23, 64
  see also under Pei, Ieoh Ming
Cossutta, Araldo 63, 65, 82–83, 83, 153, 369, 373, 374, 375, 376
Costa, Lúcio 103
Courthouse Square, Denver 52, 61, *61*, 63, *63*, 373
Creative Artists Agency, Los Angeles 231, 379
Credit Suisse First Boston, London 379
Cret, Paul Philippe 42
Crown Center, Kansas City 379
Cubism 108, 117, 251, 280

D

Dallas, Texas
  Allied Bank Tower 378
  ARCO Tower 377
  Dallas City Hall 192, *192–194*, 225, 232, *244–249*, 246–248, 375
  Mobil Research & Development Center 377
  The Morton H. Meyerson Symphony Center 231, 378
  One Dallas Center 377
  University Village, Excellence in Education Study 376
Daum, Martin *76*, 77
Demirtaş, Aslıhan 222, *222–223*, 356
Denver, Colorado 100
  16th Street Transitway Mall 377
  Courthouse Square 52, 61, *61*, 63, *63*, 373
  Denver Hilton 63, *63*
  Denver Urban Renewal 372
  Mile High Center 52, 61–62, *61–62*, 372
Derderian, Ara *73*
Des Moines Art Center 108, 118–119, *118–119*, *123*, 375
Deutsches Historisches Museum, Berlin 296, 336, *336*, 380
Development Bank of Singapore (DBS) 81, 290, 291
Dong Dayou 46
Dorner, Alexander 145, 147
Dubuffet, Jean 114
Duhart, E. H. (Emilio) 45, *45*

E

East Cove Development (unbuilt), New York 378
East-West Center, Honolulu 374
Eckbo, Garrett 103
Embassy of the People's Republic of China, Washington DC 381
Emerson, William 28–29, 43
Erieview Master Plan, Cleveland 374
Everson Museum of Art, Syracuse 77, 107, 108, 109, 115–117, *115–117*, 118, *122*, 145, 147, *147*, 152, 186–189, *186–189*, 195, 363, 365, 374

F

Federal Aviation Administration (FAA) Air Traffic Control Towers *190–191*, 191, 227, 374
Federal Housing Administration 73, 102
Fenn, William P. 302

Ferguson, Mary E. *303*
Fermigier, André *264*, 265
First Bank Place, Minneapolis 379
First Interstate Tower/Library Tower, Los Angeles 378
Fleischner, Richard 134–135
Flynn, Michael D. 153, 219, 227
Fong, H. S. 169
Four Seasons Hotel, New York 379
Fragrant Hill Hotel, Beijing 90–91, *90*, 92, 97, 109, 133, *133*, 227, 232, 252, *252–259*, 254–258, 294, 296, 298, *314–324*, 315–324, 327, 347, 366–368, *368*, 378
Frankenthaler, Helen 117
Franklin National Bank, Garden City 60, *60*, 372
Franzen, Ulrich 56
Freed, James 77, 153
Friedberg, M. Paul 78

G

Garden City, Long Island
  Franklin National Bank 60, *60*, 372
  Roosevelt Field Shopping Center 52, 59, *59–60*, *122*, 372
Gateway, Singapore 89, *89*, 232, 378
Geddes, Robert 103
Gem City Plaza, Dayton 377
General Panel Corporation 44, *45*
geometry, use of 8, 89, 109, 172, 175, 199, 202, 219, 247, 296, 313, 326, 327, 356–357, 364
Giedion, Sigfried 47
Girard, Alexander 63
Goldberger, Paul 231, 256, 379
Goodwin, Philip 145
Government Center Urban Renewal Plan, Boston 374
Graduate School of Design (GSD) *see* Harvard Graduate School of Design
Grand Louvre, Paris 51, 82, 96, *96*, 107, 109, 136–141, *136–141*, *148*, 152, 214–216, *214–218*, 219, 224, 225, 226, 231, 232, 233, 250, 260–268, *260–269*, 296, 330–333, *330–334*, 368, 378, 379
Grand Marina Hotel, Barcelona 379
Greater Shanghai Plan 18, 37, 46, 145
Gropius, Walter 19, 35–37, *36*, 39–41, *39–41*, 42, 43, 44–45, 46, 47, *47*, 107–108, 111, 145, 146, 224, 302, 364
Gruen, Victor 103
GSD *see* Harvard Graduate School of Design
Guang-yuan Construction Company 175
Guggenheim Pavilion, Mount Sinai Medical Center, New York 378
Gulf Oil Building, Atlanta 152, 159, *159*, 232, 372

H

Halaby, Najeeb 191
Hamad bin Khalifa Al-Thani, Sheikh 232, 280, 281, *281*, 380
Hamedina/Nordia Development Plan, Tel Aviv 374
Harbor Towers, Boston 375
Harvard Graduate School of Design (GSD) 18–19, 33, 35–36, 42–47, 100, 101, 103, 107, 144, 145, 147, 224, 364, 371, 372
Held, Al 108, 117
Helix (unbuilt) 41, 52, *156–158*, 157–158, 372
Herbert F. Johnson Museum of Art, Cornell University 120–121, *120–121*, *123*, 375
Hirschfeld, Al 231, 250, *250*

Ho, South *94–95*, *208–209*, *210–211*, 213, *328–329*
Hoffman Hall, University of Southern California, Los Angeles 374
Hong Kong 6, 20
  Bank of China Tower 6, 92–95, *92–95*, 153, 204–212, *205–213*, 231, 325–329, *325–329*, 378
  St Paul's College Primary School 20, 370
  Sunning Plaza 86–87, *86–87*, 377
Hough, Reginald D. 195, 227
Housing Act (1949) 51, 102
housing projects 34, 51, 68, 70, 73, 75, 78–79, 101–103, 151, 178, 225
Hoving, Thomas 258, 324
Höweler, Eric 120, 202, 326
Huatung University (unbuilt), Shanghai 19, 40–41, *40–41*, 296, 297, 300–301, *300–301*, 372
Hudec, László 23, 43
Hudnut, Joseph 42, 44, 46, 101
Hunter, Eileen *69*
Huxtable, Ada Louise 107, 242, *242*
The Hyperboloid (unbuilt), New York 52, 58, *58*, 151–152, *162–163*, 163, 196, 373

I

I. M. Pei-opoly 97, *97*
IBM Corporate Office Building, Purchase 377
IBM Headquarters Entrance Pavilion, New York 378
IBM Office Campus, New York 378
IBM Office Tower (unbuilt), New York 376
I. M. Pei & Associates 47, 51, 53, 73, 76–77, *76–77*, 224, *226*, 373, 374, 375
I. M. Pei & Partners 77, *77*, 81, *86–87*, 212, 224, *227*, 375, 365, 377, 379
Immobiliaria Refotib (unbuilt), Mexico City 378
Industrial Credit Bank (unbuilt), Tehran 85, 377
Inter-American University Chapel (unbuilt), San Germán 374
International Style 16, 19, 36
internationalisation 22, 142, 227, 281, 289, 291, 365
io Architects 222, *278*, 279
Islamic architecture 281, 356–357, 361
Islamic Revolution (1978–1979) 85, 378

J

Jacob K. Javits Convention Center, New York 378
Jacobs, Jane 103
Jacobson, Leonard *76*, 77
Jacoby, Helmut *115*, *196*
Japanese architecture 307, 341
Jencks, Charles 291
JFK International Airport, Central Terminal Complex (unbuilt), New York 379
Jianzhu xuebao (*Architectural Journal*) 90
John F. Kennedy Presidential Library and Museum, Dorchester 78, 231, 232–233, 240–243, *240–243*, 375, 379
John Hancock Tower, Boston 233, 250, 375, 376
John Portman & Associates 291
Johnson, Philip 295
Johnson & Johnson Baby Products Headquarters Complex, Montgomery Township 377
Johnson & Johnson World Headquarters, New Brunswick 377, 379
Joint Savings Society, Shanghai 18, 22, 23
Jonsson, Erik 246
Joy of Angels Bell Tower, Shigaraki 270, *270–273*, 337, *337*, 379

K

Kahn, Louis 100, 101, 103, 231
Kaplan, Craig *361*
Kapsad Development (unbuilt), Tehran 53, 85, *85*, 377
Kennedy, Jacqueline *228*, 231, 240, 241, 242, *257*, 258, 375
Kennedy, John F. 231, 246, 374
　see also John F. Kennedy Presidential Library and Museum, Dorchester
Kennedy, Robert F. 78, 79, *228*, 240, 241, 375
　see also Robert F. Kennedy Gravesite, Arlington National Cemetery
Kikukawa 153, 223
Kiley, Dan 237
Kips Bay Plaza, New York 52, *66–71*, 68, 70, *102*, 103, 113, 151, 176–178, *176–179*, 195, 225, 226, *226*, 373
Kirklin Clinic, University of Alabama 379
Kiryat Sir Isaac Wolfson Development Plan, Jerusalem 375
Korean War (1950–1953) 63, 289
Koreitem, Zeina 188
Koyama Hiroko *274*, *338*, *341*
Koyama Mihoko 233, 270, 274, *274*, 277, 339
Kubota, Naho *66–67*, *70–71*, *128–129*, *130–131*, *177*, *179*, *182*, *185*, *193*, *194*, *201*, *203*, *234–235*, *238–239*, *244–245*, *248–249*
Kung Hsiang-Hsi *20–21*
Kung, Sherman 86
Kuomintang (KMT) 313, 363, 370, 372

L

La Caixa Bank Headquarters (unbuilt), Barcelona 380
La Défense, Paris 82–83, *82–83*
Lang, Jack 266
L'architecture d'aujourd'hui 39–40, 47, 144, 146
Le Corbusier 29, 43, 47, 101, 144, 145, 152, 224, 225
Le Notre, André *333*, *333*
Lee Chu-yuan 364
Lee Kong Chian 289
Lee Kuo-Min *166–167*, *171*, *173*, *305*, *306*, *310–311*
L'Enfant, Pierre Charles 65, 101, 202, 251
L'Enfant Plaza, Washington DC 64–65, *65*, 101, 374
Leonard, Eason 76–77, *76*
Levittown, New York 102
Li Kwoh-ting 313, 363, 365
Liang Sicheng 42
Lim Chong Keat 290
Lin Bing 347
Lin Huiyin 42
Liu, Jing 22, 172
Liu Thai Ker 88
Long Beach Museum 377
Louis, Morris 108, 117
Louvre, Paris see Grand Louvre
Luce Memorial Chapel, Tunghai University 153, *164–175*, 165, 169–172, *304*, 373

M

Macau Science Center 381
McMullen, Dr Robert J. 41
Maki Fumihiko 100
materials, innovative use of
　concrete 175, 176, 178, 183, 184, 187, 192, 195, 200, 225–226
　glass 150, 199, 216, 219
　stone 159, 200, 202
　steel 214–215, 221, 223
Mardrus, Françoise 330
Marina South Development Plan, Singapore 88, *88–89*, 378
Massachusetts Institute of Technology (MIT), Cambridge 17, 18, 28–33, 42–44, 47, 107, 108, 112, *112*, 144, 151, 224, 246, 371, 374, 375, 376, 377
　Camille Edouard Dreyfus Chemistry Building 375
　Cecil and Ida Green Center for Earth Sciences 108, 112, *112*, 246, 374
　MIT Northwest Area Development Framework Plan 377
　Ralph Landau Chemical Engineering Building 376
　Wiesner Building/Center for Arts & Media Technology 134–135, *134–135*, 377
Matisse, Henri 57, 362
May, John 188
Mellon, Andrew 251
Mellon, Paul 117, 225, 232, 251, *251*, 375
'A Member's Lounge for the Museum of Modern Art' (student project) 110, *110*
Mesa Verde 181, 183, 295
Mi Youren 297, 351, 366–367, *366–367*
Mies van der Rohe, Ludwig 39, 47, 103, 145–147, *146*, 152–153, 224, 231
Miho Institute of Aesthetics Chapel, Shigaraki 153, *175*, 222–223, *222–223*, 233, *278–279*, 279, 381
Miho Museum, Shigaraki 153, *220–221*, 221, 233, 274, *274–277*, 277, *338–343*, 339, 341, 380
Mile High Center, Denver 52, 61–62, *61–62*, 372
Mill Creek Valley (unbuilt), St Louis 102, 103
Miller, J. Irwin 114
MILLIØNS *188–189*
Miró, Joan 114
Mitterrand, François 96, 138, *148*, 216, 224, 232, 260–267, *263*, 330, 378, 379
model shop 227, *227*
mixed-use developments 52–53, 59, 61, 85, 89, 100, 102, 123, 291
modern movement 17, 44, 47, 297
modernisation 27, 92, 252, 294, 332, 363
modernism 19, 37, 43, 44, 47, 82, 100, 102, 145, 147
modernity 17, 146–147, 242, 298, 363, 365
Moore, Henry 108, 114, *114*, 117, 132, *132*, *192*, 248, 290
Morford, John 320, *320*
Morris, Frederick K. *29*
Morton H. Meyerson Symphony Center, Dallas 231, 378
Moses, Robert 68, 100, 102, 103
Mosque of Ibn Tulun, Cairo 280, 295–296, 356–357
Musée d'Art Moderne Grand Duc Jean (MUDAM), Luxembourg City 335, *335*, 379
Museum of Chinese Art (unbuilt), Shanghai 18–19, 37, *37–39*, 39, 46–47, 107, 111, *111*, 144–147, *144*, 296, 297, 364–365, 372
Museum of Fine Arts, West Wing, Boston 377
Museum of Islamic Art (MIA), Doha 232, 280–286, *280–287*, 295–296, 347, *354–361*, 356–357, 361, 366, 381
museums 107–109
　see also specific museums
Musho, Theodore 242

N

Nagare Masayuki 270, 337, *337*
Nathan Road Development Plan, Singapore 377
National Airlines Terminal, Idlewild Airport, New York 374
National Bank of Commerce, Lincoln 376
National Center for Atmospheric Research (NCAR), Boulder 152, *180–185*, 181–184, 187, 232, 234–238, *234–239*, 295, 363, 374, 375
National Cheng Kung University, Tainan 364
National Defense Research Committee (NDRC) 44–45, 145, 371
National Gallery of Art East Building, Washington DC 26, 51, *104*, 106, 107, 108, 109, 117, 124–127, *124–131*, 147, 152, 197–202, *197–203*, 225, 226, 232, 250–251, 250–251, 296, 365, *365*, 368, 375
National Housing Act (1954) 102
nationalism 17, 18, 145
Navtec 215
Nesjar, Carl 113, 114
Neutra, Richard 103
New College, Sarasota 374
New York 100, 102
　88 Pine Street 375
　499 Park Avenue 377
　Asia House (unbuilt) 377
　Bedford-Stuyvesant Superblock 52–53, 78–79, *78–79*, 88, 375
　Columbia University Master Plan 375
　East Cove Development (unbuilt) 378
　Four Seasons Hotel 379
　Grand Central Terminal 52, 58, *58*, 151, 163
　Guggenheim Pavilion, Mount Sinai Medical Center 378
　The Hyperboloid (unbuilt) 52, 58, *58*, 151–152, *162–163*, 163, 196, 373
　IBM Headquarters Entrance Pavilion 378
　IBM Office Campus 378
　IBM Office Tower (unbuilt) 376
　Jacob K. Javits Convention Center 378
　Kips Bay Plaza 52, *66–71*, 68, 70, *102*, 103, 113, 151, 176–178, *176–179*, 195, 225, 226, *226*, 373
　Museum of Modern Art (MoMA) 57, 108, 145
　National Airlines Terminal, Idlewild Airport 374
　Palace of Progress (unbuilt) 373
　Radiator Building 43
　Republic of Korea Permanent Mission to the United Nations 380
　Seagram Building 86
　Solomon R. Guggenheim Museum 145
　Webb & Knapp Headquarters 55–57, *55–57*, 372
　Wilson Commons, University of Rochester 375
New York Times 107, 145, 163, 231, 242, 242, 250, 256, *379*
New York University 108, 113, *113*, 114, 374
Noland, Kenneth 134–135, *135*

O

Oare Pavilion, Wiltshire 380
oil crisis (1973) 53, 82, 85, 376
Oles, Paul Stevenson 197, 197, 262, *262*, 280
One Dallas Center 377
One Galleria Tower, Oklahoma City 377
One West Loop Plaza, Houston 377
Ong Eng Hung 291
Orchard Road Development Plan, Singapore 377

Ott, Carlos 330
Oversea-Chinese Banking Corporation (OCBC) Centre, Singapore 84, *84*, 108, 132, *132*, 152, 204, *204–205*, 288–291, *288–291*, 376

P

Page, Don *76*, 77
Palace of Progress (unbuilt), New York 373
Pan Pacific Metropolitan Tower (unbuilt), Honolulu 374
Paris 101–102
　Tête de la Défense (unbuilt) 82–83, *82–83*, 376
　see also Grand Louvre
'A Patio' (student project) 299, *299*
Pattou, Jean *264*
Pedersen, William 124
Pei, Cecilia (Pei's sister) *20*, 24
Pei, Chien Chung (Didi, Pei's son) 25, 267, *268*, 324, 372, 376
Pei, Denise (Pei's sister) *20*, 24
Pei, Eileen (Pei's wife) *34*, 35, 44, 108, 145, 147, *252*, 260, 371, 381
Pei, Ieoh Ming
　architectural education 17, 18–19, 27–39, 42–44, 46–47, 224, 371–372
　competition entries 45–46, *45–46*
　cosmopolitan upbringing and outlook 11, 17, 20, 22, 362
　early life and education 6, 18, 20, 22, *24*, *27*, 370
　honours and awards 17, 44, 378, 381
　influences 17–18, 224
　integration of staff 224, 225, 227
　on international stage 107, 144, 250
　and internationalism 17, 19
　lectures 91, *91*, 315, *315*
　library 362, *362*
　life drawings *30*
　marriage 35
　nationalism 18–19, 31–33
　retirement and death 153, 233, 281, 380, 381
　in Second World War (1939–1945) 44–45, 144–145
　see also I. M. Pei & Associates; I. M. Pei & Partners
Pei, Li Chung (Sandi, Pei's son) 134, 153, 204, *327*, 372, 377
Pei, Liane (Pei's daughter) 97, 374
Pei, T'ing Chung (Pei's son) 35, 98, 346, 371, 381
Pei, Tsuyee (Pei's father) *12–13*, 17–18, 20–21, *20–21*, 22, 24, 92, 363–364, 370, 378
Pei, Yu Kun (Pei's brother) *20*, 24
Pei, Yu Tsung (Pei's brother) 24
Pei Cobb Freed & Partners 6, 224, 379
Pei Residence, Katonah 152–153, *160–161*, 161, 372
Peng Yin-Hsuan 364
Perrault, Dominique 330
Peter, Marc Jr 44
Picasso, Pablo 70, 103, 108, 113, *113*, 114, 145
Pitney Bowes World Headquarters, Stamford 378
Place Ville Marie, Montreal 100, 373
Polaroid Office & Manufacturing Complex, Waltham 375
Polaroid Site Selection Study, Cambridge 375
Polaroid Tower (unbuilt), Cambridge 196, *196*, 376
Pope, John Russell 125, 197, 200, 202
Portland Museum of Art, Charles Shipman Payson Building 377
post-modernism 103, 295, 296, 298, 319, 324, 367
Potomac Tower, Rosslyn 379
Princeton University, Laura Spelman Rockefeller Halls 376
Pritzker Prize 378
Progressive Architecture 37, 46, 47, *59*, 107–108, 111, *111*, 117, *122*, 144, 146, *178*

Q

Qatar Museums Authority 280–281

R

Raffles City, Singapore 53, 80–81, 291, 376
Raffles International Center Redevelopment, Singapore 53, 80–81, *80–81*, 376
Rand, Christopher 337
Rappaport, Jerome 103
Regent (unbuilt), Costa Mesa 378
regionality 9, 17, 24, 37, 59, 91, 103, 255, 280, 289, 291, 298
Republic of Korea Permanent Mission to the United Nations, New York 380
Rhode Island School of Design 145
Rice, Peter 153
Roberts, Walter Orr 232, 236, *236*
Robertson, Leslie E. 153, 204, 207, 221, 325, 326, *337*
RoboCop (film) 247, *247*
Rock and Roll Hall of Fame and Museum, Cleveland 379
Rockefeller, Nelson 57
Ronald Reagan UCLA Medical Center, Los Angeles 380
Roosevelt, Franklin D. 44, 145
Roosevelt Field Shopping Center, Garden City 52, 59, *59–60*, 122, 372
Rosenfield Collection 188
Roth, Frederick G. 46
Royal Institute of British Architects 381
Rudolph, Paul 47

S

Saarinen, Eero 108, 118
Saarinen, Eliel 108, 114, 118
Safdie, Moshe 291
Saint-Gobain 150, 216
Seng Kuan 114
Sentra BDNI (incomplete), Jakarta 380
Schinkel, Karl Friedrich 336
Schwartz, Robert *81*, *83*, *100–101*, *102*
Second World War (1939–1945) 44–45, 51, 144–145, 371
Sentra BDNI, Jakarta 380
Sert, Josep Lluis 100, 101–102, 103
Shanghai 6, 17–18, 22, *22*
　Greater Shanghai Plan 18, 37, 46, 145
　Huatung University (unbuilt) 19, 40–41, *40–41*, 296, 297, 300–301, *300–301*, 372
　Museum of Chinese Art (unbuilt) 18–19, 37, *37–39*, 39, 46–47, 107, 111, *111*, 144–147, *144*, 296, 297, 364–365, 372
　Park Hotel 18, 22, 23, *23*, 43
　St John's Middle School *24*, 40, 371
　St John's University *24*, *24*, 29, 252
　Young Men's Christian Association (YMCA) 22, 23, *23*
Shidai jianzhu (*Time + Architecture*) 92
Shigaraki, Shiga
　Joy of Angels Bell Tower 270, *270–273*, 337, *337*, 379
　Miho Institute of Aesthetics Chapel 153, *175*, 222–223, *222–223*, 233, *278–279*, 279, 381
　Miho Museum 153, *220–221*, 221, 233, 274, *274–277*, 277, *338–343*, 339, 341, 380
Shilin stone forest, Yunnan 257, *327*, 366
Shinji Shumeikai 153, 221, 222, 233, 270, 274, 337, 339
Silva, Giovanna *140–141*, *217*, *218*, *269*, *331*, *334*
Singapore 91, 375
　Chung Khiaw Bank (unbuilt) 290, 376
　Collyer Quay/Raffles Square Development Study 377
　Gateway 89, *89*, 232, 378
　Marina South Development Plan 88, *88–89*, 378
　Nathan Road Development Plan 377
　Orchard Road Development Plan 377
　Oversea-Chinese Banking Corporation (OCBC) Centre 84, *84*, 108, 132, *132*, 152, 204, *204–205*, 288–291, *288–291*, 376
　Raffles City 53, 80–81, 291, 376
　Raffles International Center Redevelopment 53, *80–81*, 376
　Singapore River Development 377
　United Engineers/Robertson Quay Development Concept 378
Sino-Japanese War (1937–1945) 31, 42, 44, 371
Skidmore, Owings & Merrill 103
Slayton, William L. 64, 103
Slayton House, Washington DC 373
Smith College 18, 33, 44
Society Hill, Philadelphia 52, *72–75*, 73, 75, 101, 103, *178*, 373
Somji, Mohamed *282–283*, *286–287*, *354–355*
Spreckelsen, Johan Otto von 82, 330
'Standardized Propaganda Units for War Time and Peace Time China' (student project) 18, 31, *31–33*, 33, 43–44, 144, 151, *154–155*, 155, 371
Starr, C. V. 21
State University of New York 374
Stone, Edward Durell 145
Stone & Webster 44
Stuyvesant Town, New York 102
Süleymaniye Mosque, Istanbul 361
structural innovation 157, 158, 159, 163, 170, 176, 169, 204, 207, 212, 214–215
Sullivan, Max W. 115, *117*, 187
Sunning Plaza, Hong Kong *86–87*, *86–87*, 377
Suzhou 6, 17, 19
　Humble Administrator's Garden *344*, 346–347, 351
　Shizi Lin 25–26, 366, *367*
　Suzhou Museum 19, 98, *98–99*, 108, 109, 142–143, *142–143*, 296, 297, *344–353*, 346–351, 366–368, *368*, 381
Syracuse University, S. I. Newhouse Communications Center 374

T

Taichung see Tunghai University
Taiwan pavilion, Expo '70 297, *312–313*, 313, 363–365, *363–365*, 376
Tan Chin Tuan 288–289
Tandy Residence, Fort Worth 375
Tange, Kenzo 88, 291
Tao Shing Pee 232

Tao Yuanming *338*
TASK 18, 33, *33*, 44
Team 10 47
Tête de la Défense (unbuilt), Paris 82–83, *82–83*, 376
Texas Commerce Tower, Houston 377
The Architects Collaborative (TAC) 40–41, 46, *300*, 372
Third Church of Christ, Scientist, Washington DC 375
Thomas, Franklin 53, 78–79
Tian Fangfang *98–99*, *253*, *258–259*, *316–317*, *322–323*, *344–345*, *348–349*, *352–353*
Town Center Plaza, Washington DC 101, 373
transnationalism 11, 17, 291
Tsao, Calvin 255, 320, *320*, 366
Tunghai University, Taichung 296, 297, 302–309, *302–311*, 373
see also Luce Memorial Chapel
Turner, Tracy 97, *97*, *254*

U

United Board for Christian Colleges in China (UBCCC) 40–41, 302
United Engineers/Robertson Quay Development Concept, Singapore 378
United Nations (UN) 172, 376
United Overseas Bank (UOB), Singapore 290, 291
United States Commission of Fine Arts 240, 250
United States Embassy, Montevideo 374
United States Holocaust Memorial Museum, Washington DC 379
United States Embassy Land Use Requirements Proposal, Beijing 378
United States Plywood Corporation 45
University Gardens, Hyde Park, Chicago 373
University of Indiana, Art Museum and Academic Building 377
University of Pennsylvania (Penn) 28, 42–43, 103, 371
University of Rochester, Wilson Commons 375
University Plaza, New York University 108, 113, *113*, 114, 374
University Village, Excellence in Education Study, Dallas 376

V

van Gogh, Vincent 57, *57*, 108
Vaux-le-Vicomte 330, 333, *333*
Verhoeven, Paul 247, *247*
vernacular architecture 19, 91, 133, 255, 295, 296, 304, 315, 319, 324, 347, 367
Viksjø, Erling 114

W

W. Szeto & Partners *86–87*
Wachsmann, Konrad 44, 45, 46
Walton, William 240
Wang Da-hong 364
Wang Tianxi *91*, *315*
Warnecke, John Carl 231
Warwick Post Oak Hotel, Houston 378
Washington DC 100
    1299 Pennsylvania Avenue 379
    Columbia Square 378
    Embassy of the People's Republic of China, Chancery Building 381
    L'Enfant Plaza 64–65, *65*, 101, 374
    National Gallery of Art East Building 26, 51, *104*, 106, 107, 108, 109, 117, 124–127, *124–131*, 147, 152, 197–202, *197–203*, 225, 226, 232, 250–251, *250–251*, 296, 365, *365*, 368, 375
    Slayton House 373
    Southwest Washington Urban Redevelopment 52, 53, 64–65, *64–65*, *100–101*, 101, 373
    Third Church of Christ, Scientist 375
    Town Center Plaza 101, 373
    United States Holocaust Memorial Museum 379
    Washington Post (unbuilt) 375
Washington Plaza, Pittsburgh 373
Webb & Knapp 17, 47, 50–52, 54, 55–57, *55–57*, *60–62*, 64–65, *64–65*, 76, 100, 112, 151, 161, 224, 225, 227, 302, 372, 374
Weese, Harry 64, 101, 103
Weybosset Hill Development Plan, Providence 374
Weymouth, Yann 26, 124, *125–127*, 215, *215*, 260
Wiesner Building/Center for Arts & Media Technology, MIT 134–135, *134–135*, 377
Wong, Alfred 291
Wong, Kellogg 77, 80, 90, *90*, 254, *327*
Wong, Pershing *76*, 77
World Trade Center, Barcelona 379
Wright, Frank Lloyd 145, 224
Wu Liang-yong *346*, 347

X

Xu Bing 142

Y

Yale University 225
Yamasaki, Minoru 153, 270
Yang Yuan-loong 92, *92*, 232, 252
Yoneda Tomoko *272–273*, *275*, *340*, *342–343*
Young, Robert R. 58
YTT Tourism 92, 252, *252*, 258

Z

Zao Wou-Ki 109, 133, *133*, 142, 362
Zeckendorf, William 41, 47, 51–52, 54–55, *54*, 57, *57*, 59, 61–65, 68, 73, 76, 100–101, 102–103, 108, 151, 158, 176, 178, 225, 227, 372, 373, 375
Zhang Xinsheng 98
Zheng Zhong 255, *255*, 366, 367
Zhou Gan-shi *346*, 347

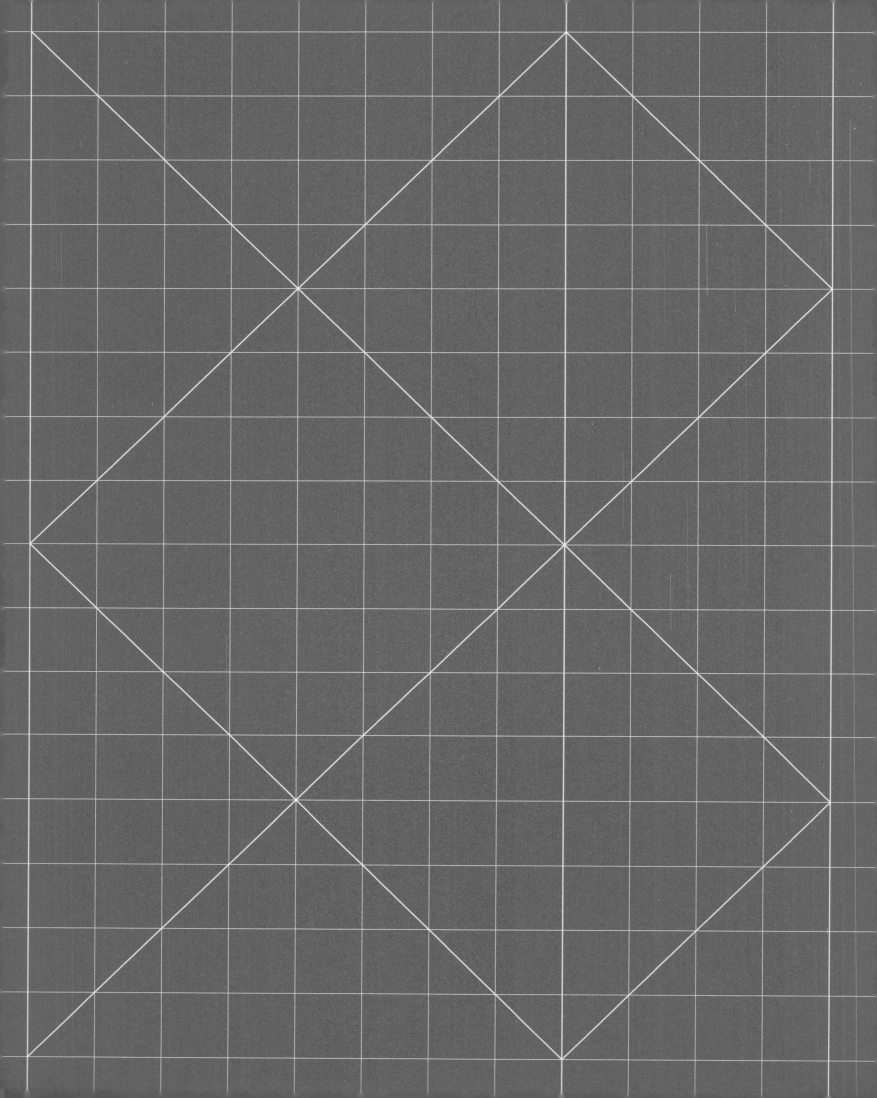